Examin
Crime and
around the

Recen
Globa

Examir
Bruce I

Examir
David J

Examining Crime and Justice around the World

JANET P. STAMATEL

Global Viewpoints

 ABC-CLIO®

An Imprint of ABC-CLIO, LLC

Santa Barbara, California • Denver, Colorado

Library of Congress Cataloging-in-Publication Data

Names: Stamatel, Janet P., author.
Title: Examining crime and justice around the world / Janet P. Stamatel.
Description: Santa Barbara, California : ABC-CLIO, an Imprint of ABC-CLIO, LLC, [2021] | Series: Global viewpoints | Includes bibliographical references and index.
Identifiers: LCCN 2019060003 (print) | LCCN 2019060004 (ebook) | ISBN 9781440860591 (print) | ISBN 9781440860607 (ebook)
Subjects: LCSH: Crime—Cross-cultural studies. | Criminal justice, Administration of—Cross-cultural studies. | Criminal behavior—Cross-cultural studies. | Punishment—Cross-cultural studies.
Classification: LCC HV6025 .S69 2021 (print) | LCC HV6025 (ebook) | DDC 364—dc23
LC record available at https://lccn.loc.gov/2019060003
LC ebook record available at https://lccn.loc.gov/2019060004

ISBN: 978-1-4408-6059-1 (print)
        978-1-4408-6060-7 (ebook)

25 24 23 22 21   1 2 3 4 5

This book is also available as an eBook.

ABC-CLIO
An Imprint of ABC-CLIO, LLC

ABC-CLIO, LLC
147 Castilian Drive
Santa Barbara, California 93117
www.abc-clio.com

This book is printed on acid-free paper ∞

Manufactured in the United States of America

Contents

Series Foreword

We are living in an ever-evolving world, one that is rapidly changing both in terms of society and in terms of our natural environment. Hot-button topics and concerns emerge daily; the news is constantly flooded with stories of climate change, religious clashes, education crises, pandemic diseases, data security breaches, and other countless issues. Deep within those stories, though, are stories of resilience, triumph, and success. The Global Viewpoints series seeks to explore some of the world's most important and alarming issues, and, in the process, investigate solutions and actionable strategies that countries are taking in order to better our world.

Volumes in the series examine critical issues, including education, war and conflict, crime and justice, business and economics, environment and energy, gender and sexuality, and Internet and technology, just to name a few. Each volume is divided into 10 chapters that focus on subtopics within the larger issue. Each chapter begins with a background overview, helping readers to better understand why the topic is important to our society and world today. Each overview is followed by eight country profiles that explore the issue at a global level. For instance, the volume on Education might have a chapter exploring literacy, honing in on literacy rates and advocacy in eight nations. The volume on War and Conflict might dedicate a chapter to women in the military, examining women's military roles in eight countries. The volume on Crime and Justice might include a chapter on Policing, focusing on police infrastructure in eight countries. Readers will have the opportunity to use this organization to draw cross-cultural comparisons; to compare how Brazil is grappling with renewable energy amidst a booming economy vs India, for instance, or how Internet access and control differs from Cuba to the United States.

Readers may read through each chapter in the volumes as they would a narrative book, or may pick and choose specific entries to review. Each entry concludes with a list of Further Readings sources to accommodate additional research needs. Entries are written with high school and undergraduate students in mind, but are appropriate and accessible to general audiences.

The goal of the series it not to make stark comparisons between nations, but instead, to present readers with examples of countries that are afflicted by various issues, and to examine how these nations are working to face these challenges.

Preface

The purpose of this book is to provide insights into how countries around the world differ with respect to the amounts and types of crimes that are most problematic, how governments respond to criminal behavior, and how countries achieve social control and administer justice. It covers ten broad topics related to crime and justice including criminal law and criminal behavior, violence against women, juvenile delinquency and juvenile justice, hate crimes, human trafficking, drug use and drug trafficking, mass atrocities and international justice, policing, gun control, and punishment. The first seven chapters focus on different types of crimes supplemented with some information about how governments respond to those crimes, whereas the last three chapters focus more heavily on social control and the delivery of justice.

Each chapter starts with an overview of the topic, an explanation of why it is important to international criminology, and background information needed to situate the country profiles into the larger issues related to the topic. After the chapter introduction, there are eight country profiles illustrating the experiences of different countries with respect to the topic. The countries were selected to highlight distinctive experiences with crime and justice and to be as inclusive as possible in terms of representing the world. The eighty country profiles feature sixty-nine unique countries covering Africa, Asia, the Caribbean, Europe, the Middle East, North America, the Pacific (Oceania), and South America. They encompass democracies and dictatorships, religious and secular societies, capitalist and communist economies, homogenous and diverse populations, and stable and conflict-ridden countries. They include countries that are popular examples of certain topics within international criminology, such as drug trafficking in Colombia, as well as countries that are often overlooked in these discussions, such as human trafficking in Malawi.

The book is written for high school and early college students, as well as for lifelong learners who are simply curious about the world. There are Sidebars in each chapter that provide popular examples of the subject matter so that readers can relate the text to what they hear about in the media. Though the book is designed to be easily understood by general readers, the information is based on contemporary scientific research. The text cautions readers about how to accurately interpret the information and alerts users to controversies in the field with the intention of encouraging critical thinking and the evaluation of evidence. There is a Further

Reading section at the end of each country entry to provide suggestions to those readers who want more information on a particular topic.

Examining crime and justice issues from an international perspective provides points of comparison to gauge how similar or different our experiences are to other countries and expands our frames of reference for interpreting domestic problems. It opens our eyes to the range of possibilities for solving crime problems or administering justice by critically examining alternative approaches to similar problems. It fosters a worldview that includes social forces beyond individual actions and rational choices including history, geography, social location, social institutions, social inequalities, and power dynamics. Finally, it acknowledges the influence that global forces, such as globalization, political unions, human rights movements, and technological advances, have on crime and justice within and between countries.

Acknowledgments

As I finished writing this manuscript on the eve of my twentieth wedding anniversary, it is fitting that I extend my first expression of gratitude to my husband, Edward (Edju) Ainsworth, whose faith in my ability to succeed at anything has never wavered. Our life together took an unexpected turn during the writing of this book and I would not have been able to complete it without my personal and professional support networks. Our families who live hundreds of miles away came to the rescue on many occasions, so a special thank you to Christina, Abby, and Randy Wrzesinski, Sandy and Steve Makela, and Marie and Saceil Sebra.

I am sincerely grateful for Holly and Mike Ashley, Erin Augis, Natalie Avant, Ann Bays, Corey Colyer, Darrell Donakowski, Jamie Fader, Tanya Johnson, Dee Jones, Christopher Kelly, Michele Kirchhoffer, Bridget McManus, Laura Makela, Stan Martin, Piper Purcell, Holli Rahl, Leigh Shapiro, Piyusha Singh, Patti Stanton, and Brenda Threloff for their emotional and intellectual support. It is not possible to thank all my friends and colleagues who were helpful in so many ways, but your kindness has not been forgotten.

I am fortunate to work in a great department at the University of Kentucky. A special thank you to my chair, Claire Renzetti, for being a fantastic mentor and to all of my colleagues for their daily support. Anna Bosch in the College of Arts & Sciences organized women's writing groups for mid-career faculty right at the time when I needed it the most. My writing group partners Clare Batty and Jennifer Cramer were great motivators.

I am especially grateful to Kaitlin Ciarmiello at ABC-CLIO and Graeme Newman for the opportunity to write this book, which was a labor of love and reminded me of all the reasons why I became an international criminologist to begin with. I also appreciate the professional networks and knowledge that I have gained through the Division of International Criminology of the American Society of Criminology.

Finally, none of this would have been possible without the perseverance of my late parents, Adele and Edward Stamatel, who truly believed in the transformative power of education and who sacrificed so much to provide their daughters with opportunities they could only dream about.

Introduction

On August 3, 2019, twenty-one-year-old Patrick Crusius of Allen, Texas, drove 650 miles to El Paso, entered a Walmart, and opened fire. Crusius killed twenty-two people before being arrested. He intentionally chose El Paso for his rampage because he was seeking to specifically harm Hispanics. This event set off a recurring debate in American politics about the availability of guns and the role of gun control legislation in curtailing violence. As part of the public dialogue, the media highlighted examples of how other countries have dealt with mass shootings and gun control, often pointing to policies adopted in Australia and Canada in response to mass violence. The aim of these international comparisons is to illustrate the range of possible causes of, and solutions to, violence that we might not consider if we only think about gun violence, domestic terrorism, or mass shootings as "American" problems. This contemporary example illustrates why this book is so important and what it aims to achieve.

The first goal of this book is to expand our frames of reference for making sense of crime and justice issues that directly and indirectly affect our lives. Americans are often reluctant to turn toward other countries to learn from their experiences on these topics because our views about them are deeply rooted in the idea of "American exceptionalism." The notion that American values, politics, and society are unique is entrenched in the history of our nation and is often used to justify unusual features of crime and justice in our country, such as the high rates of gun ownership, mass incarceration, and punitiveness. While there are certainly unique features of crime patterns and the criminal justice system in the United States, our eagerness to embrace the ideal of exceptionalism artificially narrows the way that we frame crime and justice problems, and therefore, the way we look for solutions to these problems.

American exceptionalism has not only shaped our values and beliefs about crime and justice, it has also influenced the development of the disciplines of criminology and criminal justice within the United States, which tend to be rather insular. As one prominent criminologist wrote, "for most American scholars, criminology is *American* criminology" (Marshall 2001, 238). Many academic programs in these fields focus almost entirely on American crime problems and American scholarship, most American scholars only read English-language publications, and most textbooks on the subject focus exclusively on the United States, perhaps with occasional international comparisons. This parochialism has persisted despite the internationalization of several other social sciences, and it is built into the infrastructures of the disciplines in terms of external funding opportunities, publication outlets, conference organizing, and curricular development.

This book confronts this confining view of crime and justice and offers both direct and indirect challenges to American ethnocentrism. For example, in chapter 10 on Punishment, the subject of mass incarceration in the United States is presented alongside profiles of alternative approaches to incarceration in Sweden, grassroots responses to justice in Rwanda, and even more punitive applications of punishment in Malaysia and Singapore. The juxtaposition of different attitudes toward, and methods of, punishment broadens our cognitive maps about the forms and goals of punishment and the effectiveness of different practices.

A second goal of this book is to ignite sociological imaginations to understand how broad social forces affect ordinary lives. Many current criminal justice policies emphasize, or even overemphasize, individual actions and rational choice and ignore the social and cultural contexts shaping those actions and choices. In contrast, a sociological approach to crime and justice carefully examines how historical developments, political and economic systems, cultural values and traditions, and organizations of social life create conditions that can be conducive to, or unfavorable for, illegal behavior and shape social responses to those who break the law.

Understanding the global patterns of criminal behavior and social control requires us to examine factors beyond the sum of individual actions. Why are violent crime rates higher in the Global South than the Global North? Do democracies on average have more or less crime than countries with other systems of governance? Why do so many phishing attempts come from Nigeria? Why have crime rates in the United States and many other developed countries been declining for the last three decades? Why are many Americans unaware of this crime drop? Answers to these kinds of questions require examinations into macro-level factors, such as cultural norms and values, social institutions, social inequalities, and power dynamics. These are the broad social forces that shape individual actions. Because they are more abstract than individual behaviors, they require a sociological imagination to appreciate their importance.

For example, chapter 6 illustrates how these broad social forces affect drug use and drug trafficking. The countries profiled in chapter 6 demonstrate how countries that are heavily involved in drug production and trafficking typically have weak states and/or weak formal economies (Afghanistan, Colombia, Guinea-Bissau, and Mexico). The types of political and economic systems that countries adopt and the effectiveness of these institutions can work to encourage or prohibit criminal behavior. Similarly, countries that have adopted innovative approaches to managing drug use (the Netherlands, Portugal, and Vietnam) have to balance national interests against international pressures. Progressive drug use policies in the Netherlands and Portugal have been challenged by other members of the European Union, who are concerned that those national policies could have negative outcomes for neighboring countries. The use of compulsory detention for drug users in Vietnam has attracted criticism from international human rights groups, who have the power to influence aid from international agencies.

The power dynamics within and between countries cannot be ignored when trying to understand different approaches to crime and justice problems.

Related to the sociological imagination, the third goal of this book is to specifically emphasize the importance of space (place) and time for fully understanding the social context of crime and justice issues. As a student of the Chicago School of Sociology, I firmly embrace the perspective that "social facts are *located*" and that "no social fact makes any sense abstracted from its context in social (and often geographic) space and social time" (Abbott 1997, 1152). The sociological imagination encourages careful examination of social contexts, but I argue that the fields of criminology and criminal justice need to pay particular attention to both geography and history. These features are not regularly incorporated into our representations and explanations of crime problems, in part because the American mindset regarding these issues is often immediate and local.

In contrast, an international perspective on crime and justice easily incorporates these viewpoints. Social geography plays an obvious role in terms of political and economic configurations that influence crime commission and criminal justice responses. For example, the geographic proximity of Central and Eastern European countries, such as Albania, the Czech Republic, Poland, and Slovenia, to the Soviet Union is an important factor for understanding why those countries adopted communism after World War II (1939–1945). That particular political and economic system still shapes crime patterns and responses to crime in those countries today, even thirty years after the fall of communism in Eastern Europe. The long-term effects of the social location of these countries are illustrated across almost all the chapters of this book.

Additionally, physical geography should not be overlooked when trying to understand international crime patterns, which is most clearly seen with trafficking offenses. Chapter 5 on Human Trafficking shows how Italy's geographic proximity to Northern Africa, Germany's central location as a bridge between Eastern and Western Europe, and Iraq's adjacency to countries in conflict all play a role in the types and flows of human trafficking in those countries. Internally, geography is a driving factor of sex tourism in Malawi and forced labor in the urbanization of the United Arab Emirates. Similar points can be made about arms trafficking. Chapter 9 on Gun Control shows how Albania's proximity to wars in Bosnia-Herzegovina and Kosovo, Pakistan's border with war-torn Afghanistan, and Honduras' location in the Northern Triangle of conflict-ridden Central America all contribute to the flows of illegal small arms and light weapons in those countries.

Equally important to geography is location in time. Americans view crime problems with a sense of urgency and immediacy, which tends to overlook long-term trends and prior strategies for addressing recurring problems. For example, Americans' views about the problem of crime in our country are shaped strongly by current events and stories circulating through the media. Many do not realize that rates of conventional "street crimes" have been declining in the United States since the early 1990s. Similarly, politicians calling for a renewal of the War on Drugs in 2017 have ignored lessons learned from the previous forty-six years of this failed experiment.

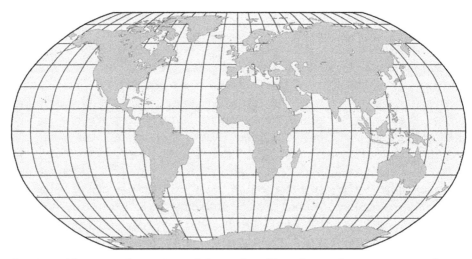

The physical locations of countries and their political boundaries play an important role in understanding the types of crimes that are most common in different countries and the varied government responses to these crimes. (Indiansummer/Dreamstime.com)

This book illustrates the importance of paying attention to historical trajectories to better understand contemporary crime problems and crime control strategies.

For example, a recurring theme throughout this book is the long-lasting effects of colonialism on contemporary societies. Chapter 1 illustrates how elements of the Ottoman and French legal systems have been combined with Islamic laws and traditions in Egypt; how the Swedish penal code shaped Finland's criminal law; and how the Japanese legal system blended Chinese, French, German, and American ideas. Chapter 7 reveals how colonialism in Southeast Asia contributed to mass atrocities in Cambodia and Myanmar by creating territorial disputes and exacerbating ethnic tensions. Chapter 8 on Policing shows how British colonialism still affects policing organizations and practices in Dominica and India.

The fourth goal of this book is to root the study of crime and justice within scientific inquiry. Professionals who engage in research within the fields of criminology and criminal justice adopt a rigorous, systematic approach to collecting and analyzing evidence. Statements such as "street crimes have been declining in the United States since the 1990s" or "immigrants have not increased crime in the United States" are not matters of opinion. They are facts supported with scientific evidence that has been tested and retested to ensure its validity and reliability. Because so many Americans rely on the media for information about crime and justice, they are given the impression that opinions about crime and justice are sufficient to drive public debate about these issues. In contrast, this book provides descriptions of facts that are grounded in scientific research. The text is written with as little scientific jargon as possible to make it more accessible to a wide audience; however, all the information in the book was thoroughly researched and based on scientific studies, unless noted otherwise.

This book also provides examples of how other countries use science to inform their criminal justice policies. For example, chapter 6 on Drug Use and Drug Trafficking exemplifies how both the Netherlands and Portugal commissioned experts to study drug problems in their respective countries before making radical changes to their drug policies. Chapter 8 on Policing illustrates how police in Slovenia collaborated with professors from major universities to implement and evaluate community-policing initiatives. Finally, chapter 10 on Punishment demonstrates how evidence-based research has been more important in shaping punishment policies in Sweden than popular opinion.

OVERVIEW OF CHAPTERS

The topics selected for the book include the most popular subjects in international criminology, as well as some emerging issues. The ten subject areas include criminal law and criminal behavior, violence against women, juvenile delinquency and juvenile justice, hate crimes, human trafficking, drug use and drug trafficking, mass atrocities and international justice, policing, gun control, and punishment. Though some important topics, such as organized crime, cybercrime, or terrorism, did not get their own chapters due to space limitations, they are nonetheless included within other chapters, as appropriate. Each chapter starts with an introduction to the topic that identifies the broad social forces at play, challenges ethnocentric interpretations of the issue, alerts readers about how to interpret the scientific data, and summarizes similarities and differences across countries.

The chapter introduction is followed by eight country profiles presented in alphabetical order. The countries were selected to illustrate diverse patterns regarding the chapter topic and to be as representative of different regions of the world as possible. Each country profile begins with an overview of the country that situates it geographically and highlights important information about population characteristics, political and economic systems, and historical events that are most relevant for understanding the country's crime problems and approaches to justice. They provide the broader context within which the topic of the chapter exists.

Chapter 1 on Criminal Law and Criminal Behavior is the starting point for most people who are generally curious about crime and criminal justice in other countries and how they differ from the United States. There are three main types of legal systems in the world: civil, common, and sacred, although in practice many countries combine elements from these three ideal types and sometimes also retain customary laws. These legal systems establish the overarching framework for viewing the law and its relationship to society. They are reflections of cultural and historical influences on different countries. Understanding how law is approached around the world helps explain how countries define and react to crime or transgressions of the law. In this chapter, Finland, France, Guatemala, and Poland are primarily civil law systems. Ghana and Jamaica are common law countries, like the United States. Egypt is an example of a mix between civil law and sacred law, and Japan has combined civil law with common law.

Crime is a social construction which means that societies decide on their rules of behavior based on their cultural values and social structures. There may be some acts that are defined as a crime in one country that may seem ridiculous to criminalize in another. However, there are some behaviors that are generally deemed wrong by most countries. These crimes are often referred to as conventional crimes or "street crimes." When people ask how much crime there is in the United States, these are the behaviors that they are usually concerned about. Conventional crimes include personal crimes, such as homicide, robbery, and assault, and property crimes, such as theft, burglary, and motor vehicle theft. These crimes are most likely to be recorded by police in most nations and are typically used to compare crime across countries. There are other behaviors that would be considered conventional crimes, such as sexual assault, fraud, or prostitution, but there is less agreement across countries about how to define these acts and whether to criminalize them. This chapter provides information about how the eight profiled countries fare in terms of the amounts of these street crimes and highlights other pressing crime problems for each of the countries, such as cybercrime or gangs.

Chapters 2 through 4 address crimes that are not included in chapter 1 but are nonetheless important in international criminology. There is generally less consensus about defining and measuring these crimes across countries and about how governments should address these problems. Chapter 2 specifically attends to the problem of Violence against Women, which includes violent crimes that are perpetrated against women largely because of the fact that they are female. Whether such behaviors are defined as crimes is strongly related to gender norms and roles and therefore varies significantly across countries. These crimes are often underreported because of women's status and power relative to men's and because of the fear and stigma often associated with them. This chapter presents a range of different types of violence against women including domestic violence in Canada, Mexico, and Russia; rape in the Democratic Republic of Congo, Haiti, and India; and homicide in China and Jordan. It discusses different risk factors for violence against women including different types of marginalization. It also provides examples of both positive and negative responses to these crimes by citizens and governments.

Chapter 3 on Juvenile Delinquency and Juvenile Justice investigates crimes committed by minors. Countries vary greatly in terms of how they define a minor and how they respond when youths break the law. Much of the information about juvenile crime focuses on low-level offenses, such as fighting, vandalism, or drug use. However, Nepal and Venezuela provide cases of youth involved in much more serious violent crimes, particularly gang activities. Countries differ greatly in terms of providing legal protections for minors, offering social services assistance, and administering punishments despite international guidelines about the treatment of minors in the criminal justice system. For example, in this chapter, Belgium, Czech Republic, Nigeria, South Korea, and Venezuela are examples of countries that have separate juvenile justice systems to process young offenders, whereas

Cyprus, Iceland, and Nepal handle cases involving minors within the adult criminal justice system, although often modifying procedures for them.

Chapter 4 on Hate Crimes tackles a topic that has the least amount of consensus among the international community on which behaviors should be criminalized. Hate crimes are a relatively new crime category for many countries, which have arisen from international human rights discourse and social movements. Hate crimes are usually a subset of conventional crimes, such as assault or vandalism, which are motivated by bias. The defining characteristic of these crimes is not the act itself, but the reason behind the act. In other words, victims are targeted because of some aspect of their identity that offenders dislike, such as race, ethnicity, religion, gender, disability, age, sexuality, or any other social category. Hate crimes are very difficult to regulate and prosecute because they hinge on the offenders' intentions. This chapter covers a broad range of hate crimes to illustrate how different countries are defining this problem. Armenia and South Africa provide examples of hate crimes based on sexuality. Australia covers the topic of hate speech. Belgium looks at the intersection of gender and religion in provoking hate crimes. Russia focuses on ethnicity and immigration status. The United States provides an example of bias crimes against persons with disabilities. Finally, the United Kingdom illustrates the challenges of broad and inclusive definitions of hate crimes.

Chapters 5 through 7 discuss crimes that are specifically violations of international laws and tend to involve more than one country. Chapter 5 tackles the difficult subject of Human Trafficking, also known as "modern slavery." It is a topic that has garnered considerable international attention in the last decade, but is very difficult to study scientifically because it is so well hidden, overlaps with other legal and illegal activities, and victims are reluctant to report it because of fear of retaliation or their dire circumstances. This chapter reports on the state of our knowledge about sexual and labor exploitation against women, men, and children. Trafficking offenses are difficult to distinguish from migration offenses, sex work, and unregulated labor practices, and therefore it is difficult to accurately estimate how frequently human trafficking occurs, even for countries with good recordkeeping practices. Therefore, this chapter outlines patterns of trafficking in the selected countries and highlights their underlying causes, rather than trying to guess their frequency. Most countries experience various forms of trafficking, but certain kinds are better documented in some countries over others. In this chapter, Brazil, Germany, Italy, Malawi, Moldova, and Thailand illustrate the problems of sexual exploitation, whereas Brazil, Iraq, Malawi, and the United Arab Emirates reveal the various causes of labor trafficking.

Chapter 6 presents two different sides of the international drug problem, Drug Use and Drug Trafficking. Drugs are a topic that most countries agree is an area of concern, but the highly lucrative businesses of drug production and drug trafficking are difficult to combat and there is disagreement among countries about how to reduce the demand for illicit substances among consumers. This chapter examines where the most popular illegal drugs are produced, how they are shipped to consumer markets, and who is benefiting from the drug trade. Afghanistan,

Colombia, and Mexico are examples of drug producing countries that have dominated the illegal drug market despite various law enforcement initiatives to reduce production. China and Guinea-Bissau are examples of countries involved in the movement of illegal drugs from producing countries to consumer countries. Finally, the Netherlands, Portugal, and Vietnam are places with relatively high levels of consumer demand for illegal drugs and illustrate very different approaches toward trying to curb this problem.

Chapter 7 on Mass Atrocities and International Justice is one of the chapters that addresses an emerging subject matter in international criminology. Mass atrocities are severe violations of international law, specifically war crimes, crimes against humanity, and genocide, which are usually perpetrated by governments against their own citizens. They differ from the other types of crimes covered in this book in terms of their scope, often harming thousands of victims, and by the fact that government actors are often involved as perpetrators. The international community has developed new regulatory mechanisms for addressing these gross human rights violations, including the establishment of the relatively new International Criminal Court, but it is still navigating difficult political terrain trying to respect national sovereignty while upholding human rights. The countries profiled in this chapter cover five decades of mass atrocities to illustrate the historical and political influences that led to these crimes. They also illustrate the different approaches to justice. El Salvador and Peru are examples of truth commissions that emphasized reconciliation over punishment. Cambodia and Bosnia-Herzegovina are examples of temporary criminal tribunals that were established to try and punish high-ranking officials responsible for coordinating and conducting large-scale violence. Georgia, the Ivory Coast, and Sudan are more recent cases that have been investigated by the International Criminal Court. Finally, Myanmar is an ongoing situation that is awaiting an international response.

Chapter 8 on Policing shifts the book's focus more directly toward social control. It examines how police forces around the world are organized and the practices they espouse to maintain public order. The chapter illustrates how these features of policing are shaped by current political systems, as well as historical trajectories. It also examines the challenges that police forces face in trying to reconcile tensions between political motivations, upholding the law, and protecting citizens. It covers a continuum of policing practices from democratic to semiauthoritarian. In this chapter, Ireland and Japan best represent the principles of democratic policing. India and Dominica have also adopted many features of democratic policing but are strongly shaped by their colonial legacies. Argentina and Slovenia demonstrate the challenges of how police forces change in response to transitions from authoritarian governments to democracies. Finally, Jordan and Turkey represent countries that struggle to find the right balance between highly centralized control and democratic policing.

Chapter 9 on Gun Control also focuses on social control and is another emerging issue in international criminology. The prevalence, types, and uses of weapons vary markedly across countries, and research on international comparisons of gun ownership, gun violence, and gun control are relatively new. This chapter documents the sources of small arms and light weapons, their uses, and their regulation in two very distinct settings. Highly developed countries, such as Australia, Canada, and Switzerland, have very different rates of gun ownership but have relatively low rates of gun violence. They are examples of countries that have developed distinct responses to gun control with the explicit goal of reducing gun violence. In contrast, developing countries, such as Albania, Honduras, Pakistan, Papua New Guinea, and Somalia, have large numbers of illegal weapons, including military-grade weapons, weak government controls over the trafficking of such weapons, and relatively high levels of gun violence.

Finally, Chapter 10 on Punishment examines how countries punish those who have been convicted of breaking laws and how they define the administration of justice. Similar to chapter 1, which illustrated how the different types of legal systems shape criminal law and criminal behaviors, chapter 10 returns to that topic to show how different legal systems also emphasize different approaches to punishments in response to criminal behaviors. It also examines divergent philosophies regarding the purpose of criminal punishments. For example, in this chapter, Hungary, Malaysia, and Saudi Arabia are examples of countries that emphasize punishment as a means of deterring others from committing crimes, whereas Trinidad and Tobago and the United States underscore the importance of incapacitating offenders to prevent them from committing additional crimes. In contrast, Rwanda and Sweden have adopted approaches to punishment that accent retribution to society and rehabilitation of offenders.

CROSSCUTTING THEMES

Although this book is divided into ten discrete topics, there are many themes that cut across several chapters in the book. For example, the fact that people who are socially marginalized are more likely to be victims of various types of crimes is apparent in a number of chapters. Social marginalization means that certain groups of society are excluded from full economic, political, and/or social benefits compared to other groups. Marginalized groups are typically defined by economic resources, ethnicity, age, religion, gender, or some combination of these categories. The relationship between marginalization and victimization is illustrated by street children in Egypt (chapter 1), indigenous women in Canada (chapter 2), poor youth (chapter 3), religious and sexual minorities (chapter 4), displaced people (chapter 5), drug users (chapter 6), and certain ethnic groups (chapter 7), who are particularly vulnerable to violence, sexual offenses, drug use, and other crimes because they lack the resources to protect themselves and also often lack government protection.

Another crosscutting theme is how different types of government systems and their effectiveness have both direct and indirect effects on criminal behaviors and crime control. Democracies are more inclined to consider human rights in the application of criminal laws, formal social control, and the administration of punishment, as seen in the criminal law of France (chapter 1), juvenile justice in Belgium (chapter 3), policing practices in Ireland and Slovenia (chapter 8), and humane punishment practices in Sweden (chapter 10). Authoritarian governments or partially free countries tend to be more concerned with upholding the law and respecting the authority of the government. Therefore, they place less emphasis on suspects' and victims' rights and tend to favor stricter punishments than fully democratic societies, as seen in Russia's approach to domestic violence (chapter 2), Armenia's response to hate crimes (chapter 4), Vietnam's treatment of habitual drug offenders (chapter 6), and Malaysia's views on criminal punishment (chapter 10).

Additionally, weak states, where governments do not have full control over public administration and public security and who are not perceived as legitimate by their citizens, are more likely to experience higher levels of violent and organized crime. This problem is apparent in the Northern Triangle of Central America, where Guatemala (chapter 1), El Salvador (chapter 7), and Honduras (chapter 9) have all experienced high rates of violence, significant gang activity, and uncontrolled weapons flows because these governments never fully recovered from political strife during the Cold War period to establish control over borders, weapons, gangs, and vigilantism. Similarly, weak states with high levels of corruption tend to facilitate organized crime, such as with drug trafficking in Guinea-Bissau (chapter 6) or arms trafficking in Albania or Somalia (chapter 9).

Finally, as mentioned above, the book could not include all topics relevant to international criminology, although several are included in other chapters in the book. For example, organized crime and gangs feature heavily in chapter 1 on Criminal Law and Criminal Behavior, chapter 3 on Juvenile Delinquency and Juvenile Justice, chapter 5 on Human Trafficking, chapter 6 on Drug Use and Drug Trafficking, and chapter 9 on Gun Control. Similarly, terrorism is discussed in the chapters on human, drug, and gun trafficking offenses (chapters 5, 6, and 9), as well as in chapter 7 on Mass Atrocities and International Justice and chapter 8 on Policing. The Index provides examples of other ways to connect across chapters, including by region of the world.

Chapter 1: Criminal Law and Criminal Behavior

Janet P. Stamatel

OVERVIEW

Why do countries differ in terms of the behaviors they criminalize? Why do some countries have more crime than others? Can we identify the common features of high-crime and low-crime countries? These questions are often the starting point for people interested in learning about crime and justice in other countries. This chapter provides a framework for understanding different legal systems around the world and for appreciating how countries vary in terms of the volume of crime that they experience.

It is important to examine diversity in national legal systems because they shape how countries define criminal behavior and appropriate responses to transgressions of the law. Legal systems are reflections of the cultural values and social systems of their respective countries and are directly shaped by historical developments. There are three main types of legal systems in the world, which establish the philosophy and structure of the law and its relationship to society. The civil law system, also known as the Romano-Germanic system, emphasizes detailed and updated written laws to clearly specify crimes and their punishments. Civil law systems usually adopt an inquisitorial process for determining innocence or guilt, where a judge leads the fact-finding investigation in search of the truth and evidence is presented in written form. This system can be found in many continental European countries such as France and Germany, as well as in the countries colonized by these nations. Of the countries profiled in this chapter, Finland, France, Guatemala, and Poland are primarily civil law systems.

The common law family also relies on written codes, but much more emphasis is placed on the interpretations of written laws by the judiciary. Prior judicial decisions, or legal precedents, are a guiding force for understanding the applications of the law. Common law systems are typically associated with an adversarial legal process where opposing lawyers advocate for their interpretation of the facts of the case. This legal system can be found in the United Kingdom, the United States, and many former British colonies. Ghana and Jamaica are examples of common law countries in this chapter.

The third type of system is sacred law, which derives legal codes directly from religious teachings. Laws are seen as directives from a higher deity, and there is little room for interpretation. The most common example of a sacred system today is Islamic law. In this chapter, Egypt is a mixed legal system that is primarily civil law but also has incorporated some influences from Islamic law. In practice, many legal systems are really mixed systems adopting features from the three main types described here, as well as customary law based on long-standing traditions. In this chapter, Japan is another example of a mixed system, combining elements of both civil and common law.

Despite the differences in types of legal systems, there are a number of behaviors that are defined as criminal across the majority of countries. These crimes are often called conventional crimes or "street crimes." Conventional crimes include personal crimes, such as homicide, robbery, and assault, and property crimes, such as theft, burglary, and motor vehicle theft. These crimes are most likely to be recorded by police in most nations and are typically used to compare crime across countries. When people wonder which countries in the world have the most crime or how crime rates in the United States compare with other countries, they are typically thinking about these types of crimes.

Our focus on this rather narrow list of crimes does not mean that others are not important. For example, many people today are concerned about credit card fraud, electronic data theft, environmental crimes, or the opioid crisis. The reason why we tend to concentrate more on street crimes than these other offenses is a matter of social constructionism. Societies decide on their rules of behavior based on their cultural values and social systems. Street crimes are behaviors that are generally deemed wrong by most countries. In other words, there is a fair amount of consensus that these acts are wrong. Additionally, street crimes were the most pressing crime problems in the 1800s and early 1900s when national police forces were becoming more formalized and more bureaucratized. When police agencies started systematically collecting data about crimes, these were the offenses that they converged on, and this tradition persists to this day. In essence, which behaviors are criminalized, which are deemed most important, and which are used to define "the crime problem" are the result of organizational decisions that are influenced by the broader society.

The emphasis on street crimes does not mean that we do not have information about other types of crimes. However, we have the most comprehensive and comparable information about a large number of countries for these crimes. Chapters 2 through 7 provide examples of other important crime problems beyond those discussed in this chapter. By investigating conventional crimes in eight countries in this chapter, we can identify some interesting patterns, such as the fact that Japan and Egypt have relatively low levels of street crimes or that violent crime is the most pressing crime problem in Guatemala and Jamaica. We can also examine how changes in political systems or legislation have affected crime rates over time in Finland, France, and Poland. Finally, we see how nonconventional crimes are becoming more important in certain countries, such as the prevalence of cybercrime in Ghana.

EGYPT

Egypt is a North African country of nearly one hundred million people, the vast majority of whom are Sunni Muslims. It lies east of Libya, north of Sudan, and west of Israel, Jordan, and Saudi Arabia. It is the home of the Suez Canal, the strategic passage connecting the Red Sea with the Mediterranean Sea. Egypt gained full independence from Britain in 1952 and has since been a presidential republic. The country's presidents have had strong ties to the military and have exhibited authoritarian tendencies. The country has a diverse economy supporting agriculture, manufacturing, and tourism, although political instability and security concerns have hampered economic development. The gross domestic product per capita in Egypt is USD 12,700, which is higher than many African countries but significantly lower than its Middle Eastern neighbors of Israel (USD 36,400) and Saudi Arabia (USD 54,500) (Central Intelligence Agency 2018). The Egyptian legal system is characterized by tensions between religious versus secular roles and the degree to which the legal system should be subject to presidential control. Information about crime trends is not always made public, but crime rates are generally considered to be relatively low, although they increased with the political turmoil of the Arab Spring in 2011. Additionally, drug use among street children and violence against women are two areas in need of further attention.

Legal System

Egypt was conquered by the Ottoman Empire in 1517 and then by the French in 1798. Both these powers shaped the development of Egypt's legal system. It is essentially a civil law system, modeled after Napoleon Code, but much of the content of the law is influenced by Islam. In the 1800s, the legal system was a mix of civil tribunals, Sharia courts, and Ottoman law. Presently, the Egyptian legal system is largely secular, and Sharia courts are limited to personal civil issues, such as marriage, divorce, and property disputes.

Sharia law is a sacred legal system where the law is seen as an instrument of God's teachings and is derived from religious texts. The degree to which Sharia influences legal systems varies greatly across Islamic countries, with Saudi Arabia as a classic example of a primarily Sharia system. Many other Muslim countries follow a model similar to Egypt's, where most legal matters, especially criminal ones, are handled by a secular civil law system.

The Muslim Brotherhood, an international organization founded by an Egyptian in 1928, aims to increase the influence of Sharia law in politics, the legal system, and society in general across Islamic countries. It has been the largest opposition group to the Egyptian government since its creation. In the 1980s and early 1990s, members of the Muslim Brotherhood began to occupy a growing number of seats on the board of the Lawyers Syndicate, a legal interest group that challenged government policies, particularly regarding civil liberties and the rule of law. As a result, President Hosni Mubarak (1928–2020) disbanded the board to limit the influence of the Brotherhood.

In 2011 large-scale public protests against Mubarak's regime broke out as part of the Arab Spring, a series of democratic protests that started in Tunisia and spread to other countries in the region, including Egypt. They resulted in Mubarak's resignation and a subsequent presidential election where Mohamed Morsi (1951–2019), who was supported by the Muslim Brotherhood, was elected. Morsi drafted a new constitution for Egypt that elevated the prominence of Sharia law. Fears that Morsi was gaining too much power and would eventually turn Egypt into a theocracy led to more protests and a military coup that removed him from power in 2013.

Despite the authoritarian nature of Egypt's government, the judiciary has a fair amount of independence. Judges serve for life and are rarely dismissed from their positions. Egypt has an inquisitorial legal system, where judges lead the investigations for cases. The Mubarak regime established a military court and an emergency tribunal system to handle cases against political opponents. Human rights advocates criticize the government's use of the legal system to suppress freedom of speech and of the press.

Crime and Delinquency

Public information about how much crime occurs in Egypt is sparse. Experts agree that street crimes are infrequent in Egypt, but money laundering, tax evasion, currency crimes, and terrorism are a problem. Egypt participated in the United Nations Office on Drugs and Crime's (UNODC) international surveys of crime and criminal justice system for some years before the 2011 Arab Spring, but not afterward. Homicide rates have historically been low in Egypt. Between 1990 and 1994, the homicide rate remained steady at less than 0.5 homicides per 100,000 people, slowly rising in the early 2000s. It was 0.7 per 100,000 in 2005, 1.1 in 2009, and then 3.15 in 2011 during the political turmoil of the Arab Spring (UNODC 2018).

Other crime rates increased around 2011 as well. According to United Nations statistics, motor vehicle theft increased from 6.1 per 100,000 in 2010 to 24.2 per 100,000 in 2011. Similarly, burglary rose from 0.3 per 100,000 in 2010 to 3.1 in 2011 (UNODC 2018). It is not unusual for crime rates to increase during periods of abrupt political and social turmoil. Because Egypt has not shared crime data with the United Nations since 2011, it is not possible to know whether crime rates decreased when the government stabilized again.

A noticeable social problem in large cities in Egypt is a sizeable presence of "street children," who are often both victims and perpetrators of crime. These homeless children are typically engaged in drug use and prostitution and are victims of harassment and physical and sexual abuse. A 2007 study of homeless children in the major cities of Cairo and Alexandria found that 35 percent of them were using alcohol, 51 percent were using drugs, and 19 percent were selling sex at the time they were interviewed. About 45 percent of the children reported experiencing physical abuse, and 12 percent revealed sexual abuse (Nada and Suliman 2010).

A 2009 study of homeless children in Asyut found that 91 percent said they used volatile substances, popularly known as "huffing," on a daily basis. They reported that the most common substance used was gas fumes from cars (68 percent), followed by paints (44 percent), gasoline (37 percent), and commercial glue (34 percent). About 75 percent of the children also reported using other illicit substances, especially prescription drugs and cannabis, when they had money to buy them (Elkoussi and Bakheet 2011).

Domestic Violence and Honor Killings

It is difficult to establish the extent of domestic violence in Egypt through official statistics for two reasons. First, women are reluctant to report it for fear of retaliation or because of a sense of shame. Second, domestic violence is captured under laws related to violence in general rather than as a separate crime. However, researchers have been able to provide estimates of this crime through surveys of women and analyses of court records and news stories. It is estimated that about 35 percent of women in Egypt have experienced domestic violence, and the most common form is beating. Economic strain and alcohol abuse are the most frequent risk factors for domestic violence. Less than half of women report their victimizations to the police. Of those who file a report, over 40 percent drop charges due to encouragement of the police, pressure from families, or fear of retaliation (Ammar 2006).

Strict gender norms and roles contribute to the perpetration and acceptance of domestic violence. Men have a superior status in Egyptian society and the responsibility to provide for and protect the family. Family law prioritizes family protection over individual rights, particularly women's rights. Women have internalized patriarchal values and often justify domestic violence if a woman disrespects her husband, spends too much money, or refuses to have sex with her husband. Additionally, Section 60 of the Egyptian penal code states that the code does "not apply to any deed committed in good faith, pursuant to a right determined by virtue of the Shari'a" (Ammar 2006). Some lawyers and judges have used this law to justify domestic violence if it was perpetrated with "good intentions."

Sexual Assault of Foreign Reporter

Lara Logan, a foreign correspondent for CBS News, was covering the mass protests in Cairo against the Mubarak dictatorship as part of the Arab Spring in 2011 with her male crew and security guards. The unruly mob suddenly turned against the foreigners and started beating them, focusing most of their attention on Logan. The crowd stripped her and repeatedly sexually assaulted her. A group of Egyptian women were eventually able to protect her until the military could help. Logan shared her story on "60 Minutes" to bring awareness to the risks of violence that women face.

Although homicide is relatively rare in Egypt, it most often occurs within the context of family violence. The most common form of homicide is honor killing, whereby family members kill one of their own, typically a female, for actions that bring shame to the family, such as premarital sex, unauthorized dating, or adultery. Honor killings are rooted in Arab customary law, whereby dishonor symbolically taints family blood and can only be cleansed by removing the source of dishonor. Homicide is illegal in Egypt, but Section 17 of the penal code gives judges sentencing discretion if conditions "necessitate" leniency, which has been a way for perpetrators of honor killings to receive light sentences, if they are even convicted.

Statistics for honor killings are also not publicly available, but one study of news reports from 1998 to 2001 found 125 cases of honor crimes. In 79 percent of these cases, a female was killed for the suspicion of dishonoring the family, 9 percent of cases involved adultery, 6 percent were attempts to hide incest, and 6 percent were due to other reasons. In 41 percent of these cases, husbands killed their wives, and in 34 percent, fathers killed their daughters (Khafagy 2005).

Some recent legal changes have improved protections for women against violence. A 2011 law increased penalties for several crimes against women, such as rape, sexual assault, and sexual harassment. A 2013 study sponsored by the United Nations found that 99.3 percent of women and girls in Egypt experienced some form of sexual harassment, nearly 60 percent of whom reported unwanted touching and about 55 percent reporting whistling and verbal abuse (El Deeb 2013). In 2014 a Presidential Decree was issued to once again increase penalties for sexual harassment.

Further Reading

Alexander, Jon, and Camy Pector. 2017. "Crime, Justice and Social Control in Egypt." In *Pan-African Issues in Crime and Justice*, edited by Biko Agozino, 17. https://doi.org/10.4324/9781315247427-4.

Ammar, Nawal H. 2006. "Beyond the Shadows: Domestic Spousal Violence in a 'Democratizing' Egypt." *Trauma, Violence, & Abuse* 7 (4): 244–59.

Central Intelligence Agency. 2018. "The World Factbook." https://www.cia.gov/library/publications/resources/the-world-factbook/.

El Deeb, Bouthaina. 2013. *Study on Ways and Methods to Eliminate Sexual Harassment in Egypt*. Vienna, Austria: United Nations Entity for Gender Equality and the Empowerment of Women. https://perma.cc/K4CG-RHQT.

Elkoussi, Alaaeldin, and Sayed Bakheet. 2011. "Volatile Substance Misuse among Street Children in Upper Egypt." *Substance Use & Misuse* 46 (suppl. 1): 35–39. https://doi.org/10.3109/10826084.2011.580202.

Khafagy, Fatma. 2005. *Honour Killing in Egypt*. Vienna, Austria: United Nations Division for the Advancement of Women.

Nada, Khaled H., and El Daw A. Suliman. 2010. "Violence, Abuse, Alcohol and Drug Use, and Sexual Behaviors in Street Children of Greater Cairo and Alexandria, Egypt." *AIDS* 24 (July): S39. https://doi.org/10.1097/01.aids.0000386732.02425.d1.

UNODC (United Nations Office on Drugs and Crime). 2018. "Crime Data." https://dataunodc.un.org/crime.

FINLAND

Finland is a Northern European country of 5.5 million people. It is bounded by the Baltic Sea to the south and a narrow strip of Norway to the north and neighbors Sweden to the west and Russia to the east. Over 90 percent of the population is Finnish and about 70 percent are Lutheran. Finland is a wealthy country with an economy supported largely by manufacturing and information and communications technology. Its gross domestic product per capita is USD 44,500, comparable to the United Kingdom and France (Central Intelligence Agency 2018).

Finland was part of the Kingdom of Sweden from the twelfth to nineteenth centuries and a grand duchy of the Russian Empire for about a century before declaring independence in 1917. It is currently a parliamentary republic with a strong welfare state. Finland's political history had a lasting impact on the development of the criminal justice system. Like many European Union countries, Finland has a relatively low crime rate, although its violent crime rates are somewhat unusual for the region.

Criminal Code

Because of its long history as a part of Sweden, the Swedish Criminal Code of 1734 greatly influenced the Finnish criminal justice system. It was not until 1894 that Finland developed its own penal code. As a new country in the twentieth century, external political and economic forces shaped Finland's criminal justice policies. The country was engaged in a civil war with Russia from its independence until the end of World War II in 1945, which did not provide a stable environment for the development of criminal justice policies and infrastructure. As part of the peace agreement with Russia, Finland had to pay war reparations in the 1950s and 1960s, which also diverted resources from the criminal justice system. It was not until the 1970s that Finland began to develop the welfare state for which it is now famous, which includes high levels of social security, an extensive public health service, low levels of income inequality, high economic growth, democratic governance, and a fair and efficient justice system emphasizing proportionality and consistency.

The Finnish criminal code includes definitions of criminal acts, sanctions for serious crimes, the age of criminal liability (fifteen years), and the scope of criminal responsibility. The code has been amended numerous times to adapt to the changing social conditions. For example, recent changes include the addition of new categories of crimes, such as organized crime, insurance fraud, abusing a victim of the sex trade, misuse of information and telecommunications data, and hacking. Additionally, Finland joined the European Union in 1995 and ratified the Treaty of Lisbon of 2009 that aims to harmonize criminal law across member countries to enhance public security in the region.

Historical Crime Patterns

Finland has been tracking annual criminal justice statistics since 1842, providing a unique look at changes in crime rates over several decades. Theft rates in

Finland were relatively low until the 1930s when they began to rise during the Great Depression (1929–1939) and the aftermath of World War II (1939–1945). They declined again in the 1960s until the mid-1970s due to changes in criminal justice policies to increase prosecutions of petty thefts. They have leveled off since the 1990s. Robbery rates followed a similar pattern, except the increase in the 1970s caused by a more permissive alcohol policy compared to previous years. In contrast to theft, robbery rates in Finland increased again in the 1990s due to an economic crisis.

Homicide data for Finland have been recorded since the mid-1700s when the rates were fairly low at about 1.5 homicides per 100,000 people. The political instability accompanying the civil war with Russia and World War II caused homicide rates to rise sharply to about 10 homicides per 100,000 people in the 1940s. They eventually returned to under 4 per 100,000 by the mid-1950s and onward. In contrast, assault rates were fairly high in Finland in the 1840s and slowly declined until about the 1960s when they increased and then leveled off. This pattern is related to changes in Finland's alcohol policies. Between 1919 and 1932, alcohol was officially prohibited in Finland. Even when prohibition was repealed, alcohol sales were highly regulated until the Alcohol Act of 1969, after which alcohol sales and consumption increased noticeably. Unsurprisingly, assault rates also increased after the policy changed, as did other violent crimes.

Contemporary Crime Patterns

Data from the UNODC can be used to compare crime rates in Finland to other Northern European countries. For example, in 2017, the assault rate in Finland was 28.63 per 100,000 compared to 39.81 in Norway and 47.27 in Sweden. Burglary rates in 2016 were 447.03 per 100,000 in Finland, 289.67 in Norway, and 905.47 in Sweden. Finally, theft rates in 2016 were 2,081.03 per 100,000 in Finland, 1,990.69 in Norway, and 3,816.87 in Sweden (UNODC 2018).

More research has been conducted on homicide in Finland than other crime types for two reasons. First, Finland has a uniquely long record of both aggregated and incident-level homicide data. Second, Finland's homicide rates have historically been higher than other Scandinavian and European Union countries, prompting investigations regarding why Finland is unique in this respect. One study reported that the homicide rate in Finland was about two or three times higher than other Nordic countries mostly due to alcohol-related violence (Lappi-Seppälä 2012). Although homicide rates have been declining since the 1990s, Finland still has the sixth highest homicide rate in the European Union.

According to the UNODC, in 2017, the homicide rate in Finland was 1.2 per 100,000, comparable to Norway (1.1) but higher than Sweden (0.5). Similar to most Western European countries that have experienced a crime drop over the last three decades, the homicide rate has been declining in Finland since the 1990s. In Finland, the homicide rate was 3.0 per 100,000 in 1990, which dropped to 2.2 by 2010 and 1.2 by 2017. Consistent with most countries, the male homicide rate in Finland (2.4 per 100,000) was higher than the female homicide rate (0.6). In 2015, about 15 percent of homicides in Finland were committed with a firearm (UNODC 2018).

The government collects comprehensive information about homicide through the Finnish Homicide Monitoring System, which is a collaborative project between the National Research Institute on Legal Policy, the Police Department of the Ministry of the Interior, and the Finnish Police College. This system collects detailed data for a thorough investigation of homicide patterns in Finland. For example, in many countries, homicide rates are higher in urban areas than those in rural ones, but this is not the case in Finland. Between 2000 and 2009, the capital of Finland, Helsinki, had an average homicide rate of 2.4 homicides per 100,000 people, which was 19 percent lower than the national average (Lehti and Kivivuori 2012).

In most homicide cases in Finland, victims knew their offenders. The majority of adult men were killed by acquaintances, whereas adult women were more likely to be killed by sexual partners or ex-partners. In Finland, it is unusual for homicides to be related to street violence. For example, robbery-related homicides were only 3 percent in Finland compared to 8 percent in Sweden and 9 percent in the Netherlands (Liem et al. 2013). Although gun ownership in Finland is higher than that in other Scandinavian countries (38 percent), firearms are only used in about 18 percent of Finnish homicides. The most common means of killing in Finland is stabbing (Lehti and Kivivuori 2012).

Alcohol plays a significant role in most homicides in Finland. Drinking patterns and volume changed with the Alcohol Act of 1969, which allowed beer to be sold in grocery stores and cafes when it was previously only available in state-owned alcohol stores. This policy increased alcohol consumption in the country. Finland is still characterized by high consumption of strong spirits and binge drinking, which tends to encourage violence. The current alcohol consumption in Finland is four times higher than it was in 1960 (Lehti and Kivivuori 2012).

Crime Prevention

In 1999, the Finnish Ministry of Justice established the National Council for Crime Prevention to monitor crime problems across the country, coordinate crime prevention practices across government agencies, and propose new crime prevention initiatives. For example, the Council promotes safety walks, whereby residents of a locality join business owners, community organizations, and local law enforcement on tours of their communities to discuss safety concerns and improvements. A new initiative by the Council aims to better inform citizens regarding fraud risks to counter the rising rates of fraud in Finland and across Europe, particularly targeting elderly people.

Further Reading

Central Intelligence Agency. 2018. "The World Factbook." https://www.cia.gov/library/publications/resources/the-world-factbook/.

Lappi-Seppälä, Tapio. 2012. "Criminology, Crime and Criminal Justice in Finland." *European Journal of Criminology* 9 (2): 206–22. https://doi.org/10.1177/1477370811424372.

Lehti, Martti, and Janne Kivivuori. 2012. "Homicide in Finland." In *Handbook of European Homicide Research*, 391–404. New York: Springer. https://doi.org/10.1007/978-1-4614-0466-8_25.

Liem, Marieke, Soenita Ganpat, Sven Granath, Johanna Hagstedt, Janne Kivivuori, Martti Lehti, and Paul Nieuwbeerta. 2013. "Homicide in Finland, the Netherlands, and Sweden: First Findings from the European Homicide Monitor." *Homicide Studies* 17 (1): 75–95. https://doi.org/10.1177/1088767912452130.

UNODC (United Nations Office on Drugs and Crime). 2018. "Crime Data." https://dataunodc.un.org/crime.

von Hofer, Hanns, and Tapio Lappi-Seppälä. 2014. "The Development of Crime in Light of Finnish and Swedish Criminal Justice Statistics, Circa 1750–2010." *European Journal of Criminology* 11 (2): 169–94. https://doi.org/10.1177/1477370813494976.

FRANCE

France is a highly developed, Western European country located north of Spain, west of Germany, and across the English Channel from the United Kingdom. The country with a population of sixty-seven million consists of thirteen regions within France proper and five overseas regions located in South America, the Caribbean, and Africa. The French Revolution of 1789 overthrew absolute monarchy and established the French Republic. Contemporary France is a semipresidential republic governed by both a president and a parliament, which has created a stable political system. The 2008 Constitution recognizes the supremacy of the presidency but also limits the powers of that position. France also has a strong economy. Its gross domestic product per capita is USD 44,100, which is comparable to the United Kingdom (USD 44,300) and Japan (USD 42,900) (Central Intelligence Agency 2018). Political stability and a strong economy have contributed to fairly low crime rates. Similar to much of Western Europe and the United States, France has been experiencing a crime drop since the early 1990s. However, high rates of youth unemployment and the marginalization of certain immigrant groups can challenge this trend.

Civil Law System

France is a model civil law country, characterized by the codification of laws and an inquisitorial legal system. Napoleon Bonaparte (1769–1821) rose to power after the French Revolution and greatly influenced the formation of the young republic. He created a strong, centralized state governed by transparent laws. Prior to Napoleon's rule, French laws were not standardized and were derived from local customs and feudal relationships. Napoleon modernized the French legal system by adopting a single set of laws for the entire country that would be understandable to the general public. The Napoleonic Code was published in 1804 and reflected the values of the French Revolutionaries, particularly the importance of the rule of law as opposed to the rule of a monarch, transparency so that all laws were visible in written code and accessible to all citizens, and checks on judicial power, as judges historically favored elite property owners.

The Napoleonic reforms also laid the foundation for the inquisitorial legal system, whereby an investigative judge is responsible for leading the collection of evidence to uncover the truth of a case. This investigative judge is independent of the public prosecutor. Contrary to the adversarial system of the United States and other common law countries, evidence is usually presented in written form rather than oral arguments.

Despite its apparent rigidity, civil law is still subject to interpretation by judges and can be amended or expanded to reflect current social conditions. For example, France amended its criminal procedural codes in 1993 and 2000 to be consistent with the standards of the European Court of Human Rights. This included increasing the participation of the defense in criminal proceedings, as well as improving the transparency of court processes.

Criminal Behavior

In 1990, the homicide rate in France was 2.4 per 100,000 people, which increased to 2.6 by 1994 before declining through the twenty-first century. The lowest homicide rate during this time was 1.2 in 2013, which increased to 1.3 in 2017. The homicide rate in France is very similar to that of Germany, Italy, and England and Wales, and about four times lower than the United States (5.3 homicides per 100,000 people in 2017). Similar to most other countries, the male homicide rate (1.6 per 100,000 males) is significantly higher than the female homicide rate (0.9 per 100,000 females). Homicides using firearms in France are quite rare, with only 0.4 per 100,000 in 2013, compared to 2.7 per 100,000 in the United States (UNODC 2018).

As a measure of nonlethal violence, serious assault in France in 2016 was 375.4 per 100,000 people, which was higher than Germany (171.0) and Italy (107.7), but lower than England and Wales (800.9). With respect to property crimes, in 2016, the burglary rate in France of 591.7 per 100,000 people was very similar to Italy, Germany, and England and Wales. However, the motor vehicle theft rate in France of 249.6 per 100,0000 was about three times higher than both Germany and England and Wales (UNODC 2018).

Because UNODC statistics are based on the number of crimes reported to the police, they do not capture criminal incidents experienced by victims but not reported to the police, which is known as "the dark figure of crime." Data from victimization surveys can capture crime incidents that victims reported or did not report to the police, as long as victims are willing to share that information with researchers. Victimization data show that crime rates for property crimes decreased in France between 1995 and 2000. For example, the percentage of people reporting having been a victim of a personal theft decreased by 11.6 percent and those reporting having been a victim of burglary decreased by 29.5 percent. However, during the same time period, the number of victims reporting a physical assault to researchers increased by 35.1 percent (Maillard and Roché 2004). Between

2001 and 2009, violent victimization rates stabilized, with 14.6 percent of survey respondents reporting being a victim of a violent crime in 2001 and 14.2 percent in 2009 (Mucchielli 2010).

Declining crime rates in France are a part of a larger international crime drop in highly developed countries since the early 1990s. In a study of fifteen European countries, including France, researchers found that property crimes and homicides have decreased steadily since 1995. For example, burglary and theft rates decreased over 30 percent during this time and homicide rates decreased about 9 percent. However, drug offenses and physical violence other than homicide increased during the same time frame. On average, robbery rates increased 23 percent, assault rates increased 125 percent, and drug offenses rose nearly 200 percent (Aebi and Linde 2010). Declining property crimes are attributed to greater private securitization (e.g., burglar and car alarms) and efforts by European Union to improve security across the union. The rise in personal violence other than homicide is believed to be due to the presence of street gangs, more leisure time among youth, and increased alcohol consumption.

Criminalization and Ghettoization

Researchers who have examined the rise in nonlethal violence in France emphasize two different processes at work. On the one hand, the French government has been criminalizing more types of violence since the 1980s. Examples of violent acts that have been added to the criminal code include torture, endangerment, malicious or repeated phone calls, sexual harassment, and hindering assistance to others in need. Expanding the definition of interpersonal violence will typically increase the number of crimes recorded by the police. However, this would not affect victimization survey data because such surveys do not cover all types of violence and consistently collect information on the same acts over time.

The second process addresses the ghettoization of neighborhoods in French cities. *Zones Urbaines Sensibles* (ZUS), sensitive urban areas, are neighborhoods on the outskirts of cities that are economically deprived and ethnically diverse. They are often referred to as housing projects or ghettos, although some French scholars bristle at inaccurate comparisons to American ghettos (Marchal and Stébé 2010). Nonetheless, these poor urban neighborhoods have higher crime rates than other urban areas. Crime victimization data from 2006 showed that in the ZUS areas the assault rate was 2.5 percent, insult and injury was 14.4 percent, and robbery with violence was 2.4 percent. In contrast, in other urban areas, the assault rate was 1.8 percent, insult and injury was 11 percent, and robbery with violence was 0.4 percent (Mucchielli 2010). This pattern of high-crime neighborhoods has given rise to fears among the public of rising insecurity and incivility.

The process of ghettoization and the resulting feelings of insecurity are tied to changes in the racial composition of France, although this is not easy to measure because the French government does not collect data on the race or ethnicity of its citizens or residents. However, rising immigration rates in France, as in many Western European countries, have increased xenophobia, particularly against

Charlie Hebdo is a satirical magazine in France that had published some religious cartoons that were perceived to be offensive to Islam. The magazine's office in Paris was targeted by terrorists in retaliation. Eleven of the seventeen people who died in the attack were employees of the magazine. (Gérard Bottino/Dreamstime.com)

immigrants from North Africa. The rising fear of crime is often driven by the rising fear of immigrants. Research, however, has shown that poverty is the driving factor for crime rates, rather than immigration status per se.

However, public opinion about immigrants and crime was strongly influenced by several high-profile terrorist attacks in France. In 2015, there was a mass shooting at the Paris magazine office of *Charlie Hebdo*. Seventeen people were killed by Islamist terrorists affiliated with Al-Qaeda Yemen and the Islamic State of Iraq and Syria (ISIS, also known as ISIL). The same year ISIS launched a series of attacks across Paris that killed 130 people and injured several hundred more. In 2016, ISIS also claimed responsibility for an attack whereby a cargo truck intentionally drove into a crowd of people in Nice, killing eighty-six and injuring hundreds more (BBC News 2016).

Aside from Muslims, who are associated with extremist violence, the other group that is often criminalized in France is the Roma. They are a historically nomadic people who have had a large presence in Central Eastern Europe and the Balkans. After the fall of communism in Eastern Europe, many Roma from Bulgaria and Romania migrated west in search of better economic opportunities. Roma in France are typically cast as criminals, especially thieves, and are socially and economically marginalized. The French government has an especially harsh policy toward Roma whereby their illegal camps are routinely demolished and thousands have been deported. Whether Roma commit more crime than other groups in France has not been clearly established, although they are often victims of crimes, especially hate crimes. For example, in 2019, rumors circulated on social media that the Roma were kidnapping children from ZUS areas. Although French authorities discredited these rumors, there were several violent attacks on Roma camps as a result of these false rumors.

Further Reading

Aebi, Marcelo F., and Antonia Linde. 2010. "Is There a Crime Drop in Western Europe?" *European Journal on Criminal Policy and Research* 16 (4): 251–77. https://doi.org/10 .1007/s10610-010-9130-y.

BBC News. 2016. "Timeline: Attacks in France." July 26, 2016, sec. Europe. https://www .bbc.com/news/world-europe-33288542.

Central Intelligence Agency. 2018. "The World Factbook." https://www.cia.gov/library /publications/resources/the-world-factbook/.

Maillard, Jacques de, and Sebastian Roché. 2004. "Crime and Justice in France: Time Trends, Policies and Political Debate." *European Journal of Criminology* 1 (1): 111–51. https://doi.org/10.1177/1477370804038709.

Marchal, Hervé, and Jean-Marc Stébé. 2010. "The New French Ghettos." *Metropolitiques.eu.* https://www.metropolitiques.eu/IMG/pdf/MET-Stebe-French_Ghettos.pdf.

Mucchielli, Laurent. 2010. "Are We Living in a More Violent Society? A Socio-Historical Analysis of Interpersonal Violence in France, 1970s–Present." *The British Journal of Criminology* 50 (5): 808–29. https://doi.org/10.1093/bjc/azq020.

UNODC (United Nations Office on Drugs and Crime). 2018. "Crime Data." https://dataunodc .un.org/crime.

GHANA

Ghana is a country of approximately 27.5 million people located on the Gulf of Guinea in West Africa, and borders the Ivory Coast, Burkina Faso, and Togo. The population is concentrated in the southern, more urban, part of the country, predominantly in the capital of Accra and the surrounding metropolitan area. The largest ethnic group is the Akan (47.5 percent), followed by Mole-Dagbon (16.6 percent) and Ewe (13.9 percent). Over 70 percent of the population is Christian and 17.6 percent are Muslim. The country is rich in natural resources including gold, timber, diamonds, and petroleum, although it has not been able to use those resources to fully develop the economy. The gross domestic product per capita in Ghana is USD 4,700, which is comparable to Sudan and Bangladesh (Central Intelligence Agency 2018). After gaining independence from Britain in 1957, Ghana experienced three decades of political instability before establishing a stable presidential republic. As a developing country, economic growth and political instability pose challenges for public safety and crime control. Technological changes have also brought cybercrime to the forefront of security concerns in the country.

Criminal Code

Ghana's legal system is a mix of common law adopted from Britain and customary law. Ghana's penal code, referred to as the Criminal Code of 1960, was first passed three years after the country gained independence and has been amended a few times since then. This code defines all criminal offenses and their maximum punishments. Ghana divides crimes into three broad categories: (1) crimes against persons, such as murder, manslaughter, rape, slavery, attempted suicide, and robbery; (2) crimes against the rights of property, such as arson, theft, burglary, pickpocketing, fraud, and embezzlement; and (3) crimes against public order, health, and morality, such as treason, smuggling, currency offenses, and alcohol and drug offenses (Appiahene-Gyamfi 2009).

Some of these criminal codes fit nearly universal definitions of these crimes. For example, the Ghanaian penal code defines murder as intentionally causing the death of another person. Robbery is defined as the intentional use of force or causing harm to another person in the act of stealing property. Falsification of accounts occurs when a public servant, clerk, or officer of a company intentionally conceals or alters financial accounts [Criminal Code 1960 (Act 29)]. However, other crimes are tailored to reflect national culture, history, and politics, as is the case in all countries. For example, a person in Ghana who attempts to commit suicide is guilty of a misdemeanor, whereas a person who assists someone in the attempt or completion of suicide is guilty of a first-degree felony. Rape is defined only as the carnal knowledge of a female aged sixteen or older, whereas defilement covers carnal knowledge of any child under sixteen years old. In another example, a person who uses force to prevent the execution of someone sentenced to death is guilty of a second-degree felony [Criminal Code 1960 (Act 29)]. Although Ghana still allows for capital punishment in its penal code, it has not executed anyone since 1993. The Ghanaian penal code has been updated periodically to adapt to new criminal justice challenges. For example, in 2012, the code was amended to specifically include crimes such as the illegal use of human body parts, sexual exploitation, illegal weapons trafficking, and organized crime (Criminal Offenses (Amendment) Act 2012).

Crime Patterns and Trends

Ghana was the first sub-Saharan country to gain independence in 1957, and government rule alternated between civilians and the military for the first few postcolonial decades. In 1981, Flight Lieutenant Jerry John Rawling (1947–) led a coup to overthrow the sitting president and oversaw a military junta until 1992. He was then elected to two terms as president and ruled the country until 2001. Between 1980 and 1999 during Rawling's rule, crime rates for most conventional crimes decreased including homicide, assault, armed robbery, theft, and drugs. For example, the homicide rate in Ghana in 1980 was 5 per 100,000 people, which dropped to 3 per 100,000 by 1984 and then stayed around 2 until 2000. Assaults decreased from 408 per 100,000 in 1980 to 308 in 1989 before returning to 407 by 1993. Theft followed a similar pattern with 426 per 100,000 in 1980, dropping to 250 in 1992, and then increasing to 456 by 1995 (Oteng-Ababio et al. 2016).

During the 1980s and 1990s, personal crimes comprised 48 percent of all crimes reported to the police, property crimes comprised 44 percent, and public order offenses comprised 8 percent. The overwhelming majority (99.7 percent) of known offenders was male between the ages of 18 and 37 (91 percent), and with little education (90 percent). Just over half of the known offenders (56 percent) were unemployed (Appiahene-Gyamfi 2009).

In 2000, the first civilian president in twenty years was elected, starting a period of democratic consolidation and economic growth. During this time, the country became significantly more urbanized. Although the middle class grew as the economy improved, income inequality also increased. Along with all of these social changes, crime also increased. Homicide rates increased from about 2 per 100,000 in 2000 to 3 in 2003 and then declined to 1.7 by 2018. The robbery rate was also about 2 per 100,000 in 2000 and increased to 9 by 2006 before declining to 6.5 in 2018 (Oteng-Ababio et al. 2016; Tankebe and Boakye 2019).

Similar to every country police statistics about crime must be interpreted cautiously because they depend upon citizens reporting crime to the police and on police discretion in recording and classifying crime. There is a low level of cooperation between citizens and police in Ghana due to widespread corruption and intimidation. Not only does this negative relationship discourage citizens from reporting crime to the police, it has also encouraged vigilantism or "street justice." Additionally, the Ghanaian police do not have the capacity to cover the entire country, leaving crimes in rural areas unreported. The police lack patrol vehicles and other equipment and have been criticized for poor recordkeeping (Appiahene-Gyamfi 2009). An alternative source of information about crime rates in Ghana would be from national crime victimization surveys, which have not been conducted yet.

Cybercrime

Despite the fact that Ghana is a developing country, cybercrime has been on the rise because of easy access to the Internet. Cybercrime became a noticeable problem in 2000 with an increasing number of credit card fraud cases, but this offense has since been surpassed by identity fraud and investment fraud. The head of the cybercrime unit of the police reported that USD 35 million was lost to cyber fraud in Ghana in 2016 and USD 105 million in 2018 (Effah 2019).

The typical offenders are young men under thirty years who are unemployed or underemployed, often with little education. They typically operate in urban areas because of easy access to Internet cafes. The offenders are popularly called "*sakawa* boys" who have developed a subcultural identity defined by stylish clothes and luxury goods bought with earnings from successful scams. These young men often engage in romance scams where they befriend Western women and convince them to send money or fake investments such as gold or real estate.

Ghana also receives considerable e-waste from abroad, such as discarded computers, monitors, cameras, and cell phones. The poor neighborhood of

Agbogbloshie near the capital of Accra has become one of the world's largest digital dumps. Some of these devices or their parts are salvaged and reused while others are stripped of valuable metals. Additionally, criminal groups have learned to sift through the waste to find hard drives that contain valuable data, such as financial accounts or social security numbers. They use the recovered information to try to extort foreigners.

The Ghanaian government passed the Electronic Transactions Act in 2008 and the Data Protection Act of 2012 to criminalize cyber offenses and give the police more authority to pursue these cases. Some communities have also provided workshops against *sakawa* to try to prevent youth from becoming involved in the activity. In 2017, the government established a National Cyber Security Secretariat to confront the problem but noted that it would require a significant amount of funding to be successful.

The majority of the population of Ghana is concentrated in the metropolitan area surrounding the capital city of Accra, which means that most reported crime in the country comes from that area. The nearby neighborhood of Agbogbloshie is the source of one of the largest digital waste dumps, making it an attractive site for cyber crimes. (Peeter Viisimaa/iStockPhoto)

Further Reading

Appiahene-Gyamfi, Joseph. 2009. "Crime and Punishment in the Republic of Ghana: A Country Profile." *International Journal of Comparative and Applied Criminal Justice* 33 (2): 309–24. https://doi.org/10.1080/01924036.2009.9678810.

Central Intelligence Agency. 2018. "The World Factbook." https://www.cia.gov/library/publications/resources/the-world-factbook/.

Effah, K. 2019. "Sakawa Boys Swindle Ghana to the Tune of $210 Million Dollars in Three Years—Police." *MSN.Com*, July 19, 2019. https://www.msn.com/en-xl/news/other/sakawa-boys-swindle-ghana-to-the-tune-of-24210-million-dollars-in-three-years-police/ar-AAEw1Rn.

"Ghana: Criminal Code, 1960 (Act 29, as Amended up to 2003)." n.d. http://www.wipo.int/wipolex/en/details.jsp.

Oteng-Ababio, Martin, George Owusu, Charlotte Wrigley-Asante, and Adobea Owusu. 2016. "Longitudinal Analysis of Trends and Patterns of Crime in Ghana (1980–2010): A New Perspective." *African Geographical Review* 35 (3): 193–211. https://doi.org/10.1080/19376812.2016.1208768.

Tankebe, Justice, and Kofi E. Boakye. 2019. "Are Murder and Robbery on the Increase in Ghana? Analysis of Police Crime Statistics." Research Brief Series, No. 1. Legon-Accra, Ghana: Africa Institute for Crime, Policy & Governance Research. https://africpgr.org/wp-content/uploads/2019/01/Africpgr-Research-Brief-Series_No-1_Jan2019.pdf.

GUATEMALA

Guatemala is a Central American country located just south of Mexico, north of El Salvador and Honduras, and west of Belize. Before the arrival of Europeans, Guatemala was part of the ancient Mayan civilization and the subsequent Mesoamerican kingdoms. In the sixteenth century, present-day Guatemala was conquered by Spain and remained a colony until 1821. As a result of this legacy, about 60 percent of the 16.5 million people in Guatemala are mestizo and European and 39 percent are Mayan. Guatemala is a relatively poor country with a gross domestic product per capita of USD 8,200, which is less than half of Mexico's (USD 19,900) (Central Intelligence Agency 2018). It has experienced long periods of political instability that have severely curtailed the government's ability to improve economic development. Most notably, the Guatemalan Civil War (1960–1996) devastated the country and created conditions for violent crime to flourish, which continues to the present.

Changing Legal System

Like most Latin American countries, Guatemala has a civil law system as a result of Spanish colonialism. As is typical for civil law countries, Guatemala also had an inquisitorial legal system where judges led investigations of facts in the pursuit of truth, and evidence was typically presented in written documents as opposed to oral arguments. In the aftermath of decades of authoritarianism and violence, many Latin American countries have been changing their criminal procedures from inquisitorial to adversarial, which is followed in the United Kingdom and the United States. The high levels of state violence and corruption among Latin American governments significantly diminished public confidence in these criminal justice systems and hindered democratic transitions. The reforms were designed to enhance the transparency of criminal justice processes and limit judicial power. Argentina was the first country in the region to make this change in 1991, followed by Guatemala in 1992.

The inquisitorial system was problematic in Guatemala because low literacy rates meant that poor people were not well represented in written legal proceedings. Additionally, the accused had no legal right to defense and no presumption of innocence. It was common for people to be imprisoned for long periods of time while awaiting trial. Vulnerable suspects were often pressured to confess.

Guatemala's new law separated the functions of the prosecutor and the judge. Suspects are presumed innocent until proven guilty and pretrial detention is supposed to be reserved for exceptional circumstances. Plea-bargaining was introduced for less serious offenses. Three judges hear all cases that go to trial and all testimony is presented orally. These procedural changes improved the rights of the accused but did not remedy all the problems of Guatemala's legal system, which are discussed below.

Crime and Violence

According to the United Nations, Guatemala has had consistently high crime rates across conventional crime categories compared to other Latin American countries. For example, the burglary rate in 2016 in Guatemala was 273.93 per 100,000 people, almost double that of Honduras, which had the second highest rate. The theft rate was 296.15 per 100,000 in Guatemala, second to Panama which had a rate of 396.28 (UNODC 2018). These statistics come from crimes reported to the police. Only 25 percent of Guatemalans said they trust the police, which means that a large number of crime incidents are most likely not reported (Brands 2010).

Violent crimes are also exceptionally high in Guatemala, which has attracted the attention of the international community. In general, Latin America has high homicide rates. Between 2000 and 2012 more than 1.5 million people in the region died from homicide, and between 60 and 73 percent of them were committed with firearms. In 2012, there were roughly 400 homicides per day in the region. In 2012, the Northern Triangle of Central America, comprising Guatemala, El Salvador, and Honduras, had homicide rates that were more than twice the average for the rest of Latin America. Homicides primarily affect young people. In Latin America, the homicide rate for ten- to fourteen-year-olds in 2012 was 2.8 per 100,000 people, which increased to 31.1 for fifteen- to nineteen-year-olds, and 48.2 for twenty- to twenty-four-year-olds, which was the age group at the highest risk for homicide (Chioda 2017). In Guatemala, the homicide rate at the end of the civil war was 31.3 per 100,000 people in 1995, which then rose to 40.8 in 2005 and declined to 26.1 by 2017. The homicide rate in 2017 was about four times higher than that of Mexico. Young males were most at risk for homicide victimization with a rate of 124.2 homicides per 100,000 males aged fifteen to twenty-nine years (UNODC 2018).

History of Violence

In the late 1800s coffee became a valuable export for Guatemala that greatly affected social relations in the country. The wealth generated from coffee led to the concentration of land into the hands of the wealthy at the expense of peasants. Small farmers who basically grew subsistence crops were primarily Mayan or belonged to other indigenous groups, whereas Ladino (mestizo) people were more likely to own land that was cultivated for export crops. Poor peasants with no land of their own were forced to work on coffee plantations for little pay in the absence of economic alternatives. Alliances between the military and the wealthy elite meant that force was commonly used to keep peasants under control.

By the 1940s leftist political parties came to power. Inspired by communist ideology, these politicians threatened the existing social order and empowered peasants to oppose their economic exploitation. With assistance from the United States, which feared the spread of communism during the Cold War, a military coup deposed the leftist government. Tensions between the alliance of elite and military, on the one hand, and leftist guerrilla groups and peasants, on the other, escalated into a full-blown civil war by 1960. Over the next thirty-six years, approximately 200,000 people were killed by leftist guerrillas, right-wing death squads, and the military. Kidnappings, disappearances, and assassinations were frequent events. Much of the violence was public and gruesome, instilling intense fear among the population (Brands 2010). The United Nations finally negotiated a peace agreement in 1996.

Current Crime Challenges

Since the end of the civil war, the Guatemalan government has gradually lost control over the country. Wealthy elites and corrupt politicians have manipulated the economy for their personal benefit. The government cannot provide security or basic services for its citizens, and has lost its monopoly on the use of violence. There is widespread unemployment, dispossessed peasants, and insufficient government revenues to support social institutions. As a result of this fragile state, the government shares control of the country with international drug cartels, domestic organized crime groups, and youth gangs, all of which contribute to high rates of violence in the country.

Two of Mexico's prominent drug cartels, Sinaloa and Los Zetas, operate in Guatemala with very little resistance. Additionally, when the U.S. government strengthened law enforcement efforts against Colombian drug cartels, Guatemala became an alternate trafficking route for drugs. It is estimated that about 90 percent of all the cocaine consumed in the United States passes through Guatemala. However, counter-narcotics measures only result in the seizure of 0.5 percent of the drugs, which is a sign of deep corruption and weak law enforcement in the country (Gutiérrez 2016).

There are also powerful domestic organized crime groups that simultaneously work with and compete against international drug trafficking organizations. They are called *poderes ocultos*, or "hidden powers," because they are embedded in legitimate social institutions. Powerful business leaders, politicians, law enforcement, and military officers engage in numerous illegal activities for profit, including drug and human trafficking, bribery, and illegal contacts. These criminals function in both legitimate and illegitimate economies because of high levels of corruption and violence.

Street gangs are a source of everyday violence in Guatemala. They are often called "youth gangs" because most members are between twelve and twenty-four years old. The estimated number of gang members in Guatemala is 14,000, slightly less than the number of soldiers in the country (15,000) or the number of police

---

The "Hidden Power" of Carlos Vielman

The former Minister of Interior, Carlos Vielman, was accused of abusing his position and ordering extrajudicial killings of prisoners. In 2010, the CICIG, which Vielman helped to create, filed criminal charges against him for approving the murders of four police officers who were in prison for killing members of El Salvador's parliament during a visit to Guatemala. Vielman fled to Spain, where he has dual citizenship. He stood trial there and was acquitted in 2016. However, the national director of police, who reported directly to Vielman, was found guilty of these murders in a Swiss court in 2014.

---

personnel (20,000) (Brands 2010). There are two types of street gangs in Guatemala. *Pandillas* are relatively small organizations with less than fifty members who typically control a single neighborhood. In contrast, *maras* are much larger groups of hundreds or thousands of members. They are hierarchically organized with a centralized leadership and often operate across several countries.

The two most violent *maras* in Guatemala are Mara Salvatrucha (MS-13) and Barrio 18. Both gangs originated in Los Angeles, recruiting El Salvadorans and Mexicans living in the United States. In the 1990s, the U.S. government increased the number of foreign, convicted felons who were deported as a domestic crime control measure. Between 1996 and 2004 approximately 500,000 Latin American felons were returned to their home countries. In 2006, Guatemala received 3,600 deportees (Brands 2010). Most of these offenders fled their home countries with their families when they were children and were raised in the United States. Many had no memories of their home countries and did not speak Spanish fluently. Upon returning to their native countries, they lacked language skills, social networks, and cultural knowledge to succeed in the legitimate world, but as they had knowledge, skills, and connections to U.S. gangs, they formed cells in Latin American countries.

The *maras* are involved in large-scale, transnational organized crime, such as drug trafficking, arms trafficking, human trafficking, racketeering, and extortion. They control major roadways and charge bus drivers fees to safely travel those roads. In 2008, gangs killed 255 bus drivers and their assistants who did not comply with this system (Brands 2010). There is also considerable competition among different organized crime groups that contributes to a significant amount of violence.

The lack of control in Guatemala prompted intervention from the international community. In 2007, the United Nations formed the International Commission against Impunity in Guatemala (CICIG) to strengthen social institutions and dismantle illegal criminal organizations. At that time, 99.75 percent of all crimes in Guatemala went unsolved including 98.6 percent of murders (Briscoe and Stappers 2012). Unlike the International Criminal Court or the International Criminal Tribunals for Rwanda or the former Yugoslavia, the CICIG was mandated to work within the Guatemalan legal system, with assistance from international staff. CICIG referred all cases to Guatemalan prosecutors, who were vetted and trained, although the CICIG often served as a private prosecutor for high-profile cases to bypass domestic corruption and reinforce the rule of law. CICIG also proposed legal reforms to strengthen the capacity and legitimacy of the criminal justice system.

Further Reading

Brands, Hal. 2010. *Crime, Violence, and the Crisis in Guatemala: A Case Study in the Erosion of the State.* Carlisle, PA: Strategic Studies Institute.

Briscoe, Ivan, and Marlies Stappers. 2012. *Breaking the Wave: Critical Steps in the Fight against Crime in Guatemala.* The Hague, the Netherlands: Cligendael Institute and Impunity Watch.

Central Intelligence Agency. 2018. "The World Factbook." https://www.cia.gov/library /publications/resources/the-world-factbook/.

Chioda, Laura. 2017. *Stop the Violence in Latin America.* Latin American Development Forum. Washington, DC: The World Bank Group. https://doi.org/10.1596/978-1-4648 -0664-3_ch2.

Gutiérrez, Edgar. 2016. "Guatemala Elites and Organized Crime." InSight Crime Foundation. https://idl-bnc-idrc.dspacedirect.org/handle/10625/55847.

UNODC (United Nations Office on Drugs and Crime). 2018. "Crime Data." https://dataunodc .un.org/crime.

JAMAICA

Jamaica is a Caribbean island of nearly three million people located south of Cuba and west of Haiti. The population is primarily black (92.1 percent) of African descent due to the country's history of slavery. Jamaica has a struggling economy that is largely dependent on tourism and the service sector. The gross domestic product per capita is USD 9,200, which is comparable to Jordan and Fiji, but lower than its neighbor Cuba (USD 12,300) (Central Intelligence Agency 2018). High rates of violent crime and corruption in Jamaica have hindered economic investment and growth.

Christopher Columbus claimed the island of Jamaica for Spain in 1494 and it remained a Spanish colony until the mid-1600s. The indigenous people of Jamaica did not survive colonization due to slavery and disease. As a result, the Spanish brought African slaves to the country. When Britain took control of the country in 1670 more African slaves were brought to work on sugarcane plantations.

Jamaica became fully independent of Britain in 1962 but remained a member of the Commonwealth of Nations, with the Queen of England as the formal head of state. The government functions as a parliamentary democracy with a common law legal system adopted from England. Criminal laws are detailed in the Jamaican Penal Code and the Prevention of Crime Law of 1963. The development of the political system in the early years of independence has had a direct effect on contemporary crime problems. Political dynamics, coupled with high unemployment, and a geographic location along international drug trafficking routes have contributed to high rates of violence in Jamaica.

Crime Patterns and Trends

Jamaica is known for high homicide rates compared to other Caribbean countries. For example, in 2017, the homicide rate in Jamaica was 57 per 100,000 people compared to 30.9 per 100,000 in Trinidad and Tobago, 11.3 in the Dominican Republic, and 10.5 in Barbados. Additionally, homicide rates have been increasing in Jamaica for nearly two decades. In 2000, the homicide rate was 33.4 per 100,000, which increased to 61 in 2005, and then dropped to 51.4 in 2010 before increasing to 57 by 2017 (UNODC 2018).

However, when comparing rates for other types of crimes between Jamaica and select Caribbean countries, Jamaica does not necessarily have the highest rates. For example, the rate of serious assault in Jamaica in 2016 was 78.54 per 100,000, which was higher than Trinidad and Tobago (44.11) and the Dominican Republic (29.52), but much lower than Barbados (547.25). The 2016 burglary rate in Jamaica of 45.41 per 100,000 was lower than all three of these countries, with the highest rate in Barbados (643.43), followed by Trinidad and Tobago (217.97) and the Dominican Republic (57.40) (UNODC 2018).

The abovementioned statistics come from police reports, which do not capture crimes that victims do not report to the police. An alternative source of information comes directly from victims' reports of their experiences. The Latin American Barometer survey questions residents in several Latin American countries about political and social issues including experiences of crime and insecurity. According to this study, the percentage of victims of robbery, theft, assault, and threat of assault in Jamaica was much higher than in Barbados and Trinidad and Tobago. In 2014, 11 percent of Jamaicans reported being a victim of robbery compared to 3.9 percent in Barbados and 3 percent in Trinidad and Tobago. Similarly, 11.5 percent of Jamaicans reported an assault compared to 6.9 percent of people in Barbados and 4.2 percent in Trinidad and Tobago (Barnes et al. 2016).

Additionally, the Jamaican government regularly conducts a National Crime Victimization Survey, which captures crimes that were and were not reported to the police. In 2016, Jamaicans claimed to have reported less than half (40.5 percent) of all crimes that they experienced to the police. That same year, one in six Jamaicans (16.9 percent) reported being a victim of a crime in the year leading up to the survey administration. The majority of crime victims experienced a property crime (13.3 percent) compared to a personal crime (3.6 percent). The victimization surveys have shown that the percentage of Jamaicans experiencing a crime within the past year declined from 30.2 percent in 2009 to 24.2 percent in 2013 to 16.9 percent in 2016. Although males are somewhat more likely (14.8 percent) than females (12.1 percent) to be victims of property crimes, exposure to personal crimes was the same for both men and women (4.6 percent) (Barnes et al. 2016).

Jamaicans were also asked about the crime problems that they believed existed in their neighborhoods, even if they were not a victim of those crimes. In 2016, about 30 percent of the respondents said that drug use was a problem, 27.5 percent reported robbery, and 23.6 percent stated drug dealing occurred in their neighborhoods. Additionally, 23 percent of respondents said that they heard gunshots in their neighborhood at least once a year (Barnes et al. 2016).

Gangs, Guns, and Violence

The overwhelming majority of violence in Jamaica is gang-related. In 1983, the number of homicides attributed to gangs was 3 percent, which increased to 79 percent by 2013. The estimated number of known gangs was 49 in 1998 and 268 by 2010 (Harriott and Jones 2016; Leslie 2010). Jamaican gangs formed as a result of postindependence politics. In the 1960s and 1970s, the two major political parties, the People's National Party (PNP) and Jamaica Labor Party (JLP), created a system of public support whereby particular inner-city neighborhoods or housing projects were "bought" by party leaders. In exchange for voter loyalty, politicians provided economic and political benefits. This system was called garrison politics. Political parties provided guns to men in the neighborhood to secure party loyalty and protect against encroachment from the other party. Neighborhood leaders, called "dons," were liaisons between residents and politicians. These leaders provided financial support, employment, and security in exchange for compliance and loyalty.

By the 1980s, an economic downturn meant that political parties had less money to distribute to dons and their garrisons. These armed and well-connected men then turned to illegal sources of income, particularly from the international drug trade, extortion, and the construction and entertainment industries. The convenient location of the island between North and South Americas made it an ideal transit for marijuana and cocaine to enter the United States and Canadian markets. The legacy of dons caring for their communities legitimized their power despite the change in income streams.

The "Kingston Kingpin"

Christopher "Dudus" Coke is a famous Jamaican don from the garrison of Tivoli Gardens in Kingston who ran the Shower Posse gang that his father helped to establish in New York. He trafficked marijuana and cocaine to the United States and weapons to Jamaica for nearly two decades. In 2011, Coke was arrested after a shoot-out between his gang and the police in which seventy people died. He was extradited to the United States and convicted of drug trafficking. He is serving a twenty-three-year sentence in the United States.

As a result of the loosening of government control over garrisons and the large sums of potential income, the number of gangs multiplied and diversified. Community gangs are typically loosely organized, youth gangs with members aged twelve to fifteen. In contrast, criminal gangs are larger, organized crime groups, typically run by dons. The nature and frequency of violence also changed from the 1960s to the 1980s. Although gangs always fought over territory and resources, the proliferation of both gangs and guns has dramatically increased incidences of violence, especially lethal violence. Guns are easily accessible. While gang members typically own the guns, they are routinely rented out to other members of the communities.

As a result of these changing dynamics, serious violence is concentrated in urban areas, particularly in the Kingston Metropolitan Region. It is also prevalent in the poorer areas of cities. Both victims and offenders of lethal violence tend to be young, poor, and uneducated men. Young men and boys under twenty-five years old commit about 40 percent of all homicides and nearly 50 percent of shootings (Leslie 2010). About 78 percent of all homicide victims are under thirty-five years old and nearly 90 percent are male (Harriott and Jones 2016). Violence results in medical expenditures of millions of dollars and increases police costs; encourages middle-class flight and discourages business investments; and decreases the quality of life for urban residents and creates high levels of insecurity.

Crime Prevention

In 2010, the Jamaican government developed a National Crime Prevention and Community Safety Strategy to develop new public safety initiatives and coordinate efforts among government institutions, nongovernmental organizations, and international partners. For example, measures were introduced to modernize the Jamaican Constabulary Force (JCF) and address problems, such as police use of force against citizens and poor police and citizen relationships. A new Crime Prevention and Community Safety and Security Branch of the JCF was formed to improve community relationship with the police. The new branch sponsored police youth clubs, neighborhood watches, and police visits to schools and churches. The JCF also established a Centre for the Investigation of Sexual Offenses and Child Abuse to improve investigations of such cases and provide much-needed victim support.

The National Crime Prevention Strategy also identified several problems with the judicial system, rendering it ineffective and inefficient. The problems included poor infrastructure, significant delays in court case processing, unequal treatment and protection, and inefficient procedures. For example, cases are often delayed or dismissed because of misplaced paperwork. Citizens are also reluctant to participate in criminal justice proceedings as witnesses or jurors.

Between 2009 and 2014 the Jamaican government passed thirty-seven laws specifically related to reducing crime and violence (Harriot and Jones 2016). Ten crime bills were passed to change the penal code or judicial system, with one directly addressing the gang problem. Four laws dealt with gender-based violence,

violence against women, child abuse, and sexual violence. The overall approach of this legislation was a "get tough" policy that increased police powers, which raised some concerns in the public about the simultaneous need to protect citizens' rights. Jamaica's crime control strategy is part of its broader National Development Plan: Vision 2030 to achieve "developed nation" status by 2030.

Further Reading

Barnes, Annmarie, Randy Seepersad, Jason Wilks, and Scot Wortley. 2016. *The National Crime Victimization Survey (NCVS) 2016 Final Report*. Kingston, Jamaica: Ministry of National Security, Government of Jamaica. https://www.mns.gov.jm/content/national-crime-victimization-survey-ncvs-2016-final-report.

Central Intelligence Agency. 2018. "The World Factbook." https://www.cia.gov/library/publications/resources/the-world-factbook/.

Harriott, Anthony D., and Marlyn Jones. 2016. "Crime and Violence in Jamaica." Technical Notes. Crime and Violence in the Caribbean. Inter-American Development Bank. https://doi.org/10.18235/0000333.

Jaffe, Rivke. 2013. "The Hybrid State: Crime and Citizenship in Urban Jamaica." *American Ethnologist* 40 (4): 734–48. https://doi.org/10.1111/amet.12051.

Leslie, Glaister. 2010. *Confronting the Don: The Political Economy of Gang Violence in Jamaica*. Occasional Paper. Geneva, Switzerland: Small Arms Survey.

UNODC (United Nations Office on Drugs and Crime). 2018. "Crime Data." https://dataunodc.un.org/crime.

JAPAN

Japan is an island country in East Asia across the Sea of Japan from North and South Korea. Japan's population of 126 million is overwhelmingly Japanese (98.1 percent), with most people adhering to Shintoism and/or Buddhism. After suffering a devastating military defeat in World War II (1939–1945), Japan's postwar recovery focused on economic development, which made it a global economic leader. Japan's gross domestic product per capita is USD 42,900 similar to the United Kingdom (USD 44,300) (Central Intelligence Agency 2018). This economic prosperity, along with a communitarian culture, has contributed to Japan's international status as a low-crime nation.

Criminal Law

Japan's contemporary legal system was shaped by several foreign powers. Before the seventeenth century, Japanese culture and society were strongly influenced by the Chinese, from whom they adopted their writing system, Buddhist religion, and many social values. Between 1603 and 1867 the military rulers of Japan, *shoguns*, were afraid of foreign influence from European traders and colonizers so they closed the country to foreigners. As a result, Japan experienced over 250 years of isolation. Throughout this period, Chinese law was the model for the Japanese legal system. In 1868, the Meiji Restoration reopened Japan to Western trade and ideas, including the adoption of some elements of the French penal code. At the end of the 1800s the Japanese legal system embraced many elements of the German civil law system, which still has the strongest influence on contemporary Japanese law. After World War II, the U.S. presence in Japan shaped the country's laws regarding the constitution and human rights. Unsurprisingly then, Japan and the United States are the only two highly developed countries that still allow the death penalty.

Low-Crime Nation

In many developed nations, including the United States and Western Europe, crime rates increased after World War II until the early 1990s because of a number of social changes including economic development, an increasing youth population due to "baby boomers," and cultural and political social movements in the 1960s and 1970s. In contrast, rates for many crimes in Japan, especially violent crimes, decreased during the postwar period, with Japan having exceptionally low crime rates compared to Western countries.

This pattern was most apparent with respect to homicide rates. In 1951, there were almost 3.5 homicides per 100,000 people in Japan, which declined to just over 1 per 100,000 by 1990 and hit a record low of 0.73 in 2013 (Roberts 2018). In contrast, the homicide rate in the United States in 1950 was about 5 per 100,000, which doubled to 10 by 1980, and then began to decline to a record low of 4.4 in 2014 (UNODC 2018). This means that the lowest postwar homicide rate in the United States was higher than the highest postwar homicide rate in Japan.

According to police statistics of recorded crime, in 2016, the robbery rate in Japan was 0.2 per 100,000, the burglary rate was 59.9 per 100,000, and the auto theft rate was 28.16 per 100,000. In comparison, in the same year in the United States, the robbery rate was 3.33 per 100,000, the burglary rate was 470.19, and the auto theft rate was 237.56 (UNODC 2018). Police statistics are not just a result of the number of crimes that come to the attention of the police but also of the amount of discretion that police use to classify and record crimes. An alternate source of information about crime rates is victimization surveys based on citizens' accounts of their experiences with crime, regardless of whether they reported it to the police. Japan participated in the International Crime Victims Survey in 1989, 1992, 2000, and 2004. In the last round of surveys, Japan had the second lowest victimization rates of all the countries that participated, just above Spain. In 2004, only 0.1 percent of Japanese respondents reported experiencing car theft compared to 1.1 percent in the United States. However, bicycle theft in Japan (5.1 percent) was higher than the United States (2.9 percent).

There are two dominant explanations for Japan's low crime rates. The first emphasizes economic performance and culture. A well-established fact in the criminological literature is that economic stress increases crime rates. In Japan, both poverty rates and income inequality dropped steadily from the 1950s to the 1990s, corresponding to declining crime rates. However, between 1990 and 2000, Japan experienced an economic recession that led to rising income inequality, fragile families, and overall economic instability. Starting in the mid-1990s, crime rates began to increase, which was about the time that the United States and Western Europe were experiencing declining crime rates. For example, the combined crime rate for the seven most serious offenses increased in Japan by 100 percent between 1995 and 2002. Specifically, the assault rate doubled and the theft rate increased by 50 percent (Johnson 2007). These patterns were highly publicized by the media, contributing to growing fear of crime among the public. As a result, politicians began emphasizing crime control on their platforms and advocating for stricter crime control policies.

As the economy rebounded and new crime control measures were implemented, crime rates in Japan began declining again. In 2017, the overall crime rate hit a record low, with an especially remarkable decline in thefts. Nonetheless, Japan still faces a number of crime challenges including organized crime, fraud, and cybercrime.

Culture and Community

Aside from economic factors, another popular explanation for Japan's historically low crime rates is its culture. The communitarian culture of Japan is often contrasted with the individualistic culture of the United States. Collective identity and group affinity are highly valued in Japanese culture. This means that the Japanese are more likely to consider the effects of their actions on others and to avoid disappointing or harming others than people raised in individualistic cultures.

Japanese culture is rooted in the religious traditions of Shintoism, Buddhism, and Confucianism, which emphasize the importance of social hierarchies and the value of accepting one's position in the hierarchy, as opposed to individualistic cultures that emphasize personal achievement and success. As such, vertical relationships define Japanese society and promote deference, group bonds, and conformity. In exchange for accepting one's role in the group, the individual earns the loyalty and continual support of other group members.

Group unity reinforces another aspect of Japanese culture derived from religious traditions, harmony. Peace and order are highly valued and individuals are rewarded for efforts to promote harmony. Japanese are socialized to be disciplined and altruistic to maintain group harmony. Cultural traditions are important for reinforcing collective identity and harmony.

These features of Japanese culture reduce the potential for interpersonal conflict and enforce a high level of social control, both of which contribute to low crime rates. But perhaps even more important than the content of Japanese values is the fact that they are highly consistent. The foundational values of Japanese culture have persisted for centuries and have been less susceptible to external influences than those of other cultures. The isolationist period of Japanese history was an important factor in solidifying Japanese culture. It is also fairly consistent across social divisions within Japanese society. Regardless of age, gender, geographic location, or social class, Japanese values are relatively constant. This continuity over time explains why Japan has been able to maintain low crime rates for so long

An important factor contributing to Japan's low crime rate is a culture that emphasizes collective identity and harmony. People are socialized to accept their positions in society and show deference to those in higher social positions, such as parents. This encourages conformity to social norms and laws. (Corel)

and why it was able to recover fairly quickly from the social disruptions of the economic recession.

Japanese cultural values permeate social institutions, including families, schools, social organizations, and even the criminal justice system. For example, all neighborhoods have a voluntary neighborhood watch group called *chokai*, in which almost all households participate by choice. People can register to be crime prevention volunteers in their neighborhoods where they work with local police to patrol problem areas and share information with residents about how to prevent crime. Because of the vertical relationships of Japanese society and respect for authority, relationships of citizens with the police are generally positive and seen as mutually beneficial.

In response to the growing fear of crime in Japan in the early 2000s, the number of people volunteering for crime preventions groups has increased significantly. In 2003, there were 177,831 registered crime prevention volunteers, which increased to 2,758,659 by 2016. Many of the volunteers are retirees over sixty years old. About 46 percent of the volunteers participate more than ten days per month. The vast majority of volunteers (79.2 percent) spend their time patrolling neighborhoods or accompanying children to school (75.1 percent), and about 41.3 percent inspect dangerous places in their neighborhoods (Herber 2018). This is an example of how the communitarian nature of Japanese culture promotes behaviors that increase social order and reduce crime.

Further Reading

Central Intelligence Agency. 2018. "The World Factbook." https://www.cia.gov/library/publications/resources/the-world-factbook/.

Herber, Erik. 2018. "Crime Prevention in Japan Orchestration, Representation and Impact of a Volunteering Boom." *International Journal of Law, Crime and Justice* 54 (September): 102–10. https://doi.org/10.1016/j.ijlcj.2018.03.005.

Johnson, David T. 2007. "Crime and Punishment in Contemporary Japan." *Crime and Justice* 36 (1): 371–423. https://doi.org/10.1086/592808.

Leonardsen, D. 2004. *Japan as a Low-Crime Nation.* New York: Palgrave Macmillan.

Leonardsen, D. 2010. *Crime in Japan: Paradise Lost?* New York: Palgrave Macmillan.

Roberts, Aki. 2018. "Revisiting Japan's Postwar Homicide Trend: 1951–2014." In *Crime and Justice in Contemporary Japan.* Springer Series on Asian Criminology and Criminal Justice Research, edited by Jianhong Liu and Setsuo Miyazawa, 99–116. Cham, Switzerland: Springer.

UNODC (United Nations Office on Drugs and Crime). 2018. "Crime Data." https://dataunodc.un.org/crime.

POLAND

Poland is a Central European country with a population of nearly thirty-nine million located east of Germany and across the Baltic Sea from Sweden. From the end of World War II (1939–1945) until 1990, Poland was a communist country under the influence of the Soviet Union, during which time the economy stagnated and people were politically oppressed. The Soviet system crumbled in 1989 in large part because of mass protests in Poland. By 1990, Poland became an independent, democratic republic that embraced a free-market economy. After a difficult decade of transition, Poland's economy began to grow and it is now a strong performer among post-communist countries. The gross domestic product per capita is USD 29,600, which is lower than Germany (USD 50,800), but comparable to many other post-communist countries like Hungary (USD 29,600) and Russia (USD 27,900) (Central Intelligence Agency 2018). In 2004, Poland joined the European Union, a political and economic alliance of twenty-eight countries. Poland's criminal justice system and crime rates were both radically affected by the massive social changes after communism collapsed and by the influence of the European Union.

Crime during Communism

The communist system in Eastern Europe was first implemented in Russia after the 1917 revolutions that brought an end to imperialism and then spread to surrounding countries with the formation of the Soviet Union in 1922. In the aftermath of World War II, the Soviet Union was able to spread its sphere of influence to Central and Eastern European countries like Poland, Czechoslovakia, and the former Yugoslavia. Soviet communism was based on the ideologies of Karl Marx (1818–1888), Friedrich Engels (1820–1895), and Vladimir Ilych Ulyanov (Lenin) (1870–1924) that promoted an end to social classes and social inequalities. All of society's problems were believed to be a result of the bourgeoisie's (wealthy class) exploitation of the proletariat (working class). Crime existed because people were demoralized by the oppressive, capitalist system. Once social classes were eliminated, crime was expected to disappear.

However, crime still persisted in communist countries like Poland because eliminating social classes was a long process and these countries had not achieved a fully communist system. Nonetheless, communist propaganda claimed that crime rates in communist countries were much lower than in the capitalist West, although the highly secretive communist governments did not share their crime statistics readily to prove this point. Research since the fall of communism has shown that crime rates were not consistently lower in communist countries compared to capitalist ones. In the case of Poland, for example, the average homicide rate from 1960 to 1964 was 0.96 per 100,000 people compared to the Western European average of 0.82 per 100,000. The homicide rate average for 1980–1984 in Poland was 1.41 compared to 1.29 in Western Europe (Stamatel 2008). Crime statistics for other types of crimes during communism are difficult to obtain and interpret because of concerns that they could have been manipulated for political reasons.

Most communist countries, including Poland, had a civil law system that was adapted to Marxist–Leninist ideology. The law was used as a tool to promote a particular political agenda. New crimes against the socialist order or the common good were defined to reflect communist ideology, and political dissidents were often arrested for "crimes" as a means of suppressing government opposition. Breaking the law was taken very seriously because it was an affront to the communitarian ideology of communism. Criminal law was very punitive and incarceration rates were high.

Transition to Democracy

Once the communist system collapsed in 1989, the new government moved quickly to establish democratic reforms and transition to a free-market economy. Because criminal law had been used by the communist government to excessively control citizens, legal reforms in the early 1990s sought to limit government power and its potential for abuse. The new criminal code was instead designed to emphasize due process and civil liberties. For example, in 1980, incarceration accounted for 32 percent of all criminal sentences, but by 1997, it was only used in 12.2 percent of all sentences (Krajewski 2004).

The first half of the 1990s was a period of massive social upheaval. Adopting a free-market economy resulted in skyrocketing inflation and unemployment, along with the loss of many social services provided by the communist government, such as free child care, free healthcare, and guaranteed retirement pensions. At the same time, opening borders to trade meant that luxury goods were available in Poland for the first time. Some people, particularly former communist politicians, were able to capitalize on the economic disarray and become wealthy very quickly and not necessarily legally. After decades of trying to eliminate social classes, inequality grew rapidly in just a few years.

Given these social conditions, crime rates increased dramatically in the early 1990s in Poland and most other post-communist countries. For example, between 1989 and 1996, the homicide rate in Poland increased from 1.5 homicides per 100,000 people to 2.9. While the numbers may still seem low, it was a doubling of the homicide rate in just a few years. Additionally, assault rates increased from 7.8 per 100,000 to 29.9 during the same period and burglary rates grew from 575.8 to 791.2 per 100,000. The number of thefts and the number of opiate addicts doubled during the same period (Krajewski 2003, 2004). The structure of criminal behavior also changed. Violent crimes became a larger portion of total crimes committed, and there was a noticeable increase in crimes committed with a firearm. The number of juveniles involved in criminal activity also increased significantly.

Although the increases in crime rates in Poland in the early 1990s were quite dramatic, they were still lower than many other countries, including the United States. Nonetheless, they were shocking for Poles and fear of crime rose considerably. As a result the public became more vocal about criminal justice policies and expressed concerns that post-communist legal reforms were too lenient. By 2000, Polish politicians had adopted America's "tough on crime" rhetoric and favored policies like zero tolerance and three-strikes laws. For example, a drug law passed in 1985 during communism did not criminalize possession of small quantities of illicit drugs for personal consumption. By 1997, as crime was increasing rapidly, possession of drugs was criminalized but not punished with criminal sanctions, instead treatment and prevention were emphasized. By 2000, drug possession was both criminalized and punished with criminal sanctions as a move to get tough on crime.

The New Order

After the initial shock of the collapse of over forty years of communist rule, which created considerable social turmoil, Poland's new democratic government and free-market economy normalized. In the second half of the 1990s crime rates began to decline. By the time Poland joined the European Union in 2004, its crime rates were comparable to many Western European nations. For example, in 2017, the homicide rate in Poland was 0.73 per 100,000, which was much lower than 2.9 in 1996 and comparable to that of neighboring Germany (0.89). In the same year, the theft rate was the lowest of the twenty-two nations that had reported data to Eurostat. At 281.6 thefts per 100,000 people, it was nearly five times lower than that of Germany (1,401.36) (Eurostat 2019).

However, the new political and economic systems created new types of crimes in post-communist countries like Poland. For example, under communism, private property was inconsistent with communal goals and equality, so there were no copyright laws. At the same time, extensive censorship and a disdain for capitalism meant that many Western products and services were not available in communist countries. This created extensive black markets and fostered a successful piracy industry for music, movies, videos, books, and video games. The ambivalence toward piracy laws changed with capitalism, a system that values private property, and with new international relationships with Western countries. As a result, Poland was pressured to sign the Anti-Counterfeiting Trade Agreement (ACTA) in 2012 that standardizes international copyright and piracy laws. This led to public protests in Poland as people feared it was a government intrusion on Internet freedom and an opportunity to increase government surveillance of citizens.

Another emerging crime problem in Poland is organized crime. Opening borders to legal trade and immigration also increases the illegal movement of products and people across countries. Additionally, Poland's close proximity to Russia makes it a convenient gateway to the west for Russian organized crime groups. Before 1989, organized crime in Poland mainly involved conventional crimes, such as burglary or motor vehicle theft, or crimes against socialism, such as black markets or illegal trade in Western currencies. However, since joining the European Union and opening borders for economic development, Poland has seen an increase in the number of organized crime groups operating in the country. These groups tend to focus on transnational crimes like drug trafficking, motor vehicle theft, and smuggling. For example, in 2019, the European Union police dismantled an organized crime ring through coordinated police raids in Poland, Spain, Lithuania, and the United Kingdom. A Lithuanian man who was arrested in a raid in Spain ran the group. This multimillion-dollar enterprise was involved in drug trafficking, smuggling cigarettes, and money laundering.

Further Reading

Central Intelligence Agency. 2018. "The World Factbook." https://www.cia.gov/library/publications/resources/the-world-factbook/.

Eurostat. 2019. "Crime and Criminal Justice." https://ec.europa.eu/eurostat/web/crime/data/database.

Krajewski, Krzysztof. 2003. "Drugs, Markets and Criminal Justice in Poland." *Crime, Law and Social Change* 40 (2): 273–93. https://doi.org/10.1023/A:1025740822452.

Krajewski, Krzysztof. 2004. "Crime and Criminal Justice in Poland." *European Journal of Criminology* 1 (3): 377–407. https://doi.org/10.1177/1477370804044006.

Pływaczewski, Emil. 2004. "Organised Crime in Poland: Its Development from 'Real Socialism' to Present Times." In *Organised Crime in Europe: Concepts, Patterns and Control Policies in the European Union and Beyond*. Studies of Organized Crime, edited by Cyrille Fijnaut and Letizia Paoli, 467–98. Dordrecht, the Netherlands: Springer. https://doi.org/10.1007/978-1-4020-2765-9_17.

Stamatel, Janet P. 2008. "Using Mortality Data to Refine Our Understanding of Homicide Patterns in Select Postcommunist Countries." *Homicide Studies* 12 (1): 117–35. https://doi.org/10.1177/1088767907311246.

Chapter 2: Violence against Women

Kathleen Ratajczak

OVERVIEW

When examining patterns of lethal violence around the world, men are 81 percent of homicide victims and 90 percent of known homicide offenders. This pattern holds for all regions of the world and is even more pronounced when considering victims and offenders under thirty years old (UNODC 2019). However, lethal violence is only a small proportion of all crime, and research has shown that women and girls experience much higher risks for sexual violence or intimate partner violence than men. Additionally, much of the violence directed at females is *driven by the fact that they are female*, as opposed to the causes of male violence, such as gangs, drugs, or substance use.

The fact that one's gender influences their risk for certain types of violence has led to a relatively new category of crimes called gender-based violence (GBV) or sexual and gender-based violence. The defining characteristic of these crimes is that victims are targeted because of their gender or sex and violence is rooted in gender inequality. Although men, women, boys, and girls can be victims of GBV, the majority of such violence targets women and girls. As such, the term violence against women (VAW) is often used to identify the subset of GBV with female victims. This chapter focuses on international examples of VAW; however, other examples of GBV with male or LGBTQ victims can be found in chapter 4 on Hate Crimes, chapter 5 on Human Trafficking, and chapter 7 on Mass Atrocities and International Justice.

According to the United Nations Global Study on Homicide, females account for only 19 percent of all homicide victims. However, of the cases of family-related homicides, females comprise 64 percent of victims, and of the cases of intimate partner homicides, females are 82 percent of victims (UNODC 2019). This implies that women are killed by current and former partners and family members (both male and female) because of gender roles and norms, as opposed to random or unplanned violence. This type of homicide is often referred to as femicide. The most well-known sources of femicide are intimate partner violence and domestic violence, but other examples include honor killings, dowry-related killings, killing women as a tool of war, and killings associating women with witchcraft.

Beyond lethal violence, the United Nations reports that about 35 percent of women globally have experienced intimate partner violence (physical or sexual) or sexual violence by a nonpartner. These types of crimes are difficult to measure because of the victims' unwillingness to report them. It is estimated that only 40 percent of victims of VAW globally sought any kind of help and only 10 percent went to the police. Women and girls are also at risk for human trafficking, and at least thirty countries still practice female genital mutilation (UNSD 2015).

Despite these bleak statistics, there have been some important initiatives to address GBV. In 1995, the Fourth World Conference for Women produced the Beijing Declaration and Platform for Action, a historic document outlining a plan to improve gender equality globally. One of the twelve critical areas addressed in the declaration was VAW. Additionally, in 2011, the Council of Europe developed the Convention on Preventing and Combating Violence against Women and Domestic Violence that was ratified by thirty-four countries and went into effect in 2014. Known as the Istanbul Convention, the document provides a legal framework of minimum standards for the prevention of VAW, the protection of victims, and prosecution of offenders (Council of Europe 2019). As of 2015, 125 countries had laws criminalizing sexual harassment, 119 had laws against domestic violence, and fifty-two made marital rape illegal (UNSD 2015).

The countries profiled in this chapter capture a broad array of acts of VAW. Domestic violence is a common theme across several countries, but with different emphases. The cases of Canada and Mexico discuss domestic violence against indigenous women, whereas Russia is an example of a country that has loosened its protections for women against their abusers. The Democratic Republic of Congo (DRC), Haiti, and India cover the topic of rape, with rape examined as a tool of war in the DRC and political rapes in Haiti. Violence associated with sex work and sex trafficking are examined in Mexico and Russia, although much more information on sex trafficking can be found in chapter 5 on Human Trafficking. Two of the less common forms of femicide are included in this chapter along with a discussion of dowry deaths in India and honor killings in Jordan. The profile of China covers different types of VAW that stem from a national population control policy including infanticide of girls, forced sterilization of women, and trafficking for marriage. All the sections consider how different kinds of marginalization increase the risks of VAW for certain groups, such as caste in India, poor children in Haiti, or sex workers in Mexico.

Further Reading

Council of Europe. 2019. "Istanbul Convention: Action against Violence against Women and Domestic Violence." https://www.coe.int/en/web/istanbul-convention/home.
UNODC (United Nations Office on Drugs and Crime). 2019. "Global Study on Homicide." https://www.unodc.org/unodc/en/data-and-analysis/global-study-on-homicide.html.
UNSD (United Nations Statistics Division). 2015. "The World's Women 2015: Trends and Statistics." https://unstats.un.org/unsd/gender/worldswomen.html.

CANADA

Canada is the northernmost country in North America and shares its southern border with the United States. It is the third largest country in landmass after Russia. It was colonized by the British and French beginning in the sixteenth century.

Canada's path to independence from Britain was not a clear event like it was in the United States. Instead, Canada started to gain autonomy from the English crown in 1867 but was not completely independent from Britain until 1982. It is a federal, parliamentary democracy and part of the Commonwealth of Nations. Canada has a diverse cultural heritage with strong French-Canadian roots in Quebec that are very different from English-Canadian culture. The majority of the nearly thirty-six million people lives close to the southern border and is heavily concentrated in urban areas, whereas native groups populate many of the northern and rural areas. About 4.4 percent of the population is aboriginal (Central Intelligence Agency 2018). Canada has a low violent crime rate, especially compared to the rest of North America, but domestic violence is a significant portion of violent crime, especially among aboriginal Canadians.

Patterns of Domestic Violence

The 2017 Family Violence Survey found that domestic violence accounted for around 30 percent of all violent crime reported to police in Canada (Government of Canada 2017). Of these instances, the overwhelming majority of domestic violence victims in Canada were women, and 45 percent of them were victims of intimate partner violence. Major risk factors of domestic violence in Canada include low socioeconomic status, economic dependence on a spouse, low educational attainment, and young age (Kaukinen and Powers 2015; Government of Canada 2017). Additionally, domestic violence is higher among indigenous women, who are also more likely to be in lower socioeconomic classes.

One rather unique aspect of domestic violence in Canada is violence against indigenous women and the large numbers of murdered and missing indigenous women and girls. Indigenous refers to the people who originated in that area and are native to the country. Some of the terms used in Canada to label this population include indigenous, aboriginal, native, first-peoples, Eskimo, and Indians, with the latter two terms considered pejorative. The Constitution Act of 1982 formally adopted the term "aboriginal," which is used in all of the country's legal

---

Honor Killing

In 2009, Rona Amir Mohammad and her three nineteen-, seventeen-, and thirteen-year-old daughters were drowned in a murder committed by Rona's husband, Mohammed Shafia, his second wife, and their son. The family immigrated to Canada from Afghanistan and Shafia was concerned about how his daughters were becoming Westernized. The prosecution had several taped recordings of Shafia discussing his disapproval of his daughters' behaviors, which he thought were shameful. He blamed his first wife for encouraging those behaviors. All three perpetrators were convicted of murder and sentenced to life in prison with no possibility of parole for twenty-five years.

documents pertaining to native peoples. There are three main indigenous groups in Canada. First Nations people are the original inhabitants of the country below the Artic Circle, while Inuit are the original inhabitants above the Artic Circle. The Métis are descendants from early interactions between the First Nations people and European settlers.

There are close to 1.4 million native people living in Canada, accounting for just over 4 percent of the population. Despite making up such a small portion of Canada's population, native people are overrepresented in the criminal justice system both as victims and perpetrators of crime. This is particularly true of native women who experience higher rates of domestic and sexual violence than their non-native peers. Some studies have found that native women in Canada have four-to-five times the risk of experiencing intimate partner violence compared to non-native women (Brownridge 2008). The main explanation for this pattern is colonization theory, which argues that the histories of colonization of native peoples and their land have lasting effects to the present day. Some of these effects include poverty, poor educational outcomes, poor health, and violence, which are all problems in native communities in Canada. Canada, like other colonizers, has a long history of human rights abuses against native peoples, including outlawing expressions of native culture, kidnapping native children and educating them elsewhere, outlawing religious ceremonies, forced removal from lands, and other legal actions.

In addition to high rates of domestic violence, there is also a large number of missing and murdered indigenous women in Canada. There have been between 500 and 1,200 missing and unsolved murders of indigenous women since the 1980s, and 24 percent of murdered women in Canada are indigenous women (National Inquiry into Missing and Murdered Indigenous Women and Girls 2017). This large range in the estimates of missing indigenous women stems from differences in defining who is indigenous, as well as in classifying murder and missing persons. Indigenous activists argue that there is less attention from police and media for cases involving indigenous victims than those involving white victims. There is some support for this argument, with one scholar finding that murdered and missing indigenous women received three and half times less media coverage than white women (Gilchrist 2010). In response to the calls to address this problem from activist groups within Canada and internationally, the Canadian government created the National Inquiry into Missing and Murdered Indigenous Women and Girls in September 2016. This inquiry is independent from the government of Canada and the governments of native peoples in Canada. It is designed to gather information and evidence of violence against both indigenous women and people who identify as LGBT in Canada. This truth-gathering process includes community and expert hearings, research, and collaboration with both indigenous peoples and police departments. This process adopts a trauma-informed, decolonizing, and families-first approach.

Responding to Domestic Violence

Canada has a relatively long history of addressing VAW. Similar to the United States, grassroots organizations in Canada began developing and opening shelters for battered women in the 1970s, as well as working to spread awareness about the different forms of violence women suffer at the hands of those close to them. These grassroots efforts came to the attention of the government in the late 1970s and early 1980s. For example, domestic violence shelters, often called transitional housing in Canada, started with grassroots organizations and eventually turned into a federally run program.

The Canadian government's history with domestic violence interventions appears to be a back-and-forth with feminist organizations. The late 1970s and early 1980s featured the government strongly incorporating the views of feminist organizations into their approach to wife battering. At the time feminists were fighting for wife battering, or domestic violence, to be viewed as a public problem rather than a private concern. This meant creating laws that criminalized this behavior and actually following through with the sentencing of offenders. Feminists pointed out frequent loopholes in the law that were designed to protect and maintain the family unit, but in reality worked to keep offenders out of jail and in their homes where they could continue abusing their wives. In 1979, the Advisory Council on the Status of Women (CACSW) conducted a survey called *Wife Battering in Canada: The Vicious Circle*. The results of the survey showed that on the surface the government's policies appeared to protect women, but in reality the laws repeatedly failed women who were abused by their partners. The Canadian government responded to the report by increasing punishments for those found guilty of wife battering, and began calling the crime "wife battering" to emphasize the gendered nature of the act. At the same time as the criminal justice system responded to feminist critiques, there was also a public health perspective on domestic violence that offered a different orientation to the problem. For example, health professionals preferred to use the gender-neutral terms of domestic violence or family violence. While the term domestic or interpersonal violence is more inclusive, as it includes men as victims and the LGBT communities, some feminists (a large portion of them in Canada) claim that this move away from the concept of wife battering de-emphasizes how gendered this abuse is (DeKeseredy and Dragiewicz 2014).

There have been two other notable government responses to domestic violence in Canada. The first was a reaction to the 1989 Montreal Massacre. On December 6, 1989, Marc Lépine targeted female students at École Polytechnique, an engineering school, in a mass shooting. He separated the female students from male students in one classroom and opened fire on the female students, and then he continued to target female students throughout the school. His attack resulted in the deaths of fourteen women, with several others injured. Lépine's mass shooting led to a quick response from the government including the creation of five research centers to study VAW, the creation of the 1993 Statistics Canada National Violence against Women Survey, and a governmental ad hoc committee to investigate the landscape of VAW in the country and create actions plans designed to address the problem.

The second notable response to VAW by the Canadian government was a more holistic approach to the problem that considers victims' needs. Most of the government's responses to the 1989 massacre involved the criminal justice system, such as dual-arrest and no-drop policies. Dual-arrest policies require that police arrest both parties in a domestic violence situation when they cannot determine who is at fault, or if they believe both parties are guilty. This has led to many women being arrested when they call the police on an abusive spouse. According to no-drop policies a domestic violence case cannot be dropped once changes are filed, even if the victim of the case wishes to drop the charges. More recently, Canada has started to investigate alternative approaches to justice outside of criminal punishment, such as restorative justice approaches currently in use in some native and tribal communities in Canada. Restorative justice is a process that includes the victim, offender, and affected community members, including family and friends of both the victim and the offender, in the pursuit of justice. This is also a different approach to justice because it allows those individuals who were harmed to collectively come to an agreement about what they believe justice should look like. A final important element about restorative justice is that the offender has to accept responsibility for their actions for restorative justice to take place.

Further Reading

Brownridge, Douglas A. 2008. "Understanding the Elevated Risk of Partner Violence Against Aboriginal Women: A Comparison of Two Nationally Representative Surveys of Canada." *Journal of Family Violence* 23 (5): 353–67. https://doi.org/10.1007/s10896-008-9160-0.

Central Intelligence Agency. 2018. "The World Factbook." https://www.cia.gov/library/publications/resources/the-world-factbook/.

DeKeseredy, Walter S., and Molly Dragiewicz. 2014. "Woman Abuse in Canada: Sociological Reflections on the Past, Suggestions for the Future." *Violence Against Women* 20 (2): 228–44. https://doi.org/10.1177/1077801214521325.

Gilchrist, Kristen. 2010. "'Newsworthy' Victims?" *Feminist Media Studies* 10 (4): 373–90. https://doi.org/10.1080/14680777.2010.514110.

Government of Canada, Statistics Canada. 2017. "Section 2: Police-Reported Intimate Partner Violence in Canada, 2017." February 16, 2017. https://www150.statcan.gc.ca/n1/pub/85-002-x/2018001/article/54978/02-eng.htm.

Kaukinen, Catherine Elizabeth, and Ráchael A. Powers. 2015. "The Role of Economic Factors on Women's Risk for Intimate Partner Violence: A Cross-National Comparison of Canada and the United States." *Violence Against Women* 21 (2): 229–48. https://doi.org/10.1177/1077801214564686.

National Inquiry into Missing and Murdered Indigenous Women and Girls. 2017. "Our Women and Girls Are Sacred: Interim Report." http://publications.gc.ca/collections/collection_2017/ffada-mmiwg/CP32-163-1-2017-eng.pdf.

CHINA

China, located in East Asia, is the world's most populous country with over 1.4 billion people. It borders fifteen countries and four seas along its eastern coast. It is located south of Mongolia, northeast of India, and north of Vietnam. As one of the oldest civilizations, China has had a long history of dynastic rule. After World War II, China became a communist country under the leadership of Mao Zedong

(1893–1976). Politically, the Communist Party controls the country, strictly controls its citizens' lives, and actively discourages political dissent. China had initially adopted the communist command economy, similar to the Soviet Union, where the government tightly controls all economic decisions and owns most of the land and businesses. However, since 1978, China has been adopting free-market economic policies to encourage economic growth, but still with more government control than typical capitalist systems. These reforms have led to an economic boom in China, which by 2017 had become the world's second largest economy (Central Intelligence Agency 2018).

Chinese society is based on a patrilineal lineage, where family and culture are based on male inheritance and power. This has led to a history in China where boys and men are granted more opportunities in society compared to girls and women. One historic instance of gender inequality and VAW in China was the tradition of foot binding for Chinese women, when women's feet were painfully bound to change their size and shape. The practice of binding feet resulted in disabilities for women that limited their mobility for the rest of their lives. Foot binding ended in the early twentieth century.

One-Child Policy

Communist China's one-child policy is another example of how gender inequality and VAW are related. The one-child policy was implemented in 1979 as a response to the rapidly growing population. While the country previously had a two-child policy in place, government officials feared that the growing population could create catastrophic conditions for the country. There were certain circumstances that allowed couples to apply for a second child, including disability of parents or the firstborn child, if their first child was a daughter, the number of siblings the parents had, and if they lived in rural areas where children were needed to help farm. The one-child policy was most strictly enforced in densely populated urban areas.

The one-child policy had some positive effects for Chinese women, which were unexpected side effects of trying to curb population growth. For example, women had expanded opportunities in life. One-child parents had only a single child to provide for, as well as to depend upon as they aged. This meant that female children from one-child families were provided a better education than women had historically been offered in the past because they were valued more as an investment for the future of the family. Research has shown that one-child families provide better education for girls than those with multiple children. There is no education gap between boys and girls from one-child families, but girls fare worse than boys in multiple-child families. While the preference for boys over girls used to disadvantage girls in terms of educational attainment and future life opportunities, those parents whose only child was female were more committed to furthering their daughter's chances in life through education and life attainment. This has led to universities with more women than men in China, as well as rates of female employment larger than other powerful countries like the United States.

This billboard promotes China's one-child family planning policy that existed from 1980 to 2015. An unintended consequence of this policy was various forms of violence against women and girls, including infanticide, selective abortions, and forced sterilization. (Corel)

China also has the largest number of female billionaires in any country, which some point to as evidence of growing gender equality.

Harm to Women

Despite some positive impacts on women's educational and life opportunities, there were other negative effects of the one-child policy on women, both on infant girls and women of childbearing age. One way women were harmed was through the means the Chinese government adopted to enforce the law. To restrict women from having more children than they were permitted to have, the government levied fines for additional children and required both contraception and sterilization of women. Women across the country were surgically fitted with an intrauterine device (IUD) after the birth of their first child. This IUD could only be removed through surgical means. After a woman had her second child she was sterilized, a surgical intervention that makes women unable to bear children. Not all women wanted to undergo these procedures, and activists from other countries have viewed this as a form of forced sterilization and contraception.

The one-child policy also heightened the preference for boys, as many families went to extreme lengths to ensure their only child would be male. Some of the methods that families used included sex-selective abortions, female infanticide, and child abandonment. Sex-selective abortions occur when a pregnant woman chooses to have an abortion depending on the sex of the baby. With the availability of ultrasound to determine a baby's sex prior to birth, families could choose to abort a fetus if it was a girl. While this practice was outlawed in China in 2005, it did not eliminate sex-selective abortions. Researchers found that the use of ultrasound to determine the sex of a baby increased for parents whose firstborn child was female, particularly in rural areas. Another avenue families have used to ensure a male child is femicide or female infanticide. Families who give birth to a female child may neglect the baby resulting in malnourishment and poor health that can result in death. If these babies are never registered, then their death goes unnoticed and the parents can try again to birth a male child. Families may also intentionally kill female children, but this is not well documented (Hong 1987). Female child abandonment is believed to be the main contributor to large number of female orphans in the country. Lastly, families can keep female children unregistered with the government to keep trying for a male child, but this child would remain hidden for the majority of their lives and experience considerable difficultly as an adult.

Social Consequences

Due to the preference for boys over girls, the use of sex-selective abortions, infant femicide, and child abandonment have led to a population with imbalanced sex ratios. There are 115 men to every hundred women, resulting in thirty-three million more men than women in China (World Economic Forum 2017). An unexpected consequence of this population shift is increased crime rates. Social scientists attribute this increase in crime to the lack of available wives for the surplus of Chinese men. When single men, primarily from low socioeconomic backgrounds, cannot find wives, they migrate to large urban city centers and may turn to crime to make their fortunes. The imbalanced sex ratio has also led to increased instances of men being raised in male-only environments, which sociological and feminist theories argue contributes to higher rates of criminality, in general, and VAW, in particular. Theories such as Male Peer Support Theory and other critical masculinity theories find that all-male spaces promote male dominance and patriarchal values that demean women and femininity and support VAW.

Additionally, the growing sex-ratio disparity between men and women in China has contributed to the trafficking of women into China for marriage. Although China has a long history of women trafficking, the more recent forms of trafficking can be traced to the shortage of women as a result of the imbalanced sex ratio. The demand for trafficked brides comes from the large number of bachelor men in the country, particularly concentrated in rural areas. Demand for trafficked brides also occurs due to financial struggles, as it is often cheaper to purchase a bride than to go through the traditional avenues of courting marriage where the bride's family is often compensated. The women who are trafficked are sometimes non-Chinese women who are brought into the country, or are Chinese women who are trafficked within the country. These women are often financially vulnerable and are either tricked, coerced, or forced into marriage. Sometimes women's families sell or coerce their daughters into such trafficked marriages when they are desperate for money or desire particular familial connections.

The Chinese government changed the one-child policy to a universal two-child policy in 2015, meaning all women can have two children irrespective of the extenuating circumstances. Their stated purpose for the policy change was to help with the sex-ratio imbalance. While this was heralded as a large victory by several news sources, some academics and activists still raised concerns about the consequences this new policy will have on women's lives. The Chinese government assumed that this relaxed policy would increase the birth rate in China; however, this expected increase has not yet occurred. The need for a larger working class to support the Chinese economy and the ever-growing elderly population has renewed pressure on Chinese women to return to the home and have children. The government has worked to create some policies to assist women in this situation, such as increasing the duration of maternity leaves. The increased duration may seem like a victory for women, but many employers do not have the funds to support these new requirements, leading to reluctance on part of companies to hire women. This growing social pressure for women to raise families and the sexual discrimination occurring in the workplace may signal a backlash to the gender equality achieved from the original one-child policy. Notably, in the relaxed policy there is still a restriction on the number of children women can bear, which is likely to continue supporting sex-selective abortions, femicide, and female child abandonment, as these practices were common in rural areas where women were already allowed to birth two children.

Further Reading

Central Intelligence Agency. 2018. "The World Factbook." https://www.cia.gov/library/publications/resources/the-world-factbook/.

Greenhalgh, Susan. 2013. "Patriarchal Demographics? China's Sex Ratio Reconsidered." *Population and Development Review* 38 (February): 130–49. https://doi.org/10.1111/j.1728-4457.2013.00556.x.

Hong, Lawrence K. 1987. "Potential Effects of the One-Child Policy on Gender Equality in the People's Republic of China." *Gender and Society* 1 (3): 317–26.

Lee, Ming-Hsuan. 2012. "The One-Child Policy and Gender Equality in Education in China: Evidence from Household Data." *Journal of Family and Economic Issues* 33 (1): 41–52. https://doi.org/10.1007/s10834-011-9277-9.

World Economic Forum. 2017. *The Global Gender Gap Report: 2017.* Geneva, Switzerland: World Economic Forum.

Zhao, Gracie Ming. 2003. "Trafficking of Women for Marriage in China: Policy and Practice." *Criminal Justice* 3 (1): 83–102. https://doi.org/10.1177/1466802503003001457.

DEMOCRATIC REPUBLIC OF CONGO

The DRC has a long and complex history of conflict and violence. Located in central Africa and west of Rwanda, it borders nine other countries. The population of eighty-five million people comprises over 200 ethnic groups. The official language is French, a remnant of Belgian colonialism. The DRC is an extremely poor country with a gross domestic product per capita of only USD 800 compared to USD 2,100 in Rwanda and USD 400 in Zambia. Minerals are the country's most valuable exports. Since gaining independence in 1960, the DRC has experienced state violence, ethnic violence, and international wars, the latter of which have been particularly brutal toward women (Central Intelligence Agency 2018).

Africa's World Wars

The DRC is a key figure in what many refer to as "Africa's World Wars." The conflict between the Hutus and Tutsis in the border country of Rwanda, which resulted in genocide, began to spill over into the DRC, culminating in two international wars starting in the 1990s. In the First Congo War (1996–1997), Rwandan forces led a coup against dictator Joseph Mobutu (1930–1997) and replaced him with Laurent Kabila (1939–2001), who changed the name of the country from Zaire to the Democratic Republic of Congo. Soon Kabila lost the support of the Rwandan government that put him in power, which led Rwanda and Uganda to attempt another coup for regaining control over the country and its valuable resources. Kabila sought support from Zimbabwe and Angola to maintain his control of the DRC. What followed was the Second Congo War (1998–2003) that involved nine African nations. Peace agreements among various countries were negotiated in 2003, and a transitional government took control in 2003. However, ethnic conflict within the country has still persisted.

While the conflict in the Congo is complicated due to the many actors involved, an important reason for the war is the valuable minerals located in the eastern part of the country. The mines in the eastern provinces contain coltan, which is used in electronic devices, such as laptops and cell phones. It is estimated that 80 percent of coltan comes from eastern DRC (Meger 2010). Most scholars argue that much of the violence in the country, both the civil wars and the continuing violence today, results from attempts to control the mines and coltan production.

Rape as a Weapon of War

While the wars in Congo are multifaceted and complex, the dominant narrative surrounding them is the widespread use of rape as a weapon of war. While the majority of studies on VAW frame rape and other forms of GBV as interpersonal in nature, rape as a weapon of war is understood differently. Rape has long been recognized as a consequence of wartime violence, with records of soldiers engaging in rape leading back to antiquity. However, the narrative change from "wartime rape" to "rape as a weapon of war" has occurred much more recently. The Bosnian War (1992–1995) is most responsible this change, as it was the first time that systematic rape was charged as a war crime and a crime against humanity. Since then, rape as a weapon of war has been documented in several violent conflicts, including in Rwanda and the DRC.

Rape as a weapon of war is different from both interpersonal rape and general wartime rape in terms of scope and purpose. Interpersonal rape is driven by an individual's power and control over another through sexual gratification. General wartime rape is also committed by individual soldiers for their own purposes, including sexual gratification and achieving masculine status. Rape as a weapon of war, on the other hand, is driven by a large group's need to dominate, eliminate, or destabilize another group of people.

Systematic rape functions to terrorize civilian populations, thus weakening their resistance to armed factions. Many cultures view rape and other forms of GBV as shameful and contaminating, oftentimes placing the blame on the victim. Therefore, systematic rape can destabilize families and entire communities, particularly when women are viewed as cultural and moral touchstones for the culture involved. Rape as a weapon of war impacts more than just the victims, as researchers find that soldiers target women and children as a means to threaten and destabilize their male family and community members. A final element that often differentiates systematic rape from other forms of rape is the brutality and extreme violence involved. When used as a weapon of war, rape is more likely to include multiple offenders (gang rape), to be committed in front of family members, to involve forced incest, and to lead to bodily injury often from using weapons to penetrate victims. This extreme level of violence is part of the strategy to conquer a civilian population by spreading fear and instilling shame in the victims and their communities.

Measuring the scope of rape during the conflict in the DRC is a difficult task. While suffering from the usual barriers in determining prevalence, such as lack of reporting and shame among victims, the decades of violent conflict in the DRC have led to a weakened government structure, which is poorly equipped to collect and maintain these statistics. Additionally, the perpetrators of rape in the DRC include rebel groups, government agents, and even peacekeeping forces. It is unlikely for a government to admit to violence against its own civilian populations. Due to these barriers, true estimates of rape during the conflict in the DRC are nearly impossible to obtain. The majority of estimates come from the United Nations (UN) and nongovernmental organizations (NGOs) who have intervened and provided aid during and after the conflict. The UN reported over 30,000 cases of sexual violence in one region over a two-year period (Schneider, Banholzer, and Albarracin 2015). These numbers are usually obtained from those who come to hospitals or organizations seeking aid. However, many of the most vulnerable victims do not have access to these facilities and cannot be counted.

Rape as a weapon of war in the DRC has devastating impacts on the victims, their families, and their communities. The effects of rape go beyond the physical injuries and violation that victims experience and include psychological, social, and financial consequences. The physical impact of rape for women in the DRC is higher than usual forms of interpersonal rape because of the brutality of the attacks. Many women suffer from injury to multiple body parts, fistula, infertility, incontinence, and sexually transmitted infections (STIs). Many of these physical ailments also contribute to psychological and social problems because many husbands and community members view women as tainted and less than a woman when they have STIs or are unable to bear children. This can lead husbands and communities to reject and ostracize women. In addition, women also experience a multitude of psychological effects that often accompany any form of sexual violence, including depression, anxiety, posttraumatic stress disorder, recurring nightmares, and intrusive memories. All of these negative effects keep women from returning to life as it existed prior to their victimization.

Foreign Aid

The conflict in the DRC quickly came to the notice of international actors such as the UN and many NGOs. The UN established a peacekeeping mission to the DRC in 1999 (MONUC) a year after the conflict began. The mission remains active to this day and is the UN's largest peacekeeping force with over 20,000 personnel deployed in the DRC (United Nations Peacekeeping 2019). UN peacekeeping missions work to assist countries in transitioning out of conflict and establishing structures to support this transition. UN peacekeepers also work to protect civilians, enforce human rights, and reintegrate combatants. Their presence in conflict areas such as the DRC also makes them primary witnesses and reporters of violations of human rights including the systematic rape occurring due to the ongoing conflict.

In addition to the UN, many NGOs have established themselves in the DRC to provide humanitarian aid to victims from the conflict. Three large NGOs, The International Rescue Committee (IRC), Malteser International, and Women for Women International (WfWI), have conducted work to specifically assist rape victims during the conflict. Each of these organizations sought to provide female rape victims assistance in the areas of health, psychological well-being, and finances. However, they each went about this very differently. The IRC's most important contribution was framing rape during conflict as a form of torture. It was this narrative that made them successful in receiving funding to create structures designed to address the multitude of needs of conflict rape victims. Malteser International, which has been active in the DRC since 1994, provides similar resources as the IRC but with two important differences. This Malta-based NGO integrates their medical, psychological, and economic services so that a victim can only access these resources through the general medical structures of the NGO. While Malteser argues that this can help to identify rape victims, it also has the dual function of limiting the number of women seeking resources who are not rape victims. Some NGOs have documented the phenomenon of women claiming to be rape victims to seek financial and food assistance they need. Malteser also created programs to help women in the DRC generate income, which are open to all women irrespective of their victim status. Lastly, the WfWI differs the most from other NGOs as they take a micro approach to assist women in the DRC. Instead of working with local structures to expand resources, they have a sponsorship program where women globally can sponsor a woman in the DRC by donating a specific amount per month.

While there is no denying that NGOs provide the much needed resources and aid in the DRC, particularly to rape victims, some scholars criticize NGOs for their unintended consequences. These scholars highlight how NGOs can become coopted by funding organizations for ulterior motives such as gaining political power and increasing profits. For example, Malteser International cut ties with some of their partner organizations after finding that many of them were viewing the work with victims as a growth market for profit. The work of NGOs is also key in framing which issues during conflicts are deemed important, as can be seen through the work on the IRC. International actors like NGOs and the UN have the ability to direct the conversation on the conflict, which means that they determine which areas and which victims will receive funding and aid. Activists and scholars have argued that this leads to a skewed view of the conflict and leaves many victims who are not a part of the popular framing without assistance, which can force some victimized women to tell stories of "false rape" to gain access to resources they need to survive (Autesserre 2012).

Further Reading

Autesserre, Séverine. 2012. "Dangerous Tales: Dominant Narratives on the Congo and Their Unintended Consequences." *African Affairs* 111 (443): 202–22. https://doi.org/10.1093/afraf/adr080.

Central Intelligence Agency. 2018. "The World Factbook." https://www.cia.gov/library/publications/resources/the-world-factbook/.

Dijkzeu, Dennis. 2015. "War, Rape and NGOs in the DR Congo." In *The NGO Challenge for International Relations Theory*, edited by William E. DeMars and Dennis Dijkzeu, 26. New York: Routledge.

Meger, Sara. 2010. "Rape of the Congo: Understanding Sexual Violence in the Conflict in the Democratic Republic of Congo." *Journal of Contemporary African Studies* 28 (2): 119–35. https://doi.org/10.1080/02589001003736728.

Schneider, Gerald, Lilli Banholzer, and Laura Albarracin. 2015. "Ordered Rape: A Principal–Agent Analysis of Wartime Sexual Violence in the DR Congo." *Violence Against Women* 21 (11): 1341–63. https://doi.org/10.1177/1077801215593645.

United Nations Peacekeeping. 2019. "MONUSCO Fact Sheet." https://peacekeeping.un.org/en/mission/monusco.

HAITI

Haiti is an island country of nearly eleven million people located in the Caribbean between Cuba and Puerto Rico. The Spanish originally colonized the island they called Hispaniola in 1492, with France taking control of the western half of the island in 1659 while the eastern half eventually became the Dominican Republic. The French began transporting African slaves in increasing numbers, with slaves soon outnumbering white landowners. Anxious white slave-owners responded to the situation by inflicting extreme violence against their slaves including frequent rapes of slave women. What occurred next in Haiti was unheard of then and even today; the slaves started a revolution that resulted in a free and independent country in 1793. Despite this important historic event, Haiti's future would be plagued by power-hungry leaders, violent conflict, and extreme poverty. The gross domestic product per capita in Haiti is USD 1,800, whereas on the other side of the island in the Dominican Republic it is USD 17,000 (Central Intelligence Agency 2018). Many recent historical events in the last fifty years have contributed to political unrest, including the thirty-year dictatorship under the Duvaliers, the violence surrounding the Aristide presidency and resulting coup, and an earthquake in 2010, all of which contribute to high levels of violence, particularly VAW.

Violence against Women

VAW in Haiti is rooted within the country's history of political unrest and poor infrastructure, and has become an expected experience in most women's lives. Most statistics of VAW come from international and domestic organizations that provide aid to victims. These organizations find that close to 50 percent of women and girls in Haiti have experienced some form of GBV (United Nations General Assembly/Security Council 2006), with a large percentage of these assaults targeting young girls. One study examining youth development in the country found that 46 percent of girls in Haiti had been sexually abused, with 33 percent between the ages of five and nine and 43 percent between the ages of ten and fourteen (Justesen and Verner 2007). VAW in Haiti occurs both inside and outside of the home, and by both strangers and community and family members. The types of violence women and girls experience range from domestic violence to political and gang rape.

Scholars who study VAW in Haiti connect the widespread violence to cultural gender norms and the high acceptability of general violence in the country. Some scholars suggest that violence has become a normalized occurrence in Haiti, with the majority of individuals reporting that they do not feel safe in their own homes. When violence becomes the norm in any society, crime rates increase as perpetrators believe that they will not be held accountable for their actions. Victims are also impacted by the normalization of violence, as they are less likely to report their victimization to authorities. Another way culture affects women's experiences of violence is through gender norms. Haitian women live in a patriarchal society where women are expected to fulfill domestic duties, such as raising children, taking care of the home, and providing meals; whereas Haitian males operate mainly in the public sphere where they are responsible for providing monetary support for the family. This strict divide in gender roles gives men power over women in both personal relationships and in the public sphere because women become dependent on men's economic support. This power imbalance contributes to VAW in the home and within intimate relationships, and is the basis of VAW in the public sphere, such as political rapes.

The connection between these gender norms and VAW occurs throughout the entire life cycle, beginning when women are very young. Many victim aid organizations in Haiti work directly with girls who have been victims of sexual abuse and find that gender roles contribute to their abuse. Haitian gender roles require that young girls work within the household, both by raising younger siblings and by doing household chores. Young girls are also less likely than their male counterparts to go to school or be engaged in apprenticeships outside of the home. This leaves girls as young as five alone at home to tend to the house, which increases the risk of sexual abuse by family and community members. Even when this abuse is known by the family, they often cover it up because acknowledging it could ruin the young girl's chance of marriage.

Political Rape

One specific form of VAW that is more common in Haiti than in most countries is politically motivated rapes. These rapes are committed by *organisations politiques* (political organizations) or gangs with political affiliations to punish and terrorize political opponents and their supporters (Duramy 2014). Politically motivated rape was common throughout the dictatorships of François "Papa Doc" Duvalier (1907–1971) and his son Jean-Claude "Baby Doc" Duvalier (1951–2014) to quell dissent among the population. Such rape incidents reappeared during the coup d'état that ousted Jean-Bertrand Aristide (1952–) from power during 1991 and 1994, and again after his return to office. There are many political organizations localized in shantytowns outside of urban centers, such as Cité Soleil outside of Port-au-Prince. It can be difficult at times to differentiate between gangs and political organizations because both groups engage in gang rape and organized crime.

Politically motivated rape is similar to rape as a weapon of war in some ways. First, wartime rape and political rape use women as pawns to harm their male relatives who are the real targets of the violence. Second, both forms of rape are used to cause terror and dismantle family structures. Raping female relatives successfully causes fear due to gender norms in the country. Women and girls are viewed as property of the male heads of household and their purity is important for their future as wives and mothers. By raping women, the perpetrators are showing that the male heads of house are unable to protect their own property and family. Oftentimes political rapes force family members to witness the violent act or force them to commit the rapes themselves. This is especially demoralizing and emasculating for the male members of the family. Third, both forms of rape frequently use gang rape as a tactic. Lastly, both wartime rape and political rape bolster the masculinity and camaraderie of the males involved.

Restavék

One reason violence against girls in Haiti is so common is the practice of *restavék*, or using children for domestic work. Restavék means "to stay with" in Creole, the common language spoken in Haiti. Restavéks are children who are sent from their homes to live in the homes of wealthier families to handle domestic work. Most restavéks come from impoverished families in provincial areas of Haiti, and

75 percent of them are girls (O'Brien 2006). Parents who send their children to live and work in these homes often believe it is going to provide their children with a brighter future, with access to better education and higher wages than they would have received if they stayed in their home town. However, many restavéks experience violence and abuse. Young female restavéks are vulnerable to abuse by their new employers because they do not have anyone to look out for them and are sold as property to the new family. Organizations working with restavéks find that many of them experience physical and sexual abuse by their employers, receive very little pay and food, and have no opportunities to gain an education. One study found that female restavéks were four-and-a-half times more likely to experience sexual assault than females who were not restavéks (Kolbe and Hutson 2006).

Impact of Aid Organizations

The UN has a long history of involvement in Haiti including three different missions in the country. The first UN mission in Haiti (UNMIH) from September 1993 to June 1996 was a peacekeeping mission designed to intervene in the military coup against the then-president Aristide. UNMIH established a multinational force to be deployed in Haiti to enforce changes in the government. The UN re-established their mission to Haiti in 2004, this time called the United Nations Stabilization Mission in Haiti (referred to as MINUSTAH) after Aristide resigned from power in 2004; the mission was extended after the 2010 earthquake. MINUSTAH was an active mission until October 2017, when it transformed into MINUJUSTH, or a mission for justice support in Haiti, which is slated to end in October 2019, at which point there should be no active peacekeeping forces in Haiti. While the UN missions in Haiti have been positive for building infrastructure and promoting democracy, they have also been at the center of a few scandals. For example, the UN led a military peacekeeping force into Cité Soleil, the shantytown in

---

UN Troops Involved in Child Sex Ring

The Associated Press investigated stories of sexual abuse by United Nations peacekeepers from 2005 to 2017 and found 2,000 allegations, 300 of which involved child victims. Between 2004 and 2007, a child sex ring operated by peacekeepers was discovered in Haiti. Nine child victims identified 134 Sri Lankan peacekeepers as perpetrators of repeated sexual assault. Most of the accused were sent home but none faced criminal charges. The United Nations does not have legal jurisdiction over peacekeepers and it is the responsibility of the member states to investigate and prosecute offenses by their own troops.

Daigle, Katy, and Paisley Dodds. 2017. "UN Peacekeepers: How a Haiti Child Sex Ring Was Whitewashed." AP NEWS, May 26, 2017. https://apnews.com/96f9ff66b7b34d9f971ed f0e92e2082c.

Port-au-Prince, to disarm a violent rebel group in 2005. This action led to the deaths of several civilians. The UN cites the mission as a success against a violent gang leader, but those who oppose the UN's presence in Haiti claim that up to eighty civilian deaths were caused by purposely targeting civilians during the raid. Critics argue that the UN is allowing violence and human rights abuses by the Haitian police forces to go unchecked.

While the UN is a large source of aid in Haiti, there are also many NGOs present in the country. NGOs have provided much needed aid and resources to the population of Haiti including victim services. However, there are some negative consequences of NGOs. For example, to receive material assistance, people must first demonstrate their status as a victim and have to tell their stories of trauma in ways that meet the mission of that NGO. NGOs use these stories of victimization and trauma to gain further funding, thus making a form of profit off of victims' trauma. The need to tell a compelling victim narrative has led to documented cases of false statements to obtain resources that women desperately need in the country, irrespective of their victim status.

Further Reading

Central Intelligence Agency. 2018. "The World Factbook." https://www.cia.gov/library /publications/resources/the-world-factbook/.

Duramy, Benedetta Faedi. 2014. *Gender and Violence in Haiti: Women's Path from Victims to Agents.* New Brunswick, NJ: Rutgers University Press.

Justesen, Michael, and Dorte Verner. 2007. "Factors Impacting Youth Development in Haiti." World Bank Policy Research Working Paper 4110. https://openknowledge .worldbank.org/bitstream/handle/10986/6884/wps4110.pdf?sequence=1

Kolbe, Athena, and Royce Hutson. 2006. "Human Rights Abuse and Other Criminal Violations in Port-Au-Prince, Haiti: A Random Survey of Households." *Lancet*, no. 368: 864–73.

O'Brien, Jane. 2006. Haiti's Children Still Struggling for Survival." https://www.unicef.org /emerg/haiti_31788.html.

United Nations General Assembly/Security Council. 2006. "Children and Armed Conflict: Report of the Secretary-General." https://www.undocs.org/S/2006/497

INDIA

India, a country in South Asia, located south of China and Pakistan, has the second largest population in the world with over 1.3 billion people. India is a culturally diverse country with many different ethnic groups and religions. The most practiced religion is Hinduism, followed by Islam, Christianity, Sikhism, and Buddhism (Central Intelligence Agency 2018). India has historically operated under a caste system, which is a social stratification system where select groups of people, determined by heredity, are relegated to certain areas of work and vocation. While this system was in place prior to colonization by the English crown, which began in the eighteenth century, the British further perpetuated the system during its rule. India gained its independence from England in 1947 under Mahatma Gandhi (1869–1948) and quickly worked to deconstruct the harmful caste system. The system has been ruled illegal, and since the 1950s the country has implemented many antidiscrimination laws based on caste. Nonetheless, castes persist and have harmful effects on people in India, particularly women.

Violence against Women

VAW in India is rooted in centuries of patriarchal gender norms and generations of divisions from caste systems and religions. Estimates from the National Family Health Survey stated that 31 percent of women between the ages of fifteen and forty-nine have experienced spousal abuse, with rural women (34 percent) experiencing higher levels of abuse than urban women (25 percent) (International Institute of Population Statistics 2016). According to the statistics from the National Crime Records Bureau (2016), there were 110,378 incidents of domestic violence from husbands or their families. In 2016, there were also 38,947 rapes that were reported to the police, and of those rapes, 2,167 were gang rapes. The actual occurrence of rape in India is much higher due to underreporting, what is called the "dark figure" of crime. India also has incidents of some more culturally specific forms of VAW, such as dowry deaths with 7,455 incidents in 2016 (National Crime Records Bureau 2016). Dowry deaths occur when a woman's husband or his family either murder her or drive her to commit suicide over conflict about her dowry, which is the property or money paid to the groom and his family when the marriage occurs. Dowry death is not a common form of VAW worldwide, and is mostly known to occur in India, Pakistan, Bangladesh, and Iran. India has the highest incidence of dowry death of these countries.

Rape

Rape in India presents an interesting case because the country simultaneously takes a progressive and conservative stance toward rape in terms of its legal and justice systems. India has experienced several mass protests in response to a few high-profile rape cases and to changes to the Indian Penal Code (IPC) to meet protestors' demands. The resulting changes are often viewed as progressive by many feminists and scholars (Chaudhary 2017); yet, India restricts who can be counted as a victim of rape. Marital rape is not criminalized, and rape is only defined within a heterosexual encounter with a male as the perpetrator and a female as a victim.

The IPC is the legal document that determines what is a crime in India and has evolved on the topic of VAW since its inception in 1860. In 1872, the Indian government implemented the Indian Evidence Act (IEA), and in 1891 it changed the age of consent for sex from ten years to twelve years. The IEA specified that women had to be able to prove physical force for an incident to be considered rape. Women also had to prove that they resisted their attacker with evidence such as injuries or eyewitnesses. Simply saying no or attempting to push an attacker off was not viewed as enough resistance by the court. There were differences in resistance qualifications depending on the social status of the victim. Women from lower caste systems or women viewed as foreigners were almost incapable of being

Protestors in India have publicly demonstrated against the occurrence of several high-profile rape cases in recent years and the criminal justice system's responses to these cases. This protest was in response to a 2018 case in which a Catholic nun in Kerala accused a bishop of repeated incidents of sexual abuse. (Saikatpaul/Dreamstime.com)

raped in the state's eyes. When presented with evidence of injuries or witnesses, courts sometimes argued that women from lower castes enjoyed rough sex to dismiss their rape claims. They also routinely used women's past sexual histories as reasons to dismiss cases, finding that women who had engaged in sexual relations with anyone, including their husbands, could not claim to be raped. This meant that the only victims with a chance of receiving a rape conviction were high-status virgins whose rape was witnessed and had left them with significant injuries.

In 1983 a sixteen-year-old girl was raped by two police officers while in their custody. The Supreme Court dismissed the charges against the officers, arguing that there was not enough evidence to prove force, the victim could not prove resistance, and the victim had a previous sexual history. Feminist groups mobilized to fight for recognition of the role of power and status as a factor in rape perpetration and prompted an amendment to the IPC. This amendment changed the circumstances of rape to include rape as a result of coercion, whereby a person with power or authority (such as police officers) can use their status to force a victim to comply against their will without physical force. One reason this occurs is due to fear from victims regarding consequences for not complying. While this amendment did not change the actual definition of rape, it added special types of rape into the law, including custodial rape, gang rape, and rape by public servants.

Another case that led to legal changes was the violent gang rape and the resulting death of a twenty-three-year-old woman. After leaving a movie theater in 2012, the woman and a male friend boarded an unmarked bus, at which time the friend was knocked unconscious and the woman was gang raped by five men, raped with an iron rod, and physically assaulted. Her assault was so severe that she ultimately died. The rape occurred in Delhi, but people across the country rose up and demanded justice. Protestors gathered outside the home of the chief minister, as well as outside the parliament and the president's home. The protestors were dispersed using different methods of force including hoses and wooden batons.

This treatment of citizens by police forces and the lackluster response from political officials caused further outrage and protests spread across the country. The increased mobilization and pressure from foreign organizations pushed India to act. As a result, the government developed courts designed to deal specifically with VAW so that they can fast track these cases. They also formed a special commission, the Justice Verma Committee, to make recommendations for future laws and structural changes to better handle VAW. The Verma committee made several recommendations, but the main legal change that occurred as a result of this case was expanding the meaning of rape, this time in terms of the meaning of penetration. One of the aspects of the case that the public found so egregious was the use of an iron rod in the rape. Under IPC law at the time of the incident, rape was defined as only penetration of the vagina by the penis, which meant that using an object to rape an individual was not actually an act of rape. The Criminal Law (Amendment) Act of 2013 expanded rape to include penetration of other body parts besides the vagina, such as the mouth or anus, and included penetration by more than just the penis, such as objects or the mouth. In addition to the expansion acts considered rape, the amendment also changed the meaning of consent. Instead of placing the burden of proof on the victim to prove resistance, burden to prove consent would be on the perpetrator.

Controversial Acquittal of Mahmood Farooqui

Mahmood Farooqui is a famous Indian author and director who was accused of raping an American doctoral student. In 2015, Christine Marrewa Karwoski brought charges against Farooqui. He was found guilty of rape and sentenced to seven years in prison. Farooqui appealed the decision in 2017. In a controversial statement, the Delhi High Court argued that "a feeble 'no' may mean a 'yes'" and Farooqui was acquitted. In 2018, the Supreme Court refused to revisit the case and upheld the acquittal. The case was controversial because it blurred the definition of consent and raised questions about whether Farooqui's fame factored into the decision.

Butalia, Urvashi. 2018. "Healing Myself: A Woman Recounts Her Struggles After a Court Acquitted the Man She Accused of Rape." *Scroll.In*, April 26, 2018. https://scroll.in/article /876788/healing-myself-a-woman-recounts-her-struggles-after-a-court-acquitted-the -man-she-accused-of-rape.

Despite the progressive nature of recent changes to rape laws in India, scholars and activists continue to point out ways the laws still fail women and other vulnerable populations. The 2012 case worked to simultaneously frame the victim as "every woman," while also highlighting her middle-class status. Cases also continue to be handled differently for marginalized women. For example, in 2004, a group of 200 women who were being continually victimized in the slums where they lived took justice into their own hands by collectively attacking their abuser in open court. The women stabbed him to death and castrated him. There were no protests or public rage about the mass rapes in a poor village and the case only received national attention because of the women's vigilante justice.

Further Reading

Central Intelligence Agency. 2018. "The World Factbook." https://www.cia.gov/library/publications/resources/the-world-factbook/.

Chaudhary, Shraddha. 2017. "Reconceptualising Rape in Law Reform." *Socio-Legal Review* 13: 156–68.

International Institute of Population Statistics. 2016. "National Family Health Survey." http://rchiips.org/nfhs/factsheet_NFHS-4.shtml.

National Crime Records Bureau. 2016. "Crime in India 2016." http://ncrb.gov.in/

Roychowdhury, Poulami. 2016. "Over the Law: Rape and the Seduction of Popular Politics." *Gender & Society* 30 (1): 80–94. https://doi.org/10.1177/0891243215613482.

Shandilya, Krupa. 2015. "Nirbhaya's Body: The Politics of Protest in the Aftermath of the 2012 Delhi Gang Rape." *Gender & History* 27 (2): 465–86. https://doi.org/10.1111/1468-0424.12134.

JORDAN

Jordan is a country in the Middle East that shares borders with Saudi Arabia in the southeast, Iraq and Syria to the north, and Israel and the West Bank to the west. Jordan's population is around ten million, and it has one of the smallest economies in the region. Culturally, Jordanians are primarily Arab, over 90 percent of the country practices Islam, and the official language is Arabic. Historically, Jordan had been ruled by the Ottoman Empire, France, and England but became an independent state in 1946 (Central Intelligence Agency 2018). In the past few decades, Jordan has started to westernize, which has caused a clash between traditional cultures in the country and the ever-growing western values. One area this clash is noticeable is in the area of women's rights.

Since the 1960s, Jordan began to advance women's positions in the country through entrance into the public sphere in the form of jobs and education. These inclusions led to shifting gender roles and relations between men and women in the country, with power shifting from male control to a more equitable position. However, this does not mean that this transition happened equally and smoothly for all women across Jordan. Instead, as seen in many countries when male power is challenged, many men responded to women's new-found access to equality with violence to maintain their dominance in both society and the family.

Women's rights in Jordan gained renewed focus in the 1990s after two igniting events: the 1995 Fourth World Conference on Women in Beijing and the news coverage of honor killings by the journalist Rana Husseini. The Conference on Women was held by the UN to review the status of women globally and develop an action plan to achieve gender equality for women. Jordan was one of the countries that held a regional conference prior to the one in Beijing. These events resulted in the creation of social and political movements to better women's position in the country and to end forms of VAW, including honor killings.

Honor Killings

Honor killings are defined as the murder of a woman by her own family to bring honor back to the family after alleged inappropriate sexual behavior of the woman. The inappropriate sexual behavior is viewed as shameful, and this loss of honor extends beyond the woman to her entire family. Cases of honor killings have resulted from women flirting with men, having a secret cell phone, and engaging in premarital sex. Other reasons for honor killings include extramarital affairs, premarital or extramarital pregnancies, and rape. In each of these instances, honor killing is usually only directed toward the woman and not the other party involved. Individuals who work on the issue of honor killings often contest the name of this violence as it appears to justify the act.

Honor killings occur most frequently in countries in the Middle East and Northern Africa but have also been found to occur in countries in the west and the Mediterranean. The most commonly cited statistic from the United Nations Population Fund states that 5,000 honor killings occur each year (United Nations Population Fund 2000). In Jordan, studies have found that between nineteen and a hundred cases of honor-related murder happen each year (Sheeley 2007), whereas Human Rights Watch has stated that around twenty honor killings happen in Jordan per year.

Accurate statistics are difficult to obtain because honor killings are often covered up and treated as accidents or suicides. Because those responsible for the murder are family members, all cases are rarely reported to the police. However, some family members turn themselves over to police after committing honor killings, usually because they know that the laws are lenient against perpetrators of honor killings in comparison to other murders.

Causes

While both Western and Muslim cultures exhibit high rates of VAW, it often manifests in different forms and relies upon different contexts and justifications. Jordan embraces a patrilineal culture, which has important differences from patriarchal culture, particularly in how VAW functions. Patrilineal culture links females to their male kin, even after they are married. This means that a woman's male kin will protect her, even against her husband and his family. However, this also means that if the woman brings shame upon her family, through alleged inappropriate sexual behavior, then shame is brought upon her blood family and they may act to bring honor back to the family through violence and murder against the shameful woman. Patriarchal culture does not retain this bloodline tie; instead it is about male power over women in general, kin or not. This is why VAW in patriarchal cultures is more likely to manifest in intimate partner violence, and femicide often occurs as a result of escalated wife beating when a woman decides to leave the relationship (Kulwicki 2002).

Although many blame honor killings on the traditional cultures of the Middle East and Islam, because of media coverage of these cases, these cultures are not solely responsible for this practice. Only associating honor crimes with Muslims leads to racism and xenophobia in Western countries and contributes to ineffective intervention and prevention strategies. Scholars and activists point out that honor killings are rooted in histories and cultures beyond Islam. There are historical records that refer to honor killings occurring in history prior to the beginnings of Islam. Today, honor killings also occur outside the Middle East and Islamic countries. Laws that permit honor killings did not originate in modern Islamic countries. Instead, laws in countries like Jordan that permit or appear to support honor killings are remnants from legal systems imposed by colonizing countries such the Ottoman Empire, England, and France. The two penal codes in Jordan that are used as a legal defense by perpetrators of honor killings were both implemented by these previous ruling entities.

Additionally, many Islamic leaders denounce honor-motivated crimes. In 2016, the Jordanian government issued a *fatwa*, or a religious decree, that prohibits the murder of women based on honor violations. Additionally, religious leaders and scholars point out that the Qur'an does not promote honor killings, VAW, or violence in general. This evidence helps to show that honor-based crimes are not a result of Islamic culture but instead are rooted in the larger patriarchal patterns of domination combined with a strong emphasis on family culture.

Legal Matters

The two laws in the penal code that activists argue support honor killings are articles 340 and 98. Article 340 of the Jordanian penal code states that a man who finds his wife involved in inappropriate sexual relations is justified in committing murder against his wife and the other party involved. This article can be used in either justifying the entire crime or diminishing the punishment. Article 340 has received the most attention from activists and organizations, both domestic and international. However, case studies of legal actions against perpetrators of honor killings find that this defense is rarely invoked. Article 98 of the penal code is similar to 340 but instead justifies the act of honor killing by stating that the perpetrator committed the act in a state of rage due to inappropriate behavior, and thus cannot be considered responsible for his actions. While Article 98 is not written specifically on honor killings, it applies to any crime committed as a result of rage due to inappropriate or dangerous actions and has been used by perpetrators of honor killings to reduce their sentences. There have been several attempts to repeal Articles 340 and 98, but they have so far been unsuccessful.

Another legal issue that deserves attention is the confinement of women at risk of honor violence. Occasionally, women who fear they may become a victim of honor-related violence are able to obtain protection from the government to prevent their murders. However, this protection often means indefinite confinement in government prisons. This confinement results in women who are victims being housed with criminal perpetrators for long periods of time. There is one case where a woman was confined for twenty-two years before finally being released. During this time, she reported being heavily abused by other inmates in prison. While the confinement itself is problematic, the options for release are also troubling. Families can obtain a woman's release if they sign a document stating that they will not perpetrate violence against her. However, there are cases of families lying on these forms and committing their intended murders once the woman is home. Another option for release is marriage. Governments sometimes search for a suitable marriage to release women from protective custody, whereas other women assent to marry their rapists (who were the reason they were confined in the first place) just to re-enter society.

Further Reading

Central Intelligence Agency. 2018. "The World Factbook." https://www.cia.gov/library/publications/resources/the-world-factbook/.

Hossain, Sara, and Lynn Welchman, eds. 2005. *"Honour": Crimes, Paradigms and Violence against Women*. London; New York: Zed Books.

Kulwicki, Anahid Devartanian. 2002. "The Practice of Honor Crimes: A Glimpse of Domestic Violence in the Arab World." *Issues in Mental Health Nursing* 23 (1): 77–87. https://doi.org/10.1080/01612840252825491.

Pope, N. 2011. *Honor Killings in the Twenty-First Century*. 2012 edition. New York: Palgrave Macmillan.

Sheeley, Ellen R. 2007. *Reclaiming Honor in Jordan: A National Public Opinion Survey on Honor Killings*. 1st ed. Amman, Jordan: Black Iris Publishing.

United Nations Population Fund. 2000. "The State of the World Population 2000: Lives Together, Worlds Apart: Men and Women in a Time of Change." https://unfpa.org/sites/default/files/pub-pdf/swp2000_eng.pdf

MEXICO

Mexico, a country of 126 million people located in North America, shares its northern border with the United States, its southern border with Guatemala, and has the Gulf of Mexico to the east and the Pacific Ocean to the West. Mexico was colonized by the Spanish empire in the sixteenth century, and after winning independence in 1821, it became a nation with a strong cultural identity based on a blend of indigenous and Spanish influences. The economy in Mexico is a mix between formal and informal sectors, with over half of the workforce working in the informal sector (Central Intelligence Agency 2018). Between the 1990s and early 2000s, workforce participation for males began to decline, and women were far less likely to be employed outside of the home. However, due to the decline in male employment, many more women were forced to become the primary wage earners for their households, creating tensions within the home. While some women were able to find work in formal sectors, such as in manufacturing plants, other women turned toward informal employment like sex work to make ends meet.

Mexican culture adheres to strict gender role expectations, supported by Roman Catholic religious beliefs. *Machismo* is the expectation that men exhibit the characteristics of being masculine, strong, aggressive, and sexual. When machismo is coupled with the expectation that women should endure suffering and be subservient to their husbands, as governed by women's goal to be like the Virgin Mary, large power imbalances occur that open opportunities for abuse. These traditional gender role expectations are challenged when male partners cannot provide economic support for their families due to the increasing inability to find work. When women become the primary financial earner within the household tensions arise, which can lead to violence.

Domestic Violence

The most recent estimates of the prevalence of domestic violence come from the 2016 National Survey of Household Relationship Dynamics, which found that 66 percent of women experienced at least one violent incident in the last year, including emotional, physical, sexual, and workplace violence. When examining violence within relationships specifically, 17.9 percent of women experienced physical violence in their current or last relationship, and 6.5 percent of women experienced sexual violence in their current or last relationship (Instituto Nacional De Estadistica Y Geografia 2016).

Young women have a higher risk of experiencing domestic violence compared to older women, with one study finding that 12.4 percent women aged fifteen to twenty-one experienced physical violence compared to 6.6 percent of women aged forty-five to forty-nine. Experiencing or witnessing violence during one's childhood increases the risk for both domestic violence victimization and perpetration. Women's engagement in the workforce is another area that increases the risk of domestic violence victimization, with one study finding that women working outside of the home had a 30 percent greater possibility of experiencing severe forms of violence compared to women who do not work outside the home (Avila-Burgos, Valdez-Santiago, and Hijar 2009).

There are two risk factors in Mexico that operate differently compared to other countries: indigenous status and the presence of other family members in the home. In countries like the United States and Canada, indigenous women are at a much higher risk for all forms of violence, including intimate partner victimization. In Mexico, however, indigenous women are less likely to be victimized at the hands of their partners and are more likely to seek help from police and other formal service providers. This may be the result of underreporting of intimate violence among this group. However, the culture among indigenous groups in Mexico is substantially different from dominant Mexican culture in that VAW is not tolerated in these communities.

In other countries, studies have found that the presence of other family members in the home decreases women's risk of experiencing intimate partner violence, thus acting as a protective factor. However, Mexico has a cultural tradition of young couples living with the male partner's parents even after marriage. Some abused women have reported that their in-laws, and mother-in-law in particular, not only excuse and justify their son's violence but also perpetrate emotional and economic violence against them. Violence in intimate relationships is frequently accepted within Mexican culture, which can lead to families and friends justifying abuse.

Violence against Female Sex Workers

Sex work is quasilegal in Mexico, meaning that there are specific areas within cities where sex may be sold commercially. These areas are called *zonas de tolerancia*, *zonas rojas*, or red-light districts. Within these districts, specific establishments, such as bars, are licensed for sex trade. Sex workers meet with clients in common areas and then use rooms in the back for the exchange of sex for money. Women also have to be licensed to work, which includes monthly health checks for STIs and human immunodeficiency virus (HIV). Illegal sex work is both sex work conducted outside of the tolerance zones and sex work conducted by women without a current health card.

One study of female sex workers in two United States–Mexico border cities found that 61 percent of the women had experienced violence while working as sex workers. Clients perpetrate the majority of violence, but sex workers also experience violence at the hands of co-workers, police, and intimate partners. For sex workers who experienced violence, 72 percent was from clients, 17 percent from other sex workers, 6 percent from police, and 3 percent from bar owners (Cepeda and Nowotny 2014). Sex workers experience four different forms of violence: physical, emotional, economic, and sexual. Violence from clients is often physical and sexual in nature, such as a client forcing a sex act not previously agreed upon or becoming physically violent when a woman refuses to participate in demanded acts. Another form of violence from clients is refusing to wear a condom, which increases the risk of STIs and HIV transmission. Violence among co-workers and bar owners is often based in workplace politics, and is most often verbal and physical violence. Violence between sex workers often occurs when one woman takes a regular client from another, whereas bar owners become violent when they feel that the women are not putting in their time and thus losing the owners money. Violence at the hands of police is more common for women who work outdoors and illegally, where police physically and sexually assault women when they do not pay a bribe to avoid being arrested.

Female sex workers in Mexico also experience increased rates of violence from intimate partners. One study found that over 40 percent of female sex workers experience violence at the hands of their intimate partners (Ulibarri et al. 2018). Many women begin sex work because their male partners cannot find work or bring home enough money to support the household. Some men respond in anger, accusing their partners of finding pleasure in their work rather than viewing it only as a job. Other partners take the role of pimps, acting as a go-between in the exchange of sex for money, which often leads to further violence when the woman does not want to comply.

The primary risk factor for experiencing violence as a sex worker is the location of their sex work. Women who perform sex work outdoors are six times more likely to experience violence from a client than women who perform sex work indoors (Katsulis et al. 2015). Outdoor sex work is more likely to occur in isolation, whereas indoor sex work often has security present and is near other workers and clients. Two additional important factors that increase the risk of violence is housing insecurity and drug use by both the sex worker and the client.

Further Reading

Avila-Burgos, Leticia, Rosario Valdez-Santiago, and Martha Hijar. 2009. "Factors Associated with Severity of Intimate Partner Abuse in Mexico: Results of the First National Survey of Violence against Women." *Canadian Journal of Public Health* 100 (6): 7.

Central Intelligence Agency. 2018. "The World Factbook." https://www.cia.gov/library /publications/resources/the-world-factbook/.

Cepeda, Alice, and Kathryn M. Nowotny. 2014. "A Border Context of Violence: Mexican Female Sex Workers on the U.S.–Mexico Border." *Violence against Women* 20 (12): 1506–31. https://doi.org/10.1177/1077801214557955.

Instituto Nacional De Estadistica Y Geografia. 2016. "National Survey on the Dynamics of Household Relationships (Encuesta Nacional Sobre La Dinámica de Las Relaciones En Los Hogares)." http://en.www.inegi.org.mx/programas/endireh/2016/.

Katsulis, Yasmina, Alesha Durfee, Vera Lopez, and Alyssa Robillard. 2015. "Predictors of Workplace Violence among Female Sex Workers in Tijuana, Mexico." *Violence against Women* 21 (5): 571–97. https://doi.org/10.1177/1077801214545283.

Ulibarri, Monica D., Marissa Salazar, Jennifer L. Syvertsen, Angela R. Bazzi, M. Gudelia Rangel, Hugo Staines Orozco, and Steffanie A. Strathdee. 2018. "Intimate Partner Violence among Female Sex Workers and Their Noncommercial Male Partners in Mexico: A Mixed-Methods Study." *Violence against Women*, 25 (5): 549–71. https://doi.org/10 .1177/1077801218794302.

RUSSIA

Russia, the largest country in the world in terms of landmass, stretches across two continents, from Eastern Europe and across Northern Asia. Throughout its history, Russia has been ruled by many different forms of governments, from the Russian Empire in the eighteenth century, to the Soviet Union in the twentieth century, to the current Russian Federation. The dissolution of the Soviet Union into the Russian Federation in 1991 created fourteen countries independent from Russia, including Ukraine, Belarus, Kazakhstan, Uzbekistan, Armenia, Azerbaijan,

Georgia, Kyrgyzstan, Moldova, Tajikistan, Turkmenistan, as well as the Baltic States of Estonia, Latvia, and Lithuania. Since this separation, the population of over 142 million people is now comprised largely of ethnic Russians, although there are over 200 ethnic groups present in the country (Central Intelligence Agency 2018). The collapse of communism in the Soviet Union and the subsequent political and economic changes have affected all aspects of social life including VAW.

Violence against Women

Russia formally adopted communism after the 1917 Russian Revolution and formed the Soviet Union in 1922. The Soviet Union was a totalitarian government with one political party, the Communist Party, which controlled almost all aspects of its citizens' lives in an attempt to provide equal living conditions for everyone and eliminate social classes. Although it never fully achieved this goal, there were some positive achievements with respect to gender equality.

Under Soviet rule women participated fully in the labor force, which was still rare in the rest of the world at that time. The Soviet Union also established women's organizations that were meant to promote women's equality, although they mainly worked toward increasing women's engagement in the political party and

Supported by an ideology of equality for all, communism in the former Soviet Union promoted women's participation in the workforce and in politics. After the break-up of the Soviet Union in 1991, Russia experienced a backlash against gender equality that put women at great risk for violence, particularly by their domestic partners. (Library of Congress)

maintaining their presence in the workforce. By focusing solely on women's workforce participation, the government neglected women's experiences in the private realm. While it may appear that gender norms were more equal under Soviet rule, differences based on sex were still enforced at home. In addition to full-time employment, women in Russia were still responsible for the majority of domestic jobs, such as cleaning the home, cooking meals, and raising children, which is referred to as "double burden." This meant that women had an even higher workload than women in countries where they could not work outside of the home. Women also had restricted rights in other arenas, such as health, reproductive rights, and even the types of jobs they could undertake.

After the fall of the Soviet Union in 1991, the situation worsened for women. The move to a market economy and change in government systems abolished the few organizations that worked for women's rights. Women were blamed more frequently for their own victimization, often for working outside of the home. Police ignored reports of domestic violence and rape, rates of gendered violence increased, sex work and trafficking of women became more common, and sexual harassment became more apparent.

Domestic Violence

Though reliable rates of domestic violence are difficult to ascertain, one study found that 26 percent of women in Russia experienced interpersonal violence from spouses or boyfriends (Stickley, Timofeeva, and Sparén 2008). Additionally, 80 percent of violent crimes in Russia are cases of domestic violence. About 14,000 women are murdered every year by family, and in most of these cases the perpetrator is the spouse (True 2012).

Although domestic violence existed under Soviet control, after the dissolution of the Soviet Union, domestic violence rates and its associated problems worsened. Government intrusion in personal and working lives was normalized under the communist government; however, under the new government, people rejected this kind of intrusion. Police no longer saw it appropriate to intervene in personal life, such as in the home where most domestic abuse occurs. Additionally, blame was more strongly placed on women for their victimization. Women who experienced violence from their spouses were told by the police and their communities that it was their own fault for working outside of the home and/or making more money than their male partners. Alcohol sales and consumption also increased after communism due to loosened state control, which is also connected to violence against partners.

Another contributing factor to the rise in domestic violence rates in the post-Soviet period is the change in women's economic dependence and available resources. The privatization of housing decreased women's likelihood of being able to leave an abusive household. Women's work status changed within the country. Whereas under Soviet control women working in full-time positions was common, after the Soviet collapse, many women starting working part-time or in underpaid fields, and others stopped working altogether. Some of this transition away from full-time work for women was the result of a return to patriarchal values that promoted women's roles in the home taking care of the household and the family. At the same time that women became more economically dependent on their male partners, resources designed to help women out of violent situations started to disappear. In 2006, the Special Rapporteur on Violence against Women reported that there were only five shelters and 120 crisis centers for around eighty million women who live in Russia.

In 2017, the government changed the law to reduce penalties for some aspects of partner violence. If a perpetrator was found guilty of beating their partner, but it was their first offense and did not lead to substantial injury (e.g., broken bones), they used to face a maximum of two years in prison. Under the new law, commonly called the "slapping law," convicted offenders can now be sentenced with a fine, community service, or a maximum of fifteen days in jail. If the perpetrator is a repeat offender, the punishment increases to up to three months in prison and an increased fine. This legal change has already impacted women's likelihood to report domestic violence to the police, with crisis centers and NGOs in Russia reporting a severe drop in reported cases. It is also likely that this kind of decriminalization may lead to an increase in the rates of domestic violence, as is signals an acceptance of violence toward women.

Trafficking and Sex Work

Another common form of VAW in Russia is the trafficking of women for sexual exploitation. It is important to note that trafficking for sexual exploitation and sex work are not the same thing. People can voluntarily choose to engage in sex work, whereas others are forced into the work through trafficking. However, there is often a gray area, where women may voluntarily enter into sex work at first, but then may be unable to leave the work because of force or coercion. This is part of a larger debate within feminism about the nature of sex work, and if there is true agency in the decision to sell one's body, or if limited agency is still a free choice.

The trafficking of women for sexual exploitation increased after the decline of the former Soviet economy due to the introduction of free markets and the opening of the country's borders. These factors made it easier for Russian women to be trafficked out of the country for both sex work and sexual exploitation in other places. Some of these women chose this voluntarily because of a popular notion in Russia that sex workers had a glamorous lifestyle, while others turned to it out of financial desperation. Even women who are trafficked for domestic labor frequently experience sexual victimization during trafficking and while on the job. Studies show that most trafficked women from Russia are from lower socioeconomic classes similar to other countries, yet they tend to be more highly educated than typical trafficking victims. The reason for this difference is that the economic fallout of the collapse of communism hurt everyone irrespective of their educational status, and the new opportunities that came with open borders left many women vulnerable to new risks.

Estimates on the numbers of women trafficked each year are highly debated. Studies show that between 20,000 and 60,000 Russian women are trafficked each year, with a total of more than 500,000 women since the fall of the Soviet Union (Tverdova 2011). Not only is Russia a main exporter and importer of trafficked women, many other countries use trafficking routes that go through Russia including smaller countries from the former Soviet Union. Most trafficked women from Russia end up in Asia, Western Europe, or North America. Many trafficked women are hesitant to contact legal services due to high levels of police corruption, police involvement in the trafficking of women, and having officers as clients.

Further Reading

Central Intelligence Agency. 2018. "The World Factbook." https://www.cia.gov/library/publications/resources/the-world-factbook/.

Lysova, Aleksandra V., and Denise A. Hines. 2008. "Binge Drinking and Violence against Intimate Partners in Russia." *Aggressive Behavior* 34 (4): 416–27. https://doi.org/10.1002/ab.20256.

Odinokova, Veronika, Maia Rusakova, Lianne A. Urada, Jay G. Silverman, and Anita Raj. 2014. "Police Sexual Coercion and Its Association with Risky Sex Work and Substance Use Behaviors among Female Sex Workers in St. Petersburg and Orenburg, Russia." *International Journal of Drug Policy* 25 (1): 96–104. https://doi.org/10.1016/j.drugpo.2013.06.008.

Stickley, Andrew, Irina Timofeeva, and Pär Sparén. 2008. "Risk Factors for Intimate Partner Violence against Women in St. Petersburg, Russia." *Violence against Women* 14 (4): 483–95. https://doi.org/10.1177/1077801208314847.

True, Jacqui. 2012. *The Political Economy of Violence against Women*. 1st ed. New York: Oxford University Press.

Tverdova, Yuliya V. 2011. "Human Trafficking in Russia and Other Post-Soviet States." *Human Rights Review* 12 (3): 329–44. https://doi.org/10.1007/s12142-010-0188-1.

Chapter 3: Juvenile Delinquency and Juvenile Justice

Janet P. Stamatel

OVERVIEW

There is not as much information about juvenile offenders and juvenile justice around the world as there is about adult crime and criminal justice systems. This is due, in part, to beliefs that juvenile crimes are not as common or as serious as adult crimes and to the fact that many countries do not have separate juvenile justice systems. Given the lack of systematic data collection for juvenile delinquents, we do not know the global prevalence or seriousness of juvenile crimes. There are enough examples of serious youth violence or substance abuse to discourage a casual dismissal of the importance of this topic. Additionally, data from some countries have shown that adult criminal offenders often engaged in juvenile delinquency in their youth, which should encourage further investigation into the long-term effects of youth violations of the law.

Obtaining information about the frequency of juvenile offenses in various countries is a challenge for a number of reasons. First, many countries do not provide detailed statistics to the public about juvenile offenses reported to the police. Second, police have a significant amount of discretion in juvenile cases, so the "dark figure" of juvenile crime is likely large. Third, the alternative source of crime data to police records are victimization surveys, but they rely on victims estimates of the age of suspects and often do not survey minors, who are likely to be victimized by other minors.

As a result of these deficiencies in data collection, many researchers use self-report surveys of schoolchildren to measure juvenile delinquency. Youth are asked to report their own illegal behaviors including fighting, stealing, bullying, vandalism, and alcohol and drug use. The first effort to collect such data from several countries was the International Self-Report Delinquency (ISRD) study. Students aged twelve to sixteen were randomly selected from schools in large or medium-sized cities in participating countries and asked to complete a self-report survey regarding their offending behaviors and victimization experiences. The first ISRD study was conducted between 1992 and 1993 in thirteen countries. The second study was conducted between 2005 and 2007 in thirty-one countries and provides data on juvenile delinquency in four countries reported in this chapter

(Belgium, Cyprus, Czech Republic, and Venezuela). The third wave is finalizing data collection in 2019 with thirty-four countries.

Information about juvenile delinquency from countries that did not participate in the ISRD comes from various sources. Some countries conduct their own self-report surveys (Nigeria, South Korea, Iceland) or have publicly available police statistics on juvenile delinquency (South Korea). In other countries, public health surveys can be used to extract information about certain problems affecting minors, such as violence and substance use (Nepal and Nigeria).

When youth violate the law and come into contact with authorities, there is considerable variation around the world regarding how to handle juvenile offenders, although there have been some efforts by the United Nations to introduce minimum standards for juvenile justice, with particular attention paid to protecting the rights of children. The United Nations Standard Minimum Rules for the Administration of Juvenile Justice, known as "The Beijing Rules," were adopted in 1985. They establish two main objectives of juvenile justice: promoting the well-being of the juvenile and administering proportional sanctions that consider the individual circumstances of the juvenile offender. The rules reinforce the notion that children are entitled to the same criminal procedural rights as adults including the presumption of innocence, the right to legal assistance, the right to confront witnesses, the right to appeal, and the right to have a parent or guardian present during criminal proceedings. They also award juveniles the additional right to privacy to avoid the harmful effects of social labeling. The rules encourage diversion from the criminal justice system at any point in case processing and support the use of sanctions that avoid institutionalization, such as probation, fines, and community service. The Beijing Rules are recommendations for member nations and not legally binding international laws.

The United Nations Convention on the Rights of the Child (CRC) is a human rights treaty that specifically outlines the rights and freedoms of children. It is based on the premise that all children should be raised in the "spirit of peace, dignity, tolerance, freedom, equality and solidarity," which are the ideals of the Charter of the United Nations (UNCHCR 1990). CRC was adopted in 1989 and has been ratified by 196 countries. The United States is the only country that has signed the treaty but has not ratified it. Article 37 of the CRC addresses issues related directly to juvenile justice. It states that children should not be subjected to torture or inhuman punishments, which include capital punishment and life in prison without the possibility of parole. Children should not be arrested and detained by the government unlawfully or arbitrarily. If they are legally deprived of their liberty, then they should be treated with dignity. Detained children should be kept apart from detained adults. They should be entitled to contact their families and get legal assistance.

In 1990, the United Nations adopted the Guidelines for the Prevention of Juvenile Delinquency, also known as "The Riyadh Guidelines." This document advocates a child-centric approach to child development, social integration, and the prevention of juvenile delinquency. It encourages countries to develop national and subnational prevention plans that encourage positive socialization through families, schools, and communities. It discourages harsh punishments for juvenile offenders and encourages diversion from the criminal justice system, whenever possible. It also warns of the harmful effects of labeling juvenile offenders as delinquents.

The countries discussed in this chapter illustrate the variations in approaches to juvenile justice and adherence to international standards. For example, five countries (Belgium, Czech Republic, Nigeria, South Korea, and Venezuela) have juvenile justice systems that are separate from adult systems, whereas three countries (Cyprus, Iceland, and Nepal) do not. Additionally, the minimum age of criminal responsibility ranges from ten in Nepal, to twelve in Belgium and Venezuela, and fourteen or fifteen in other countries. Finally, European countries (Belgium, Cyprus, Czech Republic, and Iceland) are more inclined to implement diversion or restorative justice programs for juvenile offenders compared to countries in other regions of the world (Nepal, Nigeria, South Korea, and Venezuela).

Further Reading

UNHCR (United Nations Human Rights Office of the High Commissioner). 1990. "Convention on the Rights of the Child." https://www.ohchr.org/en/professionalinterest/pages/crc.aspx.

BELGIUM

Belgium is a highly developed, democratic, Western European country located across the English Channel from Great Britain. It has a population of 11.5 million people that is divided into three language communities: Dutch, French, and German. It has a diverse economy based on a combination of manufacturing, services, transportation, and technology. Its gross domestic product per capita is USD 46,000, which is comparable to its neighbors, France and Germany. Belgium is a founding member of the European Union (EU), a political alliance among twenty-eight European countries, and the capital city of Brussels is the home of the European Parliament and other EU institutions (Central Intelligence Agency 2018).

After gaining independence from the Netherlands in 1831, Belgium became a constitutional monarchy. The population was multilingual with Flemish Dutch spoken mainly in the northern region of Flanders and French spoken in the southern Walloon region. French was the official language and the language of the bourgeoisie, and Dutch was considered an inferior language and culture at that time. A relatively small German community on Belgium's eastern border was acquired after Germany's defeat in World War II (1939–1945). In the 1960s, a Flemish movement to protect their language and culture gained momentum and political support. Since then, successive governments have wrestled with how to balance the different cultural communities in the country. In 1993, Belgium officially became a federal state with three language communities (Dutch, French, and German) and three administrative regions: Flanders (Flemish Dutch language), Walloon (French and German languages), and the bilingual capital region of Brussels. Each language community has its own government and parliament to serve the interests of their respective populations. This separation includes control over both how juvenile justice is administered and how much information is publicly available about juvenile delinquency and juvenile justice administration.

Juvenile Delinquency

Unlike other Western European countries, Belgium does not maintain comprehensive statistical data on crime and justice. Although standard information on crime rates is collected by the EU, there are no regularly published juvenile justice statistics for the entire country or the different administrative regions. This means that information on juvenile delinquency and juvenile justice comes primarily from research studies in select areas of the country.

Belgium participated in the second wave of the ISRD study (ISRD-2). Students in the seventh through ninth grades in two cities in the Dutch community and two cities in the French community participated in the survey. Overall, the study showed that 49.3 percent of males and 33.4 percent of females had engaged in some form of delinquency in their lifetimes. The most common offenses were minor violent crimes (e.g., fighting) (27.5 percent), shoplifting (20.1 percent), and vandalism (10.7 percent). Regarding substance use, 62.3 percent of youth reported ever drinking beer or wine, 31.3 percent drank hard liquor, 12 percent had tried marijuana, 2.8 percent had used hard drugs, and 4.3 percent dealt drugs (Vettenburg, Gavray, and Born 2010). Aside from alcohol consumption, the prevalence of partaking in delinquent activities was higher among students in Stream B schools (a vocational, technical track) than Stream A schools (a university track). For example, 7.8 percent of Stream A students engaged in vandalism, whereas 19.4 percent of Stream B students did the same (Vettenburg, Gavray, and Born 2010).

Another study from the third wave of the ISRD surveyed students aged thirteen to nineteen in Brussels, one Flemish city, and one French city. The vast majority of youth (77.6 percent) had downloaded something illegally from the Internet in their lifetime and almost half (49.3 percent) had ever been drunk. Students also reported shoplifting (24.1 percent), graffiti (18.1 percent), carrying a weapon to school (16.5 percent), stealing from another person (13.4 percent), participating in a group fight (13.3 percent), and selling drugs (10.6 percent). The surveyed youth reported that their parents (62.5 percent) and friends (61.5 percent) were the most important influences to prevent them from committing delinquent acts (Evenepoel and Christiaens 2013).

The Flanders Administrative Region participated in the European School Survey Project on Alcohol and Other Drugs (ESPAD) in 2015, which asked fifteen- and sixteen-year-olds about their use of illegal substances. The lifetime prevalence of cannabis among teens in this region declined from 31 percent in 2003 to 17 percent in 2015, and alcohol consumption also declined from 94 percent in 2003 to 80 percent in 2015. The lifetime use of illicit drugs other than cannabis was

6 percent, which was just slightly higher than the average for other European countries that participated in the survey; however, the lifetime use of inhalants was only 3 percent, which was less than half of the European average. In the thirty days prior to the survey, 56 percent of youth reported having used alcohol and 17 percent reported having used cannabis (EMCDDA 2019).

Juvenile Justice

Belgium has a civil law legal system based on Napoleonic code. In the 1800s, juvenile offenders were treated rather punitively, but this was changed to a protective model with the Child Welfare Act of 1912. This law eliminated judicial punishments for youth under sixteen years old. In 1965, Belgium reformed its juvenile justice policies to adopt a penal welfare model that prioritized the social roots of crime and delinquency and treated delinquents as socially vulnerable youth in need of state protection rather than punishment. The age of full criminal responsibility was subsequently increased from sixteen to eighteen.

By the 1980s, this model came under scrutiny for de-emphasizing minors' legal rights and personal responsibility and for ignoring the harm done to victims. There were some regional differences of opinion regarding how to best address these shortcomings. The Flemish community favored a restorative justice approach, whereas the French community preferred to revise the rehabilitative model. Across the country, there was widespread concern about needing more punitive responses to serious youth crimes. The initial compromise was the passage of two laws in 1994 that strengthened the rights of minors and allowed for stricter treatment of "difficult minors" who threatened public safety.

In 2006, Belgium introduced a major set of reforms to the juvenile justice system to formally adopt a restorative justice approach, allow for more alternative sanctions, increase the role of parents in dealing with juvenile delinquents, strengthen legal rights for youth, and toughen approaches to serious offenders. The current juvenile justice system consists of a youth court, a youth division of the public prosecutor, and social services. The prosecutor decides whether to drop charges

---

Violent Murder of Joe Van Hosbeeck

Joe Van Hosbeeck was a seventeen-year-old high school student who was violently killed by two teenagers in a Brussels train station in the middle of the day over an MP3 player. He was stabbed five times and died from his wounds. The suspects, sixteen- and seventeen-year-old Romani teenagers with Polish citizenship, were identified from closed-circuit televisions. The older teen was sentenced to twenty years in prison and the younger one to three-and-a-half years in juvenile detention. The public nature of the murder and its senselessness raised concerns among Belgians about how the criminal justice system should deal with serious, violent juvenile offenders.

with or without a formal warning, to suggest mediation, or to try the case in court. If the prosecutor chooses the last option, then the case is prepared for court.

As Belgium has an inquisitorial system of justice, the youth court judge is responsible for the initial investigation. The judge has six months to assess the personality, family, and social circumstances of the accused. During this time, the prosecutor can recommend parental counseling if it is deemed helpful for the youth. Parents who do not comply with the parental guidance course can be sentenced to jail for up to one week and/or be required to pay a fine of twenty-five euros.

If a minor is convicted of a crime in juvenile court, the judge can order the following measures. The first option is restorative justice, which is supposed to be the preferred route since the 2006 reforms. This could take the form of mediation, conferencing facilitated by a judge, or family or group counseling. These options are only available for cases in which all parties agree to participate. The judge must accept the resolution reached in mediation or conferencing, unless it violates public order. Usually, the case is closed if mediation or conferencing is successful.

Flanders has been using mediation for juveniles since 1994, although it used to be facilitated by nongovernmental organizations with the support of judicial officials. In 2004, there were 1,990 youth in Flanders who were referred to mediation, of which 45.7 percent agreed to participate. In 2009, this number increased to 4,050, of which 37 percent agreed to participate. Of all the juvenile cases processed in Flanders in 2010, the prosecutor dropped charged against the youth 70 percent of the time, sent 7 percent to mediation, and forwarded about 23 percent to youth court (Put, Vanfraechem, and Walgrave 2012). Comparable statistics for the French community are not available.

The second sentencing option for juveniles are measures designed to keep the youth in their own environment. All minors are eligible to receive a reprimand, supervision by a social service agency, and/or educational guidance. Additionally, youth over twelve years old can be sentenced to a maximum of 150 hours of mandatory education and/or outpatient psychiatric or substance abuse treatment.

Finally, a judge can decide to send a juvenile over twelve years old to a detention center. There is one federal facility in the country, and the communities administer others. They are typically small, housing between twenty-five and fifty people. Youths aged twelve to fourteen are typically sent to a minimum security or "open" facility, whereas older youth are sent to more secure centers. In 2006, there were 1,207 juveniles in detention centers in Flanders, with an average stay of sixty-one days. That same year there were 3,051 youth detained in the French community with an average stay of about thirty-eight days for open facilities and eighty-nine days for secure centers. The average length of stay in the federal detention center was about thirty-two days (Cartuyvels et al. 2010).

Further Reading

Cartuyvels, Yves, Jenneke Christiaens, Dominique De Fraene, and Els Dumortier. 2010. "Juvenile Justice in Belgium Seen through the Sanctions Looking Glass." In *The Criminalisation of Youth: Juvenile Justice in Europe, Turkey and Canada*, edited by Francis Bailleau and Yves Cartuyvels, 29–58. Brussels, Belgium: VUBPress.

Central Intelligence Agency. 2018. "The World Factbook." https://www.cia.gov/library /publications/resources/the-world-factbook/.

Daems, Tom, Eric Maes, and Luc Robert. 2013. "Crime, Criminal Justice and Criminology in Belgium." *European Journal of Criminology* 10 (2): 237–54. https://doi.org/10.1177 /1477370812464467.

EMCDDA (European Monitoring Centre for Drugs and Drug Addiction). 2019. "Belgium Country Drug Report 2019." http://www.emcdda.europa.eu/countries/drug-reports /2019/belgium/drug-use_en.

Evenepoel, Ann, and Jenneke Christiaens. 2013. "Giving Voice to 'Youth of Today': Young People's Views and Perspectives on Youth Crime and Its Prevention in Belgium." *Varstvoslovje: Journal of Criminal Justice and Security* 15 (4): 424–38.

Put, Johan, Inge Vanfraechem, and Lode Walgrave. 2012. "Restorative Dimensions in Belgian Youth Justice." *Youth Justice* 12 (2): 83–100. https://doi.org/10.1177 /1473225412447159.

Vettenburg, Nicole, Claire Gavray, and Michel Born. 2010. "Belgium." In *Juvenile Delinquency in Europe and Beyond: Results of the Second International Self-Report Delinquency Study*, edited by Josine Junger-Tas, Ineke Haen Marshall, Dirk Enzmann, Martin Killias, Majone Steketee, and Beata Gruszczynska, 41–46. New York: Springer.

CYPRUS

Cyprus is a small island in the Mediterranean Sea located south of Turkey, southwest of Greece, west of Syria and Lebanon, and north of Israel. The population of about 1.25 million people is divided socially, politically, and geographically into the Greek Cypriots (77 percent) and the Turkish Cypriots (18 percent). Although tensions between the two groups existed prior to 1960 when Cyprus was a British colony, they escalated after independence. In 1974, the Greek military overthrew the first president of the independent country of Cyprus in an attempt to claim the island, but the Turkish military intervened. As a result, Turkey occupied the northern part of the island and did not leave when constitutional order in Cyprus was restored. Greek Cypriots in the north were forced to move south and Turkish Cypriots were displaced to the north. In 1983, the northern region, 40 percent of the island, declared independence as the Turkish Republic of Northern Cyprus, but Turkey was the only country willing to acknowledge its sovereignty. Attempts by United Nations to reunify the country have not been successful. In 2004, Cyprus entered the EU, but the rules and benefits of membership only apply to people with Republic of Cyprus citizenship.

The official language in Cyprus is Greek and the majority of citizens are Orthodox Christians. The economy is strong, with a gross domestic product per capita of USD 37,200, which is higher than both Greece (USD 27,800) and Turkey (USD 27,000). The economy is supported largely by tourism, finance, shipping, and real estate. The global recession of 2008–2009 and the Eurozone debt crisis hit Cyprus especially hard because of its extensive banking and finance sector, but the economy has been growing again in the last few years (Central Intelligence Agency 2018).

Criminology is a relatively new field of study in Cyprus, so there is not a large volume of research on crime and justice, in general, or on juvenile delinquency and juvenile justice, in particular. However, Cyprus participated in the second wave of the ISRD study (ISRD-2). Additionally, membership in the EU and international agreements like the United Nations CRC have brought attention to areas in need of improvement in the juvenile justice system.

Juvenile Delinquency

Media coverage of crime in Cyprus has created a sensationalist portrait of rising youth crime, although the sparse research data do not necessarily support this claim. Official statistics from the police regarding the number of reported juvenile offenses show a fair amount of variation over time. For example, the number of recorded juvenile offenders was 461 in 2000, 209 in 2004, 390 in 2008, and 170 in 2011. Juveniles are most likely to commit property crimes. In 2011, 51 percent of juvenile offenders were arrested for burglary, 11 percent for other kinds of theft, 6 percent for vandalism, and 6 percent for forgery (Kapardis 2013). As in all countries, the official recording of criminal events is subject to the discretion of police, which is especially true of juvenile delinquency. Researchers in Cyprus note several factors that affect the recording of juvenile offenses independent of their occurrence, such as public pressure on the police to be tough on crime, which could increase the number of recorded offenses, or parental pressure to drop charges, which could decrease the number of recorded offenses.

Self-report delinquency studies provide an alternative source of information on juvenile delinquency that is independent of police practices. Cyprus participated in the second round of the ISRD study in 2006. Surveys were administered to 2,500 students aged twelve to fifteen in sixteen schools in the three largest cities in the free areas of Cyprus. In the capital city of Nicosia, group fighting was the most frequent delinquent act committed by the youth in their lifetime (18.7 percent), followed by vandalism (7.7 percent), shoplifting (5.7 percent), carrying a weapon to school (4.8 percent), and computer hacking (4.8 percent). Less frequent crimes included assault (3.3 percent), bicycle or motorbike theft (2.2 percent), breaking into a car (1.9 percent), and burglary (1.9 percent) (Kapardis 2012).

The ISRD-2 survey also identified risk factors for youths engaged in any form of delinquency. In Cyprus, the most important family factors related to delinquency were not having a curfew imposed by parents (53 percent) and having parents who did not know the youths' friends (29 percent). School attachment was also low among delinquents, with 44 percent stating that they did not like going to school. Delinquent youth also tended to favor violent attitudes, with 59 percent saying that they would retaliate if someone used violence against them, 30 percent claiming that life without violence was boring, and 15 percent viewing violence as a source of entertainment (Kapardis 2012).

Cyprus also participated in the ESPAD in 2015, where fifteen- and sixteen-year-old schoolchildren were asked about substance use. About 88 percent of these youth reported ever having used alcohol, a figure that has remained stable since 1995. Within the last thirty days of the survey, 50 percent of adolescents had engaged in heavy drinking. The use of illicit drugs in Cyprus is much lower than alcohol. In 2015, 7 percent of teens reported having ever used cannabis, 5 percent tried tranquilizers, 8 percent used inhalants, and 4 percent had ever taken new psychoactive drugs. The rates of illicit drug use in Cyprus were similar to other European countries that participated in the survey, except that cannabis use among teens in Cyprus was less than half of the European average (EMCDDA 2019).

Juvenile Justice

The juvenile justice system in Cyprus has not changed much since the country became independent in 1960, with two important exceptions. In 1996, the government allowed the use of community service as a sanction for juveniles. In 2007, the minimum age of criminal responsibility was raised from ten to fourteen years to be consistent with international standards. Currently, the justice system classifies minors less than fourteen years old as "children" who cannot be held criminally liable, and fourteen- and fifteen-year-olds as "young persons," who are handled through the juvenile justice system.

The legal system works closely with social welfare services in handling criminal cases involving minors. When police arrest a juvenile suspect, they request a social history and family well-being investigation by social services. That report, along with the criminal file compiled by the police, goes to the Committee for the Handling of Juvenile Offenders, which makes a recommendation about how to proceed with the case to the prosecutor. This committee consists of a local welfare officer and a deputy district police officer, who process all juvenile cases except drug offenses.

If a case is prosecuted, it goes to juvenile court, which usually consists of a district court judge who hears juvenile cases on certain days or times and sometimes in different locations than adult trials. In 2008, the police investigated 341 juvenile suspects, of which 50 percent were prosecuted. Among the juveniles who were not prosecuted, 84 percent received an official reprimand, 13.4 percent were placed under supervision, and 2.3 percent were placed in the care of social services. Of those who were prosecuted, 96 percent resulted in a conviction. The decision to prosecute was shared almost evenly between the district welfare officer and the prosecutor (Kapardis 2012).

A young person convicted of an offense can be subjected to the following measures: dismissal of charges, probation, community service, supervision, placement in the care of a guardian, fines, placement in a juvenile correctional institution, or imprisonment in extreme cases. Minors cannot be detained in adult facilities. There are no secure juvenile facilities in Cyprus. The only reform school was closed in 1986 and was never replaced. A juvenile who needs to be detained for a short period of time can only be held in a police cell with no adults. In 2008, convicted juveniles were sentenced most often to probation (40 percent), followed by community service (25.3 percent), fines (18 percent), suspended prison term (5 percent), and prison (1.2 percent) (Kapardis 2012).

Juveniles charged with drug offenses are not processed by the Committee for the Handling of Juvenile Offenders but are instead diverted to a drug treatment program. If the offender successfully completes the program, criminal charges are usually dropped. Drug treatment diversion is available for fourteen- to twenty-four-year-old offenders. If treatment is unsuccessful, a drug offender under twenty-five years old can receive a sentence of up to one year in prison.

Juvenile justice experts in Cyprus note that the Juvenile Delinquency Act has not been reformed in over fifty years. They recommend investigation into the benefits of a separate juvenile justice system. They also point to the need for specialized training for judges and a lack of social workers. While there has been some discussion about mediation and restorative justice practices for juvenile offenders, these options are currently only available in civil law cases, but not criminal law. Professionals who work with juvenile delinquents see the value of restorative justice for minor offenses but are concerned about a lack of understanding of the philosophy of restorative justice among the general public and the role that communities play in reintegration.

Further Reading

Bussu, Anna. 2016. "In Need of a Cultural Shift to Promote Restorative Justice in Southern Europe." *Contemporary Justice Review* 19 (4): 479–503.

Central Intelligence Agency. 2018. "The World Factbook." https://www.cia.gov/library /publications/resources/the-world-factbook/.

EMCDDA (European Monitoring Centre for Drugs and Drug Addiction). 2019. "Cyprus Country Drug Report 2019." http://www.emcdda.europa.eu/countries/drug-reports /2019/cyprus/drug-use_en.

Kapardis, Andreas. 2010. "Cyprus." In *Juvenile Delinquency in Europe and Beyond: Results of the Second International Self-Report Delinquency Study*, edited by Josine Junger-Tas, Ineke Haen Marshall, Dirk Enzmann, Martin Killias, Majone Steketee, and Beata Gruszczynska, 247–53. New York: Springer.

Kapardis, Andreas. 2012. "Juvenile Delinquency and Justice in Cyprus." In *Risk Assessment for Juvenile Violent Offending*, edited by Anna Costanza Baldry and Andreas Kapardis, 43–58. New York: Routledge.

Kapardis, Andreas. 2013. "Juvenile Delinquency and Victimization in Cyprus." *European Journal on Criminal Policy and Research* 19 (2): 171–82. https://doi.org/10.1007 /s10610-013-9201-y.

CZECH REPUBLIC

The Czech Republic, also known as Czechia, is a landlocked country of 10.5 million people located in Central Europe and surrounded by Germany, Poland, Slovakia, Hungary, and Austria. It has a growing economy anchored by a productive automobile industry. The majority of the population is of Czech ethnicity, although the country is religiously diverse. The Czech Republic was part of Czechoslovakia, which was under the political influence of the Soviet communist bloc until 1989. In 1993, the Czech and Slovak Republics separated into independent countries and began major political and economic transformations toward democracy and capitalism (Central Intelligence Agency 2018). This profound social change has affected both juvenile delinquency and juvenile justice in the Czech Republic. Since 2004, the country has been a member of the EU, a political and economic alliance of twenty-eight countries, and its juvenile justice policies are strongly influenced by EU laws.

Velvet Revolution and Velvet Divorce

Czech territory was part of the Habsburg Empire until the end of World War I in 1918, when it joined Slovakia to form the independent country of Czechoslovakia. In the aftermath of World War II (1939–1945), the country adopted a communist government in 1948 and was strongly influenced both politically and economically by the Soviet Union. In 1968, the citizens of Czechoslovakia launched a series of public protests, called the Prague Spring, calling for the communist government to increase the civil liberties of citizens. After eight months of unrest, the Soviet Union invaded Czechoslovakia and restored order.

By the late 1980s, economic decline in the Soviet states and a reformist government in the Soviet Union, led by Mikhail Gorbachev (1931–), led to the collapse of communist rule in the Eastern European countries and eventually brought an end to the Soviet Union itself. Anti-communist protests in Czechoslovakia in 1989 persuaded communist officials to resign, paving the way for the first democratic elections in four decades. The peaceful nature of these protests gave rise to the term Velvet Revolution. In 1993, the Czech and Slovak Republics peacefully agreed to separate into two nations, which was called the Velvet Divorce.

The sudden and rapid change in government in 1989 resulted in a period of turmoil as the new leaders sought to completely change the political system from the one-party authoritarianism of communism to a multiparty democracy. At the same time, the communist command economy, whereby the government tightly controlled the market and major industries, also collapsed, and there was little infrastructure in place to support a free-market economy. Social provisions that were commonplace during communism, such as free healthcare, childcare, education, and youth programs, as well as guaranteed employment, disappeared quickly. The result of the communist transition in the Czech Republic was a period of economic strain and social upheaval. Crime and juvenile delinquency increased during this time, and the criminal justice system was in a period of flux while the new government gained control of the country.

Juvenile Delinquency

Between 1990 and 1995, crime increased in all the former communist states in Central and Eastern Europe that were transitioning to democracies, and the Czech Republic was no exception. Rising crime was apparent in both adult and juvenile crime rates. In the 1980s, the percentage of known criminal offenders who were juveniles in the Czech Republic was 10.7 percent, which increased to 17 percent by 1994. In the second half of the 1990s, as the new political and economic systems stabilized, crime rates began to decrease. In 1999, the proportion of juvenile offenders in the Czech Republic was 8 percent, which declined to 7.2 percent by 2002 (Válková 2008). Police statistics from 2006 showed that 8 percent of known criminal offenders were less than eighteen years old. Juveniles were most likely to engage in property crimes (14 percent) than violent crimes (10 percent) and were most likely to commit pickpocketing (33 percent), followed by car theft (19 percent) and burglary (19 percent) (Burianek and Podaná 2010).

The Czech Republic participated in the second and third waves of the ISRD study (ISRD-2), although only preliminary results from the third wave have been published to date. Between 2006 and 2007, the Czech Republic administered a national survey of children in the seventh through ninth grades. According to that data, Czech youth were most likely to have shoplifted (22.5 percent) in their lifetime or participated in a group fight (19.8 percent). The next most common crimes were vandalism (11.5 percent), carrying a weapon (10.3 percent), and computer hacking (7.1 percent). The least common offenses were hard drug use (0.6 percent), car theft (0.8 percent), and burglary (1.1 percent) (Burianek and Podaná 2010). Notice that the last two numbers seem to contradict the police statistics presented earlier, but they are not directly comparable. The police statistics are the percentage of all offenders who have come to the attention of the police in a given year, whereas the ISRD numbers are the percentage of seventh through ninth graders who reported committing the criminal act in their lifetime.

The third wave of the ISRD administered in 2013 showed that the lifetime prevalence of youth participating in all of these delinquent acts decreased since 2006. In particular, only 13.3 percent reported shoplifting, 9.5 percent participated in a group fight, and 10.9 percent vandalized property. This decline is also supported by police statistics, which documented a 51 percent decline in juveniles involved in property crimes and a 45 percent decline in violent crimes (Podaná and Moravcová 2015).

Among the youth surveyed in the second wave, 86 percent had ever tried beer or wine and 40 percent had drunk beer or wine in the past month of taking the survey. Of the youth who drank within the past year, teens more than fifteen years old were much more likely than thirteen- and fourteen-year-olds to drink, particularly hard liquor. About 16 percent of the youth had ever tried cannabis, and 6 percent had used it in the month prior to the survey (Burianek and Podaná 2010). The risk factors that most strongly predicted delinquent behavior among Czech youth were divorced or separated parents, having delinquent friends, and having a tendency to take risks.

Juvenile Justice

During the communist period, court proceedings were fairly rigid, although not overly punitive. The criminal justice system in Western countries is often described as a funnel, where the number of people processed by the system decreases significantly from the initial contact (number of suspected offenders) through prosecution, conviction, and sentencing. In contrast, the communist model found in most Central and Eastern European countries, including the Czech Republic, was more of a cylinder than a funnel. The number of people who entered the system stayed relatively stable through all the stages of criminal justice processing. Juvenile justice was more flexible than the adult system, as there was more emphasis on education and child welfare than punishment. For example, in 1993, the prosecution rate for juveniles was 1,874 per 100,000 people, but the incarceration rate was 122 per 100,000 (Válková 2008).

The age of criminal responsibility was fifteen years, but there was no juvenile court for young offenders. Youth aged fifteen to seventeen were adjudicated in adult courts, but with modified proceedings. Judges tried all juvenile cases, and youth were required to have legal representation. Children's rights to a fair trial, to have a parent or guardian present, to have a lawyer, and to be able to appeal the verdict were given high priority in juvenile cases.

Changes to juvenile justice after the transition from communism to democratic governance were slow given the extensive number of legal revisions that had to be made to reform the socialist legal system to one that was based on civil liberties and political rights. However, in 2003, the Czech Republic passed the Youth Justice Act to reform the outdated system and comply with the EU standards. With this new law, the age of criminal responsibility remained at fifteen years, but youth under fifteen years of age were designated as having "limited criminal responsibility." This gives the court flexibility to prosecute minors for offenses that are deemed to be especially dangerous for society, although these cases are tried in family courts.

Importantly, the 2003 reforms created a separate juvenile court system so that youth are no longer processed in adult courts. The juvenile courts place a strong emphasis on restorative justice and mediation over punishment alone. This system aims to restore social relationships damaged by the delinquent act and to reintegrate the young offender back into their communities after completing their court sentence. Juvenile cases are also considered holistically, taking into account the youth's circumstances and personality, as well as the harm done to others.

Juvenile cases can be diverted to mediation rather than prosecuted through the criminal justice system, particularly for minor offenses. Youth who are sentenced in the juvenile justice system can be sanctioned to educational or rehabilitation programs, community service, fines (if the youth is employed), and imprisonment. Incarceration is used as a last resort for the most serious offenders. The shift in penal policy for juveniles from the communist system to the reformed system is apparent in the drop in youth incarceration rates. In 1995, there were 300 youth incarcerated, which dropped to 100 by 2006 (Dünkel 2014). Juveniles cannot be sentenced to more than five years in prison and must be held in separate facilities from adults.

In 2009, the Czech Republic passed another law to allow juveniles awaiting trial to be held in custody, but only for offenders considered to be dangerous and for no longer than two months. Legislators also proposed a law to reduce the age of criminal liability from fifteen to fourteen, but it did not pass (Dünkel 2014).

Further Reading

Burianek, Jiri, and Zuzana Podaná. 2010. "Czech Republic." In *Juvenile Delinquency in Europe and Beyond: Results of the Second International Self-Report Delinquency Study*, edited by Josine Junger-Tas, Ineke Haen Marshall, Dirk Enzmann, Martin Killias, Majone Steketee, and Beata Gruszczynska, 292–308. New York: Springer.

Central Intelligence Agency. 2018. "The World Factbook." https://www.cia.gov/library /publications/resources/the-world-factbook/.

Dünkel, Frieder. 2014. "Juvenile Justice Systems in Europe—Reform Developments between Justice, Welfare and 'New Punitiveness'." *Kriminologijos Studijos* 1 (January): 31–76. https://www.zurnalai.vu.lt/kriminologijos-studijos/article/view/3676

Neubacher, Frank, Michael Walter, Helena Válková, and Krzysztof Krajewski. 1999. "Juvenile Delinquency in Central European Cities: A Comparison of Registration and Processing Structures in the 1990s." *European Journal on Criminal Policy and Research* 7 (4): 539–62. https://doi.org/10.1023/A:1008750223844.

Podaná, Zuzana, and Eva Moravcová. 2015. "Juvenile Delinquency in the Czech Republic: First Results of the ISRD-3 Self-Report Survey." *Acta Universitatis Carolinae: Philosophica et Historica* 2012 (2): 57–68. https://doi.org/10.14712/24647055.2014.20.

Válková, Helena. 2008. "Restorative Approaches and Alternative Methods: Juvenile Justice Reform in the Czech Republic." In *International Handbook of Juvenile Justice*, edited by Josine Junger-Tas and Scott. H. Decker, 377–95. New York: Springer. https://doi.org /10.1007/978-0-387-09478-6_15.

ICELAND

Iceland is an island country in the North Atlantic Ocean, east of Greenland, west of Norway, and north of the United Kingdom. It has a population of only 350,000, half of whom live in or near the capital city of Reykjavik. The island has a large number of glaciers and active volcanoes. Icelanders are descendants of Celtic and Norse settlers from the late ninth century. The country has been independent since 1944. It is a parliamentary republic with a substantial welfare system. The economy is driven largely by the tourism and fishing industries. It is the twenty-fifth wealthiest country in the world, with a gross domestic product per capita of USD 52,200, comparable to the Netherlands (Central Intelligence Agency 2018). Despite having a relatively low crime rate, Iceland experienced a rise in juvenile delinquency in the 1990s and responded with a creative, and effective, national strategy to keep adolescents out of legal trouble.

Aggression and Drug Use

Although Iceland has historically had low violent crime rates, aggression among adolescents was fairly common in the late twentieth century. In 1997, a study called Youth in Iceland found that almost 60 percent of youth aged fifteen or sixteen had committed at least one act of violence in the past year. Of the youth who participated in the survey, nearly 34 percent said they had kicked someone, 31 percent reporting hitting another person, and almost 28 percent said they had punched someone. Additionally, nearly 4 percent claimed to have threatened another person with a weapon (Gudlaugsdottir et al. 2004).

Researchers found that most aggressive youth were males who associated with other violent peers. They identified a subculture of violence where adolescent males were encouraged to use violence as a means of protecting their reputation among their friendship networks and in their communities. Other researchers found that male delinquents were less likely to have strong parental support or attachments to school compared to nondelinquent youth. Finally, and most importantly, violent teenagers were also likely to engage in some kind of substance abuse.

Studies of substance abuse among Icelandic youth showed prevalence rates much higher than most other European countries. A 1997 survey of teenagers found that 40 percent had consumed alcohol in the previous month and 30 percent had been intoxicated during the same period (Kristjansson et al. 2010). In 1998, 17 percent of Icelandic adolescents had tried cannabis at least once and 23 percent were smoking cigarettes daily (Young 2017).

National Prevention Model

In response to the high rates of substance use among youth, the Icelandic government joined the Icelandic Centre for Social Research to develop a national plan to tackle the problem. From the outset, the strategy was based on scientific evidence regarding patterns of substance use and delinquency. It was also designed to be a community-based program recognizing the problem as a social one, and not simply an individual one.

One aspect of the prevention strategy was to pass a series of laws to discourage alcohol use and smoking and to better monitor youth. There was a national ban on alcohol and tobacco advertising, as well as restrictions on the visibility of these products in public places. Labels were added to cigarette packages warning of the risks of smoking, and cigarettes were prohibited in

In response to high rates of drug use and aggression among teenagers in the 1990s, the Icelandic government adopted a radical drug prevention model for youth that dramatically reduced both problems in the last twenty years. (ktaylorg/iStockphoto.com)

all public places. The legal age to purchase cigarettes was raised to eighteen and the alcohol age limit was raised to twenty. Finally, a curfew law was passed prohibiting youth aged thirteen to sixteen to be outside of the home past 10 o'clock in the winter and midnight in the summer. The laws were accompanied by media campaigns spreading prevention messages. The president of the country even initiated an annual substance use prevention day with organized activities and information reinforcing the prevention method.

The second part of the Icelandic national strategy was influenced by the work of American psychologist Harvey Milkman, who argued that successful prevention was based on replacing the biochemical highs of substance use with natural highs from other activities. Milkman founded a program in the United States called Project Self-Discovery, where teens were offered various classes in music, dance, martial arts, and so on that would produce these natural highs. Additionally, they received life-skills training to improve their self-image and relationship with others.

The Icelandic prevention plan was built around many of Milkman's ideas. In particular, the government identified organized activities for youth, spending time with parents, feeling attached to school, and not being away from home late at night as key protective factors against substance use and delinquency. To support this agenda, the government increased spending for organized activities, such as sports, music, and dance. Families were also given "leisure cards" with a fixed amount of money per child to be spent on family recreational activities. Parents were encouraged to increase the amount of time they spent with their children each day to get to know their children's friends. School councils also added parent representatives to forge better connections between families and schools.

The Icelandic prevention strategy has been deemed a success and serves as a model for other communities. By 2016, the percentage of fifteen- and sixteen-year-olds who had been drunk in the previous month dropped to 5 percent, and the proportion who had ever used cannabis fell to 7 percent (Young 2017). The 2015 ESPAD shows that substance use among Icelandic youth is much lower than the average for the rest of Europe. For example, the lifetime prevalence of cannabis in Iceland was 7 percent compared to 16 percent in the rest of Europe. The lifetime use of inhalants in Iceland was 3 percent compared to 7 percent in the rest of Europe. The alcohol and cigarette usage statistics are even more dramatic. In 2015, the proportion of Icelandic youth who drank alcohol in the past thirty days was 9 percent, compared to 48 percent in Europe, and cigarette use in the past month was 6 percent in Iceland compared to 21 percent in Europe.

Juvenile Justice

Iceland is part of the Nordic Council established in 1952, along with Denmark, Finland, Norway, Sweden, Faroe Islands, Greenland, and Åland. This is a long-standing political cooperative agreement among countries sharing historical and cultural roots, as well as economic and political goals. For example, the council promotes the Nordic welfare model, which supports income redistribution and comprehensive welfare programs, along with maximum labor force participation.

Participation in the Nordic Council has led to the standardization of many laws including criminal law and juvenile justice. The Nordic countries identify their legal systems as a Nordic family of law, which is similar to civil law in terms of its emphasis on written legal codes but also maintains a pragmatic view of solving social problems. The Nordic welfare model promotes high levels of trust among people and in social institutions, as well as high social tolerance. As a result, citizens in these countries tend to be less punitive than in the United States, for example.

The minimum age of criminal responsibility in Iceland is fifteen years. Juvenile delinquents under fifteen years of age are handled by child welfare services. Adolescent offenders between fifteen and seventeen years of age are dealt with by both child welfare and the criminal justice system. Young adult offenders between eighteen and twenty years are processed by the criminal justice system but may receive help with aftercare from child welfare services. Juvenile delinquents are processed in adult courts, but with different procedures and sentencing guidelines. For suspected offenders under eighteen years, authorities must notify parents or guardians and child welfare of the offense, and these parties must be present when the children are interviewed by authorities. Suspected delinquents are not allowed to be held in custody.

Juveniles aged fifteen to seventeen who are convicted of a crime are almost always given community sanctions. These include suspended sentences, probation or other supervision, community service, substance abuse or mental health treatment, or electronic monitoring. It is exceptionally rare for children to be sentenced to prison. Authorities often encourage mediation for juvenile cases. Successful mediation could result in the prosecutors dropping charges or judges reducing sentences.

Rather than emphasizing punishment for juvenile offenders, Icelandic policies focus more on crime prevention. Criminal justice policies are usually developed in consultation with professional organizations, social scientists, and nongovernmental organizations to find the most pragmatic solutions to social problems, such as adolescent substance abuse and juvenile delinquency. Iceland supports community-based prevention efforts, such as parental counseling, school programs, and legal education, as well as legislation to control factors that contribute to illegal behavior, such as alcohol.

Further Reading

Central Intelligence Agency. 2018. "The World Factbook." https://www.cia.gov/library/publications/resources/the-world-factbook/.

ESPAD (The European School Survey Project on Alcohol and Other Drugs). 2015. "Iceland." European Monitoring Centre for Drugs and Drug Addiction. http://www.espad.org/report/country-summaries#iceland.

Gudlaugsdottir, Gerdur Run, Runar Vilhjalmsson, Gudrun Kristjansdottir, Rune Jacobsen, and Dan Meyrowitsch. 2004. "Violent Behaviour among Adolescents in Iceland: A National Survey." *International Journal of Epidemiology* 33 (5): 1046–51. https://doi.org/10.1093/ije/dyh190.

Kristjansson, Alfgeir Logi, Jack E. James, John P. Allegrante, Inga Dora Sigfusdottir, and Asgeir R. Helgason. 2010. "Adolescent Substance Use, Parental Monitoring, and Leisure-Time Activities: 12-Year Outcomes of Primary Prevention in Iceland." *Preventive Medicine* 51 (2): 168–71. https://doi.org/10.1016/j.ypmed.2010.05.001.

Lappi-Seppälä, Tapio, and Michael Tonry. 2011. "Crime, Criminal Justice, and Criminology in the Nordic Countries." *Crime and Justice* 40 (1): 1–32. https://doi.org/10.1086/660822.

Young, Emma. 2017. "How Iceland Got Teens to Say No to Drugs." *The Atlantic.* January 19, 2017. https://www.theatlantic.com/health/archive/2017/01/teens-drugs-iceland/513668/.

NEPAL

Nepal is a small country nestled between India and China in southern Asia. It is the home of the Himalayan mountain range and Mount Everest, the world's tallest peak. The country has about thirty million people from 125 caste and ethnic groups speaking 123 languages, although most share a common belief in Hinduism. It is one of the poorest countries in the world with a gross domestic product per capita of USD 2,700 compared to USD 59,800 in the United States or USD 7,200 in neighboring India. The Nepali economy is largely supported by foreign aid and agriculture (Central Intelligence Agency 2018). The poor economy, as well as political instability from a decade-long civil war, is the main social factor shaping juvenile delinquency in the country and slowing the expansion of the juvenile justice system to conform to international standards.

Legacy of Violence

Nepal has neither participated in the ISRD studies nor does it have a strong university infrastructure to support criminological research. Therefore, information about illegal activities of Nepali youth must be derived from other sources, particularly from public health. One of the major concerns about youth according to medical professionals is the long-term effects of exposure to violence due to the Nepalese Civil War and the continued politicization of poor youth.

Since the eighteenth century Nepal was a monarchy that adopted a multiparty parliamentary system in 1991, which created considerable tensions among various political groups competing for power. The Communist Party of Nepal (Maoist) launched an armed attack against the Nepalese state to overthrow the monarchy and political parties controlling the relatively new parliament. This led to a ten-year civil war during which 13,000 people were killed and approximately 150,000 more were displaced from their homes (Gupte and Bogati 2014; Zia-Zarifi 2007). Civilians were the victims of much of the violence including torture, kidnapping, and executions.

The Maoist forces recruited children to join their cause. The exact number of child soldiers is disputed, with some estimates around 4,000, as are the methods of recruitment. Some children were said to have volunteered because of their extreme poverty or loss of family due to the war. Others are believed to have been recruited

During Nepal's civil war from 1996 to 2006, children were used as soldiers by the Maoist army and regularly exposed to extreme violence. Today youth are still recruited by political parties to disrupt protests or engage in other coercive activities. (Dreamstime)

through propaganda, force, or coercion. Children served in support roles in the Maoist army, for example, as porters or messengers, but they were also trained to fight and use arms (Zia-Zarifi 2007).

As a result of the civil war, and particularly the active recruitment of children as militants, large numbers of youth were exposed to extreme violence. Even those who were not directly involved in combat still witnessed killings, beatings, torture, and harassment of family members and teachers. These experiences caused a large number of people to experience psychosocial distress and mental health disorders, such as posttraumatic stress disorder, anxiety, and depression, making it difficult for youth to transition to a healthy adult life.

Even youth who were too young to participate in, or even remember, the violence are living in extremely poor economic conditions, surrounded by a culture of violence with easy access to firearms. Almost 30 percent of the Nepalese population is under thirty years old, and 54 percent of youth are unemployed. Although the war ended in 2006, homicides unrelated to war increased from 575 in 1997 to 917 in 2008, 30 percent of which were committed with a firearm. It is estimated that there are over 200,000 illegal firearms in the country (Gupte and Bogati 2014).

Vulnerable Nepalese youth are still being recruited to youth organizations affiliated with political parties and are employed for coercive activities, such as extortion, intimidation, and stirring violence during protests. These youth are also susceptible to recruitment by criminal gangs. Boys, in particular, are attracted to gangs in search of "3M," meaning money, machines (guns), and *masti* (fun). For example, in the Terai region of Nepal there were one hundred known, active military organizations, twelve of which were solely political and seventy were criminal organizations (Bennett, Karki, and Nepal 2012).

Other Types of Delinquency

Criminal groups are involved in other types of activities, particularly smuggling. The Terai region along the southern border with India is home to many youth gangs because of high levels of social exclusion, easy access to firearms, and an open border with India. Weapon and drug smuggling are common in that region and provide a source of income for poor youth. Even those who do not participate in criminal activities still tend to join gangs for self-protection against other violent youth.

Despite the presence of drug smuggling, illicit drug use is not very common among Nepalese youth. However, alcohol use in Nepal is common. There are no legal restrictions against alcohol, tobacco, or cannabis for any ages. Therefore, 60 percent of Nepalese have consumed alcohol. A study in Pokhara showed that 13.9 percent of youth aged ten to twenty-five years drank alcohol, with most starting to drink between ten and twelve years of age. Aside from alcohol, smoking tobacco and glue sniffing are preferred substances among young people (Timsinha, Kar, and Agrawal 2011).

Juvenile Justice

Like many countries in South Asia, Nepal does not have a separate justice system for juvenile offenders, although it does have separate procedures for these cases. The National Code of 1963 included punishments for juvenile delinquents, but it was only in 1992 that the first law to specifically deal with juvenile offenders was passed with the Children's Act, likely in response to Nepal ratifying the United Nations CRC in 1990. After the Comprehensive Peace Agreement was signed in 2006, the Interim Constitution of 2007 explicitly recognized the rights of children for the first time. In the same year, the Juvenile Justice Procedures Rule was passed, outlining how juvenile cases should be handled.

The minimum age of criminal responsibility in Nepal is ten years and youth aged sixteen years and older are treated as adults, which conflicts with the CRC. The law specifies that a juvenile delinquent between ten and thirteen years of age who commits an offense that would be punishable by a fine for an adult will be reprimanded instead. A child of the same age who commits a crime that would be punishable by prison for an adult can be sentenced up to six months in detention, depending on the seriousness of the offense. A child aged between fourteen and sixteen years who commits a crime will receive half of the adult sentence.

A child who is arrested cannot be put in handcuffs or other restraints. They must be informed of their rights and their parents or guardians must be informed of their offense. The child is supposed to be checked by a medical professional after arrest. A child who is awaiting court proceedings can be released to their family or a social protection organization upon the discretion of the judge. If they are to be detained prior to trial, they cannot be held in prison with adults or in solitary confinement. Parents or guardians are expected to be present during police investigations and interrogations.

A 2011 study of juvenile delinquents who had been arrested showed that many of these procedures were not followed in practice. For example, 86 percent of juveniles said they were arrested without a warrant, and 53 percent said their parents or guardians were not informed of their arrest. Additionally, 66 percent of juvenile delinquents reported being detained with adult offenders, and 25 percent said that the police had treated them cruelly (Ghimire 2013).

In 2005, the Nepalese Supreme Court requested that the government establish a juvenile bench in every court district in the country, of which there are seventy-five. This has yet to be fully implemented, and the majority of juvenile cases are heard in adult courts. They are supposed to go to trial within 120 days after filing, but this only happened in 12.5 percent of the cases in 2011 (Ghimire 2013). Juvenile proceedings are supposed to be closed to protect the identity of the youth, and they should be conducted in a manner that the child can understand.

There are no formal diversion rules for juvenile cases, although in practice local authorities handle less serious offenses without going through the formal court system. Additionally, there are no official mediation, restorative justice, or rehabilitation programs for juveniles. As of 2017, there were three Juvenile Reform Homes in Nepal, with two more under construction. In the same year 1,492 children, who had been convicted of twenty-nine different types of crimes, had been serviced by the Juvenile Reform Homes.

In 2014, the Supreme Court issued a strategic plan for further juvenile justice reforms. Their goals included having a juvenile bench in each court district and a Juvenile Reform Home in each of the country's five regions. They recommended basic training on juvenile procedures for all judges. They also requested the development of educational and rehabilitation programs for reform homes, as well as programs to reintegrate juvenile offenders into their communities. In 2011, 72 percent of juvenile offenders reported that they felt discriminated against because of their delinquency, highlighting the importance of reintegration efforts (Ghimire 2013).

Further Reading

Bennett, Ryan, Sameer Karki, and Nitu Nepal. 2012. "Youth and Peacebuilding in Nepal: The Current Context and Recommendations." DM&E for Peace. https://dmeforpeace.org/sites/default/files/NEP_CA_Jan12_Youth%20and%20Peacebuilding.pdf.

Central Intelligence Agency. 2018. "The World Factbook." https://www.cia.gov/library/publications/resources/the-world-factbook/.

Ghimire, Rajendra. 2013. "Analysis of Juvenile Justice System of Nepal in the Perspective of International Juvenile Justice Standards." *NJA Law Journal* 6: 138–65.

Gupte, Jaideep, and Subindra Bogati. 2014. *Key Challenges of Security Provision in Rapidly Urbanising Contexts: Evidence from Kathmandu Valley and Terai Regions of Nepal.* Evidence Report 69. Brighton, UK: Institute of Development Studies.

Timsinha, Sidarth, S. M. Kar, and Prashant Agrawal. 2011. "Drug Abuse and Alcohol Consumption as a Social Habit in Nepal." *Medico-Legal Update* 11 (2): 38–39.

Zia-Zarifi, Saman. 2007. "Children in the Ranks: The Maoists' Use of Child Soldiers in Nepal." Human Rights Watch, February 1, 2007. https://www.hrw.org/report/2007/02/01/children-ranks/maoists-use-child-soldiers-nepal.

NIGERIA

Nigeria is a West African nation bordering the Gulf of Guinea to the south, Niger to the north, Benin to the west, and Cameroon to the east. It is the most populous African country with over 200 million people and has one of the highest population growth rates in the world. It is a multiethnic society, with nearly 52 percent of the population practicing Islam and 47 percent adhering to some form of Christianity. Given its steadily growing population, Nigeria has a large number of children and young adults. In 2018, about 43 percent of the population was under fourteen years old and 20 percent was between fifteen and twenty-four years old. The Nigerian economy has depended heavily on income from oil, although profits have not been invested into sustaining economic growth, largely due to high levels of corruption and poor infrastructure. The gross domestic product per capita is USD 5,900, which is comparable to Honduras and Nicaragua. About 70 percent of the population lives below the poverty line, and unemployment rate is 16.5 percent (Central Intelligence Agency 2018). The large youth population, coupled with high unemployment rates, increases the risk of adolescent criminal behavior.

Juvenile Delinquency

Nigeria has been a federal republic since gaining independence from Britain in 1960. The country is divided into thirty-six states and one federal capital territory that includes the capital city of Abuja. Nigeria has neither participated in the ISRD study nor have there been any national surveys regarding the occurrence of juvenile delinquency. However, there have been some citywide studies of adolescents. One such study conducted in 2010 surveyed 200 secondary school students from Uyo, the capital of the state of Akwa Ibon in the southeast of Nigeria. Using a self-report Family Delinquency Questionnaire, the researchers found that 57 percent of the adolescents reported involvement in some form of delinquency, although the different types were not reported. Of the youth who were delinquent, 50 percent had rarely or never spent time with their parents, 71 percent had little parental supervision, and 66 percent experienced some form of violence at home (Sanni et al. 2010).

Another study from 2010 surveyed over 500 students aged thirteen to seventeen years in Owerri, the capital of the Imo state, also located in southeastern Nigeria.

This study found that 77 percent of the students reported engaging in some kind of delinquency, although once again the different forms of criminal behaviors were not shared. Of these delinquent youth, 60 percent had low parental supervision and 37 percent came from a broken home (Ugwuoke and Duruji 2015).

In 2017, Nigeria conducted its first national drug use study with assistance from the United Nations Office on Drugs and Crime (UNODC). The study found that 25 percent of men and 13 percent of women had consumed alcohol in their lifetime (UNODC 2018). Abstinence from alcohol is fairly common in Nigeria due to strong religious beliefs. Although the percentage of youth drinking was not reported, other researchers have noted heavy, episodic drinking among Nigerian youth (binge drinking). Alcohol is often produced locally from palm sap, sorghum, and maize. Additionally, the legal age to purchase alcohol is eighteen years, but experts state that this law is rarely enforced (Dumbili 2015).

The UNODC reported that 3.3 percent of youths aged fifteen to nineteen years used cannabis in the past year, 2.4 percent used pharmaceutical opioids, and 1.6 percent misused cough syrup with codeine or dextromethorphan (UNODC 2018). A 2012 study of drug users in the state of Lagos in southwestern Nigeria found that 12.9 percent of them began using drugs between the ages of ten and fourteen years and 52 percent between fifteen and eighteen years. The respondents stated that they used drugs to forget their sorrows (27.5 percent), overcome frustration (24.6 percent), and relieve stress (21.7 percent). About 29 percent of the respondents reported that their parents used drugs, and 46.2 percent said their friends introduced them to drugs. Almost 32 percent of drug users reported committing a crime other than substance abuse (Ayodele, Habibat, and Babtunde 2018).

Juvenile Justice

The Nigerian juvenile justice system was established in 1914 and modeled after the British system. The main law guiding juvenile justice is the Child and Young Persons Act (CYPA) that was initially introduced by the British in 1948. Although it was intended to be a federal law, it was instead adopted as state law. The Act was amended several times and is still the most important legislation for juvenile justice at the state level. The CYPA defines a "child" under fourteen years old and a "young person" as between fourteen and seventeen years old. The minimum age of criminal responsibility was set at fourteen years by the CYPA but has been increased to eighteen years in subsequent legislation.

In 2003, the Nigerian government passed the Child Rights Act (CRA), which was a federal legislation designed to standardize juvenile justice practices and child welfare across the country. It was also designed to make Nigeria's laws more consistent with the United Nations CRC, such as by increasing the minimum age of criminal responsibility to eighteen years. The Nigerian CRA law was meant to replace the older CYPA, but that has not been the case for all states, with both laws still in effect. For example, in the Muslim state of Kano in northern Nigeria, the minimum age of criminal responsibility in the CRA conflicts with Sharia law, which specifies that a child becomes an adult at puberty.

A child who is suspected of a criminal offense and apprehended by police is taken to the Community Development and Welfare Office. Youth cannot be held for more than one day before trial, unless they have committed a serious offense. In those cases, the youth is sent to a remand home. Although they are not supposed to be detained in these homes for more than three weeks, in practice, they often are. There is a remand home in each of the thirty-six states. These remand homes are primarily for abused and neglected children and are not an ideal location to detain juvenile criminal offenders.

The juvenile justice laws provide accused youth with the right to legal assistance and a speedy trial. Juvenile cases are heard in two courts. The first is a high court consisting of one judge, and the second is a magistrate court comprising one magistrate and two laypersons. The 2003 CRA called for the creation of a family court in each state.

Juveniles convicted of a crime can be sentenced to various measures including dismissing the charges, releasing the youth on their own recognizance, releasing the youth under the supervision of a probation officer, releasing the youth to the care of a fit person, or juvenile detention. Under the older CYPA law, young persons between fourteen and seventeen years old could be imprisoned, but the 2003 CRA does not allow incarceration for minors. There are three juvenile detention centers in Nigeria for male offenders only, with a capacity for 500 persons. These facilities are designed to be reformatory institutions that provide educational skills and training to young people aged sixteen to twenty years. The maximum sentence for juvenile detention is three years, with the possibility of another year of aftercare (Atilola 2013).

Evaluation of Juvenile Justice System

Experts agree that the juvenile justice system in Nigeria at both the federal and state levels is neglected. Juvenile facilities have been criticized for their poor conditions and overcrowding. Minors have also been sent to adult prisons in violation of the CRA. There are no mechanisms for diversion programs or noncustodial sentences like community service. Juvenile justice administrators, social welfare staff, police, and magistrates do not have the appropriate skills and training to handle juvenile cases. There is also a lack of national and state-level data on juvenile offenders and juvenile justice administration.

A study of juvenile justice professionals and delinquents across fifteen states in Nigeria assessed perceptions of the efficacy of the CYPA. When professionals were asked how well the law protected youth's rights, most respondents agreed that the current system did a good job of protecting the presumption of innocence (61.3 percent), and many thought it did well at protecting against false confessions (48.2 percent) and ensuring a prompt trial (43.7 percent). However, only 34.6 percent of the professionals thought juveniles had adequate legal representation, and 22.7 percent said that accused minors understood the legal process (Alemika and Chukwuma 2001).

Custodial staff was not very satisfied with conditions in remand homes and detention centers. Only 23 percent believed that youth had adequate healthcare, 18.8 percent said education resources were sufficient, 17.3 percent thought food services were acceptable, and 15.5 percent stated the shelter was adequate. Overall, 57.5 percent of the juvenile justice professionals believed the CYPA was not sufficiently meeting the needs of the system (Alemika and Chukwuma 2001).

Researchers also surveyed over 500 youth detained by police or staying in remand homes or detention centers. The majority of these youth reported experiencing physical abuse (64.7 percent), verbal abuse (66.5 percent), or the threat of physical abuse (68.5 percent) by the police. Additionally, 36.4 percent stated that the police forced them to confess to the charges brought against them. The youth were somewhat less likely to report abuse by custodial staff. Nonetheless, 39 percent reported physical abuse, 43.5 percent noted verbal abuse, and 45.9 percent had been threatened with physical abuse. On the positive side, 85.9 percent of youth reported receiving counseling from detention staff, and 62.2 percent believed they were treated well overall. Regarding their legal rights, only 45.7 percent of the youth had a parent or guardian present during their trial and 35.4 percent had legal representation (Alemika and Chukwuma 2001).

Many of the problems noted above prompted the 2003 CRA law, which has not yet fully replaced the older CPYA. In 2012, the government launched the Nigeria Juvenile Justice Project to evaluate and improve current practices. In addition to investigating the pretrial treatment of juveniles and the functions of juvenile courts, this project is also investigating alternative sentences to custody and juvenile delinquency crime prevention programs.

Further Reading

Alemika, Etannibi E. O., and Innocent Chukwuma. 2001. "Juvenile Justice Administration in Nigeria: Philosophy and Practice." Lagos, Nigeria: Centre for Law Enforcement Education. http://new.cleen.org/Juvenile%20Justice%20Report.pdf.

Atilola, Olayinka. 2013. "Juvenile/Youth Justice Management in Nigeria: Making a Case for Diversion Programmes." *Youth Justice* 13 (1): 3–16. https://doi.org/10.1177/1365480212474731.

Ayodele, Johnson Oluwole, Adeleke Kazeem Habibat, and Gandonu M. Babatunde. 2018. "Crime and Adolescent Drug Use in Lagos, Nigeria." *Sociology International Journal* 2 (2). https://doi.org/10.15406/sij.2018.02.00034.

Central Intelligence Agency. 2018. "The World Factbook." https://www.cia.gov/library/publications/resources/the-world-factbook/.

Dumbili, Emeka W. 2015. "A Review of Substance Use among Secondary School Students in Nigeria: Implications for Policies." *Drugs: Education, Prevention and Policy* 22 (5): 387–99. https://doi.org/10.3109/09687637.2015.1041455.

Johnson Oluwole, Ayodele, Adeleke Kazeem Habibat, and Gandonu M. Babatunde. 2018. "Crime and Adolescent Drug Use in Lagos, Nigeria." *Sociology International Journal* 2 (2). https://doi.org/10.15406/sij.2018.02.00034.

Sanni, Kudirat B., Nsisong A. Udoh, Abayomi A. Okedij, Felicia N. Modo, and Leonard N. Ezeh. 2010. "Family Types and Juvenile Delinquency Issues among Secondary School Students in Akwa Ibom State, Nigeria: Counseling Implications." *Journal of Social Sciences* 23 (1): 21–28. https://doi.org/10.1080/09718923.2010.11892807.

Ugwuoke, C.U., and Onyekachi U. Duruji. 2015. "Family Instability and Juvenile Delinquency in Nigeria: A Study of Owerri Municipality." *IOSR Journal of Humanities and Social Sciences* 20 (1): 40–45.

UNODC (United Nations Office on Drugs and Crime). 2018. *Drug Use in Nigeria*. Vienna, Austria: United Nations Office on Drugs and Crime.

SOUTH KOREA

South Korea is an ethnically homogenous country of 51.5 million people in East Asia. It is located east of China and north and west of Japan. A unified Korea gained independence from Japan after World War II (1939–1945) but quickly became a pawn of the Cold War, with Russia and China supporting a communist government in the north and the United States backing a democratic government in the south. Tensions erupted into the Korean War in 1950, which resulted in the formation of two separate countries in 1953.

South Korea is a presidential republic with a mixed legal system influenced by civil law, common law, and Chinese philosophy. South Korea experienced rapid economic development since the 1950s and is now a wealthy country with a gross domestic product per capita of USD 39,500 compared to only USD 1,700 in North Korea (Central Intelligence Agency 2018). South Korean culture places a very strong emphasis on high educational performance. On international comparisons of high school students' performance in science, reading, and math, South Korea consistently ranks above average. This focus on education has likely contributed to relatively low levels of juvenile delinquency but may also be the source of some violent incidents at schools.

Juvenile Delinquency

South Korea has not participated in the ISRD but the national police and the Korean Institute of Criminology provide some basic statistics regarding juvenile delinquency. The proportion of known juvenile offenders has been slowly declining from 5.9 percent of all offenders in 2008 to 4.5 percent in 2012 and 3.8 percent in 2015. Of the juvenile offenders arrested by the police in 2015, 3.8 percent were suspected of a serious violent crime, 24.6 percent of other types of violent crimes, 45.1 percent of property crimes, 12.1 percent of traffic violations, and 2.6 percent of counterfeiting. More than 80 percent of known juvenile offenders are male and 29.2 percent are eighteen years old. About half of all juveniles arrested in 2015 were first-time offenders, and 15.2 percent had four or more previous convictions (Korean Institute of Criminology 2018).

K-pop Scandal

Korean pop music, known as "K-pop" is a product of a government initiative in the 1990s to rebuild Korea's cultural influence after an economic crisis. Today K-pop is an international phenomenon, a multibillion dollar industry, and a teenage subculture. Teens are recruited through talent agencies and reality shows and strategically trained to be pop idols. The clean image of these idols was severely tainted in 2019 when several well-known K-pop stars were charged with brokering prostitution and filming and distributing sex videos with women without their permission. The case renewed attention to the problem of "spycam porn," which tens of thousands of Korean women had protested against in 2018.

Substance use among South Korean adolescents is especially low. The 2014 Korean Youth Risk Behavior Web-Based Survey asked over 72,000 youth aged twelve to eighteen years about their substance use. Alcohol was by far the most frequently used substance, with 48.4 percent of males and 37 percent of females reporting that they had ever drank alcohol in their lifetimes. However, in total, only 311 youth reported having ever used illicit drugs, which was only 0.4 percent of the sample, with males more likely to try drugs than females. Of those who had ever tried illegal drugs, 86.2 percent used inhalants, 53.7 percent tried stimulants, 51.8 percent used cannabis, and 50.8 percent used tranquilizers. Inhalants were often the first drug that these youths had tried (44.8 percent), followed by cannabis (10.3 percent) (Park and Kim 2016).

Research studies of South Korean adolescents have found that high levels of parental monitoring and attachment to school protect youth against involvement in juvenile delinquency. Given the high value that South Korean culture places on education, youths' strong desire to succeed in school can help suppress delinquency. However, the highly competitive environment of schools has also been cited as a source of some violent behavior, particularly bullying.

In 2011, a thirteen-year-old committed suicide as a result of severe bullying at school and at home, which became a turning point in how the country would tackle this problem. Kwon Seung-min was regularly beaten, harassed, threatened, and humiliated by other school children while at school and in his home when his parents were gone. As a result of this abuse, the teen jumped from his seventh-floor apartment and died. Since this tragedy, subsequent stories of bully suicides have generated a lot of media attention in South Korea. In 2013, another case that was featured prominently in the media shaped the political response to the problem. A fifteen-year-old boy named Choi was physically and verbally abused by five other boys for two years. In his suicide note, Choi specifically mentioned how the offenders would intentionally find places in the school to harass him that were not covered by the security cameras. Choi also killed himself by jumping from his apartment building. In response to these events, newly elected president Park Geun-hye

(1952–) declared bullying a "social evil" that required more government attention and resources. Her government implemented initiatives to install more security cameras at schools and increase security personnel. Additionally, antibullying programs were put into effect in schools and punishments for offenders were increased.

The media have portrayed school violence as a rapidly growing, new social problem in South Korea, but evidence shows that it has been an issue since the 1980s. It is difficult to measure whether the actual prevalence of bullying has increased because surveys use very different definitions of bullying, making it almost impossible to compare statistics over time. However, there seems to be some consensus that perpetrators are often abused or neglected children who do not receive enough parental monitoring. Additionally, the highly competitive educational environment tends to cause hostility among students. In the case of Kwon, the suicide note documented how the bullies tried to ruin his exam scores and destroyed his textbooks.

Juvenile Justice

The modern legal system in South Korea was formed in the late 1800s at the end of the Chosun dynasty (1392–1910). Many legal reforms were borrowed from Japan, which became more pronounced when Japan colonized Korea in 1910. The Japanese influence is apparent in the Romano-Germanic laws. After World War II, the Korean legal system adopted some features of common law from the United States. South Korea also developed its own legal codes after its formal separation from North Korea between 1953 and 1958.

The Japanese established a separate juvenile justice system with the 1942 Chosun Juvenile Law that established a juvenile court and correctional center. In 1958, an independent South Korea passed the Modern Korean Juvenile Law. Some changes were made to the law in 1988 to allow probation for juveniles and in 2012 to address school violence, but otherwise there have not been major reforms to the juvenile justice system.

South Korea defines juvenile offenders between the ages of fourteen and nineteen, whereas "law-breaking youth" aged twelve and thirteen years are not criminally responsible. There is a third category of youth called "pre-delinquency" who are between twelve and nineteen years old and are considered prone to crime. These youth are engaged in truancy, running away, or disorderly conduct, but not serious criminal offenses.

When the police arrest a juvenile, the case is immediately referred to the public prosecutor, who then gathers information about the accused and their family and school background, as well as prior criminal offenses. The prosecution then decides whether to dismiss the case, suspend the indictment so that the charges will be dropped if the youth satisfies certain conditions, or finally to send the case to court. Between 2007 and 2016, the percentage of cases that were indicted and sent to court remained fairly stable at about 10 percent, whereas the percentage of suspended sentences declined from 52.8 percent in 2007 to 34.7 percent in 2016 (Korean Institute of Criminology 2018). Cases involving law-breaking juveniles and predelinquents are heard in juvenile court, whereas juvenile offenders are tried in criminal court.

Convicted juvenile offenders can be sentenced to various measures, including supervision by parents or guardians, short-term probation of six months, long-term probation of two years, placement in child welfare, community service and education, detention, and imprisonment. In 2015, the majority of convicted juveniles (56.3 percent) were remanded to juvenile detention, 17.9 percent received an indeterminate prison sentence, 12.5 percent were sentenced to probation, 2.9 percent were fined, and 0.2 percent were given a determinate prison sentence (Korean Institute of Criminology 2018). There are two male juvenile prisons in Korea, one for first-time offenders and one for recidivists. The number of juveniles in detention centers has decreased from 356 in 2006 to 130 in 2015. As of 2017, there were fewer than twenty juveniles in prison (Korean Institute of Criminology 2018). Although South Korea has adopted a welfare approach to juvenile justice, the frequent use of detention as a punishment challenges this philosophy.

Further Reading

Bax, Trent M. 2016. "A Contemporary History of Bullying & Violence in South Korean Schools." *Asian Culture and History* 8 (2): 91–105.

Central Intelligence Agency. 2018. "The World Factbook." https://www.cia.gov/library/publications/resources/the-world-factbook/.

Chung, Jae-Joon. 2015. "Legislative Impact, Political Change, and Juvenile Detention: Comparing South Korea and Japan." In *Juvenile Justice in Global Perspective*, edited by Franklin E. Zimring, Maximo Langer, and David S. Tanenhaus, 370–80. New York: New York University Press.

Korean Institute of Criminology. 2018. *Crimes and Criminal Justice Policy in Korea (2016)*. Seoul, Korea: Korean Institute of Criminology. http://www.crimestats.or.kr/portal/crime/searchtKicFilesEngPage.do.

Lee, Hyun-Hee, and Kun Lee. 2002. "Juvenile Justice and Youth Crime: An Overview of South Korea." In *Juvenile Justice Systems: International Perspectives*, edited by John A. Winterdyk, 503–28. Toronto, ON: Canadian Scholars' Press.

Park, Subin, and Yeni Kim. 2016. "Prevalence, Correlates, and Associated Psychological Problems of Substance Use in Korean Adolescents." *BMC Public Health* 16 (1): 79. https://doi.org/10.1186/s12889-016-2731-8.

VENEZUELA

Venezuela sits at the northern tip of South America, with the Caribbean Sea and Atlantic Ocean to the north, Colombia to the west, Guyana to the east, and Brazil to the south. The thirty-one million people living in Venezuela are predominantly Spanish speaking, Roman Catholics. The government is formally a presidential republic, although since 1999, the presidents have been consolidating power at the expense of democratic institutions and civil liberties. The economy is largely supported by oil revenues, which contributed to economic growth in the 1970s and 1980s, but has proven to be unstable for the long run. The gross domestic product per capita in Venezuela is USD 12,500, which is lower than Brazil (USD 15,600) and Colombia (USD 14,400). Decreasing oil prices since 2014 have created a severe economic crisis that has caused considerable political and social unrest. Gross domestic product growth declined nearly 17 percent in 2016 and 14 percent in 2017 (Central Intelligence Agency 2018). The political and economic instability of the twenty-first century has contributed to shockingly high violent crime rates, which directly affect the country's youth and has stalled judicial reforms.

Economic Crisis and Youth Violence

Until the twentieth century, the Venezuelan economy was supported largely by agricultural exports like coffee and cocoa. However, by 1914, oil companies began drilling in Venezuela and sizable oil fields were discovered. In a very short period of time, Venezuela became one of the world's leading exporters of oil. This created an economic boom within the country, fueling industrialization and urbanization. The growth was not well planned so the large influx of people from rural to urban areas led to the creation of the *barrios*, which are poor, overcrowded neighborhoods that were marginalized from the urban elite.

The Venezuelan economy grew steadily until the 1980s when oil prices began to drop. The government tried to stabilize the economy with loans, but poverty, inflation, and economic inequality rose significantly through the twenty-first century. Although the gross domestic product per capita fluctuated in the 1990s and early 2000s, it never returned to its peak in 1980. In 2014, oil prices dropped sharply, plummeting the Venezuelan economy into a deep crisis. Between 2012 and 2017, the gross domestic product per capita dropped 40.6 percent and inflation increased over 13,000 percent. In 2017, 87 percent of the population was living in poverty and 61.2 percent in extreme poverty (OHCHR 2018).

In 1999, President Hugo Chávez (1954–2013) initiated the Bolivarian Revolution to address poverty and inequality with "twenty-first century socialism." He increased welfare spending and worked to reduce poverty and unemployment and improve education and literacy until his death in 2013. Nicolás Maduro (1962–) succeeded Chávez and has severely limited personal freedoms and civil rights and dismantled democratic institutions to consolidate his power. The fear of dictatorship and the economic crisis have led to large-scale public protests.

The economic and political crises provided the backdrop for rising levels of violence across the country. In 2016, the intentional homicide rate in Venezuela was 56.33 per 100,000 people, which is a significant increase from 19.58 per 100,000 in 1998 (UNODC 2018). The vast majority of homicide victims are young males from the barrios in large urban areas. Homicide is the leading cause of death in Venezuela for men between the ages of fifteen and thirty-four years (Zubillaga 2009). In 2012, 93 percent of homicide victims were male, 40 percent were between fifteen and twenty-four years old, 84 percent were from the poorest socioeconomic classes, and 91 percent were committed with firearms (Tremaria 2016). Gangs are largely responsible for the violence and attract poor youth because of a

---

Beauty Queen Murder

Mónica Spear was a twenty-nine-year-old actor and former beauty queen who was violently killed on a Venezuelan roadway in 2014 in a gang robbery. Spear was traveling with her ex-husband and five-year-old daughter in the evening when their car hit an object on the road and blew out two tires. They were getting assistance from a tow truck driver when a group of people opened fire on them. Spear and her ex-husband were killed at the scene, but their daughter survived a bullet wound. Ten people were arrested for the crimes including a fifteen-year-old and a seventeen-year-old. The case brought international attention to the high levels of violence in the country.

---

lack of economic opportunities, a desire to gain respect, and as a means to protect themselves against violence.

Other Forms of Juvenile Delinquency

While youth are often the victims and perpetrators of extreme violence such as homicide, there are clearly many young people who are not involved in gangs or extreme violence. Two research studies were conducted in 2008 in select Venezuelan cities to measure adolescent experiences with criminal victimization and offending. More recent studies are not available because of the political and economic crises.

The first study was the Global School-Based Health Survey administered in the state of Lara in the country's northwest. This study was concerned with student experiences with less extreme forms of violence than homicide. The most frequent form of violence that students in the seventh through ninth grades experienced as victims was bullying (43.6 percent), followed by physical fights (28.2 percent). Students reported being more likely to be robbed outside of school (22 percent) than inside (14.8 percent). About 7 percent of the students reported carrying some kind of weapon to school, and 21 percent said they would sometimes skip school out of fear of violence (Granero et al. 2011).

Venezuela also participated in the second wave of the ISRD study (ISRD-2), where students in two large cities (Caracas and Mérida) and three small urban areas were selected to participate in the study. These data showed relatively low levels of participation in juvenile delinquency. Vandalism was the most commonly reported property crime, with a lifetime prevalence of 8 percent, followed by shoplifting (4.3 percent) and pickpocketing (2.1 percent). Regarding violent offenses, 16.1 percent reported participating in a group fight, 4.2 percent said they carried a weapon to school, and 1.9 percent claimed to have robbed someone. Just over 1 percent of students said they had ever sold drugs, and 1.3 percent admitted to using marijuana in their lifetime. Less than 1 percent reported ever having tried ecstasy or speed (0.8 percent) or cocaine or heroin (0.4 percent). Similar to the previous study, students reported higher levels of criminal victimization than offending. About 24 percent of participants in the ISRD-2 reported being a victim of theft, 9.5 percent of bullying, and 7.2 percent of robbery (Birkbeck, Morillo, and Crespo 2010).

In Venezuela, like most other countries, boys (15.8 percent) are more likely than girls (6.8 percent) to participate in some form of delinquency. Unlike other countries, age was not related to delinquency. Adolescents from higher socioeconomic groups reported more delinquency than the less wealthy, which was also contrary to expectations. Dissatisfaction with school and having friends who were involved in delinquency were also strongly related to the likelihood that youth reported some delinquent activity (Birkbeck, Morillo, and Crespo 2010).

Juvenile Justice System

Until the 1900s, Venezuela and most countries in Latin America used Spanish customs for treating juveniles who came into contact with the law. Children under ten years old were not considered criminally responsible. Youth older than that threshold but under fourteen years old were subjected to different kinds of punishment, whereas those between fourteen and sixteen years only received some mitigations of adult sentences. In 1919, the American juvenile justice system was adopted in Latin America. The guiding principle was that the state was a protector of children and had a responsibility to education and rehabilitate delinquent youth, so it was called a tutelary system to emphasize this guardianship role.

Venezuela passed a Statute for Minors in 1949 that created separate courts for juveniles. These courts had a broad range of responsibilities including overseeing abused and neglected children and processing criminal cases. In contrast to the American practice, juvenile courts in Venezuela at that time used the inquisitorial system, where the judge was responsible for investigating the truth and the proceedings were confidential.

In the 1990s, the criminal justice systems across Latin America embarked on a series of reforms to emphasize due process, and, in some cases, move to an adversarial legal system. Venezuela signed the United Nations CRC in 1991 and subsequently began to reform its juvenile justice system to protect the human and legal rights of children. Two defining features of these reforms were due process and the principle of legality, which stressed that only children who have been accused of a criminal offense should be subjected to juvenile court. In particular, youth were given the presumption of innocence, and the rights to be informed of the charges against them, to have their parents or guardians informed, to have legal counsel, to have a fair trial, to be allowed to examine witnesses, and to have their court proceedings confidential.

The juvenile justice reforms also emphasized sanctions different from adult offenders that aimed for rehabilitation and social reintegration. Confinement of juveniles should only be used as a last resort. The minimum age of criminal responsibility in Venezuela was raised to twelve years and convicted offenders who are twelve or thirteen years can be confined for up to two years. Offenders who are between fourteen and seventeen years of age can be confined for up to four years. There are thirty-two juvenile detention centers in Venezuela, housing about 900 offenders in 2014 (Beloff and Langer 2015). In response to the rising levels of extreme violence in Venezuela, the government passed a law in 2014 allowing judges to double sentences for violent offenders over fourteen years old.

Juvenile delinquents are not supposed to be confined with adult offenders, but a review by the International Commission for Human Rights in 2011 found this was not always true in practice. The reviewers also found the detention centers to be in poor conditions, often lacking medical staff and equipment and having poor hygiene standards. Most detention centers also lacked drug abuse prevention and treatment programs for offenders. The reform process for juvenile justice in Venezuela has stalled because of the political and economic crises that have weakened the overall criminal justice system.

Further Reading

Beloff, Mary, and Maximo Langer. 2015. "Myths and Realities of Juvenile Justice in Latin America." In *Juvenile Justice in Global Perspective*, edited by Franklin E. Zimring, Maximo Langer, and David S. Tanenhaus, 198–248. New York: New York University Press.

Birkbeck, Christopher, Solbey Morillo, and Freddy Crespo. 2010. "Venezuela." In *Juvenile Delinquency in Europe and Beyond: Results of the Second International Self-Report Delinquency Study*, edited by J. Junger-Tas, Ineke Haen Marshall, Dirk Enzmann, Martin Killias, Majone Steketee, and Beata Gruszczynska, 385–98. Dordrecht; New York: Springer.

Central Intelligence Agency. 2018. "The World Factbook." https://www.cia.gov/library /publications/resources/the-world-factbook/.

Granero, Ricardo, Esteban S. Poni, Bertha C. Escobar-Poni, and Judith Escobar. 2011. "Trends of Violence among 7th, 8th and 9th Grade Students in the State of Lara, Venezuela: The Global School Health Survey 2004 and 2008." *Archives of Public Health* 69 (1): 7. https://doi.org/10.1186/0778-7367-69-7.

OHCHR (Office of the United Nations High Commissioner for Human Rights). 2018. "Human Rights Violations in the Bolivarian Republic of Venezuela: A Downward Spiral with No End in Sight." https://www.ohchr.org/Documents/Countries/VE/Venezuela Report2018_EN.pdf.

Tremaria, Stiven. 2016. "Violent Caracas: Understanding Violence and Homicide in Contemporary Venezuela." *International Journal of Conflict and Violence* 10 (1): 61–76. https://doi.org/10.4119/UNIBI/ijcv.393.

UNODC (United Nations Office on Drugs and Crime). 2018. "Crime Data." https:// dataunodc.un.org/crime.

Zubillaga, Verónica. 2009. "'Gaining Respect': The Logic of Violence among Young Men in the Barrios of Caracas." In *Youth Violence in Latin America: Gangs and Juvenile Justice in Perspective*, edited by Gareth A. Jones and Dennis Rodgers, 83–104. New York: Palgrave Macmillan.

Chapter 4: Hate Crimes

Chenghui Zhang

OVERVIEW

Generally speaking, hate crimes are criminal offenses motivated by bias, which is their distinguishing feature. Hate crimes can take the form of a traditional criminal act, such as assault, arson, or vandalism, with an added element of prejudice, such as ethnic, age, gender, or other social characteristics. Therefore, the term "hate crime" captures various concepts rather than a single legal definition. Bias crimes, prejudice crimes, civil rights crimes, or ethnic intimidation may all be used to describe the same criminal offense: hate crime. Hate crimes happen everywhere and occur in both small towns and big cities, from north to the south, and east to the west. They can take on many forms, from graffiti to brutal murders. A broad range of people can be at risk for victimization, often based on characteristics with which one was born.

Aside from the common harmful consequences of a nonbias criminal offense, scholars have shown that the primary victims of hate crimes experience more severe psychological harm than those suffering from similar criminal offenses without a bias motive. Victims of hate crimes are also at a higher risk for experiencing a broad range of mental health issues, such as posttraumatic stress disorder, which sometimes leads to secondary victimization when victims of hate crimes seek assistance. Healthcare service providers, criminal justice system professionals, and the community to which the victim belongs can play a role in secondary victimization if insufficient attention is given to hate incidents. Even worse, emotional and psychological impacts might spill over into the group to which the victim belongs.

A hate crime is also a sustained and systematic violation of human rights. Human rights organizations, including the Office for Democratic Institutions and Human Rights (ODIHR), Human Rights First, and the Equal and Human Rights Commission, agree that hate crimes break the shared norm that everyone enjoys equality in society. Amnesty International, a leading international human rights organization, suggests that hate crimes involve human rights violations including security rights, basic liberties, due process rights, and equality rights.

Although hate crime is a relatively well-developed term in the United States, it has a shorter history among other nations in the world. Arguably, its American origins go back to the post-Civil War period when the U.S. Constitution was being drafted (Levin 2002). Modern American antihate crime views have emerged from social movements of the 1960s, 1970s, and 1980s, especially black civil rights, women, gays and lesbians, those with disabilities, and the victims' rights lobby. Consequently, the stage was set for the awareness of hate crime as an emerging phenomenon in the United States.

The first federal hate crime statute in the United States can be traced back to 1968, which made it a crime to "use, or threaten to use, force to willfully interfere with any person because of race, color, religion, or national origin" ("Civil Rights Act of 1968"). At the state level, California provided penalty enhancements on crimes that included prejudice against race, religion, color, and national origin in 1978 (Penal Code 1978). Since then, hate crimes have gradually been criminalized in many American states and finally at the federal level with inclusive protections on multiple grounds.

Nowadays, many countries around the world have established hate crime laws and provide additional protections for minorities, along with awareness of human rights, both internationally and domestically. This chapter focuses on hate crime, covering hate crime legislation, reporting and sentencing, victim support, as well as a special focus on different protected grounds in each country. Examples of hate crimes against lesbian, gay, bisexual, transgender, and intersex (LGBTI) communities and responses to those crimes are the focus of the sections on Armenia and South Africa. Australia provides an example of how hate speech can be criminalized. Belgium illustrates how hate crimes capture the intersections of different kinds of discrimination, in this case gender and religion. Russia illustrates hate crimes related to racism, xenophobia, and immigration. The United Kingdom is an example of how laws and criminal justice systems define and record hate crimes. Finally, the United States establishes disability as a basis of a hate crime, which is not recognized in many other countries.

Further Reading

"Civil Rights Act of 1968." 1968. Public Law 90-284, 82 Stat. 73. https://legcounsel.house .gov/Comps/Civil%20Rights%20Act%20Of%201968.pdf.

Levin, Brian. 2002. "From Slavery to Hate Crime Laws: The Emergence of Race and Status-Based Protection in American Criminal Law." *Journal of Social Issues* 58 (2):227–45. https://doi.org/10.1111/1540-4560.00258.

Penal Code (CA). 1978. 190.2. https://leginfo.legislature.ca.gov/faces/codes_displaySection .xhtml?lawCode=PEN&s

ARMENIA

The Republic of Armenia is a country of three million people in the South Caucasus region of Eurasia. Ninety-eight percent of the population is ethnic Armenian and 92.6 percent adhere to the Armenian Apostolic Church (Central Intelligence Agency 2018). Located on the European and Asian border, Armenia has been influenced by many civilizations surrounding it including Arabic, Turkish, and Russian. In 1991, Armenia declared its independence from the former Soviet Union. It obtained its membership in the Council of Europe in 2001 and joined more than forty international organizations including the United Nations, the World Trade Organization, and the Asian Development Bank.

As an emerging democracy, Armenia has come a long way in allowing civil and political freedoms. Freedom House, a yearly report that attempts to measure the degree of democracy and political freedom in countries and territories around the world, has labeled Armenia as a "Partly Free" nation since 1998. Armenia allows various social and political commentary published in the media, but most print and broadcast outlets are affiliated with political or commercial interests. While private discussions on political and social issues remain relatively free and vibrant, social issues that disagree with a mainstream Armenian identity remain forbidden. One of the most prominent of these taboo issues is discrimination, intimidation, and even violence against sexual and gender minorities.

International Obligations

According to international human rights laws, states have the obligation to fully protect individuals' right to be free from discrimination, covering the grounds of "race, color, sex, language, religion, political or other opinion, national or social origin, property, birth or other status" (United Nations 1976, pt. 2). For example, the International Covenant on Civil and Political Rights (ICCPR) states that "All persons are equal before the law and are entitled without any discrimination to the equal protection of the law" (United Nations 1966, sec. 26). The United Nations Human Rights Committee along with Committee on Economic, Social and Cultural Rights both committed to nondiscriminatory treatment and protection of sexual orientation and gender identity.

The European Convention on Human Rights, of which Armenia is a party, imposed an obligation on its members to prohibit discrimination on the same grounds, as encouraged by the United Nations. More specifically, Protocol No. 12 in the Convention maintains that freedom from discrimination, as a human right, should be respected, secured, and protected. Notably, the European Convention with the protocol is incorporated into the national legal system and is applied in the domestic practices of ratified nations including Armenia.

Following these international laws, the Constitution of the Republic of Armenia defines the principle of prohibition of discrimination on similar grounds: "sex, race, color, ethnic or social origin, genetic features, language, religion or belief, political or any other opinion, membership of a national minority, property, birth, disability, age or other personal or social circumstances shall be prohibited" (The President of the Republic of Armenia 2019, sec. 14.1). Under the Criminal Code, racism is defined as a specific crime. Article 226 assigns criminal liability for incitement of national, racial, or religious hatred, as well as for actions aimed at racial superiority or humiliation of national dignity. In addition, hatred based on nationality, race, or religion is also listed as an aggravating circumstance for the liability and punishment.

The Armenian Constitution provides protection against discrimination on the basis of sex, but not specifically for sexual orientation. Hate crimes against lesbian, gay, bisexual, and transgender people are fairly common in Armenia and homophobia is institutionalized. (Algusto Cabral/Dreamstime.com)

LGBT People in Armenia

Aside from these general articles that are incorporated into the Constitution and the Criminal Code, Armenia does not have an offense of "hate crime" per se. Even within the existing legal framework, sexual orientation is not an explicitly protected characteristic in Armenia. However, hate incidents of abuse and harassment toward LGBTs occur almost on a daily basis, regardless of the fact that hate crime is not legally recognized as a criminal offense.

Public Information and Need of Knowledge (Pink Armenia, n.d.) is a community-based LGBT organization promoting public awareness on human rights protection of LGBT people that documents cases of hate crimes based on victims' sexual orientation and gender identity. For example, in 2016, three unknown persons attacked and beat five LGBT activists in one of Yerevan's central streets. Shouting profanities and sexually abusive words toward the victims, the offenders attacked them on the head, face, ear, back, and genitals. In 2014, Pink Armenia documented a case where the offender beat the victim for a "confession" about his sexual orientation. Hate incidents against the LGBT community in Armenia also take the form of property crime. A security camera captured an incident where a group threw Molotov cocktails through the windows of an LGBT-friendly bar in Yerevan in 2012. Further reports showed that the bar owner received death threats before the arson attack from the offenders who described themselves as "fascists."

Similar cases have been recorded every year. While there are no official hate crime statistics and reports available, international organizations have been tracking bias-motivated incidents in Armenia. The Organization for Security and Cooperation in Europe (OSCE) collected thirteen bias incidents that targeted victims' sexual orientation or gender identity through Pink Armenia, New Generation, and Transgender Europe.

Institutional Homophobia

The absence of official data is no coincidence. Reports show that institutional homophobia is pretty severe in Armenia. Armenian society tends to deny the existence of LGBT people, and issues of sexual identity are not discussed publicly (Carroll and Quinn 2009, 33). In 2016, Edgar Nahapetyan, a resident of Armavir region, contacted a television station to complain that he could not find a job because of his sexual orientation. One of the experts of the program, lawyer Garik Galikyan, used a number of offensive terms, threats, and hate speech at Nahapetyan during the televised show. Two other guests of the program, director Sargis Mikayelyan and psychologist Matiam Mehrabyan, also expressed hatred and bias against LGBT people during the show.

Aside from public media, the negative attitude of police and government officials toward LGBT people harms the group even more. Several victims reported uninformed and indifferent attitudes of police officers dealing with their cases. In one case, a man was robbed and threatened with a knife during a date with another man. He filed a complaint with the police, who opened an investigation. However, as soon as learning the victim's sexual orientation, the investigators became indifferent to the case. Another case documented a homosexual man who reported a robbery to the local police. In the station, the police laughed at him and threatened to reveal his sexual orientation to his parents. Later, when the offender was found, the police returned the stolen property to the victim but insulted him in the process.

In many cases, police officers become perpetrators because they demean the human rights violations against sexual and gender minorities. In one case, where a sex worker reported being forced into a car with a knife by an unknown person, instead of proceeding with the case, the police sent the victim to a psychiatric institution. In another case of a forced "confession" about sexual orientation, the victim also expressed his distrust of the police. Although Armenia decriminalized homosexuality in 2003, the situation of LGBT community has not improved much (Carroll and Quinn 2009).

Is Hate Crime Legislation Enough?

In most hate crime laws across the world, the definition of hate crime is relatively clear and easy to understand: a criminal offense and a biased motivation. However, in countries like Armenia, hate crime is not officially written in the Criminal Code. Does that simply mean hate crime does not exist in the country? The answer is yes, and at the same time, no. There is not a single crime that is defined as "hate crime" according to the legal system. Nevertheless, bias-motivated hate incidents happen regularly.

Beyond crimes against LGBT people, other forms of bias against sexual and gender minorities are prevalent across Armenian society. Healthcare institutions are often reluctant to help LGBT patients. Law enforcement officers often refuse to file reports by LGBT people. Individuals who are open about their sexual orientation or gender identity are at higher risks to face workplace harassment and social exclusion. They are also less likely to be promoted, get professional training, or approved for holidays. Other than these experiences with public service institutions and workplaces, LGBT people are suffering from discrimination and exclusion of basic needs, such as housing.

When an antidiscrimination legislation or policy is adopted, it requires protections and sanctions to be more than merely symbolic. International Organizations such as Pink Armenia, Amnesty International, and United Nations are calling for a hate crime legal framework in Armenia. Indeed, legalizing human rights through official documents is an important first step to protect vulnerable groups. However, the current response of the Armenian government and law enforcement to nondiscrimination provisions in both international laws and the constitution indicates the low priority that the government attaches to complying with these requirements.

Further Reading

Carroll, Aengus, and Sheila Quinn. 2009. "Forced Out: LGBT People in Armenia." ILGA-Europe/COC Netherlands. https://ilga-europe.org/sites/default/files/Attachments/forcedoutarmenia.pdf.

Central Intelligence Agency. 2018. "The World Factbook." https://www.cia.gov/library/publications/resources/the-world-factbook/.

ODIHR (Office for Democratic Institutions and Human Rights). n.d. "Hate Crime Reporting." Organization for Security and Cooperation in Europe (OSCE). http://hatecrime.osce.org/.

Pink Armenia. n.d. "About Us." https://www.pinkarmenia.org/en/about-us/

The President of the Republic of Armenia. 2019. "The Constitution of the Republic of Armenia 1995." https://www.president.am/en/constitution/.

United Nations. 1966. "International Covenant on Civil and Political Rights." http://www.ohchr.org/Documents/ProfessionalInterest/ccpr.pdf.

United Nations. 1976. "International Covenant on Economic, Social and Cultural Rights." https://www.ohchr.org/en/professionalinterest/pages/cescr.aspx.

AUSTRALIA

Comprising the mainland of the Australian continent, the island of Tasmania, and other smaller islands, Australia is the largest country in Oceania. Australia became free from the United Kingdom's control after the Australia Act of 1986 and remains a federal parliamentary constitutional monarchy within the Commonwealth of Nations. Australia is divided into six states and two territories. Of the population of 23.5 million people, about half are of Australian or English descent, but there is considerable ethnic, linguistic, and religious diversity across the country (Central Intelligence Agency 2018). This diversity is central to the country's development of antidiscrimination laws.

Criminalizing Hate Speech

Common law tradition values the freedom of speech. Following this principle, Australia deemed free speech as a common value and common understanding of

---

Hate Speech from Politicians

On May 15, 2019 Brenton Tarrant, a twenty-eight-year-old Australian, killed fifty people in two mosques in Christchurch, New Zealand to promote his far-right, anti-immigration agenda. Leaders around the world condemned the attack including Australia's Prime Minister Scott Morrison, who called the massacre a "rightwing extremist attack." However, Australian Senator Fraser Anning publicly blamed the tragedy on immigration policies that allowed "Muslim fanatics" into the country. The statement led to a public outcry, as well as reflection on how hate speech has become normalized in Australian politics.

Mao, Frances. 2019. "Christchurch Shooting: Australia's Moment of Hate Speech Reckoning." *BBC News*, March 20, 2019, sec. Australia. https://www.bbc.com/news/world-australia -47620391.

Martin, Eleanor Ainge Roy Lisa. 2019. "49 Shot Dead in Attack on Two Christchurch Mosques." *The Guardian*, March 15, 2019, sec. World news. https://www.theguardian.com/world /2019/mar/15/multiple-fatalities-gunman-christchurch-mosque-shooting.

---

human rights rather than protecting it through enunciated federal statutes in a bill of rights. Due to this somewhat precarious protection, there is some doubt as to the ability to protect free speech from governmental restriction. Despite these concerns, antivilification laws have faced few challenges on free speech grounds.

At the state, territory, and federal levels, antivilification laws establish the legal framework of antidiscrimination. They cover wide-ranging social characteristics including race and ethnicity, religious belief, human immunodeficiency virus and acquired immunodeficiency syndrome (HIV/AIDS) status, transgender or gender identity, sexuality or homosexuality, and disability. At all levels of government, the most common grounds for complaints under antivilification laws are with respect to race and ethnicity. New South Wales has registered numerous complaints regarding homosexuality, transgender and gender identity, and HIV/AIDS status; whereas Tasmania has reported significant complaints regarding religion, gender, sexuality, and disability.

Hate Crime Legislation

Since the 1980s, hate crime legislation has become an emerging agenda in response to diverse voices: minority group pressure, the victims' rights movement, and periodic publicity. There are two main methods to include hate crimes in the criminal justice system. The first and the most popular one adopts enhanced punishment to existing criminal law when the criminal offense is driven by a biased motive. A sentence enhancement typically imposes a penalty with additional conditions on preexisting offenses if the act is driven or aggravated by a form of bias or hostility, such as race, religion, or other forms. The enhanced penalty usually takes the form of an additional maximum or minimum term. Penalty enhancement is categorized into two types: general penalty enhancement and specific penalty enhancement. As the name suggests, general penalty enhancement provisions cover the majority of criminal offenses. One of the most common aggravating circumstances that lead to harsher penalties is for leaders or organizers of criminal offenses. Similarly, for those who have prior offenses, laws often enhance punishment. In the case of hate crime, sentence enhancements are mostly based on the wrongfulness of the biased act.

A similar practice that takes prejudicial motive into account is sentence aggravation. It also punishes hate crime during the sentencing stage, only allowing more judicial discretion than penalty enhancement. In other words, it is not necessarily the case that the offender of a hate crime receives more punishment compared to the same crime without a hate motivation. Under both enhanced punishment and sentence aggravation, hate crime is not set as a separate crime type in the criminal law, rather they influence the sentencing of a criminal case. That is, an offender must be found guilty of the accused offense before provisions under either method can be applied to the sentencing.

The second way to incorporate a bias motive in criminal law is to create a substantive offense, which places the prejudiced motive as an essential element of the crime. Compared to penalty enhancement, provisions that recognize hate crime as a substantive offense are relatively scarce. Yet, making hate crime a substantive offense has its advantages. A substantive offense on hate crime contains a symbolic message of labeling the offense by condemning the prohibited bias motive explicitly. Thus, it fulfills the expressive function of criminal law. However, under the substantive hate crime law, prosecutors are faced with more pressure and difficulties to support the charge. They are required to prove the bias motive, which is difficult to do, under a substantive hate crime law. Moreover, in some jurisdictions, the courts are restricted to the criminal act that is indicted. In other words, if a bias motive is not proven, the chances are high that the offender will not be punished for the base offense. Therefore, to convict the accused, prosecutors are more likely to avoid using hate crime laws, which implicitly weaken the symbolic value of hate crime law.

Enhanced punishment, on the other hand, is easier to incorporate into a penal code. It can be applied to a wide range of criminal behaviors, especially general enhancement. In most cases, it also only influences the sentencing without jeopardizing a conviction on the base offenses. Yet, it is not perfect either. In some jurisdictions, the reason for enhancement might not be recorded publicly, such as in Germany. Consequently, the symbolic weight of hate crime law itself is compromised, which fails to serve the expressive function of the Criminal Code.

A Mixed Approach

Australia joined the wave of reform by extending preexisting antidiscrimination statues to serious vilification. Instead of picking a single site in the debate, Australia took a third path in terms of hate crime legislation, which applies a combination of enhanced punishment and substantive offenses to achieve the best results in fighting hate crime.

In the early 2000s, Australia amended its sentencing laws and explicitly made prejudice and hatred an aggravating factor in sentencing. In 2004, Western Australia introduced penalty enhancement provisions in regard to incidents of racist graffiti and vandalism in the area, covering race as a protected ground. Most jurisdictions in Australia that have hate crime laws are taking the path of sentence aggravation. Compared to the penalty enhancement model, sentence aggravation allows more judicial discretion. In 2003, New South Wales adopted a similar approach at sentencing for offenses motivated by prejudice against religion, racial or ethnic origin, language, sexual orientation or age, or having a disability. Similarly, the Northern Territory also enacted sentence aggravation provisions in 2006.

The substantive offense model is also used in Australia. New South Wales introduced such provisions as early as 1989, regulating that vilification occurs if an offense incites hatred. Western Australia also included the offense of incitement to racial hatred in the 1990 Criminal Code as a substantive offense. Yet, Western Australia suffered from the weakness of the substantive offense approach. It was not until July 2004 that the provisions were first used to indict and convict its first case on racist graffiti attacks and promoting racial hatred.

These provisions influence fighting hate crimes in two ways. On the one hand, they translate and codify the voice of minority groups in the victims' movement globally by taking hatred or prejudice into account when sentencing an offender. On the other hand, hate crime provisions contain symbolic meanings, reminding the society of the shared social values of inclusivity, equity, and equality.

Challenges

Whereas hate crime statistics are readily available in some countries, it is not easy to get a numerical picture of hate crime in Australia. Each state has a different methodology and classification process, which makes it difficult to summarize the problem for the entire country. Moreover, jurisdictions in Australia, New South Wales, and Western Australia, for example, only break down the numbers by offenses. Within the framework of penalty enhancement and sentencing aggravation, motivations and prejudice are not reflected in the statistics. The Australian Bureau of Statistics provides some comparative figures about crime in general terms but even the substantive offense—racial hatred and vilification—is reported as common graffiti attacks.

On October 16, 2017, Australia was elected to serve on the Human Rights Council in the United Nations, promoting and protecting all human rights around the globe. Despite being portrayed as a human rights leader in the world, Australia is facing critiques on neglecting hateful actions against minority groups. For example, antihomosexual, especially antigay hate crimes were reported as an "unsolved and unacknowledged crime wave" (Sheehan 2013). Being verbally abused, assaulted, and even murdered are reported to be common among gay men. The international community also criticized the high level of abusive actions against indigenous people, particularly children.

Further Reading

Central Intelligence Agency. 2018. "The World Factbook." https://www.cia.gov/library /publications/resources/the-world-factbook/.

Chesterman, Michael. 2000. *Freedom of Speech in Australian Law: A Delicate Plant.* Burlington, VT: Ashgate/Dartmouth.

Gelber, Katharine. 2003. "Pedestrian Malls, Local Government and Free Speech Policy in Australia." *Policy and Society* 22 (2):22–49. https://doi.org/10.1016/S1449-4035(03) 70018-6.

Mason, Gail, and Andrew Dyer. 2013. "'A Negation of Australia's Fundamental Values': Sentencing Prejudice-Motivated Crime." *Melbourne University Law Review* 36 (3): 871.

NSW Legislation. 2019. "Crimes (Sentencing Procedure) Act 1999 No 92." https://www .legislation.nsw.gov.au/-/view/act/1999/92/whole.

Sheehan, Paul. 2013. "Gay Hate: The Shameful Crime Wave." *The Sydney Morning Herald*, March 4, 2013. http://www.smh.com.au/comment/gay-hate-the-shameful-crime -wave-20130303-2fe9w.html.

Western Australian Legislation. 2017. "Criminal Code Act Compilation Act 1913 Vol. 028." Government of Western Australia Department of Justice. https://www.legislation.wa .gov.au/legislation/statutes.nsf/law_a196_currencies.html&view=asmade.

BELGIUM

Located at the heart of Western Europe, the Kingdom of Belgium is bordered by France, the Netherlands, Germany, Luxembourg, and the North Sea. It is a wealthy, democratic country of about 11.5 million people. About 75 percent of the country is Belgian and is divided into three language communities: Dutch, French, and German. About half of the population identifies as Christian and about 5 percent as Muslim, making Islam the second most popular religion in the country (Central Intelligence Agency 2018). Under the constitutional framework of national religious recognition, Islam is recognized as an official Belgian religion. Mosques, clergy, chaplains, and religious teachers in state schools are funded by the state.

Islamophobia and Hate Crimes

As arguably the most culturally, religiously, and ethnically diverse continent, Europe has been struggling with deafening hostilities against Muslims. The European Network Against Racism defines Islamophobia as "a specific form of racism that refers to acts of violence and discrimination, as well as racist speech, fuelled by historical abuses and negative stereotyping and leading to exclusion and dehumanization of Muslims, and all those perceived as such" (ENAR 2015). In a survey conducted by Chatham House, an independent policy institute, an average of 55 percent of more than 10,000 respondents from ten European states objected to further migration from mainly Muslim countries (Chatham House 2017). The highest anti-Muslim sentiments were found in Poland, followed by Belgium, Austria, and Hungary. When social groups, such as Muslims, are viewed unfavorably as "others," then physical attacks and other forms of violence against those groups become more likely.

Regardless of its reputation for multiculturalism and religious tolerance, Belgium is no stranger to Islamophobia. On the morning of March 22, 2016, three coordinated suicide bombings occurred at Zaventem Airport and Maalbeek metro station in Belgium. Thirty-five people were killed during the attacks while over 300 were injured. The Islamic State of Iraq and the Levant (ISIL, also known as ISIS) claimed responsibility for the attacks. Five attackers were later identified. In the weeks after the terror attacks, the country witnessed a notable spike in anti-Muslim hate. Hate speech and prejudice by political figures and the media largely fueled Islamophobia. Jan Jambon, the Belgian Interior Minister affiliated with the New Flemish Alliance, alleged a "dancing" celebration on the terror attacks among Belgian Muslims. Shortly after the Brussels explosions, thirty-six Islamophobic incidents were recorded

Increasing immigration into Belgium from Muslim countries has heightened anti-Muslim sentiments in the country. Muslim women are particularly vulnerable to Islamophobic attacks because headscarves are easily identifiable indicators of assumed religious affiliation. (iStockPhoto)

by the Belgian Counter-Islamophobia Collective (CCIB) in one month and 120 incidents in 2016 in total (Easat-Daas 2017).

It is hard to make a direct connection between Islamophobic incidents and anti-Muslim hate crimes because anti-Muslim hate crimes are not a separate category from racism and xenophobia according to the legal framework in Belgium nor are the data available for all years. Belgium reported 615 crimes with a racist or xenophobic motive in 2012 and 375 incidents in 2013 (ODIHR, n.d.). Since then Belgium has not periodically reported reliable information and statistics on hate crime to the ODIHR, although it is obliged to report hate crime data. Meanwhile, independent research sources suggest that anti-Muslim hate crime is still occurring in Belgium.

Violence against Muslim Women

Despite the fact that no reliable data on anti-Muslim hate crime is available through official records, various studies found that Muslim women are usually at a larger risk of being victims of hate crimes. As a religious tradition, Muslim women sometimes wear a headscarf in public. This unique and visible symbol of being a Muslim contributes to women's vulnerability as suitable targets for hate crimes. Muslim women are seen as the "visible representatives" of a religion, along with the perception of greater vulnerability due to their gender. This "othering" process not only generates negative consequences for Belgian Muslims but also compromises the potential contributions these individuals may bring to society. Belgian data showed that between January 2012 and September 2015, about 63.6 percent of the registered Islamophobic hate crimes and offenses targeted women (Šeta 2016). This is not unique to Belgium. Reports conducted by European Network Against Racism confirmed a similar pattern of Islamophobic hate crimes perpetrated against Muslim women in France, Sweden, Netherlands, Germany, Denmark, and the United Kingdom.

The attacks against Muslim women are usually violent, involving the removal of headscarves, as well as a mix of racist and sexist insults and gestures, committed mostly by males not known by the victims. In one case in 2016, three Muslim women wearing headscarves were threatened and one of the victims was physically assaulted. Similarly, another case involved a Muslim woman wearing a headscarf being physically assaulted on public transport. Of the four reported incidents concerning hate crimes against individuals, all victims were Muslim women with headscarves (ODIHR, n.d.). Due to the limited data available, one cannot conclude that only Muslim women are experiencing Islamophobic hate crimes in Belgium. Nonetheless, these incidents support the reasonable assumption that Muslim women are at a greater risk of victimization than men.

Online hate speech attacks are also increasing, particularly through social media. A student at the University of Ghent in Belgium conducted a research project where she pretended to have converted to Islam and posted this information on her Facebook account. She replaced her profile image with a photo of her wearing a headscarf. The student soon became the target of racist comments and verbal violence on Facebook (Šeta 2016).

This pattern raises the question of why Muslim women are experiencing a high risk of being victims of hate incidents. Feminists throughout Europe have long debated the issue of Muslim women wearing a headscarf. Some people maintain that the headscarf is incompatible with women's rights for its unmistakable symbolic meaning of the oppression of women. Others argue that wearing headscarves is a way for women to exercise their rights. Despite the debate, one thing both sides agree on is the fact that the headscarf is a religious sign exclusively worn by women, which shows how gender and religious identity intersect. While most European countries do not register self-identified religious affiliation, the headscarf offers a visible symbol of Muslim women's religious choices, which may subsequently be a trigger in experiencing discrimination and hate crime on the grounds of religion. On the other hand, Muslim women suffer from the same inequalities as other women, such as access to education, employment, domestic, verbal, or physical violence. Their religion or ethnicity revealed by headscarves often deepens these gender gaps and inequality.

Intersecting Forms of Bias

On July 30, 1981 Belgium passed a law punishing certain acts inspired by racism or xenophobia to combat hate speech and discrimination. On February 25, 2003, the government amended the Law of 1993 to further combat discrimination and racism. The Law of 2003 offered a comprehensive protection against biased treatment of sex, supposed race, color, descent, national or ethnic origin, sexual orientation, civil status, birth, fortune, age, religious or philosophical beliefs, current or future state of health, and handicap or physical features. Additionally, on May 20, 2017, officials amended the 1999 Criminal Code to generally prohibit direct and indirect discrimination against one's race with respect to access to, and provision of, goods and public services.

Not only do these legal reforms regarding hate crimes demonstrate concern about racism, they also neglect violence against women as a separate category of hate crime. There are ongoing debates on whether violence against women should be identified as a type of hate crime, which would acknowledge that violence can be committed on the basis of multiple grounds and can be influenced by different forms of structural domination. On one hand, some feminists express reservations that women may not identify the element of "hate" during their experience with a perpetrator, who is usually a partner or an acquaintance. Moreover, legal protection under hate crime legislation may obscure and decentralize the nature of violence against women, such as domination, exclusion, and control. On the other hand, the notion of hate crime may enrich discussions regarding the nature of violence against women by considering discrimination and generalizable effects of violence.

The examples of bias crimes against Muslim women illustrate how religion, ethnicity, and gender intersect to the culmination of bias crimes. The current situation of Muslim women in Belgium is not unique. Other forms of violence and bias against women along grounds such as religion, ethnicity, or disability happen every day around the world. These unfortunate incidents require more awareness to the intersections of bias to eliminate, or at least minimize, potential hate crimes on multiple grounds.

Further Reading

Central Intelligence Agency. 2018. "The World Factbook." https://www.cia.gov/library/publications/resources/the-world-factbook/.

Chatham House. 2017. "What Do Europeans Think about Muslim Immigration?" https://www.chathamhouse.org/expert/comment/what-do-europeans-think-about-muslim-immigration#sthash.

Easat-Daas, Amina. 2017. "Islamophobia in Belgium. National Report 2016." In *European Islamophobia Report 2016*, edited by Enes Bayrakli and Farid Hafez. Istanbul, Turkey: SETA.

ENAR (European Network Against Racism). 2015. "Anti-Semitism and Islamophobia in Europe: Recent Trends." https://www.enar-eu.org/Anti-Semitism-and-Islamophobia-in-Europe-Recent-trends.

ODIHR (Office for Democratic Institutions and Human Rights). n.d. "Hate Crime Reporting." Organization for Security and Cooperation in Europe (OSCE). http://hatecrime.osce.org/.

Šeta, Ðermana. 2016. *Forgotten Women: The Impact of Islamophobia on Muslim Women.* Brussels, Belgium: European Network Against Racism.

RUSSIA

Russia is the largest country in the world in terms of landmass, spanning both Europe and Asia. It borders the Arctic Ocean to the north and the Pacific Ocean to the east, as well as fourteen other countries. Demographically, Russia comprises 81 percent of ethnic Russians and 19 percent of other ethnicities: 3.7 percent Tatars, 1.4 percent Ukrainians, 1.1 percent Bashkirs, 1 percent Chuvashes, 1 percent Chechen, and 14.1 percent other ethnic groups. More than 170 different ethnic groups and nationalities currently exist in the Russian Federation, with an estimated population of 142 million (Central Intelligence Agency 2018).

In 1917, the Russian Revolution brought an end to the Russian Empire and the beginning of communism in the country. By 1922, fourteen surrounding countries had been incorporated by Russia to form the Soviet Union. This was the largest country in the world at the time and the largest communist country. It was the primary foe of the United States during the Cold War (1947–1991). Decades of political oppression and a struggling economy led to the collapse of communism and the Soviet Union in 1991 when Russia again became a separate state. The social changes of the post-communist period had a dramatic effect on emigration and immigration flows in the country. It is estimated that there are about 500,000 legal migrants and between five and fifteen million undocumented migrants in Russia (Diène 2007). The rise in the number of foreigners has created social tensions. The political environment has also fostered a strong sense of Russian nationalism, which also tends to heighten xenophobia or the fear and dislike of foreigners.

Criminal Attacks against Ethnic Outsiders

The Russian Federation has long been criticized for its xenophobia and antimigrant movements. In 2006, the small Karelian town of Kondopoga was hit by racial violence that led to days-long intensive rioting joined by far-right group members across the country. In 2010, over 800 people were arrested on Manezh Square in central Moscow after an ethnic conflict between football fans. More recently, violent clashes in 2013 occurred in Biryulyovo in southern Moscow because of the murder of a Russian by a foreigner. Protesters were chanting "Russia for the Russians" and "White Power." Xenophobia and antimigration are central characteristics of these incidents in Russia.

Although no official statistics are available, Russian-based nonprofit research organization SOVA Center documented no less than ten people were killed in racist and neo-Nazi violence and seventy-four were beaten or injured in 2016, while estimating that the actual size of violent attacks is far higher. Compared to previous years, the number of racist attacks dropped to twelve killed and ninety-six injured in 2015 from thirty-six killed and 134 injured in 2014. Major cities, particularly Moscow and St. Petersburg, recorded the highest levels of violence (SOVA Center 2017). Research shows that Chechens, Dagestanis, and Ingushetians are the most "hated" among all the ethnicities in Russia, along with migrant workers from Central Asia.

Political and Public Response

As a response to the violence against the non-Russian ethnic populations, nationalist leaders and regional political officials called for "illegal foreigners" to be tracked down. Human Rights First recorded both political leaders and news outlets reinforcing the idea of Moscow as a city with "a Russian face" and targeting certain last names as "illegal foreigners." Other studies found that ultra-right political parties, such as the Liberal Democratic Party (LDPR) and Rodina (the Fatherland), were targeting not only illegal immigrants but all non-Slavs in Russia, which plays a significant role in disseminating racial and ethnic intolerance. Local courts took actions against foreigners as well. According to a report on mass deportation of foreigners from Russia, more than 500,000 removal orders were issued by courts between 2013 and 2015 (SOVA Center 2017; Troitsky 2016).

Political leaders and the media bear a certain responsibility for the rise of xenophobia toward ethnic minorities in Russia. Studies show that there is more hate speech in the national media than in the regional media. It also influences public opinion by exacerbating fears and prejudices. A public opinion poll conducted in 2015 by the independent Levada Analytical Center showed the high level of xenophobic sentiments in Russia. One of the questions is related to the idea of "Russia for Russians." Over 51 percent of 1,600 respondents supported the idea, while 25 percent of respondents viewed it negatively. Similarly, in another representative poll of the Russian population conducted by the Levada Center in 2013, about 73 percent of respondents supported the idea that migrants from former Soviet Republics should be deported from Russia. Polls also showed that the stigma around immigrants was still prevalent among Russians. About 64 percent of respondents made connections between immigrants and increased crime rates and 62 percent of respondents thought that immigrants take jobs away from Russians (Levada Analytical Center 2015).

Legal Response to Address Hate Crimes

While some political leaders and media participate in promoting xenophobia and racism, it is notable that many changes were introduced to the Criminal Code and other legislation since 2014. Most of them were aimed at toughening the penalties and expanding the scope of responsibility for actions related to xenophobia and racism. The Russian Federation's Criminal Code contains general penalty

Legislating Homophobia

Noticeably missing from Russia's penalty enhancements for bias crimes is any mention of gender identity or sexual orientation. Not only is homophobia common in Russian society but politicians use it to promote "traditional values." In 2013, the Russian Duma passed a law making it illegal to distribute homosexual "propaganda" to minors. The law makes gay pride events, public speaking in defense of gay rights, and treating homosexual relationships as equal to heterosexual ones as a crime, which is punishable by fines up to USD 31,000. The law has led to rising incidents of violence against the LGBT community including the murder of a gay Russian journalist in 2017.

Khazan, Olga. 2013. "Why Is Russia So Homophobic?" *The Atlantic*, June 12, 2013. https://www
    .theatlantic.com/international/archive/2013/06/why-is-russia-so-homophobic/276817/.
"Russia's New Scapegoats." 2016. *Reveal* (blog), September 24, 2016. https://www.revealnews
    .org/episodes/russias-new-scapegoats/.

enhancement provisions and substantive offenses for "committing an offense motivated by political, ideological, racial, ethnic or religious hatred or enmity or hatred or hostility toward a social group" (Criminal Code of the Russian Federation No. 63-FZ of June 13, 1996 1996, sec. 214). However, hate crime laws in Russia do not extend to criminal acts that target victim's sexual orientation or disabilities. In other words, the protected characteristics were limited compared to international treaties that Russia has signed. Despite the fact that new prosecutions against racist attacks were launched in 2016 along with ongoing cases, only nineteen convictions were made in Russia, of which forty-four people were found guilty (SOVA Center 2017).

It is worth mentioning that recorded hate violence in Russia declined since 2015; yet, the drop is slowing down compared to the trend in previous years. Due to the opaque data recording and reporting mechanisms provided by officials, the true scale of racial violence is unknown. Russian law enforcement did not break down bias motivation and type of crime. Meanwhile, studies suggest that political factors still play a role in hate crime in Russia. Russian military intervention in Ukraine since 2014 may also contribute to the lower hate-motivated cases because law enforcement agencies had targeted these groups more. On the other side, ultra-right groups had lost key activists due to differing opinions on Ukraine.

Despite the lower numbers of recorded hate violence in Russia, there are also critiques on its legislative action toward xenophobia and racism. The first one is the described as "excessive implementation," pointing out the lack of quality in law enforcement training and the excessive interest in boosting reporting statistics. The second concerns the manipulation and abuse of laws as a suppression mechanism to target political opponents. Hence, legislation can be used as a tool to suppress human rights and freedom rather than combating hate violence. For example, the 2014 Law on Bloggers demands a great amount of data through server owners. Since Russia's involvement in Ukraine, excessive law enforcement actions related to actions and speech on Ukrainian events increased significantly, especially when it comes to the charge of "incitement to hatred."

Xenophobia and Hate Crimes

The insufficient and sometimes misused antiracism legislation in Russia does not stop hate violence domestically. Xenophobia has been largely overlooked and has long been perceived as a minor problem compared to Russia's post-communist economic and social transition. Although violence is typically committed by a small population of the society, xenophobic attitudes are widespread in Russia. The hardships of economic transition, nationalism, the challenges of globalization, and history are several factors contributing to xenophobia, among which nationalism is the most popular factor in hate studies. The post-communist era of Russia not only challenged the economy but also opened the discussion of national identity. The redefining of identity led to a simplified "us" versus "them" judgment among ethnic Russians which distinguishes oneself from "others." Along with the growing economic divide and geopolitical tensions, Russia also experienced a wave of labor migration. Subsequently, immigrants were blamed for stealing jobs and became targets of violence.

While legislation against xenophobia has been drafted and enacted recently, laws on combating xenophobic crimes may not be working as designed. Scholars and civil society have been calling for more nonstate actor's participation, educational efforts, civilian oversight, and implementation of international practices in Russia to shift the negative attitude toward ethnic minorities and labor migrants.

Further Reading

Central Intelligence Agency. 2018. "The World Factbook." https://www.cia.gov/library/publications/resources/the-world-factbook/.

The Criminal Code of the Russian Federation No. 63-FZ of June 13, 1996. https://www.wto.org/english/thewto_e/acc_e/rus_e/WTACCRUS58_LEG_362.pdf.

Diène, Doudou. 2007. "Report of the Special Rapporteur on Contemporary Forms of Racism, Racial Discrimination, Xenophobia and Related Intolerance." https://documents-dds-ny.un.org/doc/UNDOC/GEN/G07/127/01/PDF/G0712701.pdf?OpenElement.

Levada Analytical Center. 2015. "Xenophobia and Nationalism." https://www.levada.ru/en/2015/09/07/xenophobia-and-nationalism/.

SOVA Center for Information and Analysis. 2017. "Racism and Xenophobia." http://www.sova-center.ru/en/xenophobia.

Troitsky, Konstantin. 2016. "Administrative Expulsion from Russia: Court Proceedings or Mass Expulsion?" Civic Assistance Committee. https://refugee.ru/en/dokladyi/administrativnye-vydvoreniya-iz-rossii-sudebnoe-razbiratelstvo-ili-massovoe-izgnanie/.

SINGAPORE

Singapore, also known as the Lion City, was a former British trading colony. Located in southeastern Asia at the southern tip of the Malay Peninsula, Singapore has one main island and sixty-two islets. Economically, Singapore is famous for its highly developed, free-market economy along with a corruption-free environment and stable prices. Singapore's per capita gross domestic product is USD 94,100, which is the seventh highest in the world, and the unemployment rate is only 2.2 percent, which is lower than most developed countries (Central Intelligence Agency 2018).

Other than the highly developed economy, Singapore is also known for its diverse population and culture. According to the 2010 census, about 23 percent of the nearly six million people in Singapore were born in a foreign country. The percentage of foreign-born reaches 43 percent of the total population if both residents and aliens are included (Statistics Singapore 2011). While nearly one-third of the resident population in Singapore practice Buddhism, other religions such as Christianity, Islam, Taoism, and Hinduism have a substantial following in Singapore.

In addition, Singapore's legal system is among the most effective, reliable, and strictest in Asia. The World Justice Project's most recent index ranks Singapore the ninth most successful "rule of law" country out of 113 countries and jurisdictions around the world and the first in Asia (World Justice Project 2016).

Hate Speech Legislation

Due to considerable racial and religious diversity, Singapore greatly values harmony among different groups. Hate speech against religion and race is regulated in Section 298 of the Penal Code and in two other statutes: the Maintenance of Religious Harmony Act and the Sedition Act.

Section 298 of the 1872 Singapore Penal Code was influenced by the Indian Penal Code of 1860, though written in different languages. It defines the harm and scope of hate speech very broadly:

> **Uttering words, etc., with deliberate intent to wound the religious or racial feelings of any person**
> 298. Whoever, with deliberate intention of wounding the religious or racial feelings of any person, utters any word or makes any sound in the hearing of that person, or makes any gesture in the sight of that person, or places any object in the sight of that person, or causes any matter however represented to be seen or heard by that person, shall be punished with imprisonment for a term which may extend to 3 years, or with fine, or with both. (Penal Code 1872)

In the revised law of 2008, Section 298A explicitly used the words "enmity" and "prejudicial," which confirms the nature of hate speech law of Section 298 (Penal Code 1872).

Enacted on July 6, 1948, the Sedition Act forbids speech that incites resistance to, hatred of, or rebellion against the government. It also includes actions that promote and help the circulation of seditious speech, which may take the form of printing, publication, sale, distribution, reproduction, and importation. The Sedition Act creates a series of substantial crimes of seditious acts to fight hate speech in the country. In addition to punishing related actions, the Act criminalizes actions and speech that promote the feelings of hostility and hatred among different racial or class groups. The Sedition Act was used less often to regulate hate speech after the revision of the Penal Code Section 298A because this amendment better defines how behaviors correspond to the act of spreading hostile and biased statements.

The Maintenance of Religious Harmony Act was enacted in 1992. It permits the minister for Home Affairs to issue a restraining order against any religious authority, such as priest, monk, pastor, imam, and elder, when the person has committed or is attempting to commit actions that may undermine harmony among religious groups. Although it only provides the minister the power of issuing restraining orders, formal sanctions from the criminal justice system may be imposed for violation of a restraining order including imprisonment and fines. An example of this gray area is the case of Amos Yee.

On March 23, 2015, Lee Kuan Yew (1923–2015), the first Prime Minister of Singapore passed away at ninety-one years of age due to ill health. As the founding father of Singapore, Lee pledged his life for the independence of the country and built a meritocratic, multiracial nation. Four days after his death, Amos Yee, a sixteen-year-old Singaporean blogger, posted a video on YouTube, demeaning Lee and comparing him to Jesus Christ. The next day, Yee created and released an indecent image of Lee and former British Prime Minister Margaret Thatcher (1925–2013) in a sexual position.

Based on these facts, the public prosecutor charged Yee under Section 298 of Singapore's Penal Code for deliberately offending Christianity and Section 292 for electronically sending an obscene image (Penal Code 1872; Global Freedom of Expression 2015). On May 12, 2015, Yee was sentenced to four weeks in prison, backdated to fifty-three days he served on remand. Yee was released right after the trial.

Reexamination of Hate Speech Laws

The three laws described above comprise the infrastructure of legal protection for racial and religious harmony in Singapore. They also raise the question of whether speech should be punished before it leads to any physical and actual harm. For example, in the case of Yee, the legal focus was whether his actions wounded the feelings of Christians. The court held the view that to wound the religious feelings "simply means to give offense to any person." Yee's comments about Christianity, using terms such as "power hunger," "malicious," and "full of bull," were regarded as "clearly offensive and derogatory to Christians." In addition, the court contended that the actual evidence of individuals being offended was not among the essential elements for a conviction under Section 298 because the offense happens when harmful speech is expressed (Global Freedom of Expression 2015).

As the case gained media attention, hate speech laws in Singapore drew new levels of criticism from human rights and free speech groups around the world. Once again, the fine line between free speech and hate speech was scrutinized. On July 6, 2015, about 500 people turned up at a protest to rally for Amos Yee's release. International human rights organizations, including the United Nations Office of High Commissioner for Human Rights, Amnesty International, Human Rights Watch, and Freedom House, commented on Yee's case and denounced the prosecution and conviction. Across the ocean, a U.S. immigration court judge granted Yee asylum during the case. The defense appealed the District Court's ruling on the ground that it impeded freedom of speech under Article 14 of the Constitution as a fundamental right. Pressure came from domestic and international civil society in recognizing the continuing presence of the offense of hate speech and sedition as somewhat incongruent in a democracy.

Nevertheless, considering the country's history of ethnoreligious riots in the 1950s and 1960s and the diverse population in Singapore today, the government's determination to protect the religious and ethnic harmony in Singapore was not waved. Justice Tay replied to the defense: "This is not freedom of speech, this is a license to hate, to humiliate others and to totally disregard their feelings or beliefs by using words to inflict unseen wounds" (Chelvan 2015). Not only Singapore but other countries around the world are facing challenges related to the coexistence of multiple religions and races, highlighting the need for legislation to cope with hatred and hostility as a state interest. Section 298, the 1992 Maintenance of Religious Harmony Act, and the 1948 Sedition Act aim to establish a solid legal infrastructure to minimize any harm that may occur to the stability of the state. Yee's case was not the first one nor will it be the last one challenging these acts.

However, studies show that banning open discussion on race and religion to maintain harmony in a society like Singapore may be counterproductive. Open communication can aid true integration and a sense of a whole community. In contrast, repressing such conversations could lead to suspicion, resentment, and division. Citizens' participation in such conversations is also critical for cultivating genuine public opinion. In a multicultural and religiously diverse society, the ultimate creation of an integrated nation cannot solely rely on repressive legislation but has to be done through collective efforts.

Further Reading

Central Intelligence Agency. 2018. "The World Factbook." https://www.cia.gov/library/publications/resources/the-world-factbook/.

Chelvan, Vanessa Paige. 2015. "Amos Yee's Appeal to Overturn Conviction and Jail Term Dismissed." Channel NewsAsia, October 8, 2015. http://www.channelnewsasia.com/news/singapore/amos-yee-s-appeal-to-overturn-conviction-and-jail-term-dismissed-8229904.

Global Freedom of Expression. 2015. "*Public Prosecutor v. Amos Yee Pang Sang.*" https://globalfreedomofexpression.columbia.edu/cases/public-prosecutor-v-amos-yee-pang-sang/.

Penal Code. 1872. Chapter 224. https://sso.agc.gov.sg/Act/PC1871.

Statistics Singapore. 2011. "Census of Population 2010, Statistical Release 1, Demographic Characteristics, Education, Language and Religion." https://www.singstat.gov.sg /publications/cop2010/census10_stat_release1.

World Justice Project. 2016. "World Justice Project Rule of Law Index 2016." https:// worldjusticeproject.org/sites/default/files/documents/RoLI_Final-Digital_0.pdf.

SOUTH AFRICA

South Africa is the southernmost country on the continent of Africa, bordering the South Atlantic Ocean, the Indian Ocean, and six other African nations. The population of over fifty-five million people comprises nearly 81 percent Black Africans, 8.8 percent mixed race, and 7.8 percent white. There are eleven official languages including Afrikaans and English. Although South Africa is an emerging economy with a modern infrastructure and many natural resources, it suffers from high rates of unemployment, income inequality, and poverty. Its gross domestic product per capita is USD 13,600, which is lower than neighboring Botswana (USD 17,000) but higher than neighboring Namibia (USD 11,200) (Central Intelligence Agency 2018).

South Africa was colonized by the Netherlands in the seventeenth and eighteenth centuries and then by Britain in the nineteenth and twentieth centuries. It gained independence in the 1930s. From 1948 until 1994, South Africa was organized under an institutionalized segregation system called apartheid, whereby the minority white population had economic, political, and social advantages over the majority nonwhite population. Because of this legacy of racial segregation, ending discrimination and violence based on skin color is a topic that has gained significant political and public attention; however, discrimination against other social groups, particularly the LGBTI community is still commonplace.

History of Homosexuality

Prior to 1994, homosexuality was illegal in South Africa, punishable with up to seven years in prison. After the fall of the apartheid regime, the equality provision of the interim Constitution included sexual orientation under its protections. South Africa became the first country in the world to provide protection against discrimination against gays and lesbians. Despite the high levels of disapproval by the general public, the 1996 Constitution codified the value of equality regarding sexual orientation, specifically disallowing discrimination on the basis of gender, sex, sexual orientation, along with other social categories such as race and ethnicity. As a result, the criminal prohibition on sodomy between consenting male adults and the ban on same-sex adoption were struck down; at the same time, equality in immigration and marriage on the basis of sexual orientation became legally protected. Additionally, a number of other provisions also ensure equality, such as the Free Speech Clause, the Limitation Clause, clauses protecting cultural, religious, linguistic minorities, and the promotion of Equality and the Prevention of Unfair Discrimination Act 2000. Thus, the 1996 Constitution provided holistic protection and established the grounds for understanding equal rights and nondiscrimination among all South Africans.

Corrective Rape

In October 2016, a South African lesbian couple experienced a violent attack: a group of men broke into their home and raped them in a bid to physically impose their ideal sexuality on the women. Similar stories are common in South Africa and around the world. These offenses are called "corrective rape." The idea of corrective rape came from the notion that being raped would correct a lesbian woman's sexuality. It can also be used more broadly against sexual and gender minorities who do not conform to perceived social norms.

Crime data for 2015 and 2016 from the national police show 51,895 reported sexual offenses or a rate of about ninety-two reported offenses per 100,000 respondents of the population (South African Police Service 2015). Research findings also suggest that physical violence, especially sexual assault, is more likely to target lesbian, gay, and bisexual individuals in South Africa than their American counterparts. Official statistics represent only the tip of the iceberg because of various social pressures that may discourage victims from reporting rape. Regardless of the number of incidents actually reported, the fear of this kind of crime is high. Two studies conducted in 2008 among a population from Western Cape found that about 44 percent of white lesbians lived in fear of sexual assault, while a higher number, 86 percent, of black lesbians shared the same fear (Triangle Project and UNISA Centre for Applied Psychology 2006).

Progressive Developments

Although incidents like corrective rape are still happening in South Africa, the country's constitution is still among the most progressive in the world that prohibits discrimination against sexual orientation and offers comprehensive human rights recognition of LGBTI people. Significant steps were also taken to form a firm alliance between government and civil society in combating violence against the LGBTI community. In March 2011, a National Task Team was established in South Africa, aiming for a well-developed and effective joint intervention strategy to address such violence. Representatives from government departments, the police service, civil society organizations, as well as the National Prosecuting Authority formed the task team to expedite cases related to the LGBTI community.

In April 2014, the Department of Justice and Constitutional Development launched a public campaign to address sexual orientation and gender-based violence and to strengthen institutional responses to such crimes. A national intervention strategy for the LGBTI community was launched during the campaign, of which one objective was to discover the pattern of sexual violence and murder perpetrated against black lesbian women. This campaign highlights the most vulnerable groups, as well as the progressive actions taken to combat such violence. Provincial task teams were also established gradually in 2015 to implement the intervention strategy.

Hate Crime Data

While hate crime statistics are not available under the current legal framework in South Africa, several LGBTI nongovernmental organizations (NGOs) have conducted surveys and case studies on victimization and discrimination experiences. For example, in 2003–2004, a survey was conducted by OUT LGBT Well-being, an NGO dedicated to empowering the LGBT community and reducing heterosexism and homophobia in society, and to document the victimization of gay and lesbian individuals in Gauteng, South Africa. Among the 487 respondents in the survey, lesbian women experienced the most hate speech, physical abuse or assault, sexual abuse or rape, as well as domestic violence incidents (Wells and Polders 2006). Results indicated that despite the legal framework that South Africa has established to protect certain groups, the reality for the LGBTI community in South Africa remains threatening. Antihomosexual hate crimes are still prevalent in South Africa.

Another study released by the Love Not Hate Campaign found that among 2,130 South African respondents, a significant proportion (41 percent) knew of murder victims who were targeted due to their sexual orientation, with females (46 percent) more likely to notice such incidents than males (36 percent) (Love Not Hate Campaign 2016). On the issue of victimization experiences, results indicated that about 44 percent of the respondents had experienced discrimination related to their sexual orientation in their daily life within the past two years. Verbal insults (39 percent) and threats of violence (20 percent) were among the most common forms of discrimination. Interestingly, there were no significant differences in sexual abuse or rape across genders (Love Not Hate Campaign 2016).

Public Attitudes

Although the LGBTI community is protected by the legal system, public attitudes are divergent. The Pew Research Center released a study in 2013 showing that 61 percent of respondents in South Africa declared that homosexuality should not be accepted by society, while 32 percent of respondents had the contrary opinion. More recently, another study found that among LGB respondents in the survey sample of South Africans, about 55 percent feared discrimination against their sexual orientation and identity, while 44 percent of respondents had experienced some kind of discrimination in their daily life over the past two years due to their sexual preferences (Love Not Hate Campaign 2016).

Case studies show some similar evidence. In a poll in Western Cape among survivors of hate incidents on the basis of their sexuality, 25 percent of women said they were afraid to expose their sexual preference to the officials and 22 percent feared potential abuse. Women reported being blamed for their victimization because of their sexuality (Martin et al. 2009, 13). The study conducted by Love Not Hate Campaign confirmed that the majority of the respondents (88 percent) did not report any incidents to the police (Love Not Hate Campaign 2016).

While the constitutional order in South Africa is established upon the inclusive principle that recognizes and respects the dignity and equity of each human being, violence against LGBTI individuals defies that principle and endangers this promising constitutional and human rights framework. Better police training, standardized procedures regarding a rape complaint, a systematic hate crime reporting system, specialized women-led sexual assault units, awareness-raising programs, among other prevention and investigation approaches can reduce the number of corrective rape cases. However, given the attitudes motivating the perpetrators who commit corrective rape, the biggest obstacle the government must overcome is educating the public on the issues of tolerance and respecting equality and human rights that are equally enjoyed by LGBTI people. Mandating that the government work to erase hatred and discrimination that lead to corrective rape may help eliminate the underlying cause of this problem and have a long-lasting effect in preventing it. The affirmative duty of the South African government should go hand in hand with the progressive legislation and efficient prosecution; ultimately, this strategy might eliminate the institutional and cultural causes of corrective rape to systemically erase hate crime against this population.

Further Reading

Central Intelligence Agency. 2018. "The World Factbook." https://www.cia.gov/library/publications/resources/the-world-factbook/.

Love Not Hate Campaign. 2016. "Hate Crimes against Lesbian, Gay, Bisexual and Transgender (LGBT) People in South Africa, 2016." https://www.gala.co.za/resources/docs/Free_Downloads/hatecrimes.pdf.

Martin, Andrew, Annie Kelly, Laura Turquet, and Stephanie Ross. 2009. "Hate Crimes: The Rise of 'Corrective' Rape in South Africa." ActionAid. https://www.actionaid.org.uk/sites/default/files/publications/hate_crimes_the_rise_of_corrective_rape_in_south_africa_september_2009.pdf.

Pew Research Center. 2013. "The Global Divide on Homosexuality." *Pew Research Center's Global Attitudes Project* (blog), June 4, 2013. http://www.pewglobal.org/2013/06/04/the-global-divide-on-homosexuality/.

South African Police Service. 2015. "SAPS Previous Crimestats." https://www.saps.gov.za/services/crimestats_archive.php.

Triangle Project, and UNISA Centre for Applied Psychology. 2006. "Overall Research Findings on Levels of Empowerment among LGBT People in the Western Cape, South Africa." http://triangle.org.za/wp-content/uploads/2020/01/levels-of-empowerment-among-lgbt-people-in-the-western-cape-south-africa.pdf.

Wells, Helen, and Louise Polders. 2006. "Anti-Gay Hate Crimes in South Africa: Prevalence, Reporting Practices, and Experiences of the Police." *Agenda: Empowering Women for Gender Equity*, no. 67:20–28. https://www.jstor.org/stable/4066789.

UNITED KINGDOM

The United Kingdom of Great Britain and Northern Ireland, consisting of England, Scotland, Wales, and Northern Ireland, is a constitutional monarchy with a parliamentary democracy. The legal system of the United Kingdom follows common law principles, which grants judges the power to legislate, interpret, and apply statutes, precedent, and common sense to the facts of a case, where decisions are binding in future similar cases. It is a highly developed, wealthy nation with a gross domestic product per capita of USD 44,300, which is comparable to Finland, France, and Japan. It is a founding member of the North Atlantic Treaty Organization (NATO) and a permanent member of the United Nations Security Council. It joined the European Union in 1973, although it is in the process of leaving the political union of twenty-eight European countries (Central Intelligence Agency 2018). The United Kingdom has broad interpretations of what it means to be a victim and how bias is determined in hate crimes, which makes the reporting of such crimes more likely in this country than others.

The Country with the Most Hate Crimes?

The OSCE's ODIHR collects official hate crime statistics and civil society group reports for forty-four participating countries. In 2016, the United Kingdom reported 80,763 total hate crimes to ODIHR, of which England and Wales reported 80,393 and Northern Ireland 370. This was an increase of about 29 percent compared with 62,518 hate crimes reported in 2015 (OSCE/ODIHR 2017; Corcoran, Lader, and Smith 2015). Among all the participating countries, the United Kingdom recorded the highest number of hate crimes reported by the police, followed by the United States. The latter reported 7,321 hate crimes in 2016 and 6,885 in 2015, nearly ten times fewer hate crimes compared to the United Kingdom. Does this mean that the United Kingdom has the most hate crimes?

The first step to answer this question is to clarify that crime statistics only record the number of hate incidents reported to and recorded by the police. Several factors could influence hate crime statistics captured by law enforcement agencies and organizations. The definitions of hate crime vary across different jurisdictions in the United Kingdom. England and Wales define hate crime as "any criminal offense which is perceived, by the victim or any other person, to be motivated by hostility or prejudice towards someone based on a personal characteristic" (O'Neill 2017). In Scotland, a hate crime is "a crime motivated by malice or ill will towards a social group" (Police Scotland 2017). Although Northern Ireland does not have a statutory definition of hate crime, it shares the same bias motivations with all jurisdictions in the United Kingdom to identify hate crime. Race or ethnicity, religion or beliefs, sexuality, disability, and gender identity are all monitored.

The legal definitions across the United Kingdom cover the most common hate motivations. Compared to other countries, the United Kingdom's definitions do not cover more characteristics. This suggests that monitored or protected characteristics are not the central reason for high hate crime reporting in the United Kingdom. However, it is important to note that England and Wales have a great degree of flexibility regarding police recording practices. The protections for groups in society that may experience antagonism and violence cover additional factors, ranging from sexual abuse to football violence. Law enforcement agencies have the freedom to extend their policy to include other hostilities to avoid further victimization from the police. According to Amnesty International, hate crime policy in the United Kingdom is grounded in a victim-based approach. While this method prioritizes the protection of victims, it may also extend the legal definitions and lead to higher hate crime reporting.

Other parts of these legal definitions may provide some clues to unravel the significant amount of hate crime reporting. In the United Kingdom, the understanding of "the victim or any other person" about the nature of the offense is the determining element in assigning an incident as a crime with bias or hostility. Under this perception-based recording mechanism, the victim may report an incident as a hate crime without providing evidence of their perception. Law enforcement first responders are not allowed to challenge this belief. Moreover, it is not necessary to provide evidence of hostility to record a hate crime.

The concept of "victim" is also fairly broad under the United Kingdom's legislation. The monitored factors of hate motivations protect the members of a minority group as well as others who may not belong to a minority group. For example, a local resident who is visiting a tourist site may well perceive hostility against foreigners if the individual is verbally abused by the local business. Although the person is not a tourist, the perception of hostility makes the incident a race-based hate incident. At the same time, anyone who is present during the verbal abuse may also report the incident as hate-motivated. "Any other person" could be police officers or staff, witnesses, family members, or even someone who has knowledge of hate crime in the area. This victim-based hate crime policy and recording mechanism in the United Kingdom encourages hate crime reporting.

On the other hand, the data collection mechanism of ODIHR also contributes to the significant reporting gap between the United Kingdom and other participant countries. ODIHR started collecting information on hate crimes in 2016. However, the organization does not collect data itself; instead, it relies on information submitted by participant states. Not all countries comply with ODHIR reporting requirements, although the United Kingdom does. Both the noncompliance and underreporting by other participating states as well as regular data submission from the United Kingdom may create a combined effect that exaggerates the gap between recorded hate crimes in the United Kingdom and other countries.

"Brexit" Effect

Though broad and inclusive legal definitions and recording mechanisms increase the reported hate crimes, one cannot ignore that major social change may also spike hate crime in society. The European Union referendum campaign for the

United Kingdom to leave the European Union (commonly known as "Brexit") began on April 15, 2016, with the result announced on June 24. Figures released after the announcement of Brexit revealed a 42 percent increase in aggravated offense data and 44 percent increase in racially or religiously motivated crimes in England and Wales in July 2016 compared to the same month in 2015 (O'Neill 2017). Data also indicated that the whole period of the European Union referendum campaign showed an increase in hate crime reporting since April with a peak in July 2016. Moreover, the number dropped in August 2016, which suggests that the European Union referendum had some impact on hate crime reporting in the United Kingdom.

Is Hate Crime Recording Enough?

The positive aspects of dealing with hate crime in the United Kingdom include a victim-based approach and attempts to provide strong and broad hate crime legislation across the country, but there are other steps that need to be taken to fully address hate crime. After an offense is classified and documented by the police as a hate crime, prosecutors determine if the evidence is sufficiently robust for prosecution. Only if the evidence is adequate and strong, is a case of hate crime built. Thus, even if a hate crime is reported, it is not always prosecuted. According to the 2016 data, 20,321 hate crimes were prosecuted in the United Kingdom, about 25 percent of the total hate crimes recorded by police (O'Neill 2017). In Northern Ireland, about 16 percent of hate crimes recorded by police resulted in a resolution, such as prosecution or police warning (Amnesty International 2017). Similarly, in 2015, England and Wales charged about 21 percent of all reported hate crime as bias-motivated (Amnesty International 2017).

Case studies also highlight the insufficient response in the United Kingdom after hate crime reporting. Cathleen Lauder was a transgender woman who had been verbally assaulted on a bus. During the incident, Lauder recorded the incident on her phone. Her evidence and report led to prosecution of one of the perpetrators. However, the court hearing was canceled because the evidence had been lost. It took eight months for her case to be heard (Amnesty International 2017). In another case, Bijan Ebranhimi, an Iranian refugee who had learning difficulties and a physical impairment, reported to the police that he had been physically assaulted and racially abused by a neighbor for years. Instead of arresting the neighbor, Ebranhimi was detained for breach of peace. Three days after his release, Ebranhimi was beaten to death and set alight by the neighbor. During the prosecution, the court found no evidence of hostility toward Bijan's disability, which disqualified the application of enhanced sentencing provided by the Criminal Justice Act 2003 (Amnesty International 2017).

Another point to consider is the victims' experiences. According to the Crime Survey for England and Wales (CSEW), among the respondents in 2012 and 2014, over half of hate crime victims were either very or fairly satisfied with the handling of the incident and about 35 percent of hate crime victims were very dissatisfied.

At the same time, 92 percent of hate crime victims reported negative emotional impact caused by the crime compared to 81 percent of all victims overall (OSCE/ODIHR 2017; Corcoran, Lader, and Smith 2015).

Further Reading

Amnesty International. 2017. "Tackling Hate Crime in the UK." https://www.amnesty.org.uk/files/Against-Hate-Briefing-2.pdf.

Central Intelligence Agency. 2018. "The World Factbook." https://www.cia.gov/library/publications/resources/the-world-factbook/.

College of Policing. 2014. "Hate Crime Operational Guidance." http://www.report-it.org.uk/files/hate_crime_operational_guidance.pdf.

Corcoran, Hannah, Deborah Lader, and Kevin Smith. 2015. "Hate Crime, England and Wales, 2014/15." GOV.UK. https://www.gov.uk/government/uploads/system/uploads/attachment_data/file/467366/hosb0515.pdf.

ODIHR (Office for Democratic Institutions and Human Rights). n.d. "Hate Crime Reporting." Organization for Security and Cooperation in Europe (OSCE). http://hatecrime.osce.org/.

O'Neill, Aoife. 2017. "Hate Crime, England and Wales, 2016/17." GOV.UK. https://www.gov.uk/government/statistics/hate-crime-england-and-wales-2016-to-2017.

Police Scotland. 2017. "What Is Hate Crime?" http://www.scotland.police.uk/keep-safe/advice-for-victims-of-crime/hate-crime/what-is-hate-crime/.

UNITED STATES

The United States of America is a country of over 325 million people located in North America with Canada to the north and Mexico to the south. It is a diverse society in terms of race, ethnicity, and religion. Approximately 72.4 percent of the population identifies as white, 12.6 percent as black, 4.8 percent as Asian, and about 1 percent as Native American or Pacific Islander. Over 65 percent of the population affiliates with Christianity, about 2 percent with Judaism, and about 1 percent with Islam. It is a constitutional federal republic with fifty states and one district, and laws are passed at both the federal and state levels (Central Intelligence Agency 2018). The diversity within the country has put discrimination and bias at the forefront of a lot of legislation throughout the country's history. The federal government has legislated against hate crimes since the 1968 Civil Rights Act and has expanded protections to various marginalized groups over time. In addition to standard protections for race, ethnicity, religion, gender, and sexual orientation, the United States includes disability as a legally protected social category.

In the first ever World Report on Disability, the World Health Organization and the World Bank reported that over one billion people in the world experience a disability, representing 15 percent of the world's population. Other than physical and mental challenges, people with disabilities also suffer from prejudice, stereotypes, and exclusion, with limited access to services and other resources. It is estimated that with the global increase in chronic health conditions and an aging population, the challenges of disabilities will escalate. The barriers to accessing basic services are exacerbated in disadvantaged communities (World Health Organization and World Bank 2011). In 2006, the United Nations adopted the Convention on the Rights of Persons with Disabilities and its Optional Protocol, which aimed to build an overarching framework to advertise, protect, and fulfill the rights of individuals with disabilities. Soon after the convention, many countries joined the campaign and took significant steps to acknowledge and promote disability rights within their own nations.

Recognition of Disability Hate Crime

The United States did not achieve consistent protections against hate crimes across all fifty states until the Matthew Shepard and James Byrd, Jr. Hate Crime Prevention Act of 2009. Granting federal officials permission to support the prosecution of a hate crime charge beyond the reach of a state statute, this legislation covers wide-ranging grounds including race, religion, national origin, sexual orientation, gender, gender identity, and disability. While other forms of hate crime have been broadly recognized in the United States, disability hate crime has drawn less public attention. There are several factors that contribute to this situation. First, disability is not a uniform nor an uncontested concept. People under similar health conditions may not be recognized under the same label. Thus, it is important to bear in mind that the notion of disability is socially constructed, as is the idea of hate crime. According to the National Crime Victimization Survey (NCVS), disability is defined as "the product of interactions among individuals' bodies; their physical, emotional, and mental health; and the physical and social environment in which they live, work, or play. . . . Disability exists where this interaction results in limitations of activities and restrictions to full participation at school, at work, at home, or in the community" (Harrell 2017, 1). Limitations that are mentioned in the definition include hearing, vision, cognitive, ambulatory, self-care, and independent living. In contrast, the Uniform Crime Reporting Program classifies disability bias into anti-mental disability and antiphysical disability. Different definitions may cause inconsistency in classification, which may lead to underreporting in disability hate crimes.

Second, although federal law allows prosecution of hate crimes without state-level legislation, some cases may not be recorded or prosecuted as disability hate crimes. Acts that could constitute disability hate crimes could be charged under other legal provisions, such as abuse, maltreatment, or neglect of a disabled person.

Finally, disability hate crimes might be perceived as rare so that little attention is warranted. However, evidence contradicts this perception. Like many other crimes, disability hate crimes may take various forms. On the one hand, it may seem like a prank, such as taking a disabled person's cane away from them. On the other hand, it can be more vicious. For example, in Cheektowaga, New York, four perpetrators drove three cars to follow victims after making numerous slurs about their developmental disabilities. During the chase, one of the cars driven by the perpetrators came dangerously close to hitting the victims' car and eventually caused a crash.

The Americans with Disabilities Act was signed into law in 1990 and prohibits discrimination against people with disabilities in the public sphere, such as employment, education, and public spaces. Disability is also a protected status in the 2009 federal Hate Crime Prevention Act. (George Bush Library)

Data on Disability Hate Crimes

As many studies have pointed out, the rate of crime against disabled people is much higher than people without disabilities. During the five-year period from 2011 to 2015, the chance of disabled people being the victim of violence was at least two-and-a-half times higher than those who were not disabled (Harrell 2017). In the Hate Crime Victimization report for 2004–2015, crimes against disability comprised about 16 percent of all reported incidents (Masucci and Langton 2017).

When it comes to disability hate crimes, the U.S. Federal Bureau of Investigation (FBI) has the world's longest-running and largest dataset on this topic. The Hate Crime Statistics Act of 1990 mandates the FBI to collect hate crime data under its Uniform Crime Reporting Program. From 1997 to 2016, the FBI recorded about 1,200 disability hate crimes, which comprises about 1 percent of total incidents recorded (Sherry 2016). While this number seems small, victimization reports are telling another story, suggesting a large number of underreported incidents. Both victims and criminal justice professionals may not correctly identify acts as hate crimes and report them accordingly.

When examining the disability hate crime data for violent offenses from 1997 to 2007, rape is thirty times more common among disability hate crimes than other hate crimes and simple assault is also much higher in disability hate crimes. The same pattern is true of property crimes, such as larceny theft, burglary, and motor vehicle theft (Sherry 2016). Interestingly, most disability hate crimes happened in the victim's home, which is also captured by other studies. For example, from 2011 to 2015, only one-third of total violent victimizations against people with disabilities were committed by strangers to the victim, whereas 40 percent offenders were people the victims knew (Harrell 2017).

Barriers to Identify Disability Hate Crimes

One of the most common barriers to identify hate crimes in general lies in the official data collecting mechanism, which not only requires the victim to identify the criminal action and bias motivation but also relies on law enforcement officers to recognize and report the offense as a hate crime. While bias motivations are usually difficult to identify, bias against disability is even trickier to recognize due to varying definitions of disability, especially when the disabilities are invisible. For example, victims with epilepsy may not express any symptoms or disability status during meetings with police. Even if the perpetrator is aware of their impairment, the incident may not be categorized as a crime with a bias motive. It is not unusual for victims or police officers to assume that the incident is bullying, maltreatment, or abuse. According to the NCVS report, about 42 percent of respondents assumed that the incident was not important enough to be a crime and the police would not help (Harrell 2017).

A special barrier for disabled people is that they often rely on caregivers to report crimes, which is especially problematic if the caregiver is committing the crime. Law enforcement officers also have difficulties in recognizing the bias motivation related to the disability when such a relationship between the victim and offender exists.

Responses to Disability in Hate Crimes

Although thousands of hate crimes have been reported every year, most were never heard by a jury. Under the new federal-level acts, only 13 percent of hate crime cases were referred to federal prosecutors between January 2010 and August 2015 (TRAC 2015). Although the fact that the individual was not federally prosecuted did not necessarily mean that the person was never charged with a crime, it reflects the difficulty to seek justice within the system. Data on disability hate crime prosecution is not available, yet it is reasonable to foresee a small number of successful prosecutions and convictions based on the general outcomes after reporting a hate crime.

Alternative support may come from communities rather than the federal government. Due to the potential barrier of recognizing hate crime against disabilities, acknowledging the nature of hate crime is critical. After a hate incident, it is important for the community to influence individuals to help others. It is also crucial to integrate disabled people within the community in cases where perpetrators rely on the isolation of the victims to carry out abuse. The wider harms of the hate crime may be prevented and tackled by involving the victims within the community and reducing tensions between groups. Lastly, although changing perception regarding the potential victims of discrimination and bigotry is challenging, it is necessary to fight against hate crimes motivated by one's mental or physical disadvantages. Stigmas and stereotypes that invade the lives of people with disabilities are still prevalent in the United States, which harms the population equally, if not more, than the hate crime itself.

Further Reading

Central Intelligence Agency. 2018. "The World Factbook." https://www.cia.gov/library/publications/resources/the-world-factbook/.

Harrell, Erika. 2017. "Crime against Persons with Disabilities, 2009–2015-Statistical Tables." Washington, DC: US Bureau of Justice Statistics. https://www.bjs.gov/content/pub/pdf/capd0915st.pdf.

Masucci, Madeline, and Lynn Langton. 2017. "Hate Crime Victimization, 2004–2015." Washington, DC: United States Bureau of Justice Statistics. https://www.bjs.gov/content/pub/pdf/hcv0415.pdf.

Sherry, Mark. 2016. *Disability Hate Crimes: Does Anyone Really Hate Disabled People?* London, UK: Routledge.

TRAC (Transactional Records Access Clearinghouse). 2015. "Convictions in Federal Hate Crime Cases since FY 2010." Syracuse University. http://trac.syr.edu/tracreports/crim/393/.

World Health Organization and World Bank. 2011. *World Report on Disability.* Geneva, Switzerland: World Health Organization. http://www.who.int/disabilities/world_report/2011/en/.

Chapter 5: Human Trafficking

Janet P. Stamatel

OVERVIEW

Stories about human trafficking fill news feeds daily. For example, in September 2019, there was a story about 165 Bulgarians who police had rescued from forced labor in French wineries and another about how female refugees from North Korea were forced into cybersex by traffickers in China. Similar stories about human trafficking within the United States are also fairly common. For example, also in September 2019, three American men who were charged with drug offenses in Oklahoma were offered a diversion program to work and receive drug treatment instead of serving time in prison. They were sent to work over forty hours a week in a chicken processing plant without pay and without any drug treatment or rehabilitation programs. The three men have filed a lawsuit against the chicken processing company and the diversion program for human trafficking because they were threatened with prison if they did not comply with the work requirements.

Common notions of slavery associate the term with white colonizers who bought or stole nonwhite people and forced them into labor against their will through violence and intimidation. This historical image of slavery leads to the illusion that the problem was eradicated with abolitionism and the passage of the Slavery, Servitude, Forced Labor, and Similar Institutions and Practices Convention of 1926 (known as the Slavery Convention). However, various forms of slavery have persisted and have been reformulated as human trafficking, which is often called "modern slavery."

Human trafficking is defined by the United Nations as "the recruitment, transport, transfer, harbouring or receipt of a person by such means as threat or use of force or other forms of coercion, abduction, fraud or deception for the purpose of exploitation" (United Nations Convention against Transnational Organized Crime 2019). To be defined as human trafficking, crimes must meet three criteria specified in this definition. First, one of the acts listed above must be present (i.e., recruitment, transport, transfer, harboring, or receipt). The word "trafficking" implies movement and is often assumed to require the transfer of people across borders, but that is not part of the legal definition according to international standards. Second, the act must be carried out against the victim's will through threat, force, coercion, fraud, or deception. Finally, the crime must have been committed with the intent to exploit the victim for personal gain.

This definition was adopted by the United Nations in the Convention against Transnational Organized Crime and its associated protocols, particularly the Protocol to Prevent, Suppress, and Punish Trafficking in Persons, especially Women and Children. This convention was adopted in 2000 in Palermo, Italy, and is often referred to as the "Palermo Protocol." It went into effect in 2003 with 175 countries agreeing to its provisions. The protocol was designed to be comprehensive in its definition of human trafficking, encompassing sexual exploitation, labor exploitation, slavery, servitude, and the removal of organs, as well as including women, men, boys, and girls as possible victims.

Since the adoption of the Palermo Protocol, human trafficking has become an important international issue that has gained the attention of policymakers, nongovernmental organizations, human rights groups, and the general public across the world. Many such organizations report large numbers of human trafficking cases, but these estimates vary wildly across sources. As these crimes are difficult to detect and measure, figures regarding their prevalence are often not accurate. As such, this chapter avoids such claims to estimated numbers of cases and instead reports cases known to governments. This approach is also problematic because it does not capture all occurrences of human trafficking, but unlike some of the other crimes discussed in chapter 1 on Criminal Law and Criminal Behavior or chapter 3 on Juvenile Delinquency and Juvenile Justice, there is no alternative measuring system to adequately capture the "dark figure" of human trafficking as there is for other types of crimes.

Much of the information available to the public about human trafficking across a large number of countries comes from the United States Department of State, which publishes an annual Trafficking in Persons (TIP) report. This report summarizes what is known about human trafficking in each participating country, the laws that have been passed to combat human trafficking, and the types of criminal justice and social service responses to the problem. The TIP ranks countries along three tiers with respect to how well they follow international standards to fight human trafficking. These evaluations are based on how well countries implement the 3Ps – prevention, protection of victims, and prosecution of offenders. Some have criticized this report for not taking a more victim-centered or trauma-informed approach to the problem of human trafficking and for using the report as a tool for political leverage. Despite these criticisms, it is an often-cited source of information on human trafficking around the world.

The countries profiled in this chapter include domestic and international trafficking, as well as both sexual and labor exploitation, although there are different emphases in each country. Germany, Italy, Iraq, and the United Arab Emirates (UAE) are examples of countries that are largely destinations for trafficked victims, whereas Malawi and Moldova are much more likely to be sources of trafficking victims; Thailand and Brazil are mixed in this respect. Brazil, Germany, and Italy are examples of countries where prostitution is legal, illustrating the difficulty to detect cases of human trafficking versus prostitution. Iraq, the UAE, and Malawi exemplify different types and sources of labor trafficking including wars, construction booms, and diseases. All the profiles summarize the legal responses to trafficking that the countries have undertaken in response to the Palermo Protocol, as well as the types of services they offer to victims of trafficking.

Further Reading

Bales, Kevin. 2005. *Understanding Global Slavery: A Reader.* Berkeley: University of California Press.

Lee, Maggy, ed. 2013. *Human Trafficking.* Portland, OR: Willan Publishing.

"United Nations Convention against Transnational Organized Crime and the Protocols Thereto." 2019. https://www.unodc.org/unodc/en/organized-crime/intro/UNTOC .html#Fulltext.

BRAZIL

Brazil is the largest country in South America, occupying the northeast portion of the continent. It borders ten countries, with Venezuela to the north, Peru to the west, and Argentina to the south. It also has a long coastal border along the Atlantic Ocean. The population of nearly 209 million people is ethnically mixed, though predominantly Catholic. Brazil has a large, diverse economy with a vibrant agricultural sector, a variety of manufacturing industries, and a large service sector. It is the eighth largest economy in the world with a gross domestic product of USD 15,600, which is higher than Venezuela (USD 12,500), but lower than Argentina (USD 20,900) (Central Intelligence Agency 2018). Brazil is also a major player in the illegal drug business as a strategic transshipment point between drug producers in South America and European consumer markets.

After gaining independence from Portugal in 1825, Brazil was run primarily by military dictatorships until the 1980s. These regimes were characterized by high levels of police brutality and corruption, creating low levels of trust in the police that still persist despite the fact that the country is now run by a civil government under a federal presidential system. Brazil's geographic location, expanding economy, and weak criminal justice system contribute to crime problems in the country, including the presence of both domestic and international human trafficking.

Nature and Extent of Human Trafficking

Brazil is a source and destination country for both labor and sex trafficking. Brazilian women are trafficked to Western Europe, the United States, and China, and Brazilian men are primarily sent to Spain and Italy for sex. Women from other Latin American countries, especially Paraguay, are trafficked to Brazil for sex and domestic work. Both men and women are trafficked from abroad, particularly from Paraguay, Uruguay, Haiti, and China, to work in debt bondage in the textile and construction industries in Brazil. Domestic trafficking has also been documented in Brazil. Men are subjected to forced labor or debt bondage, especially in the agricultural industry. Women and children are trafficked within Brazil for prostitution and sex tourism. They are often dark-skinned women from the northeast region of the country.

According to the United Nations Office on Drugs and Crime (UNODC 2018), the number of federal cases of human trafficking recorded in Brazil was seventy-eight in 2014, sixty in 2015, and thirty-nine in 2016. In 2016, these thirty-nine cases resulted in the arrests of forty-three suspects and the identification of 1,054 victims, of which 29 percent were children. It is unclear whether these numbers represent a downward trend in either the occurrence of human trafficking or the policing of it because the legal definition of human trafficking and the means for dealing with it in Brazil changed during this period. Prior to 2016, human trafficking cases were processed under broad laws regarding forced labor and sexual exploitation, which changed with the passage of a new law specifically addressing human trafficking to bring Brazil into compliance with international conventions. For example, between 1999 and 2011, the Federal Police investigated 475 cases of sex trafficking and charged 721 suspects, 54 percent of whom were women (Anselmo and Fernandes 2015). These cases were prosecuted under Section 231 of the Criminal Code regarding the movement of people for the purpose of prostitution or sexual exploitation, which is not the same as the contemporary definition of human trafficking. Another important change regarding how Brazil handles human trafficking cases is that they now tend to be concentrated at the federal level to ensure greater consistency in their processing.

Brazil is rated as a Tier 2 country by the U.S. Department of State in 2018 because it had passed this new law but it still does not fully meet the minimum international standards to eradicate human trafficking. The TIP report noted that investigations and prosecutions of human trafficking cases in Brazil were weak and the country did not sufficiently address the role of corruption in perpetuating these crimes. The report also criticized the lack of consistency in victims' services among different types of human trafficking victims. Finally, the report commented on the lack of funding and training for law enforcement to adequately address human trafficking.

Forced Labor and Debt Bondage

Brazil's agricultural industry has a long history of questionable labor practices. Debt bondage became a well-known practice once African slaves were freed. Although it was illegal, it persisted as labor demands grew. Sugarcane was discovered during the Portuguese colonization of Brazil, giving rise to the establishment of large plantations farmed by poor local and migrant workers. This practice intensified with large-scale coffee production. In the 1960s and 1970s, the military dictatorships expanded investment in agribusiness and diversified crop production to include soybean, bean, cotton, and tobacco. Although the military governments had signed international treaties abolishing slavery, they ignored the practice of debt bondage.

The civilian government that came to power in 1985 promised significant land reforms and economic justice in rural Brazil. The attorney general became a visible opponent of forced labor and raised awareness of the criminal codes related to worker exploitation. In 2003, the government developed the First National Plan

---

Fazenda Brasil Verde

Between 1988 and 2000 the Brazilian government launched twelve raids on a cattle ranch called Fazenda Brasil Verde, where hundreds of people were found working in debt bondage and forced labor. The case was never prosecuted, and by the time a nongovernmental organization tried to help victims achieve justice, the twelve-year statute of limitations had passed. The case was then filed in the Inter-American Court of Human Rights, which ruled that the statute of limitations could not be applied in cases involving international law and ordered the country to reopen the investigation and pay the victims USD 5 million for its failure to address slavery.

---

for the Eradication of Slave Labor and created a public "dirty list" of companies found to use forced labor. Businesses that violate slavery laws are put on the list for a minimum of two years and are not allowed to receive any financial support from the government during that time. This list also makes it more difficult for such companies to secure loans from private banks.

Forced labor and debt bondage are prosecuted under Article 149 of the Criminal Code that prohibits slavery-like working conditions. In 2004, the Brazilian government amended the law to define those conditions more precisely. There are now four possible actions that can qualify as a criminal offense under this law including using violence, followed by forced labor, debt bondage, excessive or exhausting work, and degrading work conditions. This law was succeeded by a National Commitment to Improve Labor Conditions in the Sugarcane Industry in 2009. Finally, in 2012, the government passed a constitutional amendment that gives the state the right to seize property from businesses that engage in slave labor. Forced labor was also specifically mentioned in the 2016 human trafficking law that also included sexual exploitation, organ trafficking, and illegal adoption. The sentence for crimes under this new law is four to eight years in prison, plus fines. These penalties can be increased in cases with child victims or international trafficking.

In terms of victim assistance, the Brazilian government provides victims of forced labor with three months of minimum wages, job training, and travel assistance. They are also eligible to receive a portion of the fines levied against their employers. In 2011, victims received a total of USD 2.9 million from fines (Hepburn and Simon 2013). However, there are no shelters to provide temporary housing for labor victims.

Sex Trafficking

Much domestic and international attention about the issue of human trafficking in Brazil has been placed on sex trafficking, even though little is known about the extent of the problem and how many cases fit the legal definition of trafficking. Until 2016, sex trafficking cases were handled under Sections 231 and 231A of the penal code, which considered prostitution and sexual exploitation as similar problems and did not specify the use of "threats, coercion, violence, fraud, or abuse," as the current law does. Given this legal ambiguity, the public's understanding of sex trafficking in Brazil was shaped by nongovernmental organizations and the media, often without scientific evidence. What emerged was a picture of excessive sexual exploitation of poor, nonwhite Brazilian women who were deceived or forced into sex work. Public awareness campaigns sought to educate the public about sex trafficking, but largely ignored male victims and labor trafficking.

The moral panic surrounding women and children as victims of sex trafficking influenced Brazil's early policy reforms to address the crime. On a positive note, much more assistance was provided to female victims of sex trafficking. They were offered temporary shelter, legal and medical assistance, educational and employment training to reintegrate them into society, and protection of their privacy. However, the government's response to the perceived problem of sex trafficking of women did not address the causes of the problem, such as poverty, gender discrimination, illiteracy, and corruption.

On the negative side, perceptions of the sex trafficking problem led to some ill-informed policy decisions. For example, as part of the country's Plan to Combat Sexual Exploitation of Children and Adolescents for 2003–2005, several campaigns were launched to rescue victims of sex trafficking. In 2003, in the city of Rio de Janeiro, police launched an initiative to intensify the monitoring of suspected trafficking operations and the apprehension of perpetrators. The campaign called "Operation Princess" initially caused confusion regarding how to separate prostitution, which is legal in Brazil, from sex trafficking, which is not. To resolve this problem, the police focused only on child sexual exploitation, which is illegal in all its forms. Operation Princess was launched as a campaign to "save children" and rid the country of its association with "new slavery" (Amar 2009). Instead, raids conducted by Operation Princess uncovered the direct involvement of the police and other civil servants in the illegal sex business and the indirect complicity of law enforcement officers who allowed these known practices to persist. Operation Princess soon became a public relations disaster that quickly lost public support.

Further Reading

Amar, Paul. 2009. "Operation Princess in Rio de Janeiro: Policing 'Sex Trafficking', Strengthening Worker Citizenship, and the Urban Geopolitics of Security in Brazil." *Security Dialogue* 40 (4–5): 513–41. https://doi.org/10.1177/0967010609343300.

Anselmo, Márcio, and Guilherme Fernandes. 2015. "An Overview of International Human Trafficking in Brazil." In *The Illegal Business of Human Trafficking*, edited by Maria Joao Guia, 61–70. Cham, Switzerland: Springer. https://link.springer.com/book/10.1007%2F978-3-319-09441-0.

Blanchette, Thaddeus Gregory, Ana Paula Silva, and Andressa Raylane Bento. 2013. "The Myth of Maria and the Imagining of Sexual Trafficking in Brazil." *Dialectical Anthropology* 37 (2): 195–227. https://doi.org/10.1007/s10624-013-9296-z.

Central Intelligence Agency. 2018. "The World Factbook." https://www.cia.gov/library/publications/resources/the-world-factbook/.

Hepburn, Stephanie, and Rita J. Simon. 2013. *Human Trafficking around the World: Hidden in Plain Sight*. New York: Columbia University Press.

UNODC (United Nations Office on Drugs and Crime). 2018. Global Report on Trafficking in Persons South America. https://www.unodc.org/documents/lpo-brazil//Topics_TIP /Publicacoes/GLOTIP_2018_SOUTH_AMERICA.pdf.

U.S. Department of State. 2018. "Trafficking in Persons Report." Washington, DC. https:// www.state.gov/reports/2018-trafficking-in-persons-report/.

GERMANY

Germany is a Western European country bordering nine other countries including France to the east, Poland to the west, and Denmark to the north. About 87 percent of the eighty million people are ethnic Germans with the largest ethnic minorities from Turkey, Poland, and Syria. Germany is a federal parliamentary democracy consisting of sixteen states. It was a founding member of the European Union, a political and economic alliance of twenty-eight countries, and the Eurozone, a common currency monetary union. Germany has the fifth largest economy in the world with a gross domestic product per capita of USD 50,800, comparable to Sweden, Taiwan, and Australia (Central Intelligence Agency 2018). Germany's geographic location in the middle of Europe, its participation in the Schengen area that eliminated border control for mutual borders among twenty-six European countries, and its strong economy make it a popular destination for immigrants, both legal and illegal.

Nature and Extent of Human Trafficking

Germany can be classified as a source, transit, and destination country for both labor and sex trafficking, although it is most often recognized as a destination. It is among the top five countries for known trafficking victims, along with Belgium, Greece, Italy, and the Netherlands. It has the third highest number of foreign migrants, after the United States and Saudi Arabia. In 2017, almost 15 percent of the population of Germany consisted of international migrants, which has been steadily increasing since 1990. It also has the fifth highest number of refugees (GMDAC 2019). This relatively large volume of people moving into and out of the country creates opportunities for human trafficking.

Much like other countries, public and law enforcement attention is much greater for sex trafficking in Germany than labor trafficking. In fact, prior to 1995, only sexual exploitation was counted as human trafficking. Police statistics recording these crimes reflect this imbalance. In 2016, Germany identified 536 trafficking victims, of which 488 were sexually exploited, or 91 percent. Nearly two-thirds of sex trafficking victims were German, and foreign victims were primarily from Hungary, Bosnia-Herzegovina, and Romania, although the number of victims from Nigeria has been increasing. Of the labor trafficking victims, most were from Ukraine and one-fourth were working for the construction industry (U.S. Department of State 2018).

In 2016, police identified 551 trafficking suspects, 95 percent of whom were investigated for sex trafficking. Of the 524 sex trafficking suspects, ninety were prosecuted and sixty were convicted. Of those convicted, thirty-five received suspended prison sentences, twenty-one were sent to prison for sentences between nine months and five years, and four were assessed fines (U.S. Department of State 2018). The United States has criticized Germany's frequent use of suspended sentences and fines in trafficking cases because they claim that they do not sufficiently hold offenders accountable for their crimes.

In 2016, Germany identified twenty-five labor traffickers, prosecuted nineteen, and convicted twelve. In these cases, eight offenders were fined, three were given a suspended sentence, and one was imprisoned (U.S. Department of State 2018). Labor trafficking victims in Germany are usually from Ukraine, Bulgaria, Romania, Afghanistan, Pakistan, and Vietnam. Forced labor cases are typically found in the food industry, agriculture, construction, transportation, fairground entertainment, and domestic work.

Legal Responses to Human Trafficking

Germany passed antitrafficking legislation in 2005 with Sections 232 and 233 of the Criminal Code that criminalized both sex and labor trafficking with penalties of imprisonment between six months and ten years. The same year the country also passed the Offenses against Personal Freedom Amendment that declared persons under twenty-one years old who were persuaded into prostitution to be considered trafficking victims. In 2017, Germany amended the human trafficking law to also criminalize forced begging and coerced criminal behavior and to increase legal penalties for trafficking cases involving child victims. Romani and unaccompanied foreign children are most susceptible to these forms of human trafficking.

Although most concerns regarding human trafficking in Germany focus on sex trafficking, it is very difficult to identify victims of trafficking among sex workers, especially because prostitution is legal in Germany. To make the issue even more complicated, it is estimated that 60–70 percent of sex workers are migrants (Shelley 2014). Traffickers recruiting victims from East European countries like Bulgaria and Romania tend to use psychological and emotional ploys to lure women to Germany for sex work, so victims may not even recognize that they have been trafficked. Others know that they will be performing sex work in Germany, but they do not understand the nature of the arrangement until they arrive and are indebted to traffickers, earn significantly less than what was promised, are not allowed to leave the job, and/or are psychologically or physically abused. For example, in 2010, it was estimated that 36 percent of identified sex trafficking victims had knowingly entered sex work (Hepburn and Simon 2013). The 2002 Prostitution Act was a means for the German government to better monitor and regulate prostitution. Sex workers are required to register and pay taxes in exchange for health insurance and legal rights. However, these rights do not cover foreign sex workers who do not have work permits.

Although Germany is ranked by the U.S. Department of State as a Tier 1 country, which means that it fully complies with international antitrafficking standards, there were two areas where further improvements were suggested. The first was victim identification and support. Current practices focus almost exclusively on sex trafficking and there are no systematic ways to identify victims of labor trafficking. Government support for victims is also tied to their willingness to participate in criminal proceedings. Those who agree to testify against their perpetrators are given temporary residency permits for three months, which are often extended to six months. They are also provided with shelter, legal assistance, job training, medical care, and psychiatric services. Victims in danger of retribution from their traffickers may be granted long-term residency permits. However, the U.S. Department of State noted that services for male and child trafficking victims were not as extensive as those offered to female sex trafficking victims.

The second suggested area of improvement is the processing of trafficking cases. Investigations often take years, which means that trials are delayed, and victims might be less likely to participate in cases that are not resolved quickly. Specialized training on how to handle trafficking cases is offered to judges, but it is not mandatory because judges are concerned that compulsory training could threaten judicial independence. Finally, once cases are tried and offenders are convicted, there is a high proportion of suspended sentences, which may undermine justice for victims and accountability for offenders. In 2016, only 30 percent of convicted traffickers served prison sentences and labor traffickers often only received fines as punishment (U.S. Department of State 2018).

Sex and Sports

As Germany was preparing to host the 2006 Fédération Internationle de Football Association (FIFA) World Cup soccer tournament, reports began to circulate that the major sporting event would put 40,000 women at risk for sex trafficking. Although the source of this statistic was not clearly established, it was repeated often enough by the media and policymakers that it became a foregone conclusion (Morrow 2008). Skeptics claimed the figure was a ploy to criticize Germany's move to legalize prostitution or to shame the country into ratifying the Palermo Protocol. Germany had signed the international trafficking protocol in December 2000, but it only ratified the agreement in 2006, less than one week before the World Cup.

Regardless of the accuracy of the statistic, the German government took the threat seriously and worked with law enforcement and nongovernmental organizations to educate, prevent, and detect sex trafficking during the World Cup. The police significantly increased their visibility in the twelve cities hosting World Cup games. They also increased training for officers to better detect human trafficking, conducted more raids on brothels and sex clubs, and dispatched numerous undercover investigations. Nongovernmental organizations launched large-scale public awareness campaigns, such as "Final Whistle—Stop Forced Prostitution" and "Red Card for Sexual Exploitation and Forced Prostitution." They also sponsored twenty-four-hour hotlines for victims to call for assistance.

A comparison of sex trafficking cases before, during, and after the 2006 World Cup showed that there was no increase in sex trafficking or forced prostitution as a result of the event. Nonetheless, the fear that major sporting events could increase the risk of sex trafficking has persisted and media stories have warned of this connection for subsequent World Cup, Superbowl, and Olympic events. Research on changes in recorded sex trafficking cases across several large sporting events still has not provided evidence that these events increase sex trafficking. Additionally, the international captivation with sex trafficking has overlooked the relationship between large sporting events and labor trafficking. The massive construction booms associated with these events increase the demand for low-wage workers, many of whom are migrant workers who are subsequently exploited (Hepburn 2017).

Further Reading

Central Intelligence Agency. 2018. "The World Factbook." https://www.cia.gov/library/publications/resources/the-world-factbook/.

GMDAC (International Organization for Migration Global Migration Data Analysis Centre). 2019. "Global Migration Data Portal." https://migrationdataportal.org/.

Hepburn, Stephanie. 2017. "It's Not Just about Sex—Human Trafficking and Sporting Events." *HuffPost*, February 13, 2017. https://www.huffpost.com/entry/its-not-just-about-sexhuman-trafficking-and-sporting_b_58a25412e4b0e172783a9fd7.

Hepburn, Stephanie, and Rita Simon. 2013. *Human Trafficking around the World: Hidden in Plain Sight*. New York: Columbia University Press.

Morrow, Katherine L. 2008. "Soccer, Sex, and Slavery: Human Trafficking the World Cup Comment." *Tulane Journal of International and Comparative Law* 17: 243–66.

Shelley, Louise. 2014. *Human Smuggling and Trafficking into Europe: A Comparative Perspective*. Washington, DC: Migration Policy Institute.

U.S. Department of State. 2018. "Trafficking in Persons Report." Washington, DC. https://www.state.gov/reports/2018-trafficking-in-persons-report/.

IRAQ

Iraq is a Middle Eastern country located south of Turkey, north of Kuwait and Saudi Arabia, west of Iran, and east of Syria and Jordan. The desert environment of Iraq is rich with oil reserves, which provide much of the country's revenues. The gross domestic product is USD 16,700, which is much lower than Turkey (USD 27,000) or Iran (USD 20,100). Iraq has a population of just over forty million people, the majority of whom are Arab, although there is a sizable Kurdish minority. Islam is the official state religion, and roughly 70 percent of the population affiliates as Shiite, while the rest are Sunni Muslims, except for a very small Christian population (Central Intelligence Agency 2018).

Iraq gained independence from the United Kingdom in 1932 and was subsequently ruled primarily by dictators, including Saddam Hussein (1937–2006), who was president from 1979 until 2003. From 1980 until the present time, Iraq has been involved in several international wars and internal insurgencies, creating a very unstable political environment. These conflicts created a large number of displaced people from Iraq, as well as from the ongoing civil war in neighboring Syria. Displacement increases the risks for domestic human trafficking in Iraq, and the use of foreign laborers to rebuild the country increases the risks for international trafficking.

Portrait of Human Trafficking

Iraq has experienced a series of violent conflicts including the Iran–Iraq War (1980–1988); Iraq's invasion of its southern neighbor Kuwait that led to the First Gulf War (1990–1991) with the United States and its allies; the Second Gulf War with the United States (2003–2009) that led to the capture and execution of Saddam Hussein and continuing insurgent violence after U.S. forces withdrew in 2011; and a civil war with the Islamic State of Iraq and ash-Sham (ISIS, also known as ISIL) since 2014. According to the USA for UNHCR (2018), 1.8 million Iraqis who were forced from their homes due to conflict or disaster are still in Iraq, known as internally displaced persons, and 360,000 Iraqis are refugees in other countries. Additionally, there are 280,000 refugees from other countries living in Iraq, most of whom fled the war in Syria.

Displaced persons are particularly vulnerable to exploitation, but so are other people suffering from poverty and poor living conditions due to persistent violence. For example, destitute families have been known to sell children for sexual exploitation or adoption. Iraqi children are subjected to forced begging or

Forced begging and forced labor are recognized as forms of exploitation covered under the Palermo Protocol. Children are particularly vulnerable to these types of human trafficking. (Kay Chernush for the U.S. State Department)

recruitment as soldiers by insurgent groups not yet under the full control of the Iraqi government. Child labor is also prevalent in Iraq, with about 12 percent of five- to fourteen-year-olds working (Hepburn and Simon 2013). Women and children are also trafficked internally and internationally for sexual exploitation. The practice of "temporary marriage," which is a traditional Islamic practice to bless a relationship, is used to manipulate families and young women into sex work. Women and girls trafficked outside of the country typically go to other Middle Eastern countries or Europe. Forced labor usually involves foreigners from East Africa and East Asia who work in construction, security, and domestic labor in Iraq.

The U.S. Department of State ranked Iraq as a Tier 2 country, meaning that it has some legislation and practices to combat human trafficking, but it is not fully compliant with international standards. In 2012, Iraq passed a human trafficking law that covers both sex and labor exploitation. People convicted under this law can face up to fifteen years in prison or a fine of up to USD 8,580 for charges involving adult male victims and up to life in prison and fines ranging from USD 12,680 to 21,440 for cases involving adult female victims or child victims.

The Iraqi human trafficking law does not criminalize all forms of child trafficking as children must be sold to qualify as victims and must experience force, coercion, or fraud, which is not required under international child trafficking laws. The Iraqi law is also difficult to implement because it mandates establishing that victims suffered "material or moral damage" (Hepburn and Simon 2013). Only judges have the authority to certify victims of human trafficking after they have testified in court in front of the accused, which many victims choose not to do for fear of retaliation.

In 2017, the Iraqi government reported that police investigated 266 possible human trafficking cases, but determined that only 108 actually involved human trafficking. Of those cases, forty were for forced labor and sixty-eight for sex trafficking. The government prosecuted sixty-eight people in those cases and convicted twenty-two. They also identified forty-one victims of trafficking, seven of whom were children, twenty-two were female, and twelve were male. In 2016, the Iraqi government established separate courts for human trafficking cases, but the Higher Judicial Council repealed that act in 2017.

The most severe criticism of Iraq's approach to human trafficking is its tendency to punish victims of these crimes. Both adults and children who experienced sexual exploitation can face prostitution charges that carry a prison term of fifteen years to life. Victims of labor exploitation usually have to pay fines for violating immigration laws. Additionally, child soldiers are often incarcerated for terrorism-related crimes.

Labor Trafficking of Third-Country Nationals

During the U.S. occupation of Iraq from 2003 to 2011, the U.S. Department of Defense contracted with a company called KBR, a subsidiary of the controversial

Halliburton corporation, to provide civilian support to the U.S. military. While this practice has existed for decades, the Iraq conflict was the first time that contractors outnumbered soldiers. In 2011, there were 64,000 people employed by private contractors in Iraq and 57 percent were third-country nationals (TCNs), that is, non-American foreigners. TCNs typically perform low-wage, menial jobs at military bases, such as food service, cleaning, and construction. What seems like a legitimate employment opportunity can be easily exploited by recruiters. Recruitment agents typically charge a fee of USD 1,000–5,000 to find employment for the laborer. For people from many East African and East Asian countries, this is an enormous amount of money that often has to be borrowed from illegal lenders. Laborers often voluntarily agree to work for the contract company and sign an employment contract. They are often told by recruiters that they will be working in the UAE or Jordan. If they want to leave once they realize that they are going to work in Iraq, they are either financially unable to do so because of the debt they owe for the recruitment fee or they are not allowed to leave because their passports are confiscated. TCNs work twelve to sixteen hours a day for low wages. They are housed in "man camps" that are overcrowded and unsanitary. They are often not allowed to leave camps except to work, and there have been reports of physical and verbal abuse.

When the conditions of TCNs became public and their situation was called "debt bondage," the U.S. contractor KRB denied responsibility because they subcontracted the recruitment of TCNs to over 200 companies in the Middle East. The Iraqi government responded by implementing an online visa system to better track migrant workers and to standardize employment contracts to include information about labor rights. In 2017, Iraq suspended fifteen migrant recruitment companies, put five more on a blacklist, and fined seven others for labor and trafficking violations (U.S. Department of State 2018).

Terrorism and Human Trafficking

The Islamic State of Iraq (ISI) is an umbrella terrorist organization formed by al-Qaeda in Iraq in 2006. In 2013, the forces in Iraq and Syria joined together to form ISIS and launched a series of successful military attacks in both countries. By 2014, ISIS controlled 81,000 square miles of territory across both countries and declared itself an independent nation, the Islamic State (BBC News 2015). ISIS could recruit soldiers from a number of Muslim countries due, in part, to its religious mission, but also because it has been able to provide a reasonable standard of living for its followers. Soldiers earn USD 200–600 a month and ISIS leaders also provide basic social services. All of the funding for ISIS comes from foreign support, looting conquered territory, and illegal activities (Bésenyő 2016).

ISIS has engaged in a very public human trafficking campaign that includes both organ trafficking and sex trafficking of women and girls, primarily "non-believers." Experts estimated that ISIS captured 3,000 women and girls in 2014 alone and approximately 25,000 in total (Kennedy 2016). These women and girls have been

Yazidi Nobel Recipient

Nadia Murad was the co-recipient of the 2018 Nobel Peace Prize for her humanitarian work to help abused and trafficked women and children and to bring attention to the use of sexual violence as a weapon of war. Murad is a Yazidi from northern Iraq whose village was attacked by ISIS in 2014. Her family was killed and she and other females were kidnapped and held captive as sex slaves. She escaped to a refugee camp and eventually found safety in Germany. She runs a nongovernmental organization called Nadia's Initiative to offer assistance to victims of abuse and help rebuild the Yazidi community in Iraq.

sexually abused and sold to soldiers from Syria, Saudi Arabia, Qatar, Chechnya, and Afghanistan. ISIS makes approximately USD 3 million per day through human trafficking. The Yazidi, who practice their own religion and live primarily in northern Iraq, were intentionally and brutally targeted by ISIS. Not only is human trafficking lucrative to fund terrorism it is also a tool of intimidation to prevent opposition to ISIS incursion. Although international forces have recovered the territory once claimed by ISIS, the organization is still functioning.

Further Reading

BBC News. 2015. "What Is 'Islamic State'?" December 2, 2015, sec. Middle East. https://www.bbc.com/news/world-middle-east-29052144.

Bésenyő, János. 2016. "The Islamic State and Its Human Trafficking Practice." *Impact Strategic* 60, no. 3: 15–21.

Brown, Amy Kathryn. 2007. "Baghdad Bound: Forced Labor of Third-Country Nationals in Iraq Notes." *Rutgers Law Review* 60: 737–68.

Central Intelligence Agency. 2018. "The World Factbook." https://www.cia.gov/library/publications/resources/the-world-factbook/.

Hepburn, Stephanie, and Rita J. Simon. 2013. *Human Trafficking around the World: Hidden in Plain Sight.* New York: Columbia University Press.

Kennedy, Paloma A. 2016. "Human Trafficking Waivers." *Women Lawyers Journal* 101: 11–25.

U.S. Department of State. 2018. "Trafficking in Persons Report." Washington, DC. https://www.state.gov/reports/2018-trafficking-in-persons-report/.

USA for UNHCR: The UN Refugee Agency. 2018. "Iraq Refugee Crisis: Aid, Statistics and News." 2018. https://www.unrefugees.org/emergencies/iraq/.

ITALY

Italy is a country of sixty-two million people located in Southern Europe. The boot-shaped country extends into the Mediterranean Sea. It lies south of Switzerland and France, north of Africa, and west of the Adriatic Sea from Croatia, Bosnia-Herzegovina, and Albania. Italy has been a parliamentary democracy since 1946 after the defeat of the fascist regime of Benito Mussolini (1883–1945). It was a founding member of the European Union, a political and economic alliance of twenty-eight countries. Italy is a relatively wealthy country with a gross domestic product of USD 38,200 due to an economy supported primarily by manufacturing in the north and agriculture in the south. Italy has been a party to the Schengen Agreement since 1990, which is an arrangement of fairly open mutual borders among twenty-six European countries. Italy's central location surrounded by Western Europe, southeastern Europe, Africa, and the Middle East, along with over 4,660 miles of coastline, contribute to fairly high volumes of irregular immigration, including human trafficking.

Migration Patterns

Historically, Italy was known as a country of emigration, with thirteen million Italians leaving the country between 1880 and 1915 in search of better economic opportunities in North America and other European countries (Scotto 2017). However, since the 1970s, the flow of migration has shifted to Italy rather than from it. In the 1990s, immigration to Italy increased significantly with the fall of communism in Eastern Europe. People fleeing political and economic uncertainty, especially in Albania and Romania, went to Italy in search of employment. Around the same time, an aging Italian population increased the need for foreign workers, particularly for domestic labor, construction, and farming. In 2002, foreigners comprised 2.7 percent of Italy's population, which increased to 5 percent in 2006 and 7.5 percent in 2010 (Scotto 2017). In the twenty-first century, a large number of migrants from Africa and the Middle East started arriving in Italy, with many seeking political asylum from conflicts in Libya, Tunisia, and Syria, although there were also many immigrants from other African countries, such as Nigeria. By 2017, there were 5.9 million foreigners living in Italy, about 10 percent of the population. About half of the migrants to Italy are female and about 17 percent are minors. The number of refugees seeking asylum increased from 5,500 in 1998 to 147,400 in 2016. The majority of migrants (51.6 percent) were from Europe, 20.8 percent from Africa, 20.3 percent from Asia, and 7.3 percent from the Americas (GMDAC 2019).

Immigration statistics document known, typically legal, immigrants, but there is no reliable way to measure irregular migration, which simply means that at some point in the migration process the rules were not followed. For example, a person may have legal permission to live in a country, but not to work there, so if they got a job, their migration status is irregular. Smuggling and human trafficking are also forms of irregular migration. Experts in human trafficking have wrestled with the problem of distinguishing human trafficking from other types of irregular migration and there are no clear ways to do that until the cases are investigated to clarify the nature of the migratory process. To understand human trafficking in Italy, it is important to consider the overall migration picture because the large inflows of legal migrants often produce illegal opportunities for migration. In addition, the extensive law enforcement, legal, and social resources dedicated to regular migration strains government efforts to deal with exploitative migration, such as human trafficking.

Types of Human Trafficking

Italy is home to both domestic and international trafficking, although many research and policy reports have emphasized international trafficking because of overall migration patterns. It is both a destination and a transit country, primarily serving as a conduit to other Schengen countries. Migrant sea crossings to Italy and Greece have received significant media attention. It only takes about two days for people to travel from the coast of North Africa to Sicily in southern Italy. There are also two common land routes to Italy. One originates in southeastern Europe, and people who take this route are often accompanied by someone from their home country. The other route originates either in Turkey or northern Europe and moves through the Balkans to reach Italy. This passage is usually controlled by Italians who act as agents to move people across borders.

Trafficked workers who stay in southern Italy typically harvest crops in the agricultural industry. In other parts of the country, laborers work in the textile industry, construction, and elder and childcare. Domestic workers typically come from Romania, Ukraine, Moldova, Albania, the Philippines, India, Peru, and Ecuador. Italy has a large Nigerian diaspora, and it is estimated that half of all prostitutes in Italy are Nigerian (Shelley 2014). Prostitution is legal in Italy, but sexual exploitation is not. The International Organization for Migration (IOM) has raised concerns that the majority of women and girls from Nigeria who arrive by sea are likely victims of sexual exploitation. However, until cases are investigated by police, it is difficult to distinguish prostitution from human trafficking.

In 2017, the Italian Department of Equal Opportunity documented 1,354 potential trafficking victims, with 71 percent from Nigeria. Less than 15 percent of the victims were subjected to labor exploitation or forced begging. Most identified victims were female (84 percent) and 11 percent were children. In the same year, police investigated 482 potential trafficking offenders and arrested thirty-three. Of those arrested, seventy-three were indicted and twenty-eight were convicted. A typical sentence for trafficking offenders was seven or eight years in prison (U.S. Department of State 2018).

Legal Responses to Trafficking

Prior to 2003, human trafficking cases fell under two existing laws in Italy's criminal code. Act 79, originally passed in 1958, makes recruitment of people in Italy or abroad for the purpose of sexual exploitation illegal. Another law adopted in 1998 made the recruitment of children for sexual exploitation illegal to be consistent with the United Nations Convention on the Rights of the Child. Importantly, these laws did not address labor trafficking. A study of legal proceedings under these older laws between 1996 and 2003 identified a total of 2,930 cases of human trafficking. The majority of victims in these cases were female (81 percent) and primarily from Albania (25 percent), Romania (10 percent), Nigeria (10 percent), and Moldova (6 percent). The large number of female victims is not surprising given the focus of these laws on sexual exploitation. Of the identified male victims,

17 percent were from Albania, 17 percent from Romania, 10 percent from the former Yugoslavia, and 9 percent from China (Curtol et al. 2004).

In 2003, Italy passed the Measures against Trafficking in Persons Law (Act 228) that explicitly criminalized both sexual and labor exploitation and emphasized the use of deception, force, and abuse of authority to obtain compliance from victims. This definition of human trafficking is consistent with international standards. The law specifies punishment for these crimes of eight to twenty years in prison. Penalties can be increased if the victims are under eighteen years old, or if the trafficking involves prostitution or organ removal.

Under the Consolidated Text of the Law on Immigration, victims of human trafficking are granted six-month residency and work permits that can be renewed if the person is employed or participating in formal job training. Victims can apply for these permits directly with the police or they can approach a nongovernmental organization that files paperwork on their behalf. Obtaining these permits is not dependent upon victims sharing information about their traffickers with the police. Between 1998 and 2000, Italy issued 726 temporary residency permits to victims, mostly from Eastern Europe (Curtol et al. 2004). In 2017, the country dispensed 418 temporary permits, 36 percent of which were given to Nigerians (U.S. Department of State 2018). Child victims automatically receive a residency permit until eighteen years of age, plus housing in a children's center, counseling, and schooling.

In response to concerns about the growing number of immigrants, a new law was passed at the end of 2018 that changed Italy's rather generous response to human trafficking victims and refugees. The humanitarian residency permits that were once given unconditionally to human trafficking victims are now only awarded if victims identify their trafficker or enter a psychological counseling program. The new law is an amendment to the previous Law on Immigration, but it is referred to as the "Salvini decree," after the Minister of Interior, Matteo Salvini, who sponsored the legislative changes. Migrants who are not eligible for refugee status are no longer eligible for these humanitarian residency permits.

It is not yet clear what the overall effect of this new law will be on human trafficking prevention and protection in Italy. As of 2017, Italy was rated a Tier 1 country in the U.S. State Department's TIP report because it fully met the minimum standards for human trafficking legislation and responses. However, the report noted some areas in need of improvement, such as underfunded nongovernmental organizations, inconsistent law enforcement training to identify human trafficking victims, and more language support for victims from African countries. On a positive note, Italy organized an exchange program with twenty-two African countries for prosecutors to come to Italy to work with domestic prosecutors on human trafficking cases for six months.

Further Reading

Central Intelligence Agency. 2018. "The World Factbook." https://www.cia.gov/library/publications/resources/the-world-factbook/.

Curtol, F., S. Decarli, A. Di Nicola, and E.U. Savona. 2004. "Victims of Human Trafficking in Italy: A Judicial Perspective." *International Review of Victimology* 11 (1): 111–41. https://doi.org/10.1177/026975800401100107.

GMDAC (International Organization for Migration Global Migration Data Analysis Centre). 2019. "Global Migration Data Portal." https://migrationdataportal.org/.

Scotto, Angelo. 2017. "From Emigration to Asylum Destination, Italy Navigates Shifting Migration Tides." Migrationpolicy.Org, August 22, 2017. https://www.migrationpolicy.org/article/emigration-asylum-destination-italy-navigates-shifting-migration-tides

Shelley, Louise. 2014. *Human Smuggling and Trafficking into Europe: A Comparative Perspective*. Washington, DC: Migration Policy Institute.

U.S. Department of State. 2018. "Trafficking in Persons Report." Washington, DC. https://www.state.gov/reports/2018-trafficking-in-persons-report/.

MALAWI

Malawi is a relatively small, landlocked country in southern Africa, just south of Tanzania, east of Zambia, and north and west of Mozambique. Much of the eastern border of the country is defined by Lake Malawi, which is a tourist destination for foreigners and, therefore, is a factor in facilitating human trafficking in the country. The population of nearly twenty million people includes various ethnic and religious groups, although the majority is Christian. High fertility rates and low life expectancy mean there is a large percentage of population less than twenty-five years old (67 percent). Malawi has a poorly developed economy that relies mostly on agricultural production. The gross domestic product per capita is USD 1,200, less than one-third of that of its neighbors Zambia and Tanzania. Nearly 51 percent of the population lives below the poverty line (Central Intelligence Agency 2018). Extreme poverty is a driving factor for both sexual and labor exploitation in Malawi.

Portrait of Human Trafficking

Malawi is primarily a source country for both sex and labor trafficking, with most of the human trafficking being domestic. Women and young girls are sold by their families or work in the sex industry out of sheer financial necessity. Men, women, and children are also victims of forced labor, as people from the southern part of the country are trafficked north to work in agriculture, herding, and brickmaking. Children are likely found begging, working for small businesses, or working in the fishing industry. There are also concerns about child sex tourism along the coast of Lake Malawi. Females are also trafficked abroad for sexual exploitation, typically to Europe, Gulf nations, or within Africa to Zimbabwe or South Africa.

Malawi passed its first antitrafficking law in 2015, which criminalized both labor and sex trafficking and imposed a penalty of up to life imprisonment for convicted offenders. The country also developed a five-year action plan to combat trafficking in 2017, with the goal of reducing the problem up to half by 2022. The top priorities that the government identified were to train professionals to better identify victims of human trafficking and to improve victim services. The country also needs a comprehensive monitoring and data collection system to track human trafficking cases, victim services, and criminal justice responses.

In 2017, Malawi reported that it had arrested forty-two suspects on human trafficking violations, but data were only reported for seven of the country's thirty-four administrative districts. Of those arrests, twenty-six people were prosecuted and convicted. The country also reported 121 victims, 71 percent of whom were adults (mostly women), and 24 percent were foreigners from Kenya, South Africa, Saudi Arabia, and Iraq (U.S. Department of State 2018).

Given these recent efforts to address human trafficking in accordance with international standards, Malawi is ranked as a Tier 2 country by the U.S. Department of State. The report recommended that Malawi fully implement its new human trafficking law and aggressively prosecute offenders. The United States also encouraged the government to follow its plan to improve training for law enforcement, prosecution, judges, and labor inspectors, and to develop a national reporting system. In the long term, the United States encouraged the country to consider ways to reduce the demand for sex trafficking and labor exploitation.

Sexual Exploitation

It is estimated that there were approximately 19,000 sex workers in Malawi in 2011, most of whom were female (Chizima and Malera 2011). Prostitution is not illegal in Malawi, although the law criminalizes third parties who are involved in facilitating sex work, such as pimps or traffickers. A study of sex workers in ten districts in the country found that 3.3 percent admitted that they were trafficked. Although the majority of sex work is legal, it raises health concerns due to infectious diseases and violence. Nearly two-thirds of sex workers in this study experienced some kind of abuse and were willing to disclose it to the researchers. Almost half of those abused encountered physical assault, 28 percent suffered rape, and 12 percent were victims of emotional abuse (Chizimba and Malera 2011). Additionally, Malawi has the ninth highest rate of human immunodeficiency virus (HIV) in the world, with 9.2 percent of the population aged fifteen to forty-nine living with the disease (Central Intelligence Agency 2018). It is estimated that the rate of HIV exposure among sex workers is at least ten times higher than the general population (Chizimba and Malera 2011).

There are economic, cultural, and legal factors that contribute to the prevalence of sex work in Malawi, both legal and illegal. The high death rate from HIV leaves many children orphaned and forced to find ways to support themselves. The poor economic conditions in the country mean that desperate families sell young girls and women for marriage, which is reinforced by cultural traditions that condone this practice. Young girls are sexualized early and taught to please men physically and materially. About 12 percent of girls marry by fifteen and 50 percent before eighteen years of age (Mwambene 2018). This practice was legal until Malawi amended its constitution in 2017 to make eighteen years the legal age for both men and women to marry. However, only 3 percent of the population registers

The high rate of HIV/AIDS in Malawi has left many children orphaned and poor, creating conditions ripe for exploitation. Orphans are vulnerable to both sexual exploitation and forced labor. (Flickr/KHym54)

births, so few people have legal documentation of their age, which makes this law difficult to enforce. These practices limit women's educational and occupational opportunities, making them more vulnerable to sex work. They also create opportunities for sexual exploitation. Traffickers make marriage offers to families who do not suspect their real motives. Rather than marriage, young women and girls are forced into prostitution.

Other trafficking networks are run by Nigerian organized crime groups. Recruiters are often local businesswomen who approach young women in markets, night clubs, or hotels and offer them jobs in Europe working at restaurants, hair salons, shopping malls, or homes as domestic workers. Once women accept the offers, they are kept in transit homes in the capital city of Lilongwe waiting to travel to Europe. Traffickers provide fraudulent travel documents and the women are usually sent to Belgium, Germany, or Italy where they are sold to Nigerian traffickers. The women are told that they must pay the debt for their travel to the traffickers with sex work. They are coerced into compliance with beatings and with customary, "magical" rituals designed to bond women to their traffickers through fears of the supernatural.

Women are also trafficked to other southern African countries for sexual exploitation. Once again, Malawian businesswomen often act as recruiters, but truck drivers also recruit women along their routes with either false promises of marriage or employment. Women are transported over land in these cases. Porous borders with neighboring countries allow women to travel without documentation. Once they arrive at their destination countries, they are coerced into sex work through fear of being exposed to the police because of their illegal immigration status.

Child Labor

Less is known about forced labor in Malawi compared to sexual exploitation, although child labor is a well-known problem that can facilitate labor trafficking. According to the U.S. Department of Labor (2018), nearly two million children aged five to fourteen years were working in Malawi in 2015, which was 43.2 percent of the children in that age group. Of those children, 67.7 percent were working in agriculture, despite a law stating that it is illegal for children under fourteen years old to work in that industry. Children are involved in the production of tea, sugar, and tobacco, and the latter is the industry most often suspected of forced labor. Children are tasked with cleaning and digging fields, making nursery beds, cutting trees, irrigating fields, applying fertilizer and pesticides, picking leaves, sorting leaves, and carrying bales. These children are exposed to hazardous substances and unhygienic conditions including unsafe drinking water.

Almost 31 percent of children under fourteen years of age work in the service industry, typically begging or selling goods. Most of these children work to support themselves and their families. The large number of children orphaned due to HIV and other health problems in Malawi makes them particularly vulnerable to exploitation, although the number of children who are victims of labor trafficking in these situations has not been well established. In 2010, Malawi passed the Child Care Protection and Justice Act to better protect children under sixteen years old from illegal labor practices and sexual exploitation. This law clearly makes child trafficking a crime punishable by up to life in prison. It also criminalizes forced marriage and forced labor of children with up to ten years in prison.

Further Reading

Central Intelligence Agency. 2018. "The World Factbook." https://www.cia.gov/library/publications/resources/the-world-factbook/.

Chizimba, Robert Mthenga, and Grace Tikambenji Malera. 2011. *Counting the Untouchables*. Lilongwe, Malawi: Family Planning Association of Malawi.

Martens, Jonathan, Maciej Pieczkowski, and Bernadette van Vuuren-Smyth. 2003. *Trafficking in Women & Children for Sexual Exploitation in Southern Africa*. Pretoria, South Africa: International Organization for Migration (IOM) Regional Office for Southern Africa.

Mwambene, Lea. 2018. "Recent Legal Responses to Child Marriage in Southern Africa: The Case of Zimbabwe, South Africa and Malawi." *African Human Rights Law Journal* 18 (2): 527–50. https://doi.org/10.17159/1996-2096/2018/v18n2a5.

Mwangonde, Martha Sika. n.d. "National Legislation, Policy and Strategy on Child Labour in Malawi—Identifying the Gaps." Lilongwe, Malawi: National Conference in Eliminating Child Labour in Agriculture.

U.S. Department of Labor, Bureau of International Labor Affairs. 2018. "Findings on the Worst Forms of Child Labor—Malawi." https://www.dol.gov/agencies/ilab/resources /reports/child-labor/malawi.

U.S. Department of State. 2018. "Trafficking in Persons Report." Washington, DC. https:// www.state.gov/reports/2018-trafficking-in-persons-report/.

MOLDOVA

Moldova is a landlocked country in Central Eastern Europe between Romania and Ukraine. In the nineteenth century, the territory shifted between being part of the Russian Empire and being part of Romania. In 1924, it became an autonomous republic within the communist Soviet Union. Of the population of 3.4 million people, 80.2 percent speak the same language, although some call it Moldovan and others call it Romanian. There are also cultural and religious ties between the Romanians and Moldovans including the fact that the majority of people in both countries are Eastern Orthodox Christians (Central Intelligence Agency 2018).

Moldova declared independence in 1991 when the Soviet Union dissolved with the end of communism in Eastern Europe. Independence has been rife with political conflict and economic crises. The country adopted free-market economic reforms to move from a communist command economy to capitalism, which caused severe financial hardship for most Moldovans. Moldova is the poorest country in Europe with a gross domestic product per capita of USD 6,700, which is comparable to Vietnam, Angola, and Myanmar, and significantly lower than the second poorest country in Europe, Ukraine, with a gross domestic product per capita of USD 8,800 (Central Intelligence Agency 2018). The poor economic conditions in the country have prompted many Moldovans to search for work abroad, which makes them susceptible to exploitation.

The State of Human Trafficking

Moldova is primarily a source country for labor and sex trafficking to Russia, Ukraine, Western Europe, the Middle East, and East Asia. Most of the research about and assistance initiatives for Moldovan trafficking victims focus mainly on women and children. Of the female victims who have been identified by the IOM, 68.3 percent were single, 68.2 percent were unemployed, and 67.5 percent were from rural areas at the time of being trafficked (Ostrovschi et al. 2011). Over 80 percent of female victims were trafficked for sexual exploitation, and 27.5 percent were exploited for over a year. Women who were victims of labor trafficking typically worked in agriculture, begging, or domestic service. Almost 40 percent of them had gone to Turkey, 27.5 percent to Russia, and 11.6 percent to European Union countries (Oram et al. 2012).

In 2005, Moldova passed the Law on Preventing and Combatting Trafficking in Human Beings and established a biennial National Action Plan to specify short-term and long-term goals for addressing this problem. Articles 165 and 206 of the Criminal Code criminalize all forms of human trafficking. Convicted offenders are subject to five-to-twelve years in prison for cases involving adult victims, eight-to-twelve years for cases with child victims, and up to twenty years for aggravating circumstances, such as grave injury or death of the victim. Article 169 of the Criminal Code also criminalizes forced labor with a sentence of up to three years in prison.

In 2017, the Moldovan police investigated 185 cases of human trafficking. Eighty-five of them led to indictments and fifty-eight to convictions. Of those convicted, fifty-two received a prison sentence, with an average duration ranging between eight and thirteen years. The police also identified 249 victims, of which forty-eight were children. The government provided shelter for assisted with repatriation for 117 victims (U.S. Department of State 2018). Victims are permitted to file civil lawsuits against their perpetrators for compensation of the harm they experienced and for lost wages; fifty-nine victims did so in 2017. In 2018, Moldova passed Law 137 that allows victims to seek restitution from the government if they cannot obtain it from convicted offenders.

Corruption as an Obstacle

Moldova is known as one of the most corrupt countries in Europe, which is a key factor preventing the country from joining the European Union. Between 2009 and 2019, Moldova became an oligarchy, where political power was heavily concentrated among a small number of people who used that power to increase their personal wealth. One of the richest people in the country, business owner Vladimir Plahotniuc (1966–), served three terms as a member of parliament and gained control over the judiciary, the national bank, fiscal and customs services, the Ministry of Internal Affairs, and the police. He manipulated these agencies to suppress his political opponents and to secure his business interests (Całus 2016). As a result of this deep-rooted corruption and weak state control, it is very difficult for Moldova to rely on the police and the judicial system to effectively control crime, especially complex and lucrative crimes such as human trafficking.

To make matters worse, a large part of the eastern border with Ukraine called Transnistria declared independence from Moldova because the predominantly Slavic population worried that their languages and cultures would be lost in Moldova. Moldova and Transnistria fought a brief war in 1992 that did not resolve the conflict. Moldova now considers Transnistria an autonomous territory within the country, but Transnistria has declared itself an independent state. It has established its own government, although it is not recognized by any other legitimate country, including Ukraine or Russia, which have sizable minority populations in the area. As a result of this confusing legal status, this break-away region has become a haven for illegal activities, such as drugs, arms, and human trafficking. High levels of corruption in Moldova, Transnistria, and Ukraine allow these activities to flourish.

Areas of Improvement

The U.S. Department of State (2018) rated Moldova as a Tier 2 country that does not yet meet the minimum international standards to fight trafficking, but that has made important strides in this area. The TIP report noted two main areas that needed further attention from the Moldovan government. The first is the problem of corruption. Within the civil service and the criminal justice system, corrupt officials either hinder prosecution or influence the outcomes of trafficking cases. For example, in 2014, it was discovered that Russian organized crime groups and politicians were laundering money through Moldovan banks between 2010 and 2014. To disguise some of these transactions, about two dozen Moldovan judges issued court orders for loan agencies to pay off bad debts that did not exist. Such cases are frequent in Moldova and erode citizens' faith in the judiciary.

The second area of improvement was better victim identification, protection, and assistance. Victims who are identified in human trafficking cases are not prosecuted for any crimes related to their trafficking experiences; however, trafficking victims can be prosecuted for immigration violations or prostitution if their case is charged under a related statute. Prosecutors are not well equipped to handle complicated trafficking cases, especially involving foreigners. Additionally, in 2016, the Constitutional Court ruled that suspects could not be detained for more than one year awaiting trial. Investigations of human trafficking cases are often slow, which means that offenders can be released and leave the country before standing trial.

Moldova has seven shelters for all victims of crime and family violence, but social worker capacities are often not sufficient to deal with all the needs of human trafficking victims. One study found that 48.3 percent of female trafficking victims identified by the IOM suffered from posttraumatic stress disorder (PTSD), 7 percent from alcohol dependence, and 5.8 percent from substance abuse (Ostrovschi et al. 2011). Victims can apply for assistance from the IOM, which includes crisis intervention; medical, psychological, legal, and social assistance; and temporary housing. The nongovernmental organization called the International Centre for Protection and Promotion of Women's Rights ("La Strada") also operates in Moldova. However, without the help of these organizations, victims do not have proper legal assistance and are often not informed of their legal rights. They are also required to confront their traffickers in person at a police station before a formal investigation can begin.

As part of its European Neighborhood Policy, the European Union has also provided Moldova assistance in dealing with human trafficking. In particular, the European Union has offered advice on judicial and legislative matters and border management. Moldova has also embraced technological assistance to fight trafficking. For example, they have been one of the first countries to adopt a blockchain digital identity system to record undocumented children who are especially vulnerable to many forms of exploitation. Finally, the country's national strategic plan to prevent trafficking recognizes the need to address the root social causes of the crime, including poverty, poor education, and discrimination against women and minorities.

Further Reading

Całus, Kamil. 2016. *Moldova: From Oligarchic Pluralism to Plahotniuc's Hegemony*. OSW Commentary 208. Warsaw, Poland: Centre for Eastern Studies.

Central Intelligence Agency. 2018. "The World Factbook." https://www.cia.gov/library/publications/resources/the-world-factbook/.

Nanu, Cezara. 2010. "Preventing Trafficking in Human Beings: The Case of Moldova." In *Human Trafficking in Europe: Character, Causes and Consequences*, edited by Gillian Wylie and Penelope McRedmond, 142–63. London: Palgrave Macmillan. https://doi.org/10.1057/9780230281721_10.

Oram, Siân, Nicolae V. Ostrovschi, Viorel I. Gorceag, Mihai A. Hotineanu, Lilia Gorceag, Carolina Trigub, and Melanie Abas. 2012. "Physical Health Symptoms Reported by Trafficked Women Receiving Post-Trafficking Support in Moldova: Prevalence, Severity and Associated Factors." *BMC Women's Health* 12 (1): 20. https://doi.org/10.1186/1472-6874-12-20.

Ostrovschi, Nicolae V., Martin J. Prince, Cathy Zimmerman, Mihai A. Hotineanu, Lilia T. Gorceag, Viorel I. Gorceag, Clare Flach, and Melanie A. Abas. 2011. "Women in Post-Trafficking Services in Moldova: Diagnostic Interviews over Two Time Periods to Assess Returning Women's Mental Health." *BMC Public Health* 11 (1): 232. https://doi.org/10.1186/1471-2458-11-232.

U.S. Department of State. 2018. "Trafficking in Persons Report." Washington, DC. https://www.state.gov/reports/2018-trafficking-in-persons-report/.

THAILAND

Thailand is a country in Southeast Asia bordering Myanmar (Burma) to the north, Laos to the north and east, and Cambodia and Malaysia to the south. There are over sixty-eight million people in Thailand, 97.5 percent of whom are Thai and 94.6 percent are Buddhist. Thailand is also home to "hill tribes," indigenous groups who typically lack citizenship, and to about 3 to 4.5 million migrants. Thailand is formally a constitutional monarchy, but it has been under the rule of the military since 2014. The country has had a growing economy since the 1980s, with some slow periods due to political unrest. Its gross domestic product per capita of USD 17,900 is much higher than most of its neighbors, but lower than Malaysia (USD 29,100). The relatively high level of economic development compared to its neighbors, plus large numbers of displaced persons in neighboring countries, and porous borders, create conditions conducive to human trafficking in Thailand.

Portrait of Human Trafficking

Thailand is known as a source, transit, and destination country for domestic and international labor and sex trafficking. Male and female adults and children from Thailand, other Southeast Asian countries, Sri Lanka, Russia, Uzbekistan, and some African countries are exploited for both labor and sex in Thailand. Labor trafficking is most common in commercial fishing, poultry, manufacturing, agriculture, domestic work, and forced begging. Prostitution is pervasive in Thailand, creating opportunities for sexual exploitation, especially among women and children. Children from Thailand, Burma, Laos, and Cambodia engage in sex work in brothels, massage parlors, hotels, and private residences. Sex tourism is also a documented problem in Thailand, often involving children.

Thailand passed an antitrafficking law that criminalized both sex and labor trafficking with punishments of up to twelve years in prison and fines up to USD 36,810 for adult victims and up to twenty years in prison and fines up to USD 61,350 for child victims. In 2017, it also amended the Human Trafficking Criminal Procedures Act to provide restitution and compensation to trafficking victims. In the same year, the Royal Thai Police Force created the Anti-Trafficking Task Force. The country drafted a law in 2018 to clearly define labor trafficking and to provide more protection and assistance to victims of forced labor, although it has not yet been passed.

These new laws demonstrate Thailand's commitment to addressing human trafficking, although it is still rated as a Tier 2 country by the U.S. Department of State, indicating that it is not fully compliant with international standards. The 2018 TIP report noted that Thailand needed to improve methods to identify human trafficking victims, especially among vulnerable populations, and to create an environment more supportive of victim reporting. Additionally, compensation for victims has not been distributed consistently and it is usually too low to encourage victims to cooperate with investigations. Finally, corruption is widespread in Thailand and government efforts to address its role in facilitating human trafficking still need improvement.

Thailand's human trafficking law specifies that officials who commit a trafficking offense are subjected to double the penalty. In 2017, Thailand investigated twenty-six officials for trafficking-related offenses, prosecuted seven, and convicted twelve, some of which were cases from the previous year. In 2018, the Thai government also convicted four police officers of bribery and sentenced them to five years in prison for accepting money for not charging offenders who were arrested for exploiting Rohingya migrants from Myanmar. Despite this example, the U.S. Department of State criticized the Thai government for using administrative punishments instead of criminal prosecutions in trafficking cases involving corruption.

In 2017, Thailand reported 302 trafficking investigations, 638 prosecutions, and 466 convictions. Much of the public and law enforcement attention regarding human trafficking focuses on sexual exploitation. In 2017, only 47 of the 302 human trafficking cases investigated by police involved labor trafficking. This imbalance may improve once the 2018 draft law is passed to clarify the conditions of forced labor. The Thai government also provided shelter for 450 victims in 2017, 228 of whom were foreigners. It repatriated 147 foreign victims, including thirty-six Rohingyas. It also provided witness protection services for fifty-two victims. Courts have worked to relieve the burdens of prosecution for victims. For example, most human trafficking cases are heard within six months of filing. Courts also allow video testimony from victims so that they do not have to face their perpetrators in open court (U.S. Department of State 2018).

Sex Trafficking

A seventeen-year-old Lao girl named Kitty went to Thailand on the promise of getting a well-paid job in a restaurant. Instead she was beaten and starved until she agreed to work as a prostitute in a karaoke bar. Kitty managed to escape and return to Laos, where she learned that she was pregnant and had syphilis. She went to a local nongovernmental organization called Village Focus International for assistance. That group notified the Thai police, leading to the arrest of two Thai women and one Lao national suspected of human trafficking.

Stories like Kitty's are fairly common in the media, but the extent of sex trafficking in Thailand is difficult to discern. Prostitution is criminalized under the 1996 Prevention and Suppression of Prostitution Act, yet sex work is pervasive in Thailand. Buying women for sex was common practice in the late 1800s, and by 1908 it was formally legalized in Thailand. The ability to purchase women for sex was a status symbol for some Thai men. During the World Wars and the Vietnam War, Thailand became known as a place where foreign soldiers would go for sex, giving the country a reputation for sex tourism. Sex services are commonly available in brothels, nightclubs, karaoke bars, and massage parlors, although it is rarely openly visible in the streets. Law enforcement officials often elect not to enforce the prostitution law or they receive bribes to ignore the problem. Many of the domestic and international women working in the sex industry are not trafficked, but rather knowingly engage in sex work to improve their financial circumstances, so trafficking cases usually only come to the attention of authorities if victims come forward.

There are also concerns about child sex tourism in Thailand. Some men believe that sex with a young girl can improve their virility or that underage sex workers are less likely to have HIV than older ones. In the 1980s and 1990s, stories of children sold into sex slavery were fairly common, but they seem to have declined after 2000 due to the government's efforts to address the problem, including the passage of the 2008 Anti-Trafficking Law. Most sex tourism today is arranged through the Internet, so the Royal Thai Police created an Internet Crimes against Children Task Force to tackle the problem. In 2014, the task force investigated forty-one allegations of online child exploitation and eighteen sex trafficking cases (U.S. Department of State 2018). The government also amended the criminal code to include possession and dissemination of child pornography. Finally, the government launched a large public education campaign about human trafficking, which includes information about the illegality of child sex tourism directed toward foreigners visiting Thailand.

Labor Trafficking

The large number of migrants seeking work in Thailand creates opportunities for labor exploitation. The fishing and shrimp industries have been scrutinized for forced labor and inhumane labor practices. The fishing industry accounts for about

24 percent of Thailand's gross domestic product. The country is also the world's largest exporter of shrimp and tuna fish, so the demand for cheap labor is high. However, much of the fishing industry is not regulated by Thailand's Labor Protection Act of 1998. About 30 percent of migrants working in the fishing industry reported working between nine and twelve hours per day and almost 18 percent said they worked fifteen to sixteen hours per day (Sorajjakod 2013). Thai, Burmese, Cambodian, Vietnamese, and Indonesian men and boys are most likely to be subjected to forced labor in the fishing industry. There have been reports of migrants forced to work at sea for years and of being drugged to allow them to work excessively long hours. Additionally, it is common for children to work in shrimp processing facilities.

As with sex work, it is difficult to identify labor trafficking within the context of migrant labor. One survey of migrants in Thailand found that 36 percent claimed that they felt that they could not leave their current job. About 12 percent said that they feared arrest, 7 percent reported that their documents had been confiscated, about 3 percent owed a debt to their employer or recruiter, and 2 percent feared violence (Sorajjakod 2013).

Domestic work is another area that is ripe for exploitation because there is usually not a formal contract between employers and employees. Additionally, most interactions between domestic workers and employers take place in private settings, so exploitation is harder to identify compared to other types of work. In one study of migrant domestic workers in Thailand, 53.6 percent reported being shouted at during work, 36 percent felt threatened in the workplace, 6.6 percent were hit or slapped by employers, and 6.8 percent were pushed by employers. These workers also reported incidents of inappropriate sexual behaviors. About 14 percent disclosed inappropriate touching, 5.9 percent reported sexual touching, and 1 percent revealed they had been raped. Additionally, 6.6 percent said that they had been confined against their will (Sorajjakod 2013).

The Thai government responded to reports of labor exploitation in 2017 by increasing penalties for employers of undocumented workers. It also required recruitment agencies to apply for a license, with a penalty of up to three years in prison and fines up to USD 1,840 for not registering. The government also conducts labor inspections of industries with large numbers of migrant workers. In 2017, these inspections uncovered 191 violations and led to twelve prosecutions (U.S. Department of State 2018).

Further Reading

Central Intelligence Agency. 2018. "The World Factbook." https://www.cia.gov/library /publications/resources/the-world-factbook/.

Hepburn, Stephanie, and Rita J. Simon. 2013. *Human Trafficking around the World: Hidden in Plain Sight*. New York: Columbia University Press.

Kranrattanasuit, Naparat. 2014. *ASEAN and Human Trafficking: Case Studies of Cambodia, Thailand, and Vietnam*. Leiden, the Netherlands: Martinus Nijhoff Publishers.

Ngamkham, Wassayos. n.d. "Lao Girl's Escape Leads to Arrest of Sex Trafficking Suspect." *Bangkok Post*, https://www.bangkokpost.com/thailand/general/1721451/lao-girls-escape -leads-to-arrest-of-sex-trafficking-suspect.

Sorajjakool, Siroj. 2013. *Human Trafficking in Thailand: Current Issues, Trends, and the Role of the Thai Government*. Chiang Mai, Thailand: Silkworm Books.

U.S. Department of State. 2018. "Trafficking in Persons Report." Washington, DC. https://www.state.gov/reports/2018-trafficking-in-persons-report/.

UNITED ARAB EMIRATES

UAE is a Middle Eastern country located between Oman and Saudi Arabia and across the Persian Gulf from Qatar and Iran. It is a federation of seven emirates formed between 1971 and 1972 after the British left the region. The population of 9.7 million consists of only 11.6 percent Emrati people, as the rest of the population is composed of immigrants, primarily from South Asia (59.4 percent). Islam is the official religion, with which 76 percent of the population identifies. The UAE is a wealthy country with a gross domestic product per capita of USD 68,600 compared to USD 59,800 in the United States (Central Intelligence Agency 2018). Much of the country's economic growth in its first decades after independence was based on oil and natural gas; however, the country has since diversified its economy to include tourism, real estate, and a large service sector. The two largest emirates, Abu Dhabi (the capital) and Dubai, have global reputations for elaborate architecture, including Burj Dubai, the tallest skyscraper in the world. The construction industry is a major pull factor for migrants searching for work, but the strict sponsorship system for visas leaves them vulnerable to exploitation.

Portrait of Human Trafficking

The UAE is primarily a destination country for the trafficking of men, women, and children. It is ranked as a Tier 2 country by the U.S. Department of State, which means that it does not fully comply with international standards to prevent and combat human trafficking. The country passed Federal Law 51 of 2006 and Federal Law 1 of 2015 to fully criminalize sex and labor trafficking, with penalties ranging from 1 year to life in prison and fines from USD 27,240 to 272,260. Convicted offenders who are not citizens are also deported. In 2017, UAE prosecuted forty-eight suspected traffickers in sixteen separate cases, all of which involved sexual exploitation. Of those indicted, seven were convicted (U.S. Department of State 2018).

The country has a national action plan to combat human trafficking and has developed training courses about the problem for law enforcement, civil service workers, migrant labor recruiting companies, and laborers. However, some of the legal provisions related to trafficking have not been consistently enforced and victim protections are not strong. Victims are not offered temporary or permanent residency visas, and most prefer to be deported than to testify in court. With the exception of one men's shelter in Abu Dhabi, shelters and other victims' services are designed for women and children victims of sexual exploitation.

Women and Human Trafficking

Government efforts regarding prosecutions and victim services primarily focus on sexual exploitation, although the prevalence of this problem compared to labor trafficking is not well established. The U.S. Department of State (2018) notes that women from Eastern Europe, Asia, East Africa, Iraq, Iran, and Morocco are the most likely sources of victims trafficked to the UAE for prostitution.

Prostitution is illegal in the UAE, although it is not well hidden, particularly in wealthy, cosmopolitan cities like Dubai. There are three tiers of sex workers, segregated largely by race, ethnicity, and cost. High-end sex workers have private apartments and operate out of expensive hotels, charging up to USD 3,000 per night. They are typically women from Iran, Morocco, and some parts of Eastern Europe. In the middle range are women from South and Southeast Asia, who tend to work in night clubs, brothels, or massage parlors and earn between USD 100 and 1,000 per night. Finally, street workers are likely to come from sub-Saharan Africa and their clients are likely to be wage laborers (Mahdavi 2011b).

As in all countries, identifying victims of human trafficking among sex workers is not easy to accomplish. While some women come to the UAE for legitimate work and may be tricked or coerced into prostitution, many others come to the country intentionally planning to work in the sex industry. They arrive on tourist visas and simply do not return home when they expire. Their illegal status makes it difficult for them to seek assistance from law enforcement or social services should they later encounter abuse or exploitation.

Women are more likely to be exploited in domestic work, although this issue has not received as much attention as sexual exploitation until recently. Experts estimate that over 600,000 migrants work in domestic services in the UAE (Mahdavi 2011b). Women who work as cleaners or caregivers in homes are likely to be isolated from other migrants and face higher risks of abuse given the privacy of their work environment. Until recently, domestic workers were not considered part of the labor force and, therefore, their employers were not subjected to labor laws.

Members of an Emrati royal family were caught in a scandal regarding the exploitation of domestic workers that brought international attention to the issue. In 2008, Princess Shekha Alnehayan and her seven daughters rented a luxury suite in a hotel in Brussels, Belgium for eight months. They brought over twenty servants with them, including women from the Philippines, Morocco, and Tunisia. These women worked around the clock without proper sleeping accommodations or food and they were not allowed to leave the hotel. One of the women escaped and reported her conditions to the Belgian police. In 2017, the princesses were tried in Belgium in abstentia and convicted of human trafficking and labor violations. They were sentenced to a suspended fifteen-month jail term and a USD 185,000 fine.

In response to international pressure, the UAE has taken steps to address the legal loopholes of domestic work with Federal Law 10 of 2017 that specified labor relationships for domestic workers. In particular, the law gave them the right to retain their personal documents, such as passports, the right to mandatory time-off, standardized labor contracts, and a process to resolve workplace disputes. Recruitment agencies or other persons who hinder police investigations into the exploitation of domestic workers or anyone who abandons a domestic worker is subjected to up to six months in jail and a fine ranging from USD 2,720 to 27,230. The U.S. Department of State (2018) noted that the new law has not yet been fully implemented and enforced.

Sponsorship Systems

Almost 90 percent of people working in the private sector in the UAE are foreigners, largely from South and Southeast Asia. To obtain a work visa and residency permit, foreign laborers must be sponsored by an Emrati citizen or authorized recruitment agency in a sponsorship system called *kafala*. While many workers come to the country willingly and legally, the sponsorship system creates a power imbalance that makes foreign workers vulnerable to exploitation. Employers have the right to cancel residence permits at their discretion, so the mere threat of losing their right to work coerces foreign workers to tolerate undesirable work conditions. If the worker decides to quit and break their labor contract, they are required to pay for their own transportation home, which is often too expensive for them to afford.

The construction boom in the large cities of the UAE, along with shortages of native labor, has provided numerous jobs for foreign workers. However, most of these workers come from poor countries and are vulnerable to labor exploitation. (Nigel Spiers/Dreamstime.com)

Child Camel Jockeys

In many Middle Eastern countries, it was common practice to use small children as jockeys for camel racing because they are lightweight. Many of these children were purchased from poor families in Afghanistan, Bangladesh, Pakistan, and Sudan. The children were often severely injured in riding accidents and many were poorly treated. A 2004 HBO documentary by Pakistani human rights activist Ansar Burney, which was updated in 2018, brought international attention to human trafficking and child abuse in the camel racing industry. Recently, countries in the region have been experimenting with using robots as jockeys to replace the demand for children.

As a result of a system that favors employers, there are numerous reports of labor exploitation. The most common offenses are underpaying employees, not paying overtime, withholding wages, confiscating passports, hazardous working conditions, unhygienic labor camps, and fraudulent employment contracts. The government is reluctant to intervene in legal matters with foreign recruiters, which give employers an additional advantage over workers.

In the UAE, it is illegal to retain another person's passport against their will, although this law is often not enforced. Many labor violations, such as underpayment, are treated as regulatory violations rather than as criminal offenses. The government has created an electronic Wage Protection System to monitor payments, but participation in this system by employers is voluntary. The country is also working with the governments of Thailand and the Philippines to improve the transparency and accountability of the recruiting process. However, given the large volume of foreigners willing to work in the UAE, employers do not have economic incentives to improve labor conditions. Without stricter government enforcement, the country has created a "deportation regime" where foreign workers are expendable (Mahdavi 2011a).

In 2018, law enforcement officials targeted gang involvement in human trafficking and significantly increased the number of suspects arrested. The same year the police arrested seventy-seven suspects and rescued forty-eight victims. Ten of the convicted offenders received a sentence of life in prison. The chair of the National Committee to Combat Human Trafficking credited the effectiveness of training 6,200 law enforcement and judicial personnel in identifying and processing human trafficking cases for this successful outcome.

Further Reading

Central Intelligence Agency. 2018. "The World Factbook." https://www.cia.gov/library/publications/resources/the-world-factbook/.

Degorge, Barbara. 2006. "Modern Day Slavery in the United Arab Emirates." *The European Legacy* 11 (6): 657–66. https://doi.org/10.1080/10848770600918307.

Hepburn, Stephanie, and Rita Simon. 2013. *Human Trafficking around the World: Hidden in Plain Sight.* New York: Columbia University Press.

Mahdavi, Pardis. 2011a. "'But We Can Always Get More!' Deportability, the State and Gendered Migration in the United Arab Emirates." *Asian and Pacific Migration Journal* 20 (3–4): 413–31. https://doi.org/10.1177/011719681102000308.

Mahdavi, Pardis. 2011b. *Gridlock: Labor, Migration, and Human Trafficking in Dubai.* Stanford, CA: Stanford University Press.

U.S. Department of State. 2018. "Trafficking in Persons Report." Washington, DC. https://www.state.gov/reports/2018-trafficking-in-persons-report/.

Chapter 6: Drug Use and Drug Trafficking

Janet P. Stamatel

OVERVIEW

Drugs that are regulated by governments are referred to as controlled substances. Such drugs are considered harmful or highly addictive and are typically limited to medical and scientific uses. Illicit or illegal drugs are regulated substances used outside of legal prescriptions. The most common illegal drugs, and the ones most prominent in this chapter, are cannabis, opium and opiates, opioids, coca and cocaine, and amphetamines and methamphetamines.

Cannabis is a plant that is smoked or eaten and produces euphoria, relaxation, and/or enhanced sensory experiences. It is often called marijuana, hash, hemp, or pot. It contains tetrahydrocannabinol (THC), which is a psychoactive substance. Opium is the juice from the opium poppy plant, while morphine and codeine are opiates, or natural derivatives of opium. These drugs are typically injected or consumed orally. Heroin is a semisynthetic opiate made from morphine. It is typically smoked or injected. These drugs produce euphoria, relaxation, and pain relief. Opioids are synthetic versions of morphine that were developed primarily for pain relief. They include hydrocodone, oxycodone, fentanyl, and methadone. Coca leaf from the coca bush is the source of cocaine, which is usually inhaled or injected. It produces exhilaration, alertness, and energy. Finally, amphetamine-type stimulants are mainly synthetic drugs that stimulate the central nervous system. They can be sniffed, smoked, injected, or consumed orally. Amphetamine and methamphetamine (commonly known as crystal meth, crank, or uppers) produce exhilaration, mental stimulation, and energy. Additionally, ecstasy (also known as E, XTC, or MDMA) increases feelings of empathy and sociability, as well as physical and emotional energy.

The United Nations Office on Drugs and Crime (UNODC) releases an annual report monitoring drug production, trafficking, and use around the world. In 2017, approximately 5.5 percent of the world's population aged fifteen to sixty-four years had used drugs in the past year. This figure is similar to that of 2016, although drug use patterns have changed in the two years. The number of people using opioids in 2017 was 56 percent higher than in 2016. Additionally, methamphetamine use increased noticeably in Southeast Asia, and the rising number of synthetic opioid deaths in North America has gained international attention. With respect to drug production, cocaine manufacturing reached a record high in 2017 with a 25 percent increase over 2016, most of which came from Colombia. The number of hectares of opium poppy also increased by 41 percent during the same time (UNODC 2017).

The problem of illicit drugs has three aspects: drug cultivation and production, drug trafficking and sales, and drug use or consumption. The ruling international laws on illegal drugs cover all three points. The United Nations Single Convention on Narcotic Drugs of 1961, as amended by the 1972 Protocol, combined previous multilateral agreements into a coherent convention and established the International Narcotics Control Board (INCB) as a central regulatory body. The treaty covers 130 narcotic drugs including both natural and synthetic drugs in addition to cannabis and coca leaf (INCB 2019). Countries that are party to the treaty agree to control the production, distribution, and use of these drugs, except for medical and scientific applications.

Two subsequent international laws have expanded the scope of the 1961 treaty. In response to changing drug preferences in the 1960s, the United Nations adopted the Convention on Psychotropic Substances of 1971 to regulate drugs that were not included in the 1961 treaty, such as amphetamines, barbiturates, and psychedelics. Finally, the United Nations Convention against Illicit Trafficking in Narcotics Drugs and Psychotropic Substances of 1988 was adopted to respond to the growth in drug trafficking in the 1980s as a result of globalization and decolonization. It especially targets organized crime groups and their roles in illicit drug production and distribution.

The eight countries profiled in this chapter cover these three dimensions of illicit drugs. Afghanistan, Colombia, and Mexico are responsible for much of the illegal drug production in the world. Political instability and weak states allow organized crime groups to control illegal drug markets, often with impunity due to high levels of government corruption and weak national security. China and Guinea-Bissau are examples of transit countries. Their strategic geographic locations facilitate their roles in the drug trafficking business, moving products from producers to consumers. However, the means of doing so are quite different in these two countries. Strict government control and stiff trafficking penalties in China have discouraged the formation of large drug trafficking organizations (DTOs) and kept violence to a minimum. In contrast, a weak government in Guinea-Bissau has created a "narco-state" characterized by corruption and violence. The last three countries illustrate different approaches to dealing with drug use. Vietnam applies compulsory detention for repeat drug offenders, which has raised concerns about human rights among the international community. The Netherlands and Portugal have both adopted public health approaches to drug use by decriminalizing it and emphasizing prevention and treatment over criminal justice responses to the problem.

Further Reading

INCB (International Narcotics Control Board). 2019. "Narcotic Drugs." https://www.incb .org/incb/en/narcotic-drugs/index.html.

UNODC (United Nations Office on Drugs and Crime). 2016. *Terminology and Information on Drugs*. 3rd ed. New York: United Nations.
UNODC (United Nations Office on Drugs and Crime). 2017. *World Drug Report 2017*. Vienna: United Nations Publications. https://www.unodc.org/wdr2017/.

AFGHANISTAN

Afghanistan is a landlocked country in South Asia surrounded by Iran, Turkmenistan, Tajikistan, and Pakistan. It is a mountainous country with about 58 percent of its land used for agriculture. The population of almost thirty-five million is predominantly Muslim. The largest ethnic group is Pashtun, but there are many ethnolinguistic groups living in Afghanistan. The country is currently an Islamic Republic, although its recent history has been defined by political turmoil (Central Intelligence Agency 2018). Afghanistan produces about two-thirds of all the illicit opium poppy in the world, and the drug production and trafficking businesses have been central to the political and economic history of the country. Between 7 and 16 percent of the country's gross domestic product (GDP) comes from opiate exports (UNODC 2017).

History of Opium in Afghanistan

Opium has been grown in Afghanistan since Alexander the Great (356–323 BCE) invaded the region in 330 BCE, but the area did not become a world supplier of the drug until the late twentieth century. Modern Afghanistan was founded in 1747 when Ahmad Shah Durrani (1722–1772) united the Pashtun tribes under a single nation. Between 1839 and 1919, Britain and Afghanistan fought three wars as Britain tried to expand its colonization of Asia. After the third war ended in 1919, Afghanistan became a fully independent state.

At that time, opium was only grown in a few provinces in the country. In the 1930s and 1940s, legal opium production expanded because traditional supplies of the drug to the West were disrupted during World War II (1939–1945). Legal sales of opium became an important source of revenue for the young nation. However, after the war, foreign governments became increasingly concerned about the illicit uses of the drug and encouraged the Afghan government to ban production in exchange for foreign assistance from the U.S. government. The Afghan government was not very successful in halting the production of such a valuable crop, and the INCB formally sanctioned it in the 1960s for its poor drug control.

In the 1970s, a series of internal and external political events emboldened opium growers and producers. The Iranian Revolution (1978–1979) and a religious ban on opium production in Pakistan disrupted opium production in neighboring countries, creating market incentives for more growth in Afghanistan. Around the same time, Afghanistan experienced a civil war followed by an international war with the Soviet Union. As the weakened central government provided few economic resources for the large rural population, opium poppy became a valuable crop for poor farmers.

In 1973, Mohammad Daud Khan (1909–1978) overthrew King Zahir Shah (1914–2007), which ended the Afghan monarchy. Khan ruled as president until 1978 when the communist People's Democratic Party of Afghanistan (PDPA) overthrew him. The new ruling party challenged some traditional Islamic laws and practices, which led to a mass rebellion supported by Pakistan and the United States. In turn, the Soviet Union supported the rule of the PDPA. In 1979, the Soviet Union invaded Afghanistan and a war ensued until 1989.

Not only was opium a profitable commodity, but rural farmers could also continue to grow it during wartime conditions, so production increased significantly in the 1980s. Cultivating opium is very labor-intensive, but it does not require highly specialized equipment. It is fairly drought-resistant, so it could be grown even if water supplies were disrupted by war. It is also a relatively low weight commodity, so it could be transported on very poor quality roads. The government's preoccupation with the war also left few resources for internal governance, such as border patrol. Given these conditions, opium cultivation expanded into new provinces in Afghanistan.

After the Soviet withdrawal from the country, civil infighting continued until the Taliban gained control in 1994. Pashtun students who had been educated in Islamic schools and had fought against the Soviets founded the Taliban, or the Islamic Emirate of Afghanistan (IEA). It is a Sunni Islamic fundamentalist movement aimed to remove foreign influences from Afghanistan and implement strict Islamic law. When the Taliban first came to power, they allowed local leaders to continue producing opium in exchange for their political allegiance and taxation. It was estimated that the Taliban initially earned USD 30 million per year taxing opium, which grew to USD 100 million per year by the late 1990s (Coyne, Blanco, and Burns 2016).

In 2000, the Taliban changed course and banned the cultivation of opium due to both religion and international pressure and promises of foreign aid. The government claimed that drug production was not consistent with the principles of Islam and threatened harsh punishments for disobeying the new law. As a result, opium production dropped by 65 percent (Coyne, Blanco, and Burns 2016). As the ban was not accompanied by economic alternatives for farmers, it caused unrest among the rural population.

In December 2001, U.S. coalition forces invaded Afghanistan and removed the Taliban from power in response to the September 11, 2001 terrorist attacks on the United States. To get local leaders to support the invasion, the coalition forces initially ignored the opium business. Hamid Karzai (1957–) became the new president of Afghanistan and formally continued the ban on opium production, but it was largely ineffective. Between 2005 and 2013, opium yields varied considerably in response to different counter-narcotics measures, but these have largely been abandoned since coalition forces left Afghanistan in 2014.

Capturing a Heroin Godfather

In 2009 the U.S. Drug Enforcement Agency captured Haji Bagcho after a four-year long operation tracking his drug operations. Bagcho had run the largest heroin operation in Afghanistan, supplying the drug to more than twenty countries, including the United States. It was estimated that he was supplying 20 percent of the world's heroin. In 2006 alone, it was believed that Bagcho sold USD 250 million of heroin and some of that money was used to support the Taliban. He was convicted of drug trafficking in the United States and sentenced to life in prison plus forfeiture of over USD 250 million in drug profits.

Patterson, Thom. n.d. "How to Catch a Heroin 'Godfather.'" CNN. https://www.cnn.com/2017 /08/10/world/afghanistan-war-opium-heroin-facts-declassified/index.html.

Current Drug Production and Trafficking

The UNODC regularly monitors opium production and trafficking around the world. In their 2017 report they noted that the number of hectares used for opium cultivation in Afghanistan increased from 57,000 in 1996 to 165,000 in 2006 and 201,000 in 2016. Similarly, the number of tons of opium produced was 2,248 in 1996, 5,310 in 2006, and 4,800 in 2016, with the decrease likely due to poor environmental conditions including drought.

Although the Taliban lost formal control of the government in 2001, they still retain control over large portions of the country and are a continuing threat to the government. About two-thirds of the world's opium supply comes from Afghanistan, and 85 percent of the cultivation of opium poppy occurs in territories under Taliban control. It was estimated that the Taliban earned about USD 150 million in 2016 from taxing opium cultivation and trafficking (UNODC 2017).

Opium is trafficked out of Afghanistan along three main routes. The oldest is the Balkan route where drugs are moved over land across Iran and Turkey into southeastern Europe. The northern route carries drugs across Central Asia into Russia, whereas the southern route runs overland through Iran or Pakistan and across the Indian Ocean to Africa, Europe, and Asia. The long porous borders of Afghanistan make it relatively easy to move drug products out of the country. For example, the border with Pakistan is 1,435 miles long and the border with China is 1,539 miles (UNODC 2017).

In addition to raw opium and drugs like morphine and codeine (opiates) that are made from the opium poppy, Afghanistan is also a major produce of opioids, which are manufactured or synthetic opium-like substances, such as heroin. In 2015, Afghanistan produced 77 percent of the world's heroin (UNODC 2017). The drug is trafficked all over the world, except Latin America. Recently, there has been an increase in opiate trafficking in Africa as domestic opiate use has increased in many African countries and organized crime groups have become more active

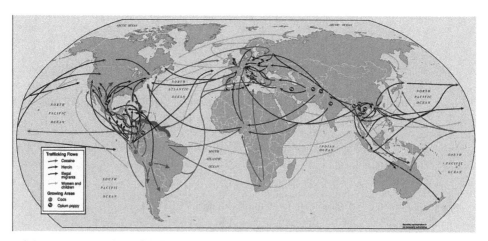

While most poppy plants for illegal drug use are cultivated in Asia and the Middle East, the resulting illicit products are trafficked throughout the continent. This map shows how drug trafficking organizations move various drugs all around the world. (University of Texas-Austin/Perry-Casteneda Library)

in drug trafficking, particularly in Western and Central Africa. Egypt, Nigeria, and South Africa have been identified as major trafficking sites in Africa.

Domestic Drug Abuse

According to the UNODC (2017), about 2.7 percent of Afghans are addicted to opiates, which is one of the highest rates in the world. Although it is difficult to get accurate drug usage statistics from remote areas of the country, researchers have been able to study the problem in urban areas. In one study conducted in 2014, 11 percent of households in urban areas tested positive for at least one illicit substance and 5.6 percent tested positive for opioids. After opioids, marijuana was the second most common substance (3.2 percent), followed by benzodiazepines (3.5 percent). Alcohol use was relatively rare (0.7 percent). Substance use is more common among men than women or children (Cottler et al. 2014).

Drug users reported that they began using illegal substances due to peer pressure, economic problems, medical problems, and the easy availability of drugs. Drug use has taken a large toll on families in Afghanistan contributing to domestic violence, truancy, and child behavioral problems. One study by the UNODC (2014) found that 60 percent of drug users were previously employed before they became addicted, and 70 percent of them suffer from financial problems because of their drug use.

Further Reading

Central Intelligence Agency. 2018. "The World Factbook." https://www.cia.gov/library/publications/resources/the-world-factbook/.

Cottler, Linda B., Shaun Ajinkya, Bruce A. Goldberger, Mohammad Asrar Ghani, David M. Martin, Hui Hu, and Mark S. Gold. 2014. "Prevalence of Drug and Alcohol Use in Urban Afghanistan: Epidemiological Data from the Afghanistan National Urban Drug

Use Study (ANUDUS)." *The Lancet Global Health* 2 (10): e592–e600. https://doi.org/10 .1016/S2214-109X(14)70290-6.

Coyne, Christopher J., Abigail R. Hall Blanco, and Scott Burns. 2016. "The War on Drugs in Afghanistan: Another Failed Experiment with Interdiction." *The Independent Review* 21 (1): 95–119.

Mansfield, David. 2016. *A State Built on Sand: How Opium Undermined Afghanistan.* Oxford: Oxford University Press.

UNODC (United Nations Office on Drugs and Crime). 2014. *Impacts of Drug Use on Users and Their Families in Afghanistan.* Vienna: United Nations Publications. https://info .publicintelligence.net/UNODC-AfghanDrugUse.pdf.

UNODC (United Nations Office on Drugs and Crime). 2016. *Afghan Opium Survey 2016.* Vienna: United Nations Publications. http://www.unodc.org/documents/crop-monitoring /Afghanistan/AfghanistanOpiumSurvey2016_ExSum.pdf.

UNODC (United Nations Office on Drugs and Crime). 2017. *World Drug Report 2017.* Vienna: United Nations Publications. https://www.unodc.org/wdr2017/.

CHINA

China is a large, East Asian country with a population of almost 4.4 billion people, the vast majority of whom is Han Chinese. It has been a communist country since the end of the Chinese Civil War in 1949. The Communist Party maintains tight political control over the country, although since the 1970s the party has gradually shifted its economy from a centrally planned system, which helped bring an end to communism in the Soviet Union, to a controlled market economy. This has led to significant economic growth in China. China has a GDP per capita of USD 16,700, comparable to Costa Rica and Iraq, with a growth of nearly 7 percent per year, compared to only 2.2 percent in the United States (Central Intelligence Agency 2018). China borders fourteen countries, making border control challenging. Importantly, it lies just east of the Golden Crescent (Iran, Afghanistan, and Pakistan) and north of the Golden Triangle (Burma, Laos, and Thailand), the two major opium-producing regions in the world, which facilitates both drug trafficking and drug use.

Opium Wars

The last imperial dynasty in China, the Qing dynasty, ruled from 1636 to 1912 and was responsible for establishing trade relationships with Europe that eventually led to the creation of an opium market in China. Although China had been trading with Europeans since the sixteenth century, it was its relationship with Britain during the early Qing dynasty years that shaped the history of opium in that country. By the mid-1700s, Chinese silk, tea, and porcelain were highly desirable goods in Europe. China was benefiting greatly from trade with Britain, although the English were experiencing a trade imbalance because European goods were not as desirable in China. By 1773, British merchants began purchasing Chinese products with opium obtained from colonies in India and Indonesia to increase their trading leverage.

The influx of large quantities of opium led to a rapid increase in recreational opium usage in China. Amid concerns of widespread addiction, the Qing dynasty banned opium trading in 1796. Instead of reducing the supply of opium, however, the ban created illegal smuggling routes. When China tried to forcibly prevent Britain from bringing opium into the country, tensions between the two countries led to the First Opium War that lasted from 1839 to 1842. Britain's victory created favorable trading agreements for Europeans and Americans conducting business in China and a continuing opium problem for the Chinese.

Drug addiction spread in China throughout the 1800s with the introduction of morphine in 1805, the hypodermic needle in 1851, and heroin in 1898. In the 1850s, as competition for the Chinese opium market increased, Britain wanted to renegotiate the Treaty of Nanking that ended the First Opium War. They demanded greater access to markets throughout China and the legalization of the opium trade. Once again, tensions escalated into violence, leading to the Second Opium War from 1856 to 1860. With assistance from France, Britain was victorious again and its commerce demands were met by China, which included continuing the opium trade.

In response to its trade losses, the Chinese government began to encourage local poppy cultivation and China soon became a leader in opium production, no longer relying on foreigners for the drug. By the late 1800s, the international community started to take opium addiction more seriously and became concerned with the spread of opium and opiates for recreational purposes. Several countries, including Britain and the United States, passed laws regulating or banning the substances, except for medical purposes. In 1908, Britain and China finally agreed on a treaty to restrict opium trade. However, efforts to control domestic production and usage in China were ineffective due to political and economic turmoil leading to the collapse of China's last imperial dynasty in 1912.

The Golden Triangle

When the Communist Party gained control of China in 1949, it banned the cultivation of poppy in the country and the exportation of opium to Southeast Asia. The government closed manufacturing facilities and drug dens and launched an extensive prohibition campaign. It also executed or imprisoned drug traffickers for lengthy periods and sentenced addicts to labor camps, sending a message that drugs were no longer tolerated in the country. However, China's prior expansions into surrounding Asian countries had already spread opium production throughout the region. When the economic reforms of the 1980s opened up China's markets and borders to legal business, they also made illegal trade easier. As a result of China's cultivation bans, the large demand for opium among Chinese drug users, as well as political instability throughout the region, a new epicenter for opium emerged. The area where the borders of Burma (Myanmar), Laos, and Thailand meet became a successful location to cultivate poppy because the land and rainfall conditions allowed the crop to grow easily, and the rugged mountains and forests made the area difficult for governments to control. The "Golden Triangle" has been a leading source of illicit opium since the early 1990s, with much of it being trafficked to and through China. In 2016, China was ranked fifth in terms of the amount of illegal opium seized by authorities, fourth with respect to morphine, and second for heroin (UNODC 2017).

By the late 1990s and early 2000s, most of the drug production in Thailand and Laos had ceased, but Myanmar remains a leading producer of opium. Most opium is made in northern Myanmar and enters China through its southern Yunnan province as heroin, which is the preferred form among drug users. Once in China, there are three main trafficking routes. The northern route through Sichuan province and the eastern route through Guizhou province move the drug to China's domestic markets. The southeast route through Guangxi to Guandong moves the product to Hong Kong, where it is transferred to global drug markets. Drug traffickers in the Golden Triangle are mostly ethnic Chinese who prefer to smuggle heroin through China rather than Thailand because of weak border control, better roads, and language familiarity.

The Chinese drug trade is different from many other major drug trafficking countries because drug cartels and large-scale, organized distributors and retailers are largely absent, which also means that there is little violence or corruption associated with the drug trade. Instead, the Chinese model for illegal drug trafficking is referred to as "ants-moving-house" because there are large numbers of small groups involved in moving drugs through the country. Wholesale trafficking is typically conducted through family groups who embrace business principles to avoid violence and detection from authorities. Retail drug sales are conducted through social networks. Most sellers move their products in small quantities to avoid detection and minimize punishments if caught. Sales transactions occur in homes or semiprivate spaces such as restaurants, rather than openly on the streets. According to Chinese law, a person caught with 50 grams of heroin could receive the death penalty, so moving small quantities of drugs through one's personal networks is considered the safest way to do business (Chin and Zhang 2015).

Drug Use and Treatment

Police in China are required to register all known drug addicts in their communities and submit statistics on drug arrests and seizures to a national registry. In 2001, the number of known drug addicts was 901,000, which increased to 1.5 million by 2010 and nearly 2.5 million by 2013. In 2001, the majority of drug users in China were heroin addicts (82.7 percent), which decreased to 53.6 percent by 2013 as other synthetic drugs became more popular among users, particularly crystal methamphetamine and ketamine. Drug users are typically young, adult males from poor families. Between 50 and 70 percent of heroin users inject the drug, increasing risks for hepatitis C and human immunodeficiency virus (HIV). In 2000, Chinese authorities reported that 72 percent of all HIV cases were due to heroin injection, prompting the launch of educational campaigns and needle exchange programs. By 2011, the percentage of HIV cases resulting from heroin injection decreased to 24 percent (Zhang and Chin 2016).

Drug users are subjected to China's Comprehensive Management of Public Order program that tracks people considered a threat to social order. Drug users are monitored through the police registration system and are subjected to either mandatory drug treatment centers or labor camps. From 1983 to 2008, China adopted a punitive approach to drug dealers with its "Strike Hard" policies emphasizing swift and severe punishments for offenders. In 1989, the government launched a moral and criminal justice campaign against the "Six Evils" of prostitution, gambling, pornography, kidnapping, superstition, and drug use. However, by 2007, the approach to drug usage in China shifted toward public health. The country passed a Drug Prohibition Law that embraced a medical approach to drug addiction and introduced needle exchange programs and methadone maintenance treatment. Although drug use is still against the law under this new policy, it is treated as an administrative sanction rather than a criminal offense. Drug users can enter rehabilitation voluntarily or they can be sanctioned by the government to community rehabilitation, coercive quarantine for drug rehabilitation (mandatory detention), or re-education through labor camps. Sending users to mandatory drug rehabilitation is a decision that is made by the police rather than by the courts. Prior to the 2007 law, drug users could be sent to mandatory rehabilitation for three months to one year, but the Drug Prohibition Law changed the initial sentence to two years. After a one-year evaluation, detainees can get an early release. After a two-year evaluation, detainees can have their sentence extended for an additional year, for a maximum of three years in total (Biddulph and Xie 2011). In 2013, the Chinese government reported that 242,000 people were sent to compulsory rehabilitation facilities (Zhang and Chin 2016).

Drug users who have completed mandatory rehabilitation and have been caught using illegal drugs again can be sent to labor camps for one to three years. In 2008, it was estimated that there were 168 such camps in China housing 69,000 drug users (Biddulph and Xie 2011). These camps were primarily located in rural areas where detainees worked on farms. As of 2009, the government started using Recovering Health Centers, a form of community-based supervision and rehabilitation, rather than labor camps. In 2013, there were 184,000 drug users admitted to community facilities.

Further Reading

Biddulph, Sarah, and Chuanyu Xie. 2011. "Regulating Drug Dependency in China: The 2008 PRC Drug Prohibition Law." *The British Journal of Criminology* 51 (6): 978–96. https://doi.org/10.1093/bjc/azr050.

Central Intelligence Agency. 2018. "The World Factbook." https://www.cia.gov/library /publications/resources/the-world-factbook/.

Chin, Ko-lin, and Sheldon X. Zhang. 2015. *The Chinese Heroin Trade: Cross-Border Drug Trafficking in Southeast Asia and Beyond*. New York: NYU Press.

Chouvy, Pierre-Arnaud. 2010. *Opium: Uncovering the Politics of the Poppy*. Cambridge, MA: Harvard University Press.

UNODC (United Nations Office on Drugs and Crime). 2017. *World Drug Report 2017.* Vienna: United Nations Publications. https://www.unodc.org/wdr2017/.

Zhang, Sheldon X, and Ko-lin Chin. 2016. *A People's War: China's Struggle to Contain Its Illicit Drug Problem.* Global Drug Policy: Comparative Perspectives and UNGASS 2016. Washington, DC: Foreign Policy at Brookings.

COLOMBIA

Colombia is a country of over forty-two million people located in northern South America. It borders Panama and the North Pacific Ocean to the north, Venezuela to the east, and Brazil, Peru, and Ecuador to the south. Colombia is an ethnically mixed, Spanish-speaking country that is predominantly Roman Catholic. It gained independence from Spain in 1819 and established its current borders in 1903 after separations from neighboring countries. The legitimate Colombian economy depends largely on oil, coal, and coffee exports. The GDP per capita is USD 14,900, which is slightly higher than its neighbors Venezuela (USD 12,500) and Peru (USD 13,500) (Central Intelligence Agency 2018). Economic development is hindered by political instability and narco-trafficking. The geography of Colombia is suitable for the cultivation of several drug crops, especially coca and marijuana. Additionally, political instability since the 1960s has allowed the drug trade to flourish as guerrilla groups used it to fund political activities and cultivate allies among rural populations. Colombia's drug cartels in the 1980s were infamous for their wealth and violence, and the country remains a leading coca producer even after the collapse of those cartels.

Current State of Drug Production

Colombia entered the international drug business in the 1960s with the cultivation and exportation of marijuana, but its global reputation is best associated with coca. According to the World Drug Report of 2017, it was estimated that 213,000 hectares of land in the world were used for coca bush in 2016, 69 percent of which was in Colombia. The number of hectares cultivating coca in Colombia in 2016 was 146,000, which was nearly double the amount in 2006. The number of hectares fluctuates annually, but there was a noticeable decrease from 2006 to 2014 before a sharp rise in 2015 and 2016. The decrease can be attributed, at least partially, to the bilateral, antidrug campaign between the United States and Colombia from 2000 to 2015. Recent increases may be due to perceptions that the risk of cultivation has declined because the government has halted aerial sprayings to eradicate drug crops. The government also reduced alternative development initiatives for rural areas, which may have increased incentives to grow drug crops. In 2016, the estimated amount of cocaine produced in Colombia was 866 tons.

Since 2000, Colombia has also become involved in opium poppy cultivation and has surpassed Asian suppliers for dominance in the American markets by reducing prices while simultaneously improving the quality of the product. Heroin has been appealing to the smaller DTOs that emerged at the end of the twentieth century because higher profits can be made per hectare of poppy versus coca. The number of hectares of opium poppy grown in Colombia in 2006 was 1,023, which declined to 287 by 2014, but started increasing again in 2015 and 2016 (UNODC 2017). Heroin production has led to a rise in drug consumption in Colombia, as well as increasing public health concerns over the use of injectable drugs, particularly with respect to the spread of HIV.

Drugs and Guerrilla Warfare

For over a hundred years after Colombia's independence from Spain in 1918, the country experienced a series of political alliances and disputes with neighboring countries and new political boundaries were drawn. The current state of Colombia was formed in 1934 when tensions with surrounding countries declined. Peace was short-lived, however, as internal conflicts started in the 1940s and lasted through the twenty-first century. Between 1948 and 1958, the country was embroiled in a civil war known as *La Violencia*. Over 200,000 people died, many of whom were peasants living in rural areas (Paul, Clarke, and Serena 2014).

Many farmers fled to the mountains of western Tolima to escape the violence, where they were recruited by the growing Colombian Communist Party to fight the sitting government for a better quality of life for peasants. One of these peasants, Pedro Antonio Marín Marín, known as Manuel Marulanda Vélez (1930–2008), became a leader of the disillusioned peasants and organized a resistance movement against the government. In 1964, Vélez became a founding member of the Revolutionary Armed Forces of Colombia—People's Army (*Fuerzas Armadas Revolucionia de Colombia—Ejército del Pueblo*, or FARC), which engaged in a guerrilla war against the Colombian government and right-wing paramilitaries until 2014.

FARC and other guerrilla groups started taxing drug producers and traffickers in the 1980s to gain revenue to fund their political and military activities. These groups also participated in extortion, fraudulent investments, and money laundering. During the same time, as Colombia's major drug cartels were starting to dominate the drug business, smaller DTOs turned to FARC for protection. By 2012, it was estimated that FARC controlled between 40 and 50 percent of the illegal drug market in Colombia (Otis 2014).

Violent Drug Cartels

The political instability in Colombia, coupled with a neglected peasantry trying to make a living, favorable conditions for growing coca, and an increasing demand for cocaine in the United States, gave rise to Colombia's notorious drug cartels of the 1970s and 1980s. The Medellín Cartel, founded by "The King of Cocaine," Pablo Escobar (1949–1993), started as a small smuggling business in the 1970s and grew into one of the most profitable, and most violent, drug cartels of the 1980s. This multi-billion dollar enterprise was the primary supplier of cocaine to the United States. The cartel operated with impunity because it used extreme violence, corruption, and extortion to maintain its dominance. Between 1979 and 1999, more than 100 judges were assassinated, along with other prominent public officials (Restrepo 2015). In the 1990s, criminals kidnapped nearly 5,000 people, and FARC and other rebel groups kidnapped another 10,000. Around the same time, the homicide rate in Colombia was about 77.5 per 100,000 people, which was nine times higher than the United States (Paul, Clarke, and Serena 2014).

When Escobar was killed in a gunfight with Colombian police in 1993, the Medellín's main rival, the Cali Cartel, became the dominant DTO in Colombia. During Escobar's reign, the Cali Cartel mainly trafficked cocaine through different routes than Medellín, such as Panama. After Escobar's death, they expanded their role in the European drug market and became the world's primary cocaine supplier, until the cartel was dismantled by law enforcement in the mid-1990s.

After Escobar's death, the Colombian government turned its full attention to the Cali Cartel. President Ernesto Samper Pizano (1950–) barely survived a scandal in which he was accused of accepting campaign money from the Cali Cartel. This spoiled relations with the United States, who accused Samper of not being tough enough against the drug traffickers. In response to political pressures, Colombian law enforcement joined forces with the U.S. Drug Enforcement Agency to target the leaders of the Cali Cartel. By 1995, most of them had been arrested. This brought an end to large-scale, extremely violent drug cartels in Colombia. Since then, the drug business has fragmented into several much smaller organizations called "cartelitos" (Paul, Clarke, and Serena 2014).

"Plan Colombia"

After the demise of the large drug cartels, the Colombian government returned their attention to the armed insurgent groups, who were still heavily involved in the drug business. In 1999, President Andrés Pastrana (1954–) proposed a collaboration with the United States to combat "narco-terrorism." To effectively fight guerrilla groups, the Colombian government recognized the role that illegal drugs played in funding the armed conflict. The goals of Plan Colombia were to provide an international collaboration that would reduce drug supplies in Colombia, drug demand in the United States, and strengthen the justice system in Colombia to be better equipped to deal with drug trafficking in the long run.

In 2000, the United States gave Colombia USD 1.6 million, most of which was spent on the Colombian army and police (Tickner and Cepeda 2015). After the terrorist attacks against the United States on September 11, 2011, the United States labeled FARC and other Colombian guerrilla groups as terrorist organizations, fueling additional monetary support for Colombia's efforts to regain control of the country. From 2000 to 2006, the United States contributed USD 5.34 billion to Colombia's counter-narcotics and counter-terrorism efforts. With the help of these funds, Colombia's military increased from 160,000 members in 2000 to 380,000 in 2017, whereas more than 31,000 paramilitary troops were demobilized. Between 2002 and 2010, Colombia reduced terrorist attacks by 7 percent (Paul, Clarke, and Serena 2014).

Plan Colombia and subsequent collaborations between the two countries were successful in bolstering the rule of law in Colombia, improving security, and demobilizing guerrilla groups, as demonstrated with a 2014 peace agreement with FARC. However, these initiatives did not successfully dismantle drug cultivation and trafficking, particularly cocaine. Coca cultivation has been on the rise in Colombia, and in 2016 it was still the largest producer of cocaine in the world.

Further Reading

Central Intelligence Agency. 2018. "The World Factbook." https://www.cia.gov/library/publications/resources/the-world-factbook/.

Otis, John. 2014. *The FARC and Colombia's Illegal Drug Trade.* Washington, DC: Wilson Center Latin American Program.

Paul, Christopher, Colin P. Clarke, and Chad C. Serena. 2014. *Mexico Is Not Colombia: Alternative Historical Analogies for Responding to the Challenge of Violent Drug-Trafficking Organizations, Supporting Case Studies.* Santa Monica, CA: Rand Corporation.

Rempel, William C. 2007. "A Daring Betrayal Helped Wipe out Cali Cocaine Cartel." *The Seattle Times,* February 25, 2007. https://www.seattletimes.com/nation-world/a-daring-betrayal-helped-wipe-out-cali-cocaine-cartel/.

Restrepo, Elvira María. 2015. "Colombia and Its War against Drug Trafficking, 1970–2010." In *Drug Trafficking, Organized Crime, and Violence in the Americas Today*, edited by Bruce M. Bagley and Jonathan D. Rosen, 139–60. Gainesville, FL: University Press of Florida. https://miami.pure.elsevier.com/en/publications/drug-trafficking-organized-crime-and-violence-in-the-americas-tod.

Tickner, Arlene B., and Carolina Cepeda. 2015. "Illicit Drugs in the Colombia-U.S. Relationship." In *Drug Trafficking, Organized Crime, and Violence in the Americas Today*, edited by Bruce M. Bagley and Jonathan D. Rosen, 161–84. Gainesville, FL: University Press of Florida. https://miami.pure.elsevier.com/en/publications/drug-trafficking-organized-crime-and-violence-in-the-americas-tod.

UNODC (United Nations Office on Drugs and Crime). 2017. *World Drug Report 2017.* Vienna: United Nations Publications. https://www.unodc.org/wdr2017/.

GUINEA-BISSAU

Guinea-Bissau is a country of 1.8 million people, strategically located in West Africa off the coast of the Pacific Ocean. It is a multiethnic country with almost 45 percent of the population following Islam and 22 percent following Christianity. It was a Portuguese colony until 1974 and has suffered from political instability and economic hardship since independence. These two factors have made Guinea-Bissau highly susceptible to corruption and illegal activities. Since the 1990s, Guinea-Bissau has become increasingly involved in the global drug trade, leading some experts to call it "Africa's first narco-state" (O'Regan and Thompson 2013).

Political and Economic Factors Behind Drug Trafficking

Guinea-Bissau is primarily an agricultural country that relies on cashew nut exports and foreign aid for its legal income. It is considered among the poorest countries in the world. Its GDP per capita is USD 1,900. In contrast, Senegal to the north has a GDP per capita of USD 3,500, and Portugal, its former colonizer, has a GDP per capita of USD 30,500 (Central Intelligence Agency 2018).

Guinea-Bissau has many natural resources that could potentially fuel economic growth including fertile land for various crops, offshore oil potential, and untapped minerals. However, it is lacking an economic and physical infrastructure to capitalize on these income sources. Only 10 percent of the roads in Guinea-Bissau are paved, the port is insufficient for global trade, and public utilities are lacking. Additionally, the relatively young population that could supply labor to new industries is largely uneducated and suffers from numerous health problems due to poor living conditions (EconomyWatch 2010). As such, Guinea-Bissau relies primarily on the cashew industry for income. It is the sixth largest producer of cashews in the world, although the lack of processing facilities means that much of this product is sold below market prices. Additionally, poor government regulation has resulted in the smuggling of cashews to neighboring countries, resulting in lost profits for Guinea-Bissau. The cashew industry employs about 85 percent of the country's workforce (EconomyWatch 2010).

The poor economic conditions are due in part to Guinea-Bissau's colonial legacy. The economy was poorly governed and underdeveloped under Portuguese rule, and the hasty exit of the Portuguese during the guerrilla war for independence between 1956 and 1974 left local leaders with little to build upon. Compounding the unfavorable conditions that the newly independent nation had to start with, perpetual political instability meant that leaders were not in power long enough or were too concerned with maintaining their power to invest in economic development. The government was subjected to several military coups throughout the end of the twentieth century, and no elected president completed their term without military interference until the current president, José Mário Vaz (1957–), who was elected in 2014 and stands for re-election in 2019.

Growing Drug Business

Various forms of illegal trafficking have been occurring in Guinea-Bissau since the sixteenth century. Portuguese Guinea was part of the "slave coast" of West Africa that sent slaves from Africa to Europe and North America. More recently, Guinea-Bissau was a transit country for illegal arms trafficked to rebel groups in southern Senegal. Since the 1990s, money from arms trafficking has been used by politicians for bribes and patronage, as well as for the personal benefit of the country's top leaders. These established trafficking routes helped fuel Guinea-Bissau's entry into the global drug trade. In the 1980s, the drug trade in West Africa was primarily run by Nigerian and Ghanaian organized crime groups, who were largely trafficking heroin. Nigeria has an extensive diaspora, with emigrants living in over eighty countries around the world, which facilitates illegal business connections (Bybee 2012).

With the turn of the twenty-first century, Guinea-Bissau began to gain ground in the drug business due to numerous factors. Drug demand in key markets like

Europe shifted from heroin to cocaine and synthetics, which increased business to South American production countries. West Africa is geographically situated as a transit from drug production in Brazil, Colombia, Venezuela, and Argentina to selling points in Europe. Guinea-Bissau is a particularly attractive business partner because it is a failed state with high levels of corruption and poor domestic and border security. The country also has ninety islands off the Pacific coast, which makes concealing illegal drugs during transport fairly easy. Finally, given the poor economic conditions in Guinea-Bissau, participating in the drug trade is a viable source of income for the poor.

Approximately one-fourth of all cocaine from South America going to European markets is shipped through Guinea-Bissau (Shaw 2015). Shipments of cocaine, primarily from Colombia, reach the coast of Guinea-Bissau where they are separated into smaller loads and sent by speedboat to Senegal or Morocco along the northern coast, or by truck through Mauritania to the north and across the Sahara Desert to the Mediterranean coast. Additionally, approximately 30–100 tons of cocaine are smuggled north by air (Brune 2011). In a similar fashion, Argentina ships ingredients to produce ephedrine and methamphetamines through Guinea-Bissau to Europe.

Narco-State

The rising influence of the drug trade in Guinea-Bissau is the result of a network of Latin American traffickers supplying illicit drugs, local entrepreneurs who operate the market in Guinea-Bissau and connect with European distributors, and the political and military leaders who directly facilitate and profit from the drug trade. A key figure in building this network was João Bernardo Vieira (1939–2009), who was president from 1980 to 1999 and benefited from illegal arms trafficking at that time. He returned to power from 2005 to 2009. As foreign aid to Guinea-Bissau had been declining since the 1990s, political and military leaders turned to illegal funding opportunities to pay people, which was needed to retain power, as well as to support their own lavish lifestyles.

Between 1999 and 2004, Vieira was living in exile in Portugal where he was cultivating business and political contacts to stage a political comeback. The money to support his political campaign and buy allegiance from high-ranking military officers came from providing Latin American drug traffickers access to transit drugs through Guinea-Bissau with little official resistance. The drug business is estimated to have been about eight times more profitable than arms trafficking, which meant that government and military leaders were becoming exceptionally wealthy, but that money was not funneled into programs that would benefit the general population. The capital city of Bissau saw a surge in construction projects and streets filled with large, expensive vehicles. The large amounts of money were laundered through various mechanisms, such as property in Senegal and the Gambia or gold and diamonds from Liberia.

The massive wealth bred more corruption and further weakened political and social institutions. For example, the understaffed Judicial Police that rarely had funds for basic needs, such as fuel, continued to try to police drug activity. However, highly successful raids were undermined by the military, which would confiscate illegal drugs and release suspects from custody (Shaw 2015). The penetration of drug money into the day-to-day functioning of basic institutions, such as the civil service, police, military, transportation, etc., has led some experts to label Guinea-Bissau as a narco-state (O'Regan and Thompson 2013). However, others have argued that the highly concentrated control over the drug market is more accurately described as a protection racket. Money is paid to a small network of people who protect the movement of drugs through the country, with violence, if necessary (Shaw 2015).

Given the extent of corruption needed to support this kind of business and the large amounts of money involved, relationships tend to be tense and fragile, contributing to the overall political instability of the country. In 2009, Vieira's top military partner, General Batista Tagme Na Waie (1949–2009), was assassinated in a bombing of his military headquarters. The offenders were never officially identified, and some experts suspect that he may have been killed by Latin American drug traffickers who feared his growing influence. However, soldiers loyal to Na Waie blamed Vieira and they brutally beat and killed him in retaliation. These deaths were followed by the killings of several other leaders of the drug trade. The deaths created a power shift, whereby weak civilian leaders controlled the government, while the military took greater control over the drug business.

The assassinations initially spurred greater attention to the drug trafficking problem by the international community. In 2009, the United Nations Office for West Africa, the United Nations Office of Drugs and Crime, Interpol, and the United Nations Department of Peacekeeping Operations created the West Africa Coast Initiative to provide technical assistance and other resources to improve local law enforcement and the judiciary, as well as to create transnational organized crime units for countries in the region to coordinate drug control activities and share intelligence. In 2011, African Union lawyers offered to assist Guinea-Bissau to draft legislation to better combat trafficking.

Another military coup in 2012, however, reinforced the military's control of the drug business. Since then, the drug trade has not only been flourishing but the military seems to have expanded operations to include human trafficking and illegal logging. In 2019, President José Mário Vaz (1957–) appealed to the international community for assistance fighting drug traffickers.

Further Reading

Brune, Nancy. 2011. "The Brazil-Africa Narco Nexus." *Americas Quarterly; New York* 5 (4): 58–62.

Bybee, Ashley Neese. 2012. "The Twenty-First Century Expansion of the Transnational Drug Trade in Africa." *Journal of International Affairs* 66 (1): 69–84.

Central Intelligence Agency. 2018. "The World Factbook." https://www.cia.gov/library/publications/resources/the-world-factbook/.

EconomyWatch. 2010. "Guinea-Bissau Economy." http://www.economywatch.com/world_economy/guinea-bissau.

O'Regan, Davin, and Peter Thompson. 2013. *Advancing Stability and Reconciliation in Guinea-Bissau: Lessons from Africa's First Narco-State.* ACS-SR-2. Washington, DC: National Defense University, Africa Center for Strategic Studies. http://www.dtic.mil/docs/citations/ADA600477.

Shaw, Mark. 2015. "Drug Trafficking in Guinea-Bissau, 1998–2014: The Evolution of an Elite Protection Network." *The Journal of Modern African Studies* 53 (3): 339–64. https://doi.org/10.1017/S0022278X15000361.

Vernaschi, Marco. 2010. "The Cocaine Coast." *The Virginia Quarterly Review* 86 (1): 43–65.

MEXICO

Mexico is a country of approximately 126 million people, sharing a nearly 2,000-mile border with the United States to the north and a much smaller border with the Central American countries of Belize and Guatemala to the south. Mexico was home to several Amerindian civilizations including the Aztecs, Olmecs, and Mayans, until it was colonized by Spain in 1535. It gained national independence in 1821. Between 1920 and 2000, a single political party characterized by oppressive control and economic instability ruled Mexico. After 2000, the government became more democratic and the economy expanded. By 2017, Mexico had the eleventh largest economy in the world with a GDP per capita of USD 19,900, comparable to Argentina and Iran (Central Intelligence Agency 2018). Amidst these positive social changes, drug cartels have gained a significant influence over both politics and economics in Mexico, which has contributed to very high levels of violence.

Drug Production and Use

Mexico is a major producer, supplier, and transit country for various drugs including heroin, methamphetamines, and marijuana. According to the 2017 World Drug Report, the cultivation of opium poppy has increased in Mexico from 2,200 hectares in 2005 to 14,000 in 2012 and 26,100 in 2015. While this volume is much lower than the 2015 estimates for Afghanistan (183,000) or Myanmar (55,500), it is also not the only drug cultivated in the country. In 2015, Mexico also produced 8,335 tons of cannabis, and the country is also known as a source of methamphetamines, particularly for the U.S. market. As the United States successfully dismantled large drug cartels in Colombia in the late 1990s, Mexico took over as a leading supplier of heroin to the United States.

Drug use within Mexico is significantly lower than in the United States. The most recent estimates show that approximately 1.2 percent of the Mexican population uses cannabis, 0.5 percent uses cocaine, 0.38 percent uses opioids, and 0.18 percent uses opiates compared to the United States where 16.5 percent uses cannabis, 2.3 percent uses cocaine, 6 percent uses opioids, and 0.5 percent uses opiates (UNODC 2017). However, government officials in Mexico are concerned that drug use has been increasing. For example, between 2002 and 2008, the number of people per year using cocaine in Mexico increased 66 percent and the number of people using marijuana increased 100 percent (Durán-Martínez 2015). In 2009, the Mexican government passed a law decriminalizing the possession of small quantities of commonly used drugs for personal consumption with the goal of steering drug users toward treatment rather than the criminal justice system.

Drug Trafficking Organizations and Violence

DTOs have existed in Mexico for decades, although their visibility and influence have increased noticeably since the 1990s. The geographic location of Mexico between the major drug producers of South America and the large consumer populations of the United States and Canada, coupled with long and porous borders, make Mexico an ideal transit country for the movement of illicit goods. Mexico played a role in alcohol smuggling during the brief prohibition era in the United States from 1920 to 1933, but it was not until the 1980s that DTOs gained prominence.

The long border between the United States and Mexico poses a challenge for law enforcement to stop the flow of illegal drugs from Latin America to the United States. Here, the U.S. Air Force is building a fence along a part of the border to improve security. (U.S. Air Force)

Félix Gallardo (1946–), known as "The Godfather" of Mexican organized crime, established the Guadalajara Cartel to smuggle marijuana and opium into the United States in the 1980s. He then expanded his business to include cocaine from Colombia and worked directly with Pablo Escobar (1949–1993) of the famous Colombian Medellín Cartel. When Gallardo was arrested in 1989, he divided his business among four lieutenants, who then created the Tijuana, Sinaloa-Sonora, Juárez, and Gulf cartels. Soon afterward, the United States and Colombian governments effectively dismantled the large Colombian DTOs, including Medellín, unintentionally allowing Mexican cartels to take control over cocaine trafficking to the United States.

Between the 1960s and 1990s, DTOs had been allowed to conduct their business with little interference by either local or federal governments. This relationship changed in the 1990s because of three factors. First, Mexican DTOs took over the cocaine business at a time when the U.S. market was expanding, making drug trafficking more profitable than ever before. Second, the shift from a single-party federal government in Mexico to a more competitive democracy diffused social control to the regional level, giving DTOs more freedom to conduct business. Third, the North American Free Trade Agreement signed in 1994 provided new opportunities to move drug cargo across borders.

The changing business and political climate in the 1990s and the "cartelization" of the drug business after Gallardo's arrest fundamentally changed the power relationships among DTOs and between DTOs and the government in a destabilizing manner that increased the amount of violence associated with the drug trade. The decentralization of power meant less control over new, competitive cartels at a time when cocaine demand was increasing and profits were large. The various crime groups also began to diversify their products to include heroin, methamphetamine, and marijuana, as well as to expand their involvement in other criminal activities, such as auto theft, human smuggling, and kidnapping.

Violence is a routine part of the drug trade, a tool to control employees and establish credibility among suppliers and buyers. It is also used to intimidate formal authorities, such as police, politicians, and the media. Competition among DTOs tends to increase the use of violence, provoking a response by the government to better regulate drug trafficking. Between 2000 and 2007, homicide rates in Mexico actually declined, reflecting relative stability in the illicit economy. However, several high-profile cartel wars that resulted in large numbers of deaths in 2005 renewed the call for political intervention.

Government Responses to DTOs

The Institutional Revolutionary Party (PRI) ruled Mexico from 1929 until 2000 when President Vicente Fox (1942–) of the National Action Party (PAN) was elected. This was accompanied by changes in the ruling parties at the municipal level that destabilized political arrangements with DTOs. In 2006, President Felipe

Calderón (1962–) of PAN won the election based on a law-and-order platform that specifically targeted DTOs. In light of the wave of violence in 2005, this message was well received by the public. In particular, Calderón used military and federal police troops to target cartel leaders. The United States supported him through a bilateral initiative signed in 2008 to supply equipment to Mexico and strengthen police and judicial reforms.

During Calderón's six-year presidency, the Mexican government arrested nine high-level cartel leaders and 149 lieutenants (Germá-Bel and Holst 2016) and killed several others, but there were no significant increases in drug seizures or crop eradication. This strategy also had the unintended consequence of increasing violence as the removal of the cartel leadership created power struggles among the lower ranks. The shifting alliances, creation of new cartels, and new leaders eager to prove themselves contributed to rising violence. Between 2006 and 2012, the homicide rate increased dramatically from 9.4 to 22.6 per 100,000 people (UNODC 2019).

When the PRI regained power in 2012 with the election of President Enrique Peña Nieto (1966–), the government's antidrug strategy changed from direct military action against cartel leaders to reducing violence against citizens and businesses. Although violent crime decreased during his presidency, to 16.4 homicides per 100,0000 (UNODC 2019), Peña Nieto's administration was nonetheless criticized for not doing enough to combat DTOs. For example, vigilante groups formed among business owners and farmers to protect themselves against cartel violence. Additionally, a highly publicized mass killing of forty-three students by an organized crime group in 2014 and the prison escape of renowned drug lord Joaquín Guzmán ("El Chapo") soured public sentiment against Peña Nieto.

In December 2018, President Andrés López Obrador (1953–) from the National Regeneration Movement (AMLO) came to office with a controversial plan to end Mexico's War on Drugs. In direct response to a 33 percent increase in homicides between 2017 and 2018, Obrador shifted attention away from targeting DTOs toward improving public safety (Quackenbush 2019). He also proposed an amnesty plan for drug cultivators and dealers to reduce incentives to work for the

---

El Chapo

Joaquín Guzmán is one of Mexico's most famous drug cartel leaders, who is popularly known as "El Chapo" or "Shorty" because of his short stature. He worked for Gallardo early in his career and then founded the Sinaloa cartel. He was arrested in 1993 and sentenced to twenty years in prison, but he bribed prison officials to help him escape in 2001. He was arrested again in 2014 but escaped a year later after having a tunnel built under the prison. He was caught again in 2016 and extradited to the United States where he faced ten criminal charges related to drug trafficking. He was convicted and sentenced to life in prison and USD 12.6 billion in forfeiture.

drug cartels. Although the details of Obrador's new strategy for combating DTOs are still being developed, his ideas have so far been met with skepticism.

Further Reading

Central Intelligence Agency. 2018. "The World Factbook." https://www.cia.gov/library /publications/resources/the-world-factbook/.

Durán-Martínez, Angélica. 2015. "Drugs around the Corner: Domestic Drug Markets and Violence in Colombia and Mexico." *Latin American Politics and Society* 57 (3): 122–46. https://doi.org/10.1111/j.1548-2456.2015.00274.x.

Germá-Bel, and Maximilian Holst. 2016. "A Two-Sided Coin: Disentangling the Economic Effects of the 'War on Drugs' in Mexico." IREA Working Papers 201611. University of Barcelona, Research Institute of Applied Economics. https://ideas.repec.org/p/ira /wpaper/201611.html.

Quackenbush, Casey. 2019. "Mexico's President Declares an End to the Drug War." *Time*, January 31, 2019. http://time.com/5517391/mexico-president-ends-drug-war/.

UNODC (United Nations Office on Drugs and Crime). 2017. *World Drug Report 2017.* Vienna: United Nations Publications. https://www.unodc.org/wdr2017/.

UNODC (United Nations Office on Drugs and Crime). 2019. *Global Study on Homicide."* Vienna: United Nations Publications. https://www.unodc.org/gsh/.

THE NETHERLANDS

The Netherlands is a northern European country located across the English Channel from the United Kingdom and shares land borders with Germany to the east and Belgium to the south. The country of seventeen million people has a predominantly Dutch population that subscribes to varying religious beliefs. The head of state is a monarch, King Willem-Alexander (1967–) as of 2014, although the functioning of the government is the responsibility of a constitutional parliament. The Netherlands is one of the original six members of the European Union, a political and economic alliance of twenty-eight countries. It is a very wealthy country with a high standard of living. It has a GDP per capita of USD 53,900, just below the United States (USD 59,800). The Netherlands has been a world leader in liberal drug policies, which sometimes conflicts with the preferences of some of its partners in the European Union.

Historical Origins of Drug Policy

The Dutch became involved in the global drug trade in the early 1600s as the United Dutch East Indies Company developed trading posts in Asian colonies and became involved in the opium market. Between 1816 and 1915, opium sales comprised approximately 10 percent of the income generated by the Dutch colonies (de Kort 1994). Opiates were used as painkillers in the Dutch medical community throughout the 1800s, but by the end of the century, doctors and pharmacists were becoming concerned about the recreational use of opiates. Around the same time, opium-leasing profits were declining, so the government took control over the sale and distribution of the drug.

Colonies also provided the Netherlands with access to cocaine. Coca was grown in the colonies in Indonesia and harvested from Peru and Bolivia in South America. A cocaine factory was opened in Amsterdam to process the drug, mainly for medical purposes. By the 1920s, the Netherlands was a world leader in cocaine production. Around the same time, the international community started to lobby for tighter regulation of the drug trade in the colonies. The Netherlands was reluctant to embrace uniform legislation because the drug trade was very profitable.

The political and economic landscape changed dramatically after the end of World War II, and the independence of Indonesia brought the Netherlands opium trade to an end. Instead the marijuana market expanded as it was legal until 1953. By the 1960s, psychoactive drugs also grew in popularity, especially as part of youth countercultures.

"Two-Track" Drug Policy

In the 1960s, the cultural attitudes toward drug use in the Netherlands were not punitive, as they were in the United States. Most Dutch viewed drug use as a personal choice rather than as deviant behavior. When the government commissioned a formal study of drug use and its individual and social consequences, experts warned against using criminal law to regulate behaviors that primarily harmed people participating in such activities. They also recommended carefully considering the risks of different kinds of drug use, rather than treating all illicit drugs as equally harmful. Finally, experts advocated for a public health response to drug use, rather than a criminal justice response.

As a result of these expert opinions, the Baan Committee issued a report in 1972 making recommendations to update drug policy in the Netherlands. Most importantly, the committee recommended a "two-track" policy. They argued that the government's response to drug use should depend on the type of drugs involved. "Soft drugs," such as cannabis, were considered fairly harmless. Casual users and small-quantity dealers should largely be left alone. "Hard drugs," such as cocaine or heroin, should elicit a different response. Addicts should be treated through the health system rather than the criminal justice system, but large-scale dealers of hard drugs should be sanctioned by the criminal justice system.

These recommendations informed the revision of the Opium Act of the Netherlands, which was originally adopted in 1919 in response to international pressure to better regulate the opium trade from colonies. The 1976 Revised Opium Act adopted the two-track recommendation of the Baan Commission. It was considered a "pragmatic and normalizing" drug policy based on the philosophy that illegal drugs will never be completely eliminated and drug use is a normal social problem (Leuw 1994). This approach embraces education and prevention to reduce illegal drug use, as well as social and medical assistance for drug addicts. As a result of this new policy, the Netherlands has since adopted relatively progressive drug programs including needle exchanges, free testing of pills for harmful additives, free methadone, and medical uses of marijuana.

"Coffee Shops"

The revised Dutch drug policy did not legalize soft drugs, but rather decriminalized them. This meant that the national government was not going to pursue legal action against users and small-quantity drug dealers of soft drugs, but instead would let local authorities deal with these matters. As most local police and prosecutors did not find pursuing these cases very efficient or effective, casual use of soft drugs like cannabis was largely accepted.

In the 1970s, local coffee and tea shops began selling small quantities of marijuana to customers. Initially, the sales were fairly discreet, but by the 1980s, the availability of soft drugs in these shops was well known. For the most part, as long as these shops were not selling hard drugs or causing problems for local residents, they were largely left unregulated.

Government attitudes toward coffee shops shifted somewhat in the 1990s, partly due to international pressure. When Sweden joined the European Union, they lobbied for more punitive drug policies, putting pressure on the Netherlands to do more to control drug use within its borders. Additionally, authorities were concerned about the possibility of organized crime groups taking control over coffee shop markets. In 1995, a national law was passed to add regulations to coffee shops. In particular, it became clear that selling marijuana to youth under eighteen years old would not be tolerated. Shops were also required to stock less than 500 grams of cannabis, and customers were only allowed to purchase five grams a day. The prohibition against hard drugs was also reinforced with the new regulations. Finally, coffee shops were not allowed to advertise drugs and they could not cause nuisance in their local neighborhoods. In 1999, another law was passed giving mayors the power to close local coffee shops (Grund and Breeksema 2013).

Another wave of regulation over coffee shops came between 2002 and 2012, driven largely by conservative politicians who advocated for stronger drug enforcement. In 2002, a law was passed to build stronger relationships between law enforcement and local communities to abolish and prevent the cultivation of cannabis. In 2012, legislators tried to establish a "weed pass" to make coffee shops available only to local residents, but initial experiments with this policy only increased illegal drug sales in public and increased nuisance problems. In 2013, a law was passed to limit coffee shop sales to residents of the Netherlands to decrease drug tourism. Another law was proposed to change the classification of cannabis with more than 15 percent THC to a hard drug, which was not adopted.

As of 2017, there were 567 coffee shops in the Netherlands (European Monitoring Centre for Drugs and Drug Addition 2018). Only about 25 percent of municipalities in the country allow coffee shops, and half of all such shops are located in the five largest cities (Grund and Breeksema 2013). Despite some political trends to regulate coffee shops more strictly, the Dutch public still supports the two-track drug policy. Government reviews of the policy in the late 2000s confirmed that separating the drug markets and respective government responses was a successful strategy that reduces the harm of illegal drug use.

Drug Use Patterns

According to the Netherlands Drug Report (European Monitoring Centre for Drugs and Drug Addition 2018), in 2016, there were 21,118 registered drug offenses. More than half of these offenses were for soft drugs (List I), and most of the hard drug (List II) offenses were for possession. By and large, the most common drug used by adults in the Netherlands is cannabis. In 2017, the percentage of fifteen- to thirty-four-year-olds who used cannabis was 15.7, whereas 7.4 percent used ecstasy, 3.7 percent used cocaine, and 3.6 percent used amphetamines. Drug use is highly concentrated among this age group, and men are one-and-a-half times more likely to use illegal drugs than women in the Netherlands.

The number of drug-related deaths increased from 95 in 2006 to 235 in 2016, with 31 percent of those in 2016 due to opioids. The incidence of HIV and hepatitis among drug users in the Netherlands is quite low, largely because the country has had free needle and syringe exchange programs for over three decades. There are also thirty-one drug consumption facilities in twenty-five cities in the Netherlands, where drug users can inject, smoke, or inhale drugs under the supervision of trained staff (European Monitoring Centre for Drugs and Drug Addition 2018).

Further Reading

Central Intelligence Agency. 2018. "The World Factbook." https://www.cia.gov/library/publications/resources/the-world-factbook/.

Chatwin, Caroline. 2018. "Mixed Messages from Europe on Drug Policy Reform: The Cases of Sweden and the Netherlands." *Journal of Drug Policy Analysis* 11 (1). https://doi.org/10.1515/jdpa-2015-0009.

de Kort, Marcel. 1994. "A Brief History of Drugs in the Netherlands." In *Between Prohibition and Legalization: The Dutch Experiment in Drug Policy*, edited by Ed Leuw and Ineke Haen Marshall, 3–22. Amsterdam, the Netherlands: Kugler Publications.

Dolin, Benjamin. 2001. *National Drug Policy: The Netherlands*. Prepared for the Special Committee of the Senate on Illegal Drugs. Ottawa, ON: Library of Parliament.

European Monitoring Centre for Drugs and Drug Addiction. 2018 "Netherlands Country Drug Report." http://www.emcdda.europa.eu/countries/drug-reports/2018/netherlands_en.

Grund, Jean-Paul, and Joost Breeksema. 2013. "Coffee Shops and Compromise." https://repub.eur.nl/pub/50745/.

Leuw, Ed. 1994. "Initial Construction and Development of the Official Dutch Drug Policy." In *Between Prohibition and Legalization: The Dutch Experiment in Drug Policy*, edited by Ed Leuw and Ineke Haen Marshall, 23–40. Amsterdam, the Netherlands: Kugler Publications.

PORTUGAL

Portugal is a small country located in southwestern Europe, to the east of the Atlantic Ocean, west of Spain, and north of Morocco. The majority of the nearly 10.5 million people are Catholic Portuguese. The country has been a democracy since 1974 when a military coup overthrew the ultraconservative, nationalist dictatorship that had been in power since 1933 (Central Intelligence Agency 2018). The sudden opening of the country to the international community and the accompanying economic modernization of the 1970s and 1980s brought about rapid social changes including rising drug use. Against this backdrop, Portugal implemented a radical, and controversial, drug policy at the beginning of the twenty-first century.

Harm Reduction and Decriminalization

Portugal's geographic location, straddling Europe and North Africa and bordering the Atlantic Ocean, makes it an ideal location for drug trafficking. It is a key transit nation for cocaine and ecstasy from Brazil, cocaine from Mexico, hashish from Morocco, and cannabis from southern Africa to navigate to European markets. Despite this activity, Portugal has not developed large-scale organized crime groups involved in drug trafficking nor does it have a large problem with domestic drug use.

In fact, the prevalence of drug usage among the Portuguese has historically been low relative to other European countries, although systematic data collection in Portugal was not available before the 1990s. However, after the end of the dictatorship in 1974 and the independence of Portuguese colonies in 1975, the country experienced dramatic social changes. Large numbers of people moved from rural areas to the two main cities, Porto and Lisbon. Soldiers returned from former colonies with exposure to various drugs. The country opened its borders for travel and trade as part of its democratization and economic modernization, which also made it easier for illicit products like drugs to enter the country.

By the 1990s, drug use in general was still fairly low in Portugal, but grew quickly into a crisis. In particular, heroin became more popular among the Portuguese. As an injectable drug, heroin usage led to an increase in related health problems, notably hepatitis and HIV. Heroin was also consumed in public spaces and was highly visible to the general population. It was a preferred drug across all social classes, and was not just a problem among the economically marginalized.

According to police statistics, in 1991, 4,667 people in Portugal were arrested for drug offenses. This number increased to 6,380 in 1995 and 11,395 in 1998. Of the arrests in 1998, 45 percent were related to heroin (Van Het Loo, Van Beusekom, and Kahan 2002). What was more alarming was the fact that the number of drug users diagnosed with acquired immunodeficiency syndrome (AIDS) increased from 47 in 1990 to 590 in 1997, and drug-related deaths reached a peak of 369 in 1999 (Hughes and Stevens 2010).

In response to the heroin and public health crises, the Portuguese government appointed a commission of experts in 1998 to study the problem and make

An increase in injectable drug use in Portugal in the 1990s led to a public health crisis with rapidly rising rates of hepatitis and HIV. In response the country adopted a radical decriminalization drug policy that significantly reduced these health problems. (iStockPhoto.com)

recommendations for changes. The commission advocated for an evidence-based strategy that emphasized harm reduction. In particular, the commission recommended the decriminalization of drug use and increased resources for prevention, harm reduction, treatment, and social reintegration.

The Portuguese government turned the commission's report into the first national drug strategy. The plan emphasized a humanistic and pragmatic approach to drug use. Realizing that a drug-free society was unrealistic, the strategy instead aimed for a reduction in drug consumption along with minimizing the health and social risks associated with drug usage. While drug users had been marginalized in Portuguese society, the new plan reframed drug users as people who needed help and who could recover and be reintegrated into society.

The national drug strategy led to the passage of a law in 2001 that decriminalized drug use and drug possession for *all* illicit substances. The law did not distinguish between "hard" and "soft" drugs. Legalization was not a realistic option given Portugal's participation in United Nations conventions prohibiting illicit drugs, as well as concerns among the international community that legalization could increase drug problems in neighboring countries. Instead, drug possession for personal use became an administrative offense rather than a criminal one.

Prior to 2001, possessing, acquiring, or growing drugs for personal use were crimes punishable by up to one year in prison. After the new law went into effect, newly formed Commissions for Dissuasion of Drug Addiction (known as CDTs) became responsible for sanctioning drug offenders. Importantly, decriminalization was limited to personal use and possession of up to a ten-day supply of a drug. Possessing larger quantities, selling, mass producing, or trafficking illicit drugs were still criminal offenses handled by the legal system. For example, a conviction for trafficking drugs could bring a sentence of either one-to-five years or four-to-twelve years, depending on the substance and quantity involved.

The CDTs are regional panels of three experts, such as health professionals, social workers, or lawyers, who review cases of drug use and possession for personal use and administer sanctions to the offender. Their main purpose is to discourage drug use and encourage treatment for addicts. The CDTs have a range of sanctions to choose from, which includes community service, fines, suspension of professional licenses, location restrictions, and treatment (both outpatient and inpatient). Panels consider numerous factors specific to the case before deciding on the appropriate sanction, such as the severity of the offense, if the offender was a recreational or habitual offender, the type of drug involved, and the social and financial circumstances of the offender.

Importantly, the national drug strategy also increased resources for prevention and treatment of drug abuse. Healthcare and drug treatment are available free of charge to drug users. The country implemented needle and syringe exchange programs for the general public and in prisons to reduce the transmission of infectious diseases. It also adopted opioid substitution therapy, mainly methadone maintenance treatment, for both the public and prisoners. Subsequent five-year action plans for the national drug policy have continued to support these efforts. Additionally, in 2013, a new drug law was passed to prohibit the production, advertisement, sale, or distribution of new psychoactive substances (NPS).

Controversies and Evaluations

The passage of the 2001 law raised concerns among the Portuguese public and the international community that decriminalization would be a "green light" for drug use and would increase usage rather than deter it. As part of the national drug strategy, Portugal began a regular, systematic collection of data related to drug use, drug crime, and treatment. In fact, after 2001, the data showed small-to-moderate increases in drug use among the Portuguese. However, researchers have argued that the increase seems likely caused by recreational users rather than addicts, and that by reducing the stigmatization associated with drug use, people may be more willing to report their usage after the law was passed compared to before.

Early evaluations of the effectiveness of the 2001 law also produced conflicting conclusions depending on what data were used and how they were interpreted. While it is true that there has not been a dramatic decline in overall drug use in Portugal since decriminalization, many experts still argue that the benefits of the policy outweigh the costs. For example, between 2001 and 2009, problematic drug use, which was the main concern prompting legal changes, declined from 7.6 per 100,000 to 6.8 per 100,000 among fifteen- to sixty-four-year-olds. Equally important, injecting drugs decreased from 3.5 per 100,000 people to 2 per 100,000 during the same time period (Hughes and Stevens 2010).

Health benefits of the national drug plan have also been very positive. There have been significant reductions in overdose and opiate-related deaths, as well as in cases of HIV, hepatitis, and tuberculosis since 2001 (Hughes and Stevens 2010). Additionally, decriminalization has freed up criminal justice resources. Between 1999 and 2008, the percentage of drug offenders in prison decreased from 44 percent to 21 percent. Police also report being able to focus more resources on trafficking rather than possession (Hughes and Stevens 2010).

Drug Use and Treatment

The most common illicit drug used in Portugal is cannabis, followed by cocaine and ecstasy. In 2017, it was estimated that 8 percent of the population used cannabis within the last year, about twice as many men as women. Cocaine use in the past year was 0.3 percent and ecstasy was 0.2 percent. Of the people arrested for drug offenses in 2017, 72 percent were for possession, mainly cannabis followed by cocaine and heroin (European Monitoring Centre for Drugs and Drug Addiction 2018).

A study of fifteen- and sixteen-year-old students found that alcohol was the most common substance used within the last month (41 percent). About 16 percent of the youth reported using cannabis within the last month, and less than 5 percent reported using other illicit drugs. The lifetime use of cannabis by students in Portugal was only slightly lower than most European countries; however, the use of NPS in Portugal was much lower than other countries (European Monitoring Centre for Drugs and Drug Addiction 2018).

There are fifty-nine inpatient therapeutic drug treatment centers in Portugal offering three-to-twelve-month programs. The number of patients treated in an outpatient drug center in 2017 was 27,150, whereas 2,046 were treated in therapeutic communities, and 1,140 in prisons. About three out of five patients entering treatment in 2017 were first-time clients. In the same year, about 16,000 patients received opioid substitution treatment, typically methadone maintenance (European Monitoring Centre for Drugs and Drug Addiction 2018).

Further Reading

Central Intelligence Agency. 2018. "The World Factbook." https://www.cia.gov/library /publications/resources/the-world-factbook/.

European Monitoring Centre for Drugs and Drug Addiction. 2018. "Portugal Drug Report." http://www.emcdda.europa.eu/countries/drug-reports/2018/portugal_en.

Hughes, Caitlin Elizabeth, and Alex Stevens. 2010. "What Can We Learn From The Portuguese Decriminalization of Illicit Drugs?" *The British Journal of Criminology* 50 (6): 999–1022. https://doi.org/10.1093/bjc/azq038.

Hughes, Caitlin Elizabeth, and Alex Stevens. 2015. "A Resounding Success or a Disastrous Failure: Re-Examining the Interpretation of Evidence on the Portuguese Decriminalization of Illicit Drugs." In *New Approaches to Drug Policies: A Time for Change*, edited by

Marten W. Brienen and Jonathan D. Rosen, 137–62. London: Palgrave Macmillan UK. https://doi.org/10.1057/9781137450999_9.

Van Het Loo, Mirjam, Ineke Van Beusekom, and James P. Kahan. 2002. "Decriminalization of Drug Use in Portugal: The Development of a Policy." *The ANNALS of the American Academy of Political and Social Science* 582 (1): 49–63. https://doi.org/10.1177/000271620258200104.

"Want to Win the War on Drugs? Portugal Might Have the Answer." n.d. *Time.* http://time.com/longform/portugal-drug-use-decriminalization/.

VIETNAM

Vietnam is a country of approximately ninety-seven million people located in Southeast Asia, south of China, and east of Cambodia and Laos. It is located across the South China Sea from the Philippines. The majority of the population is Kinh (Viet), although there are fifty-four recognized ethnic groups in the country. Vietnam was part of French Indochina during the nineteenth century but has been an independent, communist country since the reunification of North and South Vietnam in 1976, shortly after the end of the Vietnam War (1955–1975). In 1986, the communist government introduced some limited free-market reforms to boost the struggling economy. It is still a relatively poor country, with a GDP per capita of USD 6,900, which is similar to its neighbor Laos (USD 7,400) but much lower than China (USD 16,700) (Central Intelligence Agency 2018). Much like other countries in this region, drug production, trafficking, and use in Vietnam have been strongly shaped by its colonial legacy, geographic location, and changing political and economic environments.

Colonization and Drugs

Between 929 and 1885, Vietnam was ruled by a series of imperial dynasties. In the early 1800s, as the Hmong from China were migrating south, they introduced British opium from Burma (currently Myanmar) into North Vietnam. The Vietnamese monarchy was concerned that habitual opium use would have a negative impact on the country's economy, so smoking opium and smuggling it across the border were criminalized.

France gained control of Vietnam in 1885 after the Sino-French War (1883–1885) and combined it with Cambodia and later Laos to form French Indochina. The French financed their colonial activities through the opium trade, which then introduced the drug to the southern provinces of Vietnam. It is estimated that by 1940, when Vietnam was occupied by Japan during World War II, about 2 percent of the Vietnamese population was addicted to opium, with especially high rates of use among elites (Nguyen and Scannapieco 2008).

When Japan was defeated in World War II in 1945, France regained control over Vietnam but communist leader Hồ Chí Minh (1890–1969) led a resistance movement against the foreign power. For nine years the Vietnamese fought against colonial rule in the First Indochina War and finally won independence in 1954. The role of drugs in the new country was debated, as some argued they should be banned because they were part of colonial history, whereas others saw the economic potential of opium production. A compromise was reached whereby opium cultivation and consumption were tolerated in the highlands, but not in other parts of the country.

The General Accords of 1954 divided French Indochina into three independent countries: Vietnam, Cambodia, and Laos. It also divided Vietnam into two administrative regions that were supposed to be temporary until elections could be held. Instead the country remained separated as the communist Democratic Republic of Vietnam (North Vietnam) and the anti-communist Republic of Vietnam (South Vietnam). Tensions between the two states escalated and Vietnam became the center of the Cold War battle between the Soviet Union and China supporting North Vietnam and the United States backing South Vietnam. The result was the Vietnam War (also called the Second Indochina War) that lasted until 1975.

The United States' War on Drugs

During the course of the Vietnam War, American government officials were concerned with drug production across Southeast Asia and its harmful effects on soldiers fighting in Vietnam. As early as the 1950s, the U.S. Federal Bureau of Narcotics set up an office in the region to better prevent the supply of illegal drugs to Americans and train the South Vietnamese police to enforce drug laws. In 1969, the U.S. military launched a campaign to destroy marijuana plants and succeeded in eliminating half a million plants. However, this policy created resentment among local farmers, who not only earned a living from marijuana cultivation but were also concerned about the effects of crop spraying on their livestock.

In 1971, U.S. president Richard Nixon (1913–1994) launched the War on Drugs in the United States that had a direct impact on Vietnam. The U.S. government threatened to end military and economic aid to countries that would not assist its efforts to control illegal drug production, trafficking, and use. Estimates about drug usage among U.S. military personnel in Vietnam were exaggerated to gain public and political support for the War on Drugs (Kuzmarov 2008). The U.S. threats spurred South Vietnamese president Nguyen Van Thieu (1923–2001) to increase antidrug activity, which he assigned to Admiral Chung Tan Cang (1926–2007).

Cang created a Joint Narcotics Investigation Division (JNID) to improve police practices regarding drug enforcement. He fired hundreds of police officers that he believed were corrupt or ineffective. He sent promising police officers to the United States for counter-narcotics training. This strategy was accompanied by a cultural campaign highlighting the harmful effects of drugs, which included parades and speeches celebrating the country's victories over drugs. Finally, Thieu also increased the penalty for trafficking opium, morphine, or heroin to a mandatory life sentence.

These strategies appeased American officials, but they were not truly effective. In the midst of the social upheaval from decades of war and thriving drug economy, the efforts to reduce drug supplies in Vietnam were not successful (Kuzmarov 2008). The Vietnam War ended with the victory of the North Vietnamese, who reunited the country under communist rule in 1976. The new communist government quickly banned illegal drug use and had some success in reducing the number of drug addicts, particularly among Vietnamese soldiers.

Changing Drug Patterns and HIV

In 1986, the Communist Party of Vietnam introduced major economic changes to move Vietnam away from the communist planned economy toward a free-market economy, following China's lead. These reforms not only improved the economy but also increased urbanization and globalization, which in turn increased drug markets and drug use. Between 1994 and 2004, the number of drug addicts per 100,000 people in Vietnam increased from 78 to 208; one-third of the drug addicts lived in the two largest cities in the country; two-thirds of addicts were ethnic minorities; and two-thirds were between eighteen and twenty-five years old (Nguyen and Scannapieco 2008). The 1980s and 1990s also brought about a change in the drug preferences of users from smoking opium toward injecting heroin and taking methamphetamines. In 2009, it was estimated that 83 percent of the 150,000 people using illegal drugs in Vietnam were injecting heroin, and half of all drug users tested positive for the HIV (Vuong et al. 2012).

Prior to 1995, drug policy in Vietnam focused mainly on punishing drug suppliers. Drug users were typically subjected to home- and community-based treatment that included detoxification and moral teachings. However, this policy changed in response to the HIV epidemic. In 1995, an Ordinance on Administrative Violations was passed that required detention for drug users for three months to one year if other treatment programs were not successful. This law did not include harm reduction services for drug addicts, such as safe sex education or HIV treatment. The country's HIV policy was updated in 2005 to focus more on prevention by promoting condom use, needle and syringe exchange programs, and maintenance treatment for opioid addiction.

Compulsory Detention

Vietnam has continued to use compulsory detention for drug addicts since the mid-1990s, especially for repeat offenders. In 2005, there were eighty such centers around the country capable of serving 55,000 people. By 2010, there were 129 treatment centers housing up to 70,000 drug users (Vuong et al. 2012). Between 2006 and 2010, the government reported that 169,000 people were sent to compulsory drug treatment centers (Amon et al. 2014).

Vietnam's detention policy is controversial in the international community. On the one hand, some countries provide money to build new facilities in Vietnam or provide staff training or vocational programs, including the United States and the UNODC. On the other hand, drug addicts can be sent to detention centers for up to five years without legal due process (Vuong et al. 2012). Human rights groups advocate for closing these centers because people are being detained without a trial or legal representation, and there are numerous human rights abuses occurring in the centers. The Vietnamese government has responded to these concerns with a 2012 law that prohibits the detention of sex workers and allows drug addicts the right to a court hearing and a lawyer. Nonetheless, the government still does not allow independent international monitors to evaluate the living conditions and treatment of detained drug users.

Further Reading

Amon, Joseph J., Richard Pearshouse, Jane E. Cohen, and Rebecca Schleifer. 2014. "Compulsory Drug Detention in East and Southeast Asia: Evolving Government, UN and Donor Responses." *International Journal of Drug Policy* 25 (1): 13–20. https://doi.org/10.1016/j.drugpo.2013.05.019.

Central Intelligence Agency. 2018. "The World Factbook." https://www.cia.gov/library/publications/resources/the-world-factbook/.

Kuzmarov, Jeremy. 2008. "From Counter-Insurgency to Narco-Insurgency: Vietnam and the International War on Drugs." *Journal of Policy History* 20 (3): 344–78. https://doi.org/10.1353/jph.0.0019.

Nguyen, Van T., and Maria Scannapieco. 2008. "Drug Abuse in Vietnam: A Critical Review of the Literature and Implications for Future Research." *Addiction* 103 (4): 535–43. https://doi.org/10.1111/j.1360-0443.2007.02122.x.

UNODC (United Nations Office on Drugs and Crime). 2017. *World Drug Report 2017.* Vienna: United Nations Publications. https://www.unodc.org/wdr2017/.

Vuong, Thu, Robert Ali, Simon Baldwin, and Stephen Mills. 2012. "Drug Policy in Vietnam: A Decade of Change?" *International Journal of Drug Policy* 23 (4): 319–26. https://doi.org/10.1016/j.drugpo.2011.11.005.

Chapter 7: Mass Atrocities and International Justice

Janet P. Stamatel

OVERVIEW

The field of criminology has historically been concerned with documenting and explaining conventional crimes, also known as "street crimes," such as homicide, robbery, assault, burglary, fraud, drug offenses, etc., which are covered in chapter 1 of this volume. It was not until the end of the twentieth century that the discipline began to include the study of large-scale atrocities, such as genocide and crimes against humanity, within its domain. This shift in scope has been due, in part, to the growing globalization of criminology, which has brought more attention to international crimes and the evolving standards of international justice. Mass atrocities differ from conventional crimes in terms of their size, with numbers of offenders and victims in hundreds or thousands, and in terms of their relationship to national governments. Crimes are violations of state laws that sovereign governments have the authority to investigate, prosecute, and punish. In contrast, most mass atrocities implicate sovereign governments as perpetrators or accomplices in extreme violence, which presents a problem as to who will hold government leaders accountable for violating laws they are expected to enforce.

This issue became especially salient in the aftermath of World War II (1939–1945) when the international community was wrestling with the sheer scope of the Holocaust and Germany's systematic killing of approximately six million Jews and other ethnic and social groups deemed undesirable by the Nazi regime. Between 1945 and 1949, the Allied countries of France, Britain, the Soviet Union, and the United States held a series of military trials to hold Axis leaders, particularly Nazis, accountable for violations of international laws.

Numerous issues were raised during these trials that prompted the newly formed United Nations (UN) (1945) to codify certain human rights. In 1948, the UN developed a Universal Declaration of Human Rights that, among other protections, boldly sates that every person is entitled to "the right to life, liberty, and security of persons" (United Nations 2015). In the same year, the UN also adopted the Convention on the Prevention and Punishment of the Crime of Genocide, which confirmed that genocide is a violation of international law and defined the acts that constitute genocide. More directly related to the Nuremburg Trials, the Geneva Conventions of 1949 articulated human rights within the context of wars and their aftermath. They specifically protect wounded and sick military personnel, prisoners of war, and civilians against murder, torture, and inhumane treatment. Two additional protocols were added in 1977 to broaden the scope of violent conflicts including international, civil, and guerrilla wars.

These laws were important for establishing a consensus regarding acts that are so egregious that they violate nearly universal norms regarding basic human rights. However, they raised a lot of questions about how they would be enforced. From the 1970s through the early 2000s, truth commissions were often used to hold governments accountable for their crimes, to publicly acknowledge the harm done to victims, and to carve a path for peace. Truth commissions are sanctioned by governments to investigate mass atrocities, document crimes, identify perpetrators and victims, and recommend strategies to reconcile political differences and restore peace. The goal of the commissions is to acknowledge wrongdoing and not to directly punish offenders. For example, the Truth and Reconciliation Commission of South Africa established in 1995 was instrumental in documenting the harmful impact of apartheid and facilitating the transition to democratic governance. In this chapter, El Salvador and Peru are examples of countries that have used truth commissions to address mass atrocities.

By the 1990s, the international community began to emphasize a stronger criminal justice response to mass atrocities, with a shift toward punishing perpetrators. In response to the atrocities committed during the Bosnian War, the UN established an International Tribunal to investigate criminal violations of international law. These tribunals were temporary legal structures with limited jurisdiction to deal with specific crimes. Two examples of international tribunals in this chapter are Bosnia-Herzegovina and Cambodia. A similar tribunal was also established in the aftermath of the genocide in Rwanda, which is discussed in chapter 10 on Punishment.

The experiences of these limited courts prompted discussions of a more permanent international court to try cases of certain violations of international law, particularly those related to mass atrocities. In 2002, the UN Rome Statute went into effect, which created the International Criminal Court (ICC) located in The Hague, the Netherlands. The ICC has jurisdiction over cases of genocide, crimes against humanity, war crimes, and crimes of aggression. As of 2019, the ICC has heard twenty-seven cases (International Criminal Court, n.d.).

The countries presented in this chapter address mass atrocities that occurred in the 1970s (Cambodia) through the present day (Myanmar). The events vary greatly in terms of the length of the conflicts, the number of deaths, the types of harms victims experienced, and the international responses. Cambodia, El Salvador, and Peru represent historical examples from the Cold War era of the 1970s through the early 1990s when communist ideology, economic inequality, and the treatment of rural peasants triggered long and violent conflicts. The case of Bosnia-Herzegovina was the result of the end of the Cold War in the 1990s and represents the shift in international justice from truth commissions to international tribunals. Georgia, the Ivory Coast, and Sudan are cases from the first decade of the twenty-first century that have been referred to the ICC. Finally, Myanmar is an ongoing conflict that highlights the difficulties of labeling mass atrocities and the international community's discomfort in doing so, even after the establishment of the ICC.

Further Reading

"International Criminal Court." n.d. https://www.icc-cpi.int/Pages/Main.aspx.

Rafter, Nicole. 2016. *The Crime of All Crimes: Toward a Criminology of Genocide*. New York: NYU Press.

Savelsberg, Joachim. 2010. *Crime and Human Rights: Criminology of Genocide and Atrocities*. Thousand Oaks, CA: SAGE.

United Nations. 2015. "Universal Declaration of Human Rights." https://www.un.org/en /universal-declaration-human-rights/index.html.

BOSNIA-HERZEGOVINA

Bosnia-Herzegovina is a country of nearly four million people located in southeastern Europe, across the Adriatic Sea from Italy. It was once a republic of Yugoslavia, a multiethnic, multireligious, communist country formed after World War I (1914–1918). When the communist system in Central and Eastern Europe collapsed in the late 1980s due to economic troubles and political uprisings, the country of Yugoslavia broke apart into six independent countries (Bosnia-Herzegovina, Croatia, the Former Yugoslav Republic of Macedonia, Montenegro, Serbia, and Slovenia), and one partially recognized state, Kosovo. The population comprises three main ethnic groups: Bosniaks (50.1 percent), Serbs (30.8 percent), and Croats (15.4 percent). The majority of the population is Muslim (50.7 percent), although 30.7 percent are Orthodox Christian and 15.2 percent are Catholic (Central Intelligence Agency 2018). The dissolution of Yugoslavia was peaceful in some cases, led to brief civil wars in others, and most notably involved a series of mass atrocities and violations of international humanitarian laws in Bosnia-Herzegovina. The Bosnian tragedy led to the formation of the International Criminal Tribunal for the former Yugoslavia (ICTY), which was a predecessor to the current ICC.

The End of Yugoslavia

In January 1990, a meeting of the League of Communists of Yugoslavia was held to address the growing economic and political unrest that had been spreading throughout the communist countries of Central and Eastern Europe including the former Soviet Union. At this meeting, the Serbian representative, Slobodan Milošević (1941–2006), advocated for a voting system of one vote per person, which would favor the republic with the largest population that happened to be Serbia. In contrast, the Slovenian and Croatian representatives sought a more even distribution of power across the republics. The issue could not be resolved to everyone's satisfaction and led to the dissolution of the Yugoslav Communist Party.

In 1991, the republics of Slovenia and Croatia declared their independence from Yugoslavia. This led to a brief Ten-Day War between Slovenia and the Yugoslav military, resulting in fewer than fifty deaths (Mennecke 2012). This also sparked a war between Croatia and Serbia that was fought on and off between 1991 and 1995. Approximately 20,000 people died in that war, and about 250,000 had to flee their homes (BBC News 2003). Both sides of the conflict sought to forcibly remove opposing ethnic groups from their territories using inhumane and illegal tactics, which led to the indictments against both Croats and Serbs by the ICTY, although the majority of the ICTY cases were against Serbs, in large part because of their subsequent actions in Bosnia-Herzegovina.

The Bosnian War

Following Slovenian and Croatian independence, the republic of Macedonia peacefully declared autonomy in 1991 (and formally adopted the name of "Former Yugoslav Republic of Macedonia" (FYROM) due to a conflict with Greece over the name of "Macedonia"). This was followed by a referendum for self-governance in Bosnia-Herzegovina that was passed in 1992. In sharp contrast to the relatively uncontested separation of Macedonia, the Bosnian case escalated ethnic and religious tensions, resulting in a bloody conflict over territory and identity.

At the time of the war, Bosnia-Herzegovina was the most ethnically diverse Yugoslav Republic. The country was also situated geographically in the middle of Yugoslavia, with Croatia and Slovenia to the north and west; Serbia to the east; and Montenegro, Kosovo, and the FYROM to the south. These two features meant that the secession of Bosnia-Herzegovina from Yugoslavia would be hotly contested. The referendum for independence passed but was not supported by the Bosnian Serbian politicians.

In response to the declaration of independence, Serbian politician Radovan Karadžić (1945–) announced the formation of an independent Serbian Republic of Bosnia, of which he was president. Fighting ensued involving three main factions: Bosnian Muslims, Bosniaks, who wanted an independent Bosnia-Herzegovina, Croats who aimed to establish a Croatian Republic, and Serbs (Yugoslavs) loyal to an independent Serbian Republic of Bosnia who were supported by Serbia.

The violence included acts of ethnic cleansing by Bosnian Serb forces against Muslims in Bosnia-Herzegovina. These tactics were designed to create a "greater Serbia," in which all Serbs would be united in the same state. To that end, Karadžić explicitly announced his plans to physically separate Serbs from the other two ethnic communities. In particular, Bosnian Serbs enacted the Ram Plan, which included, among other things, a strategy to target Muslim women and children to instill fear in the Muslim enclaves and encourage military withdrawal. This was accompanied by the Bram Plan that forced Muslims to move out of areas that the Serbs wanted to control, isolating the Muslim population in selected geographic areas. By June 1992, Bosnian Serb and Serbian forces controlled two-thirds of Bosnia-Herzegovina, leading to the displacement of 1.3 million people (Mennecke 2012).

In response to reports of ethnic cleansing and other mass atrocities, the UN Security Council declared Sarajevo, Goradze, Srebrenica, and three other Muslim communities in Serb-controlled areas as "safe zones" that were protected by UN peacekeepers. Additionally, in May 1993, the UN Security Council established the ICTY to address violations of humanitarian law that had been occurring in the territories of the former Yugoslavia since its dissolution in 1991. This was a historic decision as it was the first organized international effort to address such crimes since World War II.

Unfortunately, these steps by the UN did not immediately quell the violence. Large-scale massacres that began in 1992 continued throughout the war. The most notable of these events was ethnic cleansing in the Prijedor region, resulting in nearly 20,000 deaths; the nearly four-year long siege of Sarajevo, the capital of Bosnia-Herzegovina, during which approximately 14,000 people were killed; and the massacre in Srebrenica, in which nearly 8,000 Bosnian men and boys were systematically killed in 1995 (Mennecke 2012; United Nations, n.d.). Despite the numerous incidents of mass killings, it was the case of Srebrenica that drew the most attention from the international community and eventually led to the formal end of the war in November 1995. It is estimated that more than 100,000 people died during the course of the Bosnian War (Mennecke 2012).

Genocide in Srebrenica

Srebrenica is a small mountain town in the eastern part of Bosnia. Before the war, its population was 5,800 people, most of whom were Bosniaks. As Serbian forces made headway in Bosnia, Srebrenica soon became home to nearly 50,000 Bosnian refugees (Wagner 2010). When Serbs took control over the area, they first removed Bosniaks from the local police forces and had them surrender their weapons to minimize resistance. Next they cut off access to the community by closing all roads and other access points, planting minefields, and shelling the towns regularly. Bosniaks trying to escape were either killed by snipers or mines, or captured and taken to concentration camps in Sušica and Karakaj, where they were tortured and killed. Food supplies were also cut off, starving the trapped civilians.

The UN declared Srebrenica and five other areas as "safe areas" in April 1993 to prevent the Bosnian Serbs from taking control over these areas. However, this designation did not stop shelling and forced starvation. In early July, 1995 Bosnian Serb forces assumed control over the town and put more than 20,000 people, mostly women, children, and the elderly, on buses to deport them to other Muslim-controlled territories. Many of the women were raped either before deportation or taken to "rape camps" instead of Bosniak territories (Allen 1996). Between July 13 and 19, 1995 nearly 8,000 "battle-age" boys and men, many of whom were civilians, were systematically killed by the Bosnian Serb army under the control of Ratko Mladić (1942–) and a Serbian military unit called the Scorpions (Bećirević 2010). Most victims were shot and buried in mass graves.

The Srebrenica massacre was a breaking point for the international community and the North Atlantic Trade Organization (NATO) began bombing Serbian-controlled parts of Bosnia in August 1995. By November 1995, Bosnian Serbs agreed to a negotiated peace settlement that was drafted in Dayton, Ohio and signed in Paris, France. The Dayton–Paris agreement brought an end to the Bosnian War.

International Justice

In 1993, long before the Srebrenica massacre, the UN had already formed the ICTY to deal with a range of humanitarian crimes that had occurred since 1991. This was the first court of its kind since the Nuremberg and Tokyo tribunals following World War II, and it was the precedent for the International Criminal Tribunal of Rwanda and eventually the ICC. The court was given jurisdiction over individuals only, not militaries, political parties, or other organizations, for war crimes, crimes against humanity, genocide, and grave breaches of the Geneva Conventions. Rape and sexual abuse were not included in the ICTY's jurisdiction. Between 1993 and 2017, the ICTY indicted 161 people, ninety of whom were convicted and sentenced, thirty-seven had their proceedings terminated or their indictments withdrawn, nineteen were acquitted, thirteen were referred back to the countries of the former Yugoslavia, and two were retried by the UN (United Nations, n.d.).

The most well-known case of the ICTY was against Slobodan Milošević, who was the President of the Federal Republic of Yugoslavia from 1997 to 2000 and the sitting President of Serbia at the time of his indictments. It was the first time that the UN brought criminal charges against a sitting head of state. Numerous charges were brought against Milošević regarding Serbian activities in Kosovo, Croatia, and Bosnia-Herzegovina, including genocide in Srebrenica. The trial against Milošević began in 2002 but never reached a decision because Milošević died in custody in 2006 from a heart attack.

The most notable case related to Srebrenica was the indictment and conviction of Ratko Mladić, who was the commander of the Army of Republika Srpska in Bosnia-Herzegovina. He was indicted in 1995, arrested in 2011, and convicted in 2017.

Suicide in Court

Slobodan Praljak was a general in the Croatian Army who was convicted by the International Criminal Tribunal of the Former Yugoslavia for crimes against humanity, war crimes, and grave breaches of the Geneva Convention for his role in the persecution, murders, and inhumane treatment of Bosnian Muslims in the historical town of Mostar. He was sentenced to twenty years in prison in 2013. Praljak appealed his sentence, and when he appeared in court to learn that his appeal was denied, he declared his innocence and drank poison in the open courtroom, leading to his death.

He was found guilty of numerous crimes, including "genocide and persecution, extermination, murder, and the inhumane act of forcible transfer in the area of Srebrenica in 1995" (United Nations, n.d.). He was sentenced to life in prison, which was the most severe punishment the Tribunal had the authority to administer.

Further Reading

Allen, Beverly. 1996. *Rape Warfare: The Hidden Genocide in Bosnia-Herzegovina and Croatia.* Minneapolis: University of Minnesota Press.

BBC News. 2003. "Presidents Apologise over Croatian War." September 10, 2003. http://news.bbc.co.uk/2/hi/europe/3095774.stm.

Bećirević, Edina. 2010. "The Issue of Genocidal Intent and Denial of Genocide: A Case Study of Bosnia and Herzegovina." *East European Politics and Societies* 24 (4): 480–502.

Central Intelligence Agency. 2018. "The World Factbook." https://www.cia.gov/library/publications/resources/the-world-factbook/.

Mennecke, Martin. 2012. "Genocidal Violence in the Former Yugoslavia: Bosnia Herzegovina and Kosovo." In *Centuries of Genocide: Essays and Eyewitness Accounts*, edited by Samuel Totten and William S. Parsons, 507–54. New York: Routledge.

United Nations. n.d. "International Criminal Tribunal for the Former Yugoslavia." http://www.icty.org/en.

Wagner, Sarah. 2010. "Identifying Srebrenica's Missing: The 'Shaky Balance' of Universalism and Particularism." In *Transitional Justice: Global Mechanisms and Local Realities after Genocide and Mass Violence*, edited by Alexander Laban Hinton, 25–48. New Brunswick, NJ: Rutgers University Press.

CAMBODIA

Cambodia is a country of sixteen million people located in Southeast Asia, surrounded by Thailand, Laos, and Vietnam. It was part of French Indochina until it gained independence in 1953. Decades of internal and external conflicts hindered economic development, making Cambodia one of the poorest countries in Asia. The gross domestic product in Cambodia is USD 4,000, which is much lower than Thailand (USD 17,900), Laos (USD 7,400), and Vietnam (USD 6,900) (Central Intelligence Agency 2018). In the 1970s, Cambodia was caught in the middle of the Cold War between the democratic West and the communist East. As part of this political struggle, approximately two million people died in a systematic effort to eliminate people of certain ethnicities and social classes from the country. More than forty years later, the country and the international community are still trying to bring justice to the victims of this mass atrocity.

Civil War

Between 1887 and 1953, Cambodia belonged to French Indochina, along with Vietnam and parts of Laos and Thailand. It gained independence in 1953 as the Kingdom of Cambodia, ruled by King Norodom Sihanouk (1922–2012). During this political transition, Cambodia lost territorial control over the Mekong Delta to

Vietnam, which created diplomatic tensions between these two young countries. In 1955, the Vietnam War started, pitting the communist North Vietnamese, supported by the Soviet Union, against the non-communist South Vietnamese, supported by the United States and its allies. Cambodia officially declared neutrality in that war, although unofficially its position was more ambiguous.

Ten years into the Vietnam War, the United States began bombing parts of Cambodia to disrupt the supply routes of North Vietnam. Between 1965 and 1973, the United States had conducted at least 230,000 bombings, which served to alienate the Cambodian people from their king (Cox 2017). In 1970, King Sihanouk was overthrown in a peaceful coup. The new military government demanded that the North Vietnamese stop transporting supplies through Cambodia, and the North Vietnamese began attacking the new government and inciting a civil war. The North Vietnamese supported the Khmer Rouge, a communist political faction seeking to gain political power.

Pol Pot, born as Saloth Sar (1925–1998), was the leader of the Khmer Rouge. He was from an affluent family and received an elite education. While studying in France in the 1940s, he joined the Communist Party. He returned to Cambodia in 1953 with a radical vision for his country. Pol Pot believed that the ancient culture of the Khmer people, as epitomized by the great Angkor Empire in the eleventh through thirteenth centuries, had been tainted by foreign influences, particularly from surrounding countries. He called himself "The Original Khmer" and spearheaded a nationalist movement that prioritized race and nation.

Pol Pot encouraged the North Vietnamese to attack the Cambodian government, which also brought the United States and South Vietnamese forces into Cambodia to fight the North Vietnamese. While the Cambodian government and military were preoccupied with these international conflicts, Pol Pot and the Communist Party of Kampuchea, which means "Kingdom of Cambodia," continued to gain supporters and military strength. Eventually, they became strong enough that they no longer relied on North Vietnamese assistance. On January 1, 1975, Pol Pot launched a final attack on Phnom Penh, the capital of Cambodia, and the supply routes in the Mekong Region and succeeded in taking over the government on April 17, 1975. He immediately changed the name of the country to Democratic Kampuchea.

The Killing Fields

Pol Pot was strongly influenced by the Maoist version of communism that viewed the peasantry as the key to successful and rapid economic development. He aimed to collectivize agriculture and abolish money and markets. Additionally, he promoted a nationalist agenda of "Cambodia for Cambodians" and was highly paranoid of internal and external enemies. On his first day as the ruler of Cambodia, he ordered all cities to be evacuated. The government classified people as either "base people" or the peasantry and "new people" or city-dwellers. Urban Cambodians were seen as a threat to Pol Pot's new vision for Cambodia because they did not work the land and embraced multiculturalism. Urban residents were forced to leave their possessions and relocate to rural areas to work in the fields. These forced marches of citizens out of the cities led to tens of thousands of deaths through execution, starvation, and disease. Professionals, intellectuals, those with ties to foreign governments, and anyone believed to be a threat to the new regime were killed.

In addition to this class warfare, Pol Pot's regime targeted religious and ethnic groups other than Khmer. Massacres of Vietnamese had started under the military dictatorship, but Pol Pot eliminated all remaining Vietnamese in the country. Additionally, 300,000 Muslims (Chams) and 59,000 Buddhist monks were murdered, which was nearly the entire population of monks in Cambodia (Robertson 2013). Religion and education were outlawed to ensure loyalty to Angkor and the Communist Party. Executions were often brutal using poison or agricultural tools to save ammunition. There were so many mass graves that the Cambodian countryside was referred to as "the killing fields."

Pol Pot also established about 150 extermination camps. The most famous was a high school in Phnom Penh that was converted to Security Prison 21. It was called Tuol Sleng or "Hill of the Poisonous Trees." Of the 15,000 prisoners sent to Tuol Sleng, only five were known to have survived (Robertson 2013). Many of the prisoners worked for the previous government or were city-dwellers who were perceived as a threat to the new regime. The prisoners were cruelly tortured before execution.

The exact death toll inflicted by Pol Pot's regime is difficult to determine. The Yale University Genocide Studies program found evidence of over 1.3 million victims of execution (2018). The UN estimated two to three million deaths, including those from disease and starvation. At the beginning of Pol Pot's rule, there were approximately eight million people living in Cambodia, so he is accused of killing approximately one-fourth of the population.

Pol Pot's killings continued throughout his rule. On December 25, 1978, Vietnam invaded Cambodia and established the People's Republic of Kampuchea, which was under the direct influence of Vietnam and the Soviet Union. Pot went into hiding near

Tuol Sleng Prison was a notorious extermination camp built by Pol Pot in Phnom Penh where political prisoners were brutally tortured and killed. Only five people were known to have survived their experiences in the prison. (Danielal/Dreamstime.com)

the Thai border and tried to rebuild a military with support from China, but he was not successful.

Criminal Prosecutions

In the wake of the 1992 genocide in Bosnia-Herzegovina and the 1994 genocide in Rwanda, the international community was increasingly sensitive toward the need to achieve justice and reconciliation after mass atrocities. To establish an international tribunal to investigate the humanitarian crimes of the Khmer Rouge, the UN Security Council had to justify the need "to maintain or restore international peace and security," but the conflict in Cambodia had already ended (United Nations 2015). Instead, the UN argued that Cambodian legal professionals were poorly trained and subject to corruption and, therefore, could not adequately handle the investigation and prosecution of such a large and complicated case.

The Cambodian prime minister Hun Sen (1951–) objected to any court that Cambodia did not control, so it took several years to reach a compromise. In June 2003, the Extraordinary Chambers in the Courts of Cambodia (ECCC) was established to prosecute crimes committed during the existence of Democratic Kampuchea, or the Pol Pot regime. To balance power between international and Cambodian interests, the trial court consisted of five judges, three of whom were Cambodian, and the appeals court had seven judges, four of whom were Cambodian; however, all decisions required a super-majority (four of five trial judges and five of seven appeal judges) so that Cambodian judges could not solely determine all rulings. Cambodia also appointed the prosecutor and registrar of the court, but the UN assigned their deputies. Similar to other international tribunals, the death penalty was not allowed, and the court had no jurisdiction over corporate or political bodies. Unlike other tribunals, the ECCC included the destruction of cultural property in its jurisdiction.

The first case by the ECCC was in 2007 against Kaing Guek Eav (1942–), who was the head of Tuol Sleng, or Security Prison 21. He was convicted of several counts of crimes against humanity and grave breaches of the Geneva Conventions. He was sentenced to thirty-five years in prison in 2012. The second case began in 2011 against Nuon Chea (1926–), former Deputy Secretary of the Communist Party of Kampuchea, and Khieu Samphan (1931–), former Head of State of Democratic Kampuchea, for crimes against humanity, grave breaches of the Geneva Convention, and genocide against the Muslim Cham and Vietnamese. In 2013, both defendants were found guilty of crimes against humanity and sentenced to life imprisonment. The cases for other charges were still ongoing as of 2018. There were initially two other defendants in the case: Ieng Sary (1925–2013), former Deputy Prime Minister of Foreign Affairs, and his wife Ieng Thirith (1932–2015), former Minister of Social Affairs. Ieng Sary died during the trial, and Ieng Thirith was deemed unfit to stand trial due to dementia.

The third case began in 2015 against Meas Muth (1938–) for genocide, crimes against humanity, and grave breaches of the Geneva Convention. He was a former

Central Committee member of the Khmer Rouge. The same charges were brought against Yim Tith and Ao An, both former zone sector secretaries, in the same year. Those cases were still ongoing as of 2018. It is likely that these will be the last cases heard by the ECCC due, in part, to the fact that the offenders and many of the victims are either deceased or elderly considering that these crimes occurred about forty years ago.

Further Reading

Central Intelligence Agency. 2018. "The World Factbook." https://www.cia.gov/library/publications/resources/the-world-factbook/.

Cox, John. 2017. *To Kill a People*. Oxford: Oxford University Press.

ECCC (Extraordinary Chambers in the Courts of Cambodia). "Introduction to the ECCC." https://www.eccc.gov.kh/en/introduction-eccc

Robertson, Geoffrey. 2013. *Crimes against Humanity: The Struggle for Global Justice*. New York: The New Press.

United Nations. 2015. "Chapter VII: Action with Respect to Threats to the Peace, Breaches of the Peace, and Acts of Aggression." Charter of the United Nations, June 17, 2015. https://www.un.org/en/sections/un-charter/chapter-vii/.

Yale University Genocide Studies. 2018. "Cambodian Genocide Program." https://gsp.yale.edu/case-studies/cambodian-genocide-program.

EL SALVADOR

El Salvador is a small, Central American country of just over six million people. It borders the Pacific Ocean to the south, Guatemala to the northwest, and Honduras to the northeast. Over 85 percent of the population is mestizo and Christian, and Spanish is the official language. El Salvador is a relatively poor country whose economy relies heavily on agricultural exports, such as coffee and sugar. In 2017, the gross domestic product per capita of El Salvador was USD 8,000, about half that of nearby Costa Rica (Central Intelligence Agency 2018). A long history of state violence culminating in a twelve-year civil war has hampered economic development in the country and contributed to exceptionally high violent crime rates.

State Violence and Civil War

El Salvador gained independence from Spain in 1821 and joined other Central American countries in various alliances until becoming a separate state in 1898. From that time until the 1990s, El Salvador experienced a number of military coups, riots, and general political upheaval. The main sources of instability were power struggles over control of the land and the country's main export, coffee. Since the colonial period, estates owned by the wealthy continually spread into indigenous lands, depriving peasants of opportunities to own their own lands and forcing them to work on plantations for little money and with no hope for upward social mobility. Wealthy landowners also controlled coffee processing and wielded significant political influence.

In 1932, thousands of peasants in the western part of the country rioted against their oppressors, attacking the police, military, government officials, and wealthy landowners, and killing thirty-five people. The government responded by sending the National Guard and armed forces to the area and authorizing the killing of anyone suspected of having participated in the riot. This meant that people who looked indigenous or dressed like a peasant were presumed guilty. The government retaliation resulted in the killings of 10,000 to 25,000 people (Stanley 2010). The massacre was referred to as the *matanza* or "slaughter." This extreme violence intimidated peasants, which dampened active resistance to the government for a while. Additionally, the massacre forged an understanding between the military and wealthy landowners against the peasantry and against anyone promoting ideologies that would threaten the existing social order, such as communism.

Class tensions rose again in the 1970s as the country's economic situation worsened. The military regimes were unable to improve the economy or appease the peasants. The number of poor farmers without their own land increased significantly because more than 100,000 Salvadoran farmers were expelled from Honduras as a result of a war between the two countries in 1969. At the same time, agricultural practices became more mechanized (Wood 2003). The state continued to use violence against citizens to subdue any signs of unrest, but this time the strategy did not work. Much of the state violence was public and often very gruesome, such as death squads and beheadings, in an attempt to frighten civilians into pacification. Instead of scaring peasants, the brutality of the state violence increased the conflict as it radicalized leftist guerrilla groups, who then responded with assassinations and kidnappings. Around the same time, liberation theory, which was a religious belief system that incorporated Marxist ideas about social inequality and economic justice into Christianity, had become popular in Latin America. This provided an ideology for resisting government oppression that many poor Christians found relatable.

As the violence escalated in the late 1970s, a military junta overthrew the government in 1979 and tried to introduce agrarian reforms to appease the opposition groups, but the wealthy landowners objected to such measures. In 1980, five of the leftist guerrilla groups joined as the Farabundo Martí National Liberation Front (FMLN). The same year several prominent leaders calling for compromise between the two factions were assassinated, including the popular Archbishop Óscar Romero (1917–1980), which paved the way for civil war. In 1980 alone, about 12,000 civilians died. During the peak years of violence between 1978 and 1983, government forces killed over 42,000 people, which was about 1 percent of the total population (Stanley 2010).

The United States supported the Salvadoran government against the communist rebels and encouraged a transition to civilian rule in 1982. Americans supplied weapons, vehicles, helicopters, and attack jets to the Salvadoran military. To obtain U.S. Congressional approval for military aid, the Salvadoran government was pressured to reduce its violence against civilians. In total, the United States provided USD 4.5 billion in military assistance during the civil war (Hayner 2001).

The Assassination of Archbishop Óscar Romero

Óscar Romero, a Jesuit priest who became archbishop of San Salvador, was an outspoken advocate for peace between the left and right political factions and for economic reforms to help the poor. He broadcast his sermons about reducing violence and poverty over the radio and gained a large following throughout the country. He was a vocal critic of the military junta in control of the country. Romero was assassinated during mass on March 23, 1980 on the orders of Roberto D'Aubuisson, a death squad leader whose political party replaced the junta in 1982. Romero's death weakened support for the junta and escalated violence between the government and guerrilla groups. In 2018, Pope Francis canonized Romero into sainthood.

Despite American assistance, the FMLN had several military victories in the late 1980s that prompted the United States to encourage the Salvadoran government to negotiate a peace treaty. The UN and the Roman Catholic Church facilitated the talks, which led to a peace agreement in 1992, bringing an end to the civil war. This treaty significantly reduced the power of the military and created a separate civilian police force to handle internal security. This led to reforms of the judicial system, with a focus on improving the protection of human rights. Finally, the treaty also allowed the FMLN to transform into a political party and participate in elections.

Truth Commission

The FMLN and the Salvadoran government agreed to the formation of a truth commission as part of the peace negotiations to provide transparency and accountability for the mass killings of civilians. A three-person commission headed by Belisano Betancur (1923–2018), the former president of Colombia, was given six months to investigate "serious acts of violence" that occurred between 1980 and 1991. The commission documented 22,000 complaints and heard testimony from 2,000 victims. About 60 percent of the complaints were about extrajudicial executions, 25 percent were related to disappearances, and 20 percent addressed torture. Witnesses accused government agents in 85 percent of the complaints. The military was blamed in 60 percent of those cases, with security forces, civil defense, and death squads comprising the rest of the complaints. Importantly, the commission's report named more than forty high-ranking military and judicial officials directly involved in the violence. The commission also documented more than 8,000 complaints against the FMLN. About half of them were extrajudicial killings, and the rest were disappearances and forced recruitment. The commission concluded that approximately 75,000 people were killed during the civil war (Betancur, Planchart, and Buergenthal 1993).

The truth commission did not have any legal authority to prosecute anyone; instead, they had the power to investigate what had happened and to make recommendations for the government to prevent further atrocities. First, the commission recommended that the individuals identified in the report as perpetrators of mass violence be dismissed from the military or civil service and barred from holding any other public office. Second, the commission proposed major reforms to the armed forces and the judiciary to create a more balanced power structure within the government. Finally, the commission recommended both financial and moral compensation to the victims, with the latter consisting of a memorial to those killed and a national day of mourning.

The truth commission's report was not well received by the Salvadoran government or the military. President Alfredo Cristiani (1947–) criticized the commission for not allowing the country to "forgive and forget," while the military attacked the report as biased and unfair (Hayner 2001). Military officials who were named in the report were allowed to retire with full honors. Not even a week after the report was released, the government passed a law providing amnesty for all of the alleged perpetrators. The international community strongly criticized the truth commission for not explicitly discouraging amnesty, but its members argued that the judicial system at the time was not capable of ensuring fair trials. Judicial reforms were slow to materialize, but pressure from the UN finally brought some changes in that area in 1996. An independent Council of the Judiciary was formed to oversee the election and removal of judges, and a new Criminal Procedures Code was passed to better protect the rights of defendants and victims. The truth commission recommended that the government establish a reparations fund for victims comprising 1 percent of the El Salvador's foreign aid receipts that would be administered by an independent body, but it was never created.

Although the peace accords brought an end to the civil war, they did not end violence in the country altogether. Homicide rates in El Salvador were 61 per 100,000 in 2000, which rose to 105 per 100,000 by 2015 before declining to 62 by 2017 (UNODC 2018). Gangs grew their influence after the war, fueled in part by a young population, high unemployment and underemployment, and easy access to weapons after the war. Additionally, many Salvadorans who fled to the United States during the war became involved in American gangs, especially in Los Angeles. The U.S. government passed a law allowing convicted foreigners to be deported back to their home countries. Between 2000 and 2004, approximately 20,000 young people from Central America were deported to countries they hardly knew. They brought knowledge of drugs and weapons trafficking and connections to international gangs back with them, thereby increasing the power of Central American gangs. The El Salvadoran gang Mara Salvatrucha (MS-13) originated in Los Angeles, but has since become an international criminal organization that contributes to high levels of violence in El Salvador and surrounding countries.

Further Reading

Betancur, Belisario, Reinaldo Figueredo Planchart, and Thomas Buergenthal. 1993. "From Madness to Hope: The 12-Year War in El Salvador: Report of the Commission on the Truth for El Salvador." UN Security Council. United States Institute of Peace. https://www.usip.org/sites/default/files/file/ElSalvador-Report.pdf.

Central Intelligence Agency. 2018. "The World Factbook." https://www.cia.gov/library /publications/resources/the-world-factbook/.

Hayner, Priscilla B. 2001. *Unspeakable Truths: Confronting State Terror and Atrocity.* New York: Routledge.

Stanley, William. 2010. *The Protection Racket State: Elite Politics, Military Extortion, and Civil War in El Salvador.* Philadelphia, PA: Temple University Press.

UNODC (United Nations Office on Drugs and Crime). 2018. "Global Study on Homicide." https://www.unodc.org/unodc/en/data-and-analysis/global-study-on-homicide.html.

Wood, Elisabeth Jean. 2003. *Insurgent Collective Action and Civil War in El Salvador.* Cambridge, UK: Cambridge University Press.

GEORGIA

Georgia is a country of about four million people located in Europe, to the east of the Black Sea, bordering Russia, Azerbaijan, Armenia, and Turkey in a region called the Caucasus. It was a republic of the Soviet Union from 1921 to 1991. When the Soviet Union dissolved in 1991, several republics like Georgia became independent states. The present country of Georgia is comprised mainly of ethnic Georgians (87.6 percent), with Azeri and Armenians as the two largest ethnic minorities. Its economy relies heavily on agricultural production, with a gross domestic product per capita of USD 10,700, less than half of Russia (USD 27,900) (Central Intelligence Agency 2018).

The political separation from the Soviet Union was not a smooth process in Georgia as there were internal struggles over political power and external conflicts regarding the new country's borders. Several of these clashes involved the severe mistreatment of civilians, which some have interpreted as international law violations. The most recent conflict in 2008 led to an official investigation of charges of crimes against humanity and war crimes against multiple parties by the ICC.

History of Violence

The short history of the independent country of Georgia consists of a series of violent conflicts. The country declared independence from the Soviet Union on April 9, 1991, and on May 26 of that year Zviad Gamsakhurdia (1939–1993) was elected as the first president. His tenure, however, was short-lived as a faction of the National Guard overthrew the government on December 22, 1991, leading to a civil war for political power that lasted until 1995.

At the same time, there was an ongoing history of tensions between Georgia and two of its border regions, South Ossetia and Abkhazia. With Georgia's quest to build a new nation independent of the Soviet Union, some ethnic minority groups accustomed to certain political, economic, and cultural rights under the old regime feared that their interests would be ignored or threatened in the establishment of a distinct Georgian identity. South Ossetia, which is a northern region of Georgia bordering Russia, declared independence from Georgia in 1991, but Georgia did not acknowledge its claim. This disagreement led to a war between a militia of ethnic South Ossetians and the Georgian National Guard accompanied by a militia of ethnic Georgians. The war ended in 1992 when Russia negotiated a ceasefire that divided power over the region between the two sides.

Human Rights Watch documented several violations of international law by both sides of this conflict, including pillage, violations of personal dignity, physical violence, forced displacement, widespread shelling and artillery fire, and hostage-taking. They also documented discrimination and violence against South Ossetians living in Georgia. For example, homes of South Ossetians were raided and livestock, guns, and other valuable items were stolen. Approximately 1,000 people died during this conflict and thousands were displaced (Human Rights Watch 1992).

Soon after, Georgia became embroiled in another war with Abkhazia, a region in the northwest bordering the Black Sea. On August 14, 1992, Abkhazia declared independence from Georgia resulting in a military conflict between the Abkhaz militia and the Georgian National Guard. A ceasefire was negotiated by the United Nations in December 1993. Abkhazia declared independence again in 1994, but foreign governments did not recognize it as a sovereign nation.

Similar to the war with South Ossetia, the war with Abkhazia also resulted in severe human rights violations, including hostage-taking and indiscriminate fire. However, in this case, there were also claims of ethnic cleansing. Georgians were approximately half of the population of Abkhazia in 1992, but during the conflict an estimated 8,000 to 10,000 Georgians were killed and approximately 250,000 were expelled from the region (Chervonnaya 1994). Human Rights Watch documented large-scale, sophisticated hostage exchanges on both sides designed to create ethnically homogenous territories.

Several cease-fires were negotiated by Russia between 1993 and 1994 and Georgia eventually lost control over the region, although it does not recognize Abkhazia as an independent territory. The international community acknowledged the perpetration of war crimes and ethnic cleansing, although little action was taken to pursue justice. Although the political tensions between Georgia and these two regions were not resolved, the large-scale violence subsided for a few years as Georgia focused on internal political matters and economic development.

Human Rights Violations in the War of 2008

With the Rose Revolution of November 2003, Georgia once again tried to shed its Soviet past and install a democratic, pro-Western government with the election of Mikheil Saakashvili (1967–) as president. The new government sought to diminish Russia's influence in the country, including the removal of Russian peacekeeping forces in South Ossetia and Abkhazia that had been present since the conflicts in the early 1990s. This political shift strained relations with Russia, which had already been antagonizing Georgia by supporting the independence movements of South Ossetia and Abkhazia. Georgia's efforts to join NATO increased tensions with Vladimir Putin (1952–), the President of Russia. Russia responded by issuing large numbers of Russian passports to citizens of South Ossetia and Abkhazia to establish a future claim to these territories. Russia also supported South Ossetia with economic and military aid.

By 2008, diplomatic relations between Georgia and Russia were strained. In early August 2008, there were some border skirmishes between Georgia and South Ossetia that led to South Ossetian separatists shelling Georgian villages, thereby violating the 1992 ceasefire agreement. Georgia responded by invading Tskhinvali, the capital of South Ossetia on August 7, 2008. Russia then accused Georgia of attacking South Ossetia and responded with military force under the pretense of peacekeeping. Russian forces prevented Georgia from occupying the South Ossetian capital and proceeded to attack and occupy several Georgian cities and villages near the region. The Russian military even attacked Tbilisi, the capital of Georgia, which the Western media described as a revenge attack. After several days of fighting, French President Nicolas Sarkozy (1955–), who was also the President of the European Union at the time, negotiated a ceasefire on August 12, 2008. On August 25, 2008, Russia formally recognized South Ossetia and Abkhazia as independent states, although the international community did not agree. Georgia responded by ending diplomatic ties with Russia.

Following the conflict, there were charges of violations of international humanitarian laws by all parties of the war. Many claims were made to gain political leverage, but others were substantiated with evidence from investigations conducted by the Organization for Security and Cooperation in Europe (OSCE), the UN, and independent organizations like the Human Rights Watch. There were 199 documented violations of international laws for humanitarian treatment in war outlined by the Geneva Conventions. Of these offenses, 47 percent were committed by South Ossetia, 42 percent by Russia, 10.5 percent by Georgia, and less than 1 percent by Abkhazia (Mullins 2011). Many of the South Ossetian offenses were charges of ethnic cleansing that continued even after the ceasefire agreement was signed. South Ossetia and Russia were also accused of mistreating prisoners of war. The charges against Russia included failure to maintain order, which facilitated the crimes of South Ossetians; indiscriminate and disproportionate use of military force including targeting cultural objects; and intentionally targeting civilians in military actions. The majority of charges against Georgia were related to inappropriate target selection. Although Russia accused Georgia of ethnic cleansing, the evidence does not support its claim. While it was clear that Georgia wanted to regain control over the region, it does not appear that their goal was to eliminate non-Georgian ethnic groups. Most of the criminal violations that occurred during this conflict were acts of "one-sided violence," where armed forces attacked civilians who could not adequately defend themselves. Hundreds of people died during the conflict and almost 200,000 people were displaced, including about 90 percent of the people living in South Ossetia (Stepanova 2009).

International Justice

Because Georgia signed the Rome Statute in 2003, it is subject to the jurisdiction of the ICC. In January 2016, the ICC opened an investigation into crimes against humanity and war crimes committed between July 1 and October 10, 2008 in the territory of Georgia, which also includes South Ossetia. Specifically, the ICC identified crimes against humanity as murder, forcible removal of a population, and persecution; and war crimes as attacks against civilians, attacks against peacekeepers, willful killing, destruction of property, and pillaging. The ICC does not investigate crimes if the national authorities have already begun such investigations, which was initially the case in Georgia. However, when the national investigations failed, the ICC decided to launch its own proceedings. Over 6,000 victims filed claims of wrongdoing with the ICC (International Criminal Court 2018). The court is investigating charges against Georgia, South Ossetia, and Russia, although Russia is not a signatory of the Rome Statute, which gives the ICC its authority. As of 2019, the investigation was ongoing and no official criminal charges were levied.

The situation in Georgia illustrates the difficulties of identifying and substantiating criminal acts in the context of ongoing political conflicts. It also challenges the application and authority of international law in a situation in which all the potential offenders do not formally recognize the legitimacy of those laws.

Further Reading

Central Intelligence Agency. 2018. "The World Factbook." https://www.cia.gov/library/publications/resources/the-world-factbook/.

Chervonnaya, Svetlana. 1994. *Conflict in the Caucasus: Abkhazia, Georgia, and the Russian Shadow*. Glastonbury, UK: Gothic Images Publications.

Human Rights Watch. 1992. *Bloodshed in the Caucasus: Violations of Humanitarian Law and Human Rights in the Georgia-South Ossetia Conflict*. New York: Human Rights Watch.

International Criminal Court. 2018. "Situation in Georgia." https://www.icc-cpi.int/georgia.

Mullins, Christopher W. 2011. "War Crimes in the 2008 Georgia–Russia Conflict." *The British Journal of Criminology* 51 (6): 918–36.

Stepanova, Ekaterina. 2009. "Trends in Armed Conflicts: One-Sided Violence against Civilians." In *SIPRI Yearbook 2009: Armaments, Disarmament and International Security*, 39–68. Stockholm, Sweden: Stockholm International Peace Research Institute (SIPRI).

IVORY COAST

The Ivory Coast, also known as Côte d'Ivoire, is a relatively small West African country off the coast of the North Atlantic Ocean, bordering Liberia, Guinea, Mali, Burkina Faso, and Ghana. Its population of about twenty-four million comprises many ethnic groups, although about 30 percent of the population is Akan. Almost 43 percent of the population is Muslim and 34 percent are Christian, but the majority of foreigners who come to the Ivory Coast to work are Muslim (73 percent) (Central Intelligence Agency 2018). The Ivory Coast declared independence from France in 1960 and enjoyed three decades of economic development and political stability until the 1990s when economic pressures coupled with a large immigrant population created political pressures that resulted in a civil war. The presidential election of 2010 triggered a period of intense violence that has resulted in charges of crimes against humanity by the ICC.

Background Tensions

The Ivory Coast was a French colony from 1893 until independence in 1960. Félix Houphouët-Boigny (1905–1993) became the first president of the country after independence. He was a politically moderate leader who was devoted to the economic development of the new country. Coffee and cocoa exports, along with strong economic ties to France and other Western countries, led to a period of prosperity called the "Ivoirian miracle." However, the excessive agricultural production damaged the country's natural resources, particularly land and forests, making this plan for economic growth unsustainable for the long term. At the same time, the country's period of prosperity attracted a large number of poor immigrants from surrounding countries. Between 1960 and 2000, the population of the Ivory Coast grew from three million to sixteen million, and one-fourth of the population were foreigners (Chirot 2006). By the 1980s, the economy had stagnated and the country faced large foreign debts.

When Houphouët-Boigny died in 1993, the National Assembly president, Henri Konan Bédié (1934–) succeeded him and was re-elected in 1995. Bédié's political opponent was Allassane Dramane Ouattara (1942–), who was the Prime Minister under Houphouët-Boigny. To diminish Ouattara's influence and prevent him from running in the 1995 election, Bédié passed a law in 1994 stating that presidential candidates had to prove that they and both their parents were born in the Ivory Coast. This was one of several new citizenship laws called Ivoirité that were designed to distinguish "indigenous Ivoirians" from "Ivoirians of immigrant ancestry" to concentrate political power (Bah 2010). As most immigrants were Muslim and more northerners were Muslim than southerners, the Ivoirité laws tended to favor Christians and southerners. The new laws also affected voting rights, national identification, land rights, and employment opportunities. To complicate matters, unreliable birth records and fluid borders made it difficult, if not impossible, for people to prove their ancestry and citizenship. These new laws served Bédié's political agenda, as he won the 1995 presidential election with 96 percent of the vote (Chirot 2006).

Civil War

The first forty years of independence for the Ivory Coast were relatively peaceful, but political maneuvering and economic decline in the 1990s led to the country's first military coup. The Ivoirité laws excluded many people from key military posts. Additionally, the declining economy and high levels of corruption resulted in unpaid military bonuses, which contributed to dissatisfaction among the military.

In December 1999, the Ivoirian military initiated a bloodless coup and instated retired General Robert Gueï (1941–2002) as president. Although Gueï lost the October 2000 election to Laurent Koudou Gbagbo (1945–), he initially refused to accept the election results. Northerners, who were once again excluded from voting, protested in the streets, encountering violence with the police. Former Prime Minister Ouattara, who was also prevented from running for office because of the Ivoirité policies, called for peace and recognition of the Gbagbo presidency.

Gbagbo was a militant evangelical Protestant who further alienated northern Muslims, including purging them from the military, police, and civil service. In September 2002, a group of Muslim former army officers who had been living in neighboring Burkino Faso attempted to overthrown Gbagbo's weak government. The rebels attacked the capital of Abidjan, but could not secure it. However, they succeeded in controlling the northern part of the country. Guillaume Soro (1972–), a Christian northerner, became the leader of the rebel movement known as Forces Nouvelles de Côte d'Ivoire (New Forces).

Fighting between the northern rebels and Gbagbo regime lasted until 2004. Both sides of the civil war were accused of committing massacres. An estimated 10,000 people were killed and one million displaced (Chirot 2006). France sent troops to protect French citizens in the country and assist the Gbagbo government. The UN, Economic Community of West African States, and African Union also contributed peacekeeping troops. The French negotiated a peace settlement that was accepted in November 2004. The peace agreement focused on sharing power across rival groups, disarming rebels, and setting a date for new elections, but it did not tackle the underlying citizenship issues related to ethnicity and religion. Elections were supposed to take place in 2005, but continuing instability delayed them until 2010. Another peace agreement developed by Ivoirians was signed in March 2007 that finally addressed the citizenship problem. In the law, citizenship was defined as having been born in the Ivory Coast or having at least one parent who had been born in the Ivory Coast. Additional provisions were made for adoption, marriage, and naturalization. A new identity system was established and mobile courts traveled the country issuing birth certificates.

Flailing Democracy and Crimes against Humanity

In November 2010, the first presidential elections since Gbagbo came to power were held, as agreed upon in the 2007 peace accord. Gbagbo lost the election to Ouattara, who was Houphouët-Boigny's Prime Minister in the early 1990s and had been prevented from running for president in previous elections because of the Ivoirité laws regarding citizenship. Gbagbo claimed fraudulent voting in the north and declared himself the winner despite the fact that the UN and many other countries accepted Outtara's victory, as did Soro who was the Prime Minister and leader of New Forces.

The contested elections led to another round of violence in the country, reigniting earlier tensions. In large, urban areas the violence was largely committed by pro-Gbagbo forces who used excessive force and unwarranted killings to dispel public protests over the elections. West Africans, Muslims, and northerners were specifically targeted for harassment and violence. The state-controlled media was promoting racist and inflammatory speech. Pro-Ouattara forces were also accused of massacres and reprisal killings, particularly against ethnic communities supporting Gbagbo. Most notably, a massacre in the western city of Duékoué resulted in hundreds of civilian deaths (Straus 2011). Human Rights Watch (2012) estimated at least 30,000 deaths and more than 150 rapes, and 180,000 Ivorian refugees fled to Liberia.

Pro-Ouattara forces took over the western part of the country and succeeded to capture the capital of Abidjan in April 2011. On April 11, Gbagbo and his wife Simone Gbagbo (1949–) were captured and Ouattara assumed his role as President with Soro as his Prime Minister. Ouattara created a Dialogue, Truth, and Reconciliation council headed by the former Prime Minister Charles Konan Banny to investigate crimes committed during the postelection crisis, but it was criticized as being one-sided.

International Justice

The Ivory Coast was not a signatory of the Rome Statute until 2013 but President Gbagbo accepted the jurisdiction of the ICC in 2003 and President Ouattara confirmed it in 2011 when he asked the ICC to investigate crimes committed after November 2010. Ivoirians objected to the limited scope of the investigation and requested the court to consider events since the first civil war in 2002. The prosecutor for the ICC immediately announced the court's intention to investigate possible crimes by both sides of the conflict.

On November 23, 2011, Gbagbo was charged with four counts of crimes against humanity, including murder, rape, other inhumane acts, and persecution committed after the November 2010 election. In 2014, the same charges were brought against Charles Blé Goudé, who was the Minister for Sports and Youth in Gbagbo's administration. He was in charge of recruiting young people to fight for Gbagbo through a group called the Young Patriots. Their cases were combined in 2015, and the court proceedings began in January 2016. In January 2019, both men were acquitted of all charges, although the prosecutor is expected to appeal the decision.

In November 2012, the ICC also issued an arrest warrant for the former president's wife, Simone Gbagbo, for the same four counts of crimes against humanity, but the Ivory Coast has not yet transferred her to the ICC. In 2015, she was tried and convicted in the Ivory Coast for crimes against the state and undermining state security during the 2010 postelection crisis and was sentenced to twenty years in prison. Witnesses accused her of personally distributing arms to death squads (BBC News 2015). In 2017, she was tried for crimes against humanity in the Ivory Coast. She was initially acquitted, but that decision was later overturned. In 2018, President Ouattara pardoned Simone Gbagbo to promote peace in the country. To date, the ICC has not brought any charges against Ouattara supporters.

Further Reading

Bah, Abu Bakarr. 2010. "Democracy and Civil War: Citizenship and Peacemaking in Côte d'Ivoire." *African Affairs* 109 (437): 597–615. https://doi.org/10.1093/afraf/adq046.

BBC News. 2015. "Ivory Coast Former First Lady Jailed." March 10, 2015, sec. Africa. http://www.bbc.com/news/world-africa-31809073.

Central Intelligence Agency. 2018. "The World Factbook." https://www.cia.gov/library /publications/resources/the-world-factbook/.

Chirot, Daniel. 2006. "The Debacle in Côte d'Ivoire." *Journal of Democracy* 17 (2): 63–77.

Human Rights Watch. 2012. "World Report 2012: Côte d'Ivoire." January 22, 2012. https:// www.hrw.org/world-report/2012/country-chapters/cote-divoire.

Straus, Scott. 2011. "'It's Sheer Horror Here': Patterns of Violence during the First Four Months of Côte d'Ivoire's Post-Electoral Crisis." *African Affairs* 110 (440): 481–89.

MYANMAR

Myanmar is a country in Southeast Asia that is often referred to by its pre-1989 name, Burma. The country of fifty-five million people is located on the Bay of Bengal and Andaman Sea and borders Bangladesh, China, Laos, and Thailand. The military has been in control of the government since the 1960s, struggling to meet the needs and demands of the country's ethnic and religious minorities. The Burman ethnic group comprises 68 percent of the population, but there are 135 recognized ethnic groups, with the Shan (9 percent), Karen (7 percent), and Rakhine (4 percent) being the largest. Almost 88 percent of the population is Buddhist, with 6.2 percent Christian and 4.3 percent Muslim (Central Intelligence Agency 2018). Since the country gained independence from Britain, the government has been accused of multiple humanitarian violations against different ethnic and religious minorities, but the international community has wrestled with how to label these conflicts and, therefore, how to respond to them.

Historical and Political Background

Prior to the British occupation starting in 1824, Myanmar consisted of feudal societies ruled by kings. Ethnic divisions existed and in some cases non-Burman ethnic groups were treated as slaves. However, ethnic identity was not as important as being a Buddhist or having an alliance with the ruling dynasty. When Britain colonized the area, it bureaucratized the governance of the state and introduced administrative rules and regulations that categorized people in ways that suited the new state structure. In particular, people in Myanmar were divided between lowland Burmese and highland ethnic minorities. British rule solidified ethnic identities and fostered opposition to the Burman majority.

The British controlled Myanmar until 1948, although the Japanese briefly occupied the country during World War II from 1942 to 1945. After achieving independence in 1948, Myanmar became a parliamentary republic, and several ethnic minority groups lobbied for independence or federalism. Importantly, most minority groups were granted citizenship in the new republic at the time of independence, except for the Rohingyas, which would become a persistent source of tension that later contributed to ethnic persecution.

In 1962, the government was overthrown in a military coup led by General Ne Win (1911–2002), who instituted martial law for the next twelve years. Win was a Burman who only saw Burman Buddhists as loyal citizens. Win introduced a socialist economic system and nationalized all major industries. This proved to be a disaster and quickly transformed Myanmar from one of the largest exporters of rice to one of the poorest countries in the region. Antigovernment protests and rising ethnic conflicts led to another coup, in which General Saw Muang (1928–1997) became the new leader. Muang declared martial law, ended the socialist economic experiment, and changed the country's name from Burma to Myanmar.

The government allowed free elections in 1990 but refused to cede power when the National League for Democracy party, led by Aung San Suu Kyi (1945–), won a large majority of the seats. In 2007, public protests erupted again in response to rising prices and soon turned into opposition against military rule. Buddhist monks spearheaded the peaceful protests, which were named the Saffron Revolution due to the color of the monks' robes. At that time, more than 90 percent of the country's population was living on less than USD 1 per day, less than half of the children completed primary education, and one-third of adults were unemployed. The government spent only 11 percent of the country's budget on health and education and over 40 percent on the military (Kingston 2008). The government responded to the protests with force, as it had done with previous incidents throughout the military's reign. However, this time the government's response was broadcast on television and the Internet to Western audiences, eliciting economic sanctions and calls for democratic reform from the international community. Approximately six months later in May 2008, Cyclone Nargis hit the densely populated farmland of Myanmar, killing hundreds of thousands of people and causing billions of dollars of damage. The government's inability to handle this crisis further diminished its legitimacy.

In 2008, a constitutional referendum declared the intent to establish a democracy. Elections were held in 2010 and the political party supported by the military declared victory. The next general election in 2015 was the most open in the country's history, and the National League for Democracy won the majority of seats. The party's leader, Ang San Suu Kyi, who had won a Nobel Peace Prize in 1991, was prevented from becoming president because she had married a foreigner, so she was appointed state counselor instead.

The decline of the military junta and the bumpy road to democratic reform intensified tensions with ethnic minority groups. Since 2008, Myanmar has been involved in violent conflicts with several such groups, including the Christian Kachins and Karens, Muslim Rohingyas, Chinese rebels, and others. While ethnic violence has a long history in Myanmar, the country's new political status has brought increased scrutiny of human rights abuses by the international community.

Ethnic Violence against the Karen

The Karen ethnic group first migrated to Burma in 739 BC and now comprises about 7 percent of the population of Myanmar (Pedersen 2011). They were oppressed by the Burmese dynasties before colonization and solidified a collective identity in opposition to the Burmese majority during Britain's colonial rule when the lowland Burmese were separated from the highland ethnic minority groups. Western missionaries converted many Karen to Christianity, further separating them from the Buddhist Burmese.

When Japan briefly occupied Myanmar between 1942 and 1945, both the Japanese and the Burmese carried out attacks against Karen villages. Britain regained control in 1945 and the Karen petitioned for a British state, but they were denied the right to secede. Persecution against the Karen continued after independence from Britain in 1948, including an attack against Insein, the home of the Karen National Union. The attacks against the Karen intensified when Win, an ethnic Burmese, became chief of staff of the armed forces in 1949, replacing an ethnic Karen in the position.

The Karen National Defense Organization, formed in 1947, led an insurgency against the military dictatorship, along with several other minority ethnic groups in Myanmar. The international community had largely ignored attacks against Karen civilians until 1984 when thousands of Karen refugees fled to Thailand. Some human rights advocates refer to the attacks against the Karen as genocide, but the international community has not officially labeled this crime. Nonetheless, mass killings, rape, torture, and forced labor of the Karen have been ongoing for decades. One newspaper estimated that approximately one million people were displaced by the conflicts between 1996 and 2007. An offensive against the Karen launched in 2007 destroyed 232 villages and forced 27,000 Karen to become refugees (Pattisson 2007). A preliminary ceasefire was signed between the Myanmar government and Karen leaders in 2012, but this was not the end of ethnic violence in the country.

Suspected Genocide against Rohingya

The Rohingya are an Indo-Aryan ethnic group living primarily in western Myanmar in the Rakhine State, just south of Bangladesh. They are predominantly Muslim, although a minority are Hindu. Similar to the Karen, the Rohingya supported the British government during the Japanese invasion in 1942 and were persecuted as a result. It has been estimated that 100,000 Rohingya died during the three-year Japanese occupation and 80,000 became refugees (Ibrahim 2016). When the British regained power, they rewarded most ethnic groups for their support with citizenship, except for the Rohingya. This separate distinction persisted after independence and laws passed in 1974, 1982, and 2014 continued to deny Rohingya citizenship and labeled them foreigners.

Major military attacks against the Rohingya occurred in 1978 under General Win and again in 1991 after Suu Kyi's electoral victory, resulting in hundreds of thousands of refugees fleeing to Bangladesh. From 2012 onward, a series of events escalated violence against the Rohingya to the point of garnering calls for international intervention. In 2012, riots erupted between Rohingya Muslims and Buddhist Rahkines in the Rakhine State, resulting in hundreds of thousands of Rohingya segregated into refugee camps in Myanmar where they were subjected to numerous human rights abuses, which resulted in more people leaving the country.

Fighting with the military resumed in 2016 in response to terrorist attacks at three border patrol posts, resulting in the deaths of nine officers (BBC News 2016). In 2017, the military began large-scale efforts to forcibly remove the Rohingya from Rakhine, leading to an estimated 1,000 deaths and the displacement of 120,000 people (Haltiwanger 2017). The UN labeled the events as "ethnic cleansing" and since then there have been investigations into whether the actions constitute genocide. In 2019, the UN released a report following a two-year investigation that claimed that hundreds of thousands of Rohingya are still at risk for genocide. The report also accused Myanmar of failing to comply with the Geneva Convention and recommended that the UN Security Council refer the case to the ICC.

Further Reading

BBC News. 2016. "Myanmar Policemen Killed in Rakhine Border Attack." October 9, 2016, sec. Asia. https://www.bbc.com/news/world-asia-37601928.

Central Intelligence Agency. 2018. "The World Factbook." https://www.cia.gov/library/publications/resources/the-world-factbook/.

Haltiwanger, John. 2017. "Is Genocide Occurring against the Rohingya in Myanmar?" Newsweek, September 5, 2017. https://www.newsweek.com/genocide-occurring-against-rohingya-myanmar-experts-weigh-659841.

Ibrahim, Azeem. 2016. *The Rohingyas: Inside Myanmar's Hidden Genocide*. Oxford: Oxford University Press.

Kingston, Jeff. 2008. "Burma's Despair." *Critical Asian Studies* 40 (1): 3–43. https://doi.org/10.1080/14672710801959125.

Pattisson, Pete. 2007. "On the Run with the Karen People Forced to Flee Burma's Genocide." *The Independent*, January 16, 2007. http://www.independent.co.uk/news/world/asia/on-the-run-with-the-karen-people-forced-to-flee-burmas-genocide-6229182.html.

Pedersen, Daniel. 2011. *Secret Genocide: Voices of the Karen of Burma*. Dublin, Ireland: Maverick House.

South, Ashley. 2008. *Ethnic Politics in Burma: States of Conflict*. Abingdon, UK: Routledge.

PERU

Peru is a South American country lying west of the Pacific Ocean, south of Ecuador and Colombia, and west of Brazil. The majority of the thirty-one million people in Peru is of mixed Amerindian and white descent (60.2 percent), but there is a sizable Amerindian population (25.8 percent). Spanish, Qecha, and Aymara are official languages. Peru is a developing country with a gross domestic product of USD 13,500, lower than neighboring Brazil (USD 15,600) but higher than Ecuador (USD 11,500). Its economy relies heavily on mineral and metal exports, especially silver and copper. Although economic development was hampered by political turmoil, the country's economy has been growing since 2009 (Central Intelligence Agency 2018).

Peru was the home of the Incan Empire in the thirteenth century until it was conquered by Spain in 1572. It remained a Spanish colony until 1824. Peru's political history as an independent nation is characterized by ongoing struggles between civilian and military governments. In the 1960s and 1970s, military dictators largely ran the country. Economic depression and civil unrest during this time led to the formation of several militant groups advocating for government reforms. One of these groups, Shining Path, launched a twenty-year guerrilla campaign against the government, which drew a brutal military response and led to the deaths of nearly 70,000 people, most of whom were Andean peasants. A Truth and Reconciliation Commission was formed in 2001 to document human rights violations and assign responsibility for this mass atrocity.

Shining Path

Shining Path was a Peruvian militant organization formed in 1970 by Abimael Guzmán (1934–), a philosophy professor inspired by Marxist and Maoist ideologies. The antigovernment movement originally started among intellectuals interested in cultivating a communist revolution, but by 1980, it had transformed into a guerrilla group operating out of the city of Ayacucho. In 1975, General Francisco Morales-Bermúdez (1921–) took over the Peruvian government at a time of severe economic crisis and political unrest. Although he supported socialism at first, the unstable political conditions pressured him to embrace democratization. He called for the first democratic election in over a decade to be held in 1980. Shining Path opposed the election, preferring a people's revolution that would represent peasants' economic and political interests instead.

In the 1980s, Shining Path gained support among the rural areas of the Andean highlands. It is estimated that there were 530 Shining Path militants and sympathizers in 1980 and 2,700 a decade later (Degregori et al. 2012). Peruvians living in these areas were extremely poor and felt neglected by the central government, so Guzmán's message of equality and improving living standards were welcomed. Shining Path's strategy to destabilize the government involved violently taking over rural areas and driving out government officials. Their plan was to initiate a series of guerrilla fights to gain territory and mobilize the peasantry against the government. The group's tactics against government supporters were brutally violent and typically public, designed to demonstrate the power of the group and spread fear across the country.

At first the government ignored Shining Path until it boldly attacked the National Police, which forced the government to respond. Newly elected president Fernando Belaúnde Terry (1912–2002) entrusted the military to forcefully eliminate Shining Path from the highlands. The military's tactics were callous including torture, rape, and mass murder. Shining Path responded with several massacres of their own. Many victims from both sides of the violence were peasants, who were labeled as terrorists.

The military also tried to gain the support of peasants by arming and organizing them into militias to fight Shining Path on behalf of the government. The Shining Path guerrillas responded severely to such attacks, which meant that the group that was formed to advocate for peasants ended up violently attacking them. Fighting among these factions escalated in 1983 and 1984 when approximately 4,000 people were killed (Degregori et al. 2012).

Around the same time, Shining Path extended its activities beyond the highlands and into Lima, the capital of Peru. They assassinated prominent political and business leaders, bombed civilian areas, and sabotaged the electrical grid. In 1986, the government responded by executing 300 imprisoned militants who were suspected of terrorism. By the late 1980s the military had control over only 32 percent of the country (Degregori et al.

The Amerindian peasantry in Peru lives largely off the land. The exploitation of rural highlanders contributed to the rise of Shining Path, a communist guerrilla group that fought against the Peruvian government for two decades, contributing to tens of thousands of civilian deaths. (Antonella865/ Dreamstime.com)

2012). When President Alberto Fujimori (1938–) took office in 1990, the government was not effectively combating Shining Path. In 1992, Fujimori called a constitutional crisis, suspended the constitution and congress, and purged the judiciary. He withdrew from human rights conventions and allowed the military and intelligence services to use whatever means necessary to regain control of the country, which ultimately led to more violence. During his regime, the Peruvian judiciary issued 51,684 arrest warrants for 12,858 people, and nearly 90 percent of them did not include necessary identifying information to ensure that the correct people were apprehended. Unknown numbers of innocent people were arrested and imprisoned without a trial. Once in prison, these civilians were tortured and treated as suspected terrorists (Faverio and Naimark 2013).

Fujimori's tactics worked. In 1992, the National Counterterrorism Directorate captured Guzmán in Lima and eventually captured the majority of Shining Path's commanders. Within twelve days, Guzmán was convicted of terrorism by a military tribunal and sentenced to life in prison. Some of the remaining members of Shining

Path continued to fight the government, but the organization lost its momentum after Guzmán's arrest, and the number of attacks significantly declined by 1994.

Fujimori's success over Shining Path led to his re-election in 1995, but he did not restore democracy. Instead he consolidated his power, limited the freedoms of Peruvians, and continued to use the National Intelligence Service and military to oppress citizens. Fujimori attempted to disregard the constitutional limit of his presidency to two terms and ran for a third term in 2000. However, popular support for him eroded amidst heavily publicized corruption scandals. In 2001, Fujimori fled the country to Japan and resigned as president.

Truth and Reconciliation

Interim president Valentín Paniagua (1936–2006) established a Truth and Reconciliation Commission in 2001 to investigate the numerous human rights abuses committed by both the Peruvian government and militant groups like Shining Path between 1980 and 2000. Truth commissions are a form of transitional justice that facilitate government changes during periods of mass violence. They aim to provide a transparent, historical record of the crimes committed and the victims affected, assigning responsibility for the crimes to the parties involved. Unlike traditional court proceedings, they are not focused on punishing offenders. Instead truth commissions aim to restore peace after conflict, help victims heal, and repair social divisions.

The Peruvian Truth Commission consisted of twelve members, many of whom were academics. They conducted a two-year investigation that included fourteen public hearings and 17,000 testimonies. They concluded that 69,280 people had been killed or disappeared during the conflict, and that Shining Path was responsible for 54 percent of the deaths and the government was responsible for 37 percent. Importantly, they noted that the vast majority of the victims were poor farmers whose native language was not Spanish (Laplante and Theidon 2007).

To restore trust in government and reduce fears of more violence, the truth commission established the Program of Integral Reparations to make amends with victims. Because the Peruvian government is not an individual, it cannot be directly prosecuted for the crimes documented by the truth commission. Instead reparations are a means to hold the state accountable and assist in the recovery of victims. The truth commission recommended monetary compensation to victims, as well as victim services, such as health and education, the restoration of rights, and symbolic reparations, such as memorials to publicly acknowledge the government's failure to protect its citizens.

While the plan for reparations presents a reasonable path to reconciliation, the reality is that few reparations have actually been paid. The government allocated money to social programs and gave land to some of the Andean peasants, but the Minister of Economy and Finance has not released funds for monetary reparations. Researchers have documented the ongoing damage to the Andean peasantry as a result of the mass atrocities including difficulties finding employment because of a criminal record, stigmatization from being labeled a terrorist by the government, psychological damage from torture, and continuing poverty.

In 2001, President Alejandro Toledo (1946–) brought criminal charges against Fujimori including corruption, murder, kidnapping, and crimes against humanity. However, Japan granted Fujimori citizenship upon his arrival and refused to extradite him to stand trial. In 2005, he flew to Chile with the intention of mounting a campaign for president of Peru in 2006. Instead he was arrested and extradited to Peru in 2007. He was convicted of multiple charges and sentenced to twenty-five years in prison.

Further Reading

Central Intelligence Agency. 2018. "The World Factbook." https://www.cia.gov/library /publications/resources/the-world-factbook/.

Degregori, Carlos Iván, Steve J. Stern, Nancy Appelbaum, Joanna Drzewieniecki, Héctor Flores, and Eric Hershberg. 2012. *How Difficult It Is to Be God: Shining Path's Politics of War in Peru, 1980–1999*. Madison: University of Wisconsin Press.

Faverio, Aida, and Anna Naimark. 2013. "Perpetual Injustice: The Twenty-Year Battle for Reparations in Peru." *Human Rights Brief* 20 (3): 32–36.

Hunefeldt, Christine. 2014. *A Brief History of Peru*. New York: Infobase Publishing.

Laplante, Lisa J., and Kimberly Susan Theidon. 2007. "Truth with Consequences: Justice and Reparations in Post-Truth Commission Peru." *Human Rights Quarterly* 29 (1): 228–50. https://doi.org/10.1353/hrq.2007.0009.

SUDAN

Sudan is a large country of forty-three million people in northern Africa. It borders seven countries including Egypt to the north and Chad to the west, with some eastern coastline along the Red Sea. It is a relatively poor country with a gross domestic product per capita of only USD 4,300, about one-third of Egypt (Central Intelligence Agency 2018). Historically, the Sudanese economy had relied largely on oil production, but the secession of South Sudan in 2001 meant that Sudan lost most of its access to oil, and the economy has been struggling since then. Sudan has been embroiled in civil wars, genocide, rebel conflicts, and other forms of state violence since its independence in 1956, with very few periods of peace. The sources of the conflicts are complex including ethnic tensions heightened by colonialism, pan-Arabism imported from Libya and Saudi Arabia, climate change affecting the availability of natural resources, and international conflicts and relations. All these factors contributed to extreme violence against citizens in the western region of Darfur that the international community has called genocide. This mass atrocity became the first test of the newly formed ICC.

Violence in Darfur

Sudan has always been an ethnically and religiously diverse country. The capital of Khartoum is run primarily by descendants of Arab migrants who rose to a ruling class under British colonialism. The northern part of the country is home to mostly non-Arab camel nomads. The western part of the country is home to non-Arab, Muslim Africans of different ethnic groups living primarily as farmers. Finally, the southern part of the country consists of cattle and camel nomads of Arab descent, in addition to various other ethnic and religious groups, which includes Christians and animists. The southern region was part of Sudan during the Darfur genocide, but has since become an independent country.

When Colonel Omar Hassan Ahmad al-Bashir (1944–) took over the country in a military coup in 1989, he adopted the ideology of pan-Arabism and sought to make Sudan a definitively Arab country aligned with other Arab nations in North Africa and the Middle East. This led to the adoption of political and economic policies that disadvantaged non-Arab groups in the west and south. A severe drought in the 1980s wreaked havoc on the livelihood of people from north and central Sudan, who then moved to other parts of the country in search of water and grazing areas to maintain their livelihood. This increased tensions between these regions and Khartoum, as people felt the government was ignoring their needs.

In response to decades of social exclusion and the mounting economic threats to farmers in the western region of Darfur, leaders from the largest ethnic groups in the region joined forces to protect their people from the government. These groups formed the Sudan Liberation Army (SLA), one of the several rebel groups opposing the unfair rule of the government of Sudan, including the Justice and Equality Movement (JEM). The SLA claimed to be fighting for a united country that accepted all diverse ethnic and religious groups in Sudan, as well as for a democratic government that respected the separation of church and state.

Although there had been skirmishes between the rebel groups and the Sudanese government for a few years, the violence escalated in 2003 when Darfur rebels attacked a government military garrison, killing 200 soldiers. This prompted a violent response from the Sudanese military. While fighting rebel groups, the government also attacked villages in Darfur under the pretense that they were supporting the rebels. The Sudanese government hired a militia group called the Janjaweed to carry out most of the attacks against civilians. The Janjaweed comprised Arabs from within Sudan and neighboring countries who traveled the country on horses and committed horrific acts of violence against Darfurians. When the Janjaweed descended on a village, they typically killed and mutilated men and raped and sometimes killed women. Then they killed the livestock, burned all of the homes and other structures, burned the fields, and sometimes poisoned water wells to ensure that any survivors could not return to their villages. The Janjaweed specifically targeted the non-Arab African groups of the Fur, Masalit, and Zaghawa. Just a year after the conflict had begun, it was estimated that at least 300,000 people had been killed, 200,000 refugees from Darfur had fled across the western border to Chad, and another million refugees were displaced within Sudan (Collins 2006).

There was much debate in the international community about what was happening in Darfur and who was responsible. By 2004, the United States openly declared that the violence in Darfur constituted genocide and pressured the

Sudanese government to end the conflict. The UN claimed that war crimes and crimes against humanity had occurred and engaged the African Union to negotiate peace in the country. It was not until May 2006 that the government of Sudan and the SLA signed a peace agreement, although the other rebel groups did not sign until a month later after intense international pressure. Between 2007 and 2018, a joint African Union and UN peacekeeping force was present in Sudan. Although the violence in Darfur significantly declined after 2006, it did not end altogether.

Determination of Genocide

Deciding whether a mass atrocity is genocide is both a legal and a political matter. The UN Convention on the Prevention and Punishment of the Crime of Genocide, adopted in 1951 in direct response to the Holocaust of World War II, defines genocide as one of five acts of violence committed with the intent to destroy a national, ethnic, racial, or religious group. The most obvious of the five acts is killing, but the legal definition also allows for serious bodily or mental harm, creating conditions that will eventually lead to the demise of a group (e.g., destroying farmland), preventing births within the group, and forcibly removing children from the group (Hagan and Rymond-Richmond 2008). While the evidence of acts of violence can be fairly easily established (e.g., mass graves, burned fields, violence against women), proving the intent of the violent acts is more challenging. For example, in the case of Darfur, President al-Bashir claimed that military violence was directed at rebel groups as part of war and not directed at any particular ethnic groups. From a political viewpoint, the formal designation of a mass atrocity as genocide requires action on the part of the UN and the signatories of the Genocide Convention. As a result, terms such as "ethnic cleansing" are often used instead of "genocide" to sidestep both the question of criminal intent and the political obligations to respond to the crisis.

Evidence of mass atrocities occurring in Darfur came from numerous sources. Initially, foreigners from nongovernmental organizations and the media raised concerns about the spread of violence. Subsequently, more systematic documentation of deaths, injuries, disease, and malnutrition among refugees came from the World Health Organization and Doctors without Borders, who had already been working in Sudan prior to the conflict in Darfur. Satellite images became an important source of visual evidence of the destruction of villages and farmland. These various sources provided confirmation about death, violence, and destruction of property, but they could not identify the perpetrators or their intentions.

To obtain this information, the U.S. Department of State's Bureau of Democracy, Human Rights, and Labor, in conjunction with the international nongovernmental organization the Coalition for International Justice, and the American Bar Association, fielded a survey of refugees' experiences modeled after victimization surveys used by criminologists in the United States and other countries to measure crime. For two months in the summer of 2004, researchers interviewed 1,200 refugees from Darfur who were living in refugee camps in Chad as part of the Atrocities

The violent conflict in Darfur caused over a million people to leave their homes in fear of their safety. Many fled to internal displacement camps in other regions of Darfur or settled in refugee camps in neighboring Chad. (Manoocher Deghati/IRIN)

Documentation Survey. These surveys were important for calculating the number of people who had died in the conflict, documenting other types of violence and destruction of property, and identifying who was committing the violence. Victims clearly indicated events that involved the Sudanese military, such as bombings of villages, and those that were largely the responsibility of the Janjaweed. Most importantly, victims recounted what they heard during the attacks, which included the frequent use of derogatory racial terms to distinguish Black Africans from Arabs. This was important information to establish that perpetrators targeted specific racial and ethnic groups. The documentation of sexual assault was also important to counter government claims that the violence was only a result of war, as one would expect deaths as an inevitable byproduct of war, but not sexual abuse.

Prosecuting Genocide

The ICC was officially established on July 1, 2002 when the UN Rome Statute was ratified. Sudan did not sign this statute, but it has been a member of the UN since independence in 1956. When the UN Security Council investigated the situation in Darfur and referred the case to the ICC, it gave the court jurisdiction over Sudan for the case of Darfur. The prosecutor for the ICC initially brought charges against President al-Bashir and several high-ranking military officials for crimes against humanity (e.g., murder, rape, torture) and war crimes (attacks against civilians) because of concerns that the evidence for genocide was not strong enough to lead to a conviction. Al-Bashir was the first president in power to be charged for a crime by the ICC. In 2010, the prosecutor added charges of genocide due to mounting evidence from the Atrocities Documentation Survey, information from Janjaweed militia, and documents with incriminating evidence pointing to the government targeting specific groups of people. Al-Bashir was the first person to be charged with genocide by the ICC. The court issued arrest warrants for six individuals, including al-Bashir, but none have faced trial. As the ICC has no arrest powers, it relies on suspects to appear before court voluntarily, or for domestic governments or signatories to the Rome Statute to arrest suspects so that they can stand trial. Because al-Bashir was president of Sudan until 2019, the Sudanese government would not acknowledge the authority of the ICC.

On April 11, 2019, a military coup in Sudan ended al-Bashir's presidency. Economic decline since the separation with South Sudan and a pro-democracy movement spurred by the Sudanese Professionals Association led to a series of mass protests starting in late 2018 that proved disastrous for the legitimacy of al-Bashir's rule. The military took over as a two-year transitional government, but protests continued in support of civilian rule. Some of these protests have ended with the military's use of violence against citizens, once again. Military officials have charged al-Bashir with corruption and are holding him in custody, but they have publicly stated that they will not turn him over to the ICC to stand trial for the genocide in Darfur.

Further Reading

Central Intelligence Agency. 2018. "The World Factbook." https://www.cia.gov/library /publications/resources/the-world-factbook/.

Collins, Robert O. 2006. "Disaster in Darfur: Historical Overview." In *Genocide in Darfur: Investigating the Atrocities in the Sudan*, edited by Samuel Totten and Eric Markusen, 3–24. New York: Routledge.

Goldstein, Joseph. 2019. "The Revolutionary Force behind Sudan's Protest Movement? Doctors." *The New York Times*, April 20, 2019, sec. World. https://www.nytimes.com /2019/04/20/world/africa/sudan-doctors-protest.html.

Google Earth Outreach. n.d. "United States Holocaust Memorial Museum: Crisis in Darfur." https://www.google.com/earth/outreach/success-stories/united-states -holocaust-memorial-museum/.

Hagan, John, and Wenona Rymond-Richmond. 2008. *Darfur and the Crime of Genocide.* New York: Cambridge University Press.

International Criminal Court. n.d. "Darfur, Sudan." https://www.icc-cpi.int/darfur,

Chapter 8: Policing

Joseph M. Calvert

OVERVIEW

The policing models adopted by countries are a reflection of historical influences, such as colonialism, as well as contemporary political and legal systems. In democracies, law enforcement officers are accountable to the rule of law and the citizenry. Their power is legitimized by the recognition and consent of those over whom it is exercised. This is starkly contrasted by policing in authoritarian and repressive regimes where police legitimacy is based on force. Democratic policing also stresses upholding the rule of law, police accountability and transparency, ethics, and the protection of human rights.

Community policing is both a philosophy and a strategy for law enforcement closely aligned with the ideals of democratic policing. Community policing is noted for its proactive approach to policing, the establishment of lasting community ties, and working with the community to collaboratively prevent crime and address problems related to security, disorder, and the fear of crime. To achieve this end, community policing efforts often involve establishing a decentralized police structure, committing to finding tailored solutions to community problems, de-emphasizing the image of the police as paramilitary officers, and engaging the community as an active participant in public safety and crime prevention. Community policing is also concerned with providing local level accountability to establish and maintain police legitimacy.

In contrast, authoritarian regimes, such as absolute monarchies or dictatorships, and military regimes tend to have highly centralized, hierarchical police forces. They often have a militaristic quality and structure. They emphasize maintaining public order over individual rights or community relationships. These police forces are accountable to higher political officials rather than the public. They gain their legitimacy directly from the government. Relationships with citizens are often more strained under this type of policing model, with frequent complaints of human rights abuses. Countries that have had histories of military or other authoritarian governments, but have more recently transitioned to democracies, often have police forces with a mixture of features from these different models.

This chapter includes democracies that embrace the community policing model (Ireland and Japan), countries whose police forces have been shaped by colonial legacies (India and Dominica), countries that have transitioned from authoritarian regimes to democracies (Argentina and Slovenia), and countries strained by tensions between authoritarian tendencies and democratic pressures (Jordan and Turkey). Each country profile includes an overview of the organizations responsible for fulfilling police duties and an examination of policing practices that are implemented. The country descriptions also include comments on notable issues and controversies related to police and security, such as corruption, scandals, scarce resources, or terrorism. Finally, each country survey addresses aspects related to the nature of police–citizen interactions, including public attitudes toward the police, use of force and firearms by the police, and human rights abuses.

This chapter focuses primarily on public police agencies, or those operated by the government at the local, provincial, state, or national level. These tend to be the most visible expression of the government and perform the bulk of general police duties in society, such as crime prevention, control, and investigation; order maintenance and preserving the peace; provision of social services; and traffic regulation and control. This chapter is less concerned with special jurisdiction police or private police.

Further Reading

Haberfeld, M. R., and Ibrahim Cerrah, eds. 2008. *Comparative Policing: The Struggle for Democratization.* Los Angeles, CA: SAGE Publications.

Senior Police Adviser to the OSCE Secretary General. 2008. *Guidebook on Democratic Policing.* Vienna: Organization for Security and Co-operation in Europe. https://www.osce.org/spmu/23804.

ARGENTINA

Argentina is a federal constitutional republic located in the southern half of South America. It borders Chile, Bolivia, Paraguay, Brazil, Uruguay, and the South Atlantic Ocean. The population of over forty-four million is primarily of Spanish and Italian descent or mixed European and Amerindian descent. Argentina has a diverse economy rebounding from a series of economic crises in the twentieth century. The gross domestic product per capita is USD 20,900, which is comparable to Chile (USD 24,600) and higher than Brazil (USD 15,600). The territory that is now Argentina was colonized by Spain in the sixteenth century until the United Provinces of the Rio Plata declared independence in 1816. The contemporary Argentine Republic was formed in 1861. Though the first half of the twentieth century was characterized by political instability, periods of military rule, and state violence, the country has been a relatively stable democracy since 1983. The long history of military influence and authoritarian rule still affects the role of the police in Argentina, despite important strides toward democratization.

Police Structure and Practices

Policing in Argentina is decentralized and carried out at the provincial and federal levels of the government. Both police bodies fulfill security and judicial police functions. The former entails activities related to order maintenance, crime prevention, traffic control, and criminal intelligence. The latter refers to activities involving criminal investigation or judicial supervision. Argentina is a representative democracy divided into twenty-three autonomous administrative units or provinces. The bulk of policing occurs at the provincial level, with each provincial government operating its own police force that answers to the provincial governor and minister of security. Each provincial force's legal jurisdiction is limited to its own geographic borders and the enforcement of nonfederal crimes. Additionally, the autonomous city of Buenos Aires and a handful of other cities operate their own municipal police forces.

All policing at the federal level occurs under the Ministry of Security. The Policía Federal Argentina (PFA), or the Argentine Federal Police, is the primary and most powerful law enforcement agency at this level. Similar to all federal agencies, its jurisdiction extends geographically beyond provincial boundaries but is limited to violations of federal law. The PFA is headquartered and operates primarily in Buenos Aires, the capital and the largest city. The Gendarmería Nacional (GN), or the National Gendarmerie, and the Prefectura Naval Argentina (PNA), or the Argentine Coast Guard, are the two major federal police agencies. While the PFA is a civilian police force, like the provincial forces, the GN and PNA have a more militarized organizational form. The GN primarily performs tasks related to protection, security, and judicial policing. The PNA fulfills similar security-related functions on the nation's waterways.

National attention to increased crime rates and police abuses led to public calls for reform in the early twenty-first century, especially in Buenos Aires and Mendoza. In both instances reforms focused on increasing civilian participation, protecting civil liberties, and decentralizing authority, all of which are in line with community and democratic policing principles. However, the highly centralized structure of the PFA and ties to the political regime hinder community-policing efforts. For instance, the position of chief of police within the PFA is politically appointed. Other factors besides political influence that have inhibited policing reform include organizational resistance to change, tolerance for corruption, intergovernmental disputes between the levels of government (i.e., federal, provincial, and local), and the potential illicit benefits of unreformed police agencies.

Terrorism is a key concern for police agencies in Argentina. Terrorism-related activities are primarily performed at the federal level. In 1997, the PFA created a Department of Antiterrorist Investigations Unit (DUIA) in response to two terrorist attacks in the early 1990s. In 2001, the PFA created the General Directorate for International Terrorism and Complex Offences. The GN's Intelligence Directorate and Special Counter-Terrorism Intelligence Unit are primarily responsible for collecting terrorism-related intelligence. The GN also includes a Special Forces Section, Bomb Disposal Group, Scientific Police Department, and Special Unit for Judicial Investigations. Additionally, the PNA collects intelligence through its Intelligence Service and Antiterrorist Division. Since 2000, members from each agency also work together on a special investigations unit. Argentina has received support from other nations, such as the United States, in establishing and carrying out counter-terrorism and drug interdiction activities.

Police Violence

Argentina has a long history of human rights abuses at the hands of government security agencies including extrajudicial kidnappings, torture, and killings. Much of this occurred during military rule and the Dirty War (1976–1983), when the junta used extreme violence against insurgent groups and citizens in a fight against communism and Peronism, a social justice movement started by the former president Juan Domingo Perón (1895–1974). Government forces used kidnapping, torture, and murder to suppress political opposition. For example, it is estimated that during this time the military kidnapped between 10,000 and 30,000 Argentines. These people became known as *los desaparcidos*, or the disappeared. Many women were pregnant at the time of their abduction. It is reported that the government then stole and sold approximately 500 children who were born in captivity. These children became known as *los desaparcidos con vida*, or the living disappeared (Haberman 2015).

The Argentine government reopened cases of human rights violations that allegedly occurred during the junta. By 2014, the government had completed more than 121 trials and convicted 503 perpetrators (Human Rights Watch 2015). An

Mothers of the Plazo de Mayo is a social movement that originally aimed to hold the Argentine government accountable for children who went missing during the Dirty War. It has since evolved into an organization advocating for human and civil rights more generally. (Shutterstock)

additional 1,611 persons suspected of human rights abuses are still being investigated. Similarly, Argentina is working to identify children who disappeared and reunite them with their families. More than 100 grandchildren of *los desaparacidos* have been located as of August 2014.

By some measures, contemporary Argentina is one of the least violent countries in a particularly violent region. However, even after the dictatorship ended, violent clashes between citizens and police remain a problem in Argentina. Between 1993 and 2001, four civilians died in clashes with security forces in Buenos Aires City and Greater Buenos Aires for every one police officer who died (Das 2006). It was not until 2002 that police and security forces were legally barred from using live ammunition against public protestors.

Though the use of such violence has declined over the last few years, Human Rights Watch reported that police abuse was still a significant problem. In May 2014, the police fired rubber bullets at a workers' demonstration in the Tucumán province, injuring twenty-two people. The next month, more than 100 people were injured in a similar event in the Chaco province. In 2016, GN officers fired rubber bullets at children in Buenos Aires, and mounted police officers fired upon unarmed protestors in the Tucumán province. An Argentine human rights report noted that 126 citizens died in violent confrontations with security personnel in 2015. Approximately thirty-six security personnel died during the same events. Citizens killed in these confrontations were likely to be young and male. For instance, 95 percent of those killed by security forces between 1996 and 2015 were male, and 87.5 percent were no older than thirty-five years (CELS 2016).

Human Rights Watch also reported instances of police abuse of citizens in custody. In addition to generally poor prison conditions, citizens have reported coercive interrogation tactics employed by the police. These include physical torture, threats of violence against family members, threats of sexual abuse, and other forms of ill treatment designed to coerce confessions from suspects.

Public Attitudes toward Police

The Argentine public has exhibited relatively low levels of trust in the police over the last few decades. During the 1990s, estimates on the percentage of the population that trusts the police ranged from 16 to 24 percent (Hinton 2006). According to a 2012 survey, public confidence in police reached only 43.3 points, the tenth highest score of a sample consisting of twenty-six nations in the region (International Security Sector Advisory Team 2015). For reference, the highest score of 65.7 points was earned by Chile. The militarized GN and PNA tend to receive more favorable evaluations by the public than the PFA and provincial police forces. Experiences with police abuse and increased media coverage of police violence contributed to low levels of trust. Public confidence was also negatively affected, and citizens became reluctant to report criminal victimizations to authorities. Perceived police criminality and incompetence has also contributed to poor public attitudes in more recent years.

Further Reading

CELS (Centro de Estudios Legales Y Sociales). 2016. "Human Rights in Argentina: 2016 Report." http://www.cels.org.ar/especiales/informeanual2016/en/#prologue.

Central Intelligence Agency. 2018. "The World Factbook." https://www.cia.gov/library /publications/resources/the-world-factbook/.

Das, Dilip K. 2006. "Argentina." In *World Police Encyclopedia*. Vol. 1, edited by Dilip K. Das, 28–34. New York: Routledge.

Eaton, Kent. 2008. "Paradoxes of Police Reform: Federalism, Parties and Civil Society in Argentina's Public Security Crisis." *Latin American Research Review* 43 (3): 5–32.

Haberman, Clyde. 2015. "Children of Argentina's 'Disappeared' Reclaim Past, with Help." *The New York Times*, October 11, 2015. https://www.nytimes.com/2015/10/12/us /children-of-argentinas-disappeared-reclaim-past-with-help.html.

Hinton, Mercedes S. 2006. *The State of the Streets: Police and Politics in Argentina and Brazil*. Boulder, CO: Lynne Riener Publishers.

Human Rights Watch. 2015. "World Report: 2015." https://www.hrw.org/sites/default/files /wr2015_web.pdf.

International Security Sector Advisory Team. 2015. "Argentina Country Profile." September 1, 2015. https://issat.dcaf.ch/Learn/Resource-Library/Country-Profiles/Argentina -Country-Profile.

DOMINICA

The Commonwealth of Dominica is an independent parliamentary democracy situated in the Caribbean between Puerto Rico and Trinidad and Tobago. It has a small population of 74,000 people, most of whom are of African descent. Dominica has a struggling economy based largely on agriculture and ecotourism. Its gross domestic product per capita is USD 11,000, which is comparable to Ecuador (USD 11,500) but much lower than neighboring Puerto Rico (USD 39,400). The country suffered severe damage from Hurricane Maria in 2017, which hindered economic development (Central Intelligence Agency 2018). The colonial history of Dominica and the lack of financial resources have played important roles in shaping policing in the country.

Police Structure and Practices

Having established independence from the British Empire in 1978, law enforcement is structured according to the British Westminster legal system. Policing in the Commonwealth of Dominica is a highly centralized institution, with a national police force fulfilling all police duties on the island. This agency, the Commonwealth of Dominica Police Force (CDPF), operates under the Ministry of Justice, Immigration, and National Security. Dominica is divided into two divisions for policing purposes, which are further subdivided into twenty districts. As the only police force, CDPF officers may perform their duties in any district on the island. The top law enforcement officer in the CDPF is the commissioner of police who is assisted by the deputy commissioner of police. At the bottom of the rank structure are the constables, who are the uniformed line officers who fulfill patrol and other general police functions in the community. Constables are based out of police stations. Headquartered in Roseau, the capital and largest city in Dominica, the CDPF is a relatively small force compared to those of other Caribbean nations. Specifically, the force claimed 444 officers in 2018 (Government of the Commonwealth of Dominica 2018). While this number has doubled since 1978, it is still half the average force in the Caribbean.

The Police Act (1940) outlines the powers and duties granted to the CDPF by the government. It also specifies the organizational structure of the CDPF, which is hierarchical and militarized in nature. According to the Police Act, the CDPF performs the following tasks: preserving public peace and protecting public property; investigating, apprehending, and prosecuting perpetrators of criminal offenses and other wanted persons; maintaining public order and assemblies in public places; controlling and regulating traffic; carrying out revenue, quarantine, emigration, excise, and immigration laws; executing summons and warrants; protecting lost property; providing animal control; escorting detainees; and carrying out other tasks defined by laws. Notably, Dominica does not have a standing military force. As such, the Police Act also charges the CDPF with national security and defense responsibilities. Specifically, the paramilitary Special Service Unit (SSU) and the Coast Guard perform functions related to external security. Other specialized units include intelligence and investigative squads tasked with surveillance and protection duties.

Roseau is the capital city of Dominica and the home of the headquarters of the Commonwealth of Dominica Police Force. (Irishka777/Dreamstime.com)

In line with the principles of democratic policing, the CDPF has engaged in reform efforts designed to increase professionalism and transparency. These include ventures to include community participation in crime and order maintenance. For instance, the CDPF established a Community Outreach Programme on Crime in 2012 designed to elicit community feedback through public meetings between the public, the national security minister, and the attorney general. Other community-based programs include outreach initiatives in various neighborhoods and a radio show designed to inform the public about crime and security matters. Another effort is the "Crime Stoppers Dominica" program that solicits public help in solving various crimes. However, none of these efforts has been evaluated to determine effectiveness and whether they should be continued, modified, or halted. In late 2017, the National Security Minister announced that the government would initiate a review of the CDPF to assess its capabilities and efficiency. The intent of this review is to create lasting solutions that modernize and strengthen the nation's only police force.

One impediment to this process is the government's reticence to release recent crime statistics to the public. This makes it difficult to assess the level of crime and analyze trends in criminal behavior over time in Dominica. It also impedes assessing police performance and estimating other crime-related statistics, such as the number of firearms in the country. Another impediment to democratic policing is the highly centralized structure of the police force. The tenets of community policing emphasize a decentralized structure that provides local governments a role in crime prevention and community safety. There are forty-one local authorities in Dominica that do not have their own police forces.

Challenges

A major problem for policing in Dominica is lack of resources dedicated to supporting the CDFP. However, the government has made strides to remedy this situation. For instance, Dominica entered into the Caribbean Basin Security Initiative (CBSI), which aims to improve efficiency, and has allowed the CDPF to receive updated equipment. The CDPF has accepted support from other nations, such as China, which donated ninety motorcycles in 2012. Dominica also recently provided twelve new vehicles for the CDPF to replace aging police vehicles. This means that all but one police station in the country has a vehicle assigned to it. Similarly, a Motor Cycle Unit was introduced to facilitate efficient traffic control and enforcement in Roseau. The CDPF has also collaborated in training efforts with China, the United States, and Barbados. Finally, a new E-911 system was established in an effort to increase emergency response times. This new system is monitored twenty-four hours per day, seven days a week and responded to 97 percent of the 10,800 calls it processed in fiscal year 2016–2017.

Drug trafficking is another challenge for the CDPF as Dominica acts as a drug transshipment point. The number of drug trafficking convictions increased from 47 in 2006 to 225 in 2009. Police engaged in nearly 500 drug seizures in 2011

(International Security Sector Advisory Team 2015). Notable substances confiscated include 1.7 tons of marijuana and 62 kilograms of cocaine. Drug trafficking is linked to violent crime in Dominica. For instance, the number of confiscated firearms related to drug trafficking increased from four in 2006 to twenty-five in 2009. Marijuana is also cultivated and consumed in Dominica. Marijuana was grown on an estimated 210 acres in 2011, with CDPF officers eradicating thirteen acres. It is estimated that one-quarter of the marijuana transported through Dominica is consumed domestically, with the remaining three-quarters exported.

The CDPF created a Drug Squad in 2012 in response to the growing threat of drug-related crime. This unit consists of twenty officers and engages in various activities related to drug interdiction. As noted above, the Coast Guard is tasked with maintaining external security. Therefore, it also performs drug interdiction operations. Because drug trafficking is a significant concern for many Caribbean nations, security forces in Dominica are involved with the Regional Security System (RSS), in which various Caribbean countries cooperate in drug interdiction efforts. Through the CBSI, the CDPF has acquired modern equipment to combat drug crimes, such as computer systems, boats, and technical assistance.

Finally, as a small island in the Caribbean, Dominica is vulnerable to a wide variety of natural hazards, such as floods, volcanoes, and landslides. However, the most severe threats are tropical storms and hurricanes. Between 2007 and 2015, three major events negatively affected 23,500 residents and killed fifteen (Assessment Capacities Project 2017). Tropical Storm Erika in 2015 directly killed thirteen people and resulted in floods that killed an additional thirty people. Damages associated with Tropical Storm Erika were estimated to exceed USD 480 million. In 2017, Hurricanes Irma and Maria descended upon the Caribbean in a matter of weeks, devastating the island of Dominica. Maria was a category five hurricane that damaged the vast majority of the country's structures, including the CPDF training facility and various police stations. These events have the potential to overwhelm the resources of the CDPF, which is tasked with protecting property, preserving peace, maintaining order, and controlling traffic. Looting in the wake of such events is a particularly significant problem.

Crime Rates and Public Attitudes

The crime rate in Dominica is relatively low compared to other Caribbean nations. For instance, the average murder rate in Dominica between 2000 and 2010 was 10.4 per 100,000 inhabitants, which was lower than Jamaica (51.7), Trinidad and Tobago (26), St. Lucia (21), St. Kitts and Nevis (29.2), and Belize (35.8) during the same time period. The average murder rate for the entire region between 2000 and 2010 was 22 per 100,000 citizens. During the same time period, Dominica ranked among the lowest crime rates for a variety of crime types. It was only among countries with the highest crime rate for burglaries and break-ins (Seepersad 2013).

Despite these relatively low levels, the crime rate in Dominica has seen an upward trend over the last few decades. For instance, Dominica only had two murders in 2000 (Seepersad 2013). Over the next ten years, it averaged seven murders per year. However, the number of murders rose to thirteen in 2009 and remained high at eleven in 2010. The number of murders in 2009 represented a record high for the nation (Hill 2013). During this period, Dominica exhibited one of the most significant increases in the murder rate for the entire region. Specifically, the murder rate increased from 2.1 per 100,000 in 2000 to 7.3 in 2006 and 22.1 in 2010 (International Security Sector Advisory Team 2015). Additionally, between 2000 and 2010, Dominica saw an increase in other violent crimes, such as shootings (0.9), robbery (1.4), and kidnapping (0.3).

A related concern is an increasing trend in gun-related crimes and the possession of illicit firearms. Between 2000 and 2010, the average rate of shootings in Dominica was 5.6 per 100,000 inhabitants. However, the rates for years 2007 through 2009 were all above average, with 10 shootings per 100,000 people in 2009 (Seepersad 2013), which is likely related to gang activity. It is estimated that there are ten gangs in the country with about 113 members (International Security Sector Advisory Team 2015). In response, the CDPF launched an initiative to reduce the number of illegal firearms on the streets of Dominica. This has seen some success as significantly more firearms and rounds of ammunition were seized in 2016 compared to 2015. Specifically, the police confiscated forty-four firearms and 1,198 rounds of ammunition in 2016 compared to the twenty-six firearms and 327 rounds of ammunition seized in 2015.

Further Reading

Assessment Capacities Project. 2017. "Dominica Country Profile." https://www.acaps.org /sites/acaps/files/slides/files/20171019_acaps_dominica_country_profile_0.pdf.

Central Intelligence Agency. 2018. "The World Factbook." https://www.cia.gov/library /publications/resources/the-world-factbook/.

Government of the Commonwealth of Dominica. 2018. "Home." http://www.dominica .gov.dm.

Hill, Sheridon. 2013. "The Rise of Gang Violence in the Caribbean." In *Gangs in the Caribbean*, edited by Randy Seepersad and Ann Marie Bissessar, 36–79. Newcastle upon Tyne, UK: Cambridge Scholars Publishing.

International Security Sector Advisory Team. 2015. "Dominica Country Profile." December 1, 2015. https://issat.dcaf.ch/Learn/Resource-Library/Country-Profiles/Dominica -Country-Profile.

Seepersad, Randy. 2013. "Crime in the Caribbean." In *Gangs in the Caribbean*, edited by Randy Seepersad and Ann Marie Bissessar, 2–35. Newcastle upon Tyne, UK: Cambridge Scholars Publishing.

INDIA

India is the second most populous country in the world, behind China, with a population of 1.3 billion people. It is the eighth largest country in the world in terms of landmass, located in southern Asia, south of Pakistan and southwest of Nepal and China. It is a federal parliamentary republic with twenty-nine states and seven union territories. Its gross domestic product per capita is USD 7,200, less than half that of China (USD 16,700) but greater than neighboring Pakistan (USD 5,400). India was under the influence of British colonial rule for over 100 years, gaining independence in 1947, when British India was divided into two separate countries, India and Pakistan (Central Intelligence Agency 2018). The British colonial legacy still strongly shapes contemporary policing practices, and economic hardships make it difficult for India to fully modernize its police force.

Police Structure and Practices

As a legacy of colonialism, India's police system was modeled after the Royal Irish Constabulary and designed to further Britain's reign over India. The modern Indian police system was established with the passage of the Police Act (V) of 1861, which placed policing duties in the hands of civil officers, rather than the military. India's constitution places the responsibility for policing and corrections in the hands of state governments. However, the constitution also mandates that the central government is ultimately responsible for national security. As a result, policing is largely decentralized, with most traditional police activities occurring at the state level.

In addition to maintaining its own police forces, the central government is responsible for advising, training, coordinating, and financially assisting state police activities. Central police forces are supervised by the Ministry of Home Affairs (MHA) and may be categorized as either armed or unarmed. The former includes central armed police forces that provide national security and emphasize order maintenance. The latter includes organizations that investigate interstate crimes, collect intelligence, provide training, and conduct research. The Indian Police Service (IPS) is an all-India service that provides centrally trained officers to lead both state and central police forces.

State police forces are divided between armed and civil branches. Armed police are paramilitary units that receive separate training and have a separate rank structure than civil police. Armed police are headed by a commandant and are organized into battalions. These units are reserved for emergency situations requiring physical force, such as security, protection, and crowd control. These forces typically have heavier weaponry and armor than armed officers for districts. Civil forces are unarmed and responsible for standard policing duties and criminal investigation. Though they do not carry firearms, civil police are often armed with wooden staffs, or *lathis*, as a means of protection. These officers include uniformed patrol constables and are based in police stations and other criminal investigation, training, and intelligence agencies.

In 2016, there were 1,731,666 civil (1,363,497) and armed (368,169) police officers in India. Of the total police population, 21.3 percent were armed, 66.5 percent were constables, and 7.1 percent were women. The past decade has seen a steady increase in the ratio of police to civilians, rising by nearly 27 percent. The number of armed police battalions has also increased from 344 in 2005 to 443 in 2016 (Bureau of Police Research and Development 2016).

The Indian police engage primarily in traditional, reactive policing. Their central focus is on order maintenance rather than crime prevention or service provision. Critics argue that the structure, policies, and practices of India's police are outmoded and not fit for a democratic country. For example, armed police officers do not live among or interact with the community on a regular basis. Instead, they live in military-style barracks and only venture into the community when responding to emergency situations. The Supreme Court of India has suggested reforms that would push the policing model toward community policing. These include setting minimum training standards, de-emphasizing the role of order maintenance, focusing on crime prevention and service, including the community in police activities, and overhauling the current mission and goals of the police to better reflect those of a modern democracy.

Use of Force

India exhibits a high level of social unrest with frequent public political, religious, and ethnic demonstrations. These present almost daily opportunities for violent confrontations between the citizens and the police. For instance, in 2016, state police were criticized for responding to rock-throwing from protestors by firing teargas, rubber bullets, and even real bullets into crowds. As a result, thirty civilians were killed and hundreds were injured (Human Rights Watch 2016). In 2017, a police chief with magisterial powers found a popular Guru of the Dera Sacha Sauda sect guilty of raping two women in 2002. The conviction sparked outrage among his followers, resulting in a protest of over 100,000 in Panchkula, Haryana (*The Guardian* 2017). The riotous behavior of protestors led to a violent confrontation with armed police. In the end, thirty-eight civilians were killed and another 200 were wounded.

This problem is exacerbated by India's emphasis on armed, rather than civil, policing. Another factor that contributes to violence between police and the public is a lack of appropriate training and protective equipment. State officers do not receive adequate training to address affronts to their authority. A final contributing characteristic is an air of impunity found in the policing culture. This culture encourages the use of violent tactics as a means of law enforcement and permits such tactics to go unpunished. In 2015, forty-two civilians were killed by police gunfire and thirty-nine were injured, with the majority of injuries occurring during riots (National Crime Records Bureau 2016). Additionally, most police officer injuries caused by civilian gunfire were sustained during riots.

Aside from police killings, another measure to examine is the number of complaints against police lodged by citizens. In 2015, police received almost 55,000 complaints, resulting in 1,100 trials and twenty-five convictions (National Crime Records Bureau 2016). Of those not going to trial, 447 officers were dismissed and 18,000 received some form of punishment. Further, in the same year, ninety-four cases of human rights violations were investigated, resulting in thirty-four officers being charged and zero convictions. Such a low proportion of convictions to complaints fuels public perceptions that police are above the law and not accountable for their misconduct.

Additionally, a Human Rights Watch (2009) study interviewed a sample of police officers and abuse victims at various police stations in India. Many police officers admitted feeling that illegal methods are necessary to enforce law and solve crimes. They further admitted regularly committing human rights abuses, such as torture, unlawful arrests, prolonged detentions, and even extrajudicial encounter killings. Encounter killings refer to unplanned killings of civilians by armed police officers allegedly for self-defense. Officers have faked such killings in the past as a means of doling out "street justice." Another study corroborated this finding, reporting that police consider such tactics to be effective and are often not treated as deviant. Among citizens who suffer the most are members of minority groups, as they are often unable to pay when being extorted. As a result, they do not receive the police services they need or are punished.

Other Challenges

Because it borders nations like Pakistan, Bangladesh, and Nepal, India faces threats from external and internal terror organizations. India experiences the second highest number of terror attacks and lives lost due to terrorism in the world. Jammu and Kashmir is the area most devastated by terrorism. In 2015, 95 percent of Indian civilian fatalities caused by terror attacks occurred in this state. Of the police line of duty deaths in 2016, excluding accidents, 63 percent were killed in terrorism or extremist-related incidents (National Crime Records Bureau 2016). Terrorism remains unconstrained in this region because of a lack of infrastructure necessary for police to effectively operate, and because local citizens are fearful, often refusing to cooperate with law enforcement or report crime.

The central government is primarily responsible for responding to terrorism-related activities as they are perceived as a threat to national security. Traditionally, the MHA has addressed terrorism through legislation grants to police and enhancing security forces, such as the Prevention of Terrorist Activities Act (POTA) of 2002, the Armed Forces Special Powers Act of 1958, and the Unlawful Activities Prevention Act of 1967. Critics point out that these so-called "black laws" appear to sacrifice civil liberties in the name of national security. For example, they allow the central government to label an area as "disturbed" without judicial review, granting their forces broader use of lethal force in such regions. Moreover, officers are prohibited from prosecution even when misconduct has been verified.

Another major problem facing the police in India is scarcity of resources. State governments are often unable to provide their officers modern equipment, maintain standards of training, or build the infrastructure necessary to effectively prevent and fight crime. Many rural areas remain virtually unpatrolled, as the police have neither the communications systems nor vehicles necessary to do so. Recognizing this problem, the MHA has engaged in a modernization scheme designed to supplement state policing resources since 1969, with its current iteration running from 2012 to 2017. The goals of this program are to provide state police with modern equipment and training infrastructure, such as housing, weapons, forensic equipment, and training centers.

Further Reading

Bureau of Police Research and Development. 2016. *Data on Police Organisations*. New Delhi, India: Ministry of Home Affairs, Bureau of Police Research and Development. http://bprd.nic.in/WriteReadData/userfiles/file/201701090303068737739DATABOO K2016FINALSMALL09-01-2017.pdf.

Central Intelligence Agency. 2018. "The World Factbook." https://www.cia.gov/library /publications/resources/the-world-factbook/.

The Guardian. 2017. "Indian States in Lockdown for Guru's Rape Sentencing after Deadly Protests." *The Guardian*, August 27, 2017. https://www.theguardian.com/world/2017 /aug/27/indian-states-in-lockdown-for-gurus-sentencing-after-deadly-protests.

Human Rights Watch. 2009. "India: Overhaul Abusive, Failing Police System." August 4, 2009. https://www.hrw.org/news/2009/08/04/india-overhaul-abusive-failing-police-system.

Human Rights Watch. 2016. "India: Investigate Use of Lethal Force in Kashmir." 2016. July 12, 2016. https://www.hrw.org/news/2016/07/12/india-investigate-use-lethal-force -kashmir.

National Crime Records Bureau. 2016. "Crime in India 2015." Ministry of Home Affairs. http://ncrb.gov.in/.

IRELAND

The Republic of Ireland is a country of five million people occupying much of the Island of Ireland to the south of Northern Ireland and the west of the United Kingdom. Eighty-two percent of the population is Irish and more than three-fourths are Catholics. Ireland has a small, trade-dependent economy with a high standard of living. The gross domestic product per capita is USD 73,200, which is higher than both the United Kingdom and the United States (Central Intelligence Agency 2018). Since gaining independence in 1921, Ireland has been a parliamentary republic with a common law legal system. It has embraced democratic policing initiatives, most notably in the form of community policing.

Structure and Practice

Law enforcement in the Republic of Ireland is highly centralized, featuring a unitary police service. This means that general policing duties across the nation are carried out by a single, national police force rather than separate local (e.g., county, province, state, city) police agencies. This stands in stark contrast to the highly decentralized structure of law enforcement in the United States, which incorporates over 20,000 separate law enforcement agencies. In Ireland, this national force is An Garda Síochána, or the Guardians of the Peace. Following the Anglo-Irish Treaty (1921), in which the Irish Free State (now the Republic of Ireland) gained independence from the United Kingdom, the Royal Irish Constabulary once responsible for policing unified Ireland was dissolved so that the Republic of Ireland and Northern Ireland could each establish its own service. Out of this was born the Civic Guard in 1922, which merged with the Dublin Metropolitan Police to form the Garda Síochána in 1925. Presently, it is responsible for all law enforcement duties across Ireland, including order maintenance, crime prevention, crime detection and investigation, traffic control and regulation, and national security.

In 2016, the Gardaí ("Guardians") employed nearly 13,000 law enforcement officers, 750 reserve officers, and 2,000 civilian employees (An Garda Síochána 2018). Personnel in the Gardaí are organized in a pyramidal, civilian rank structure, with uniformed police officers equivalent to a patrol officer in the United States in the bottom tier. At the top of the pyramid is the Garda Commissioner who reports to the Minister of Justice, Equality, and Law Reform.

The primary policing model employed in Ireland is community policing, emphasizing community participation in public safety activities. This organizational ethos informs policing strategies that proactively target the underlying sources of crime and disorder. It is reflected in the Gardaí's mission statement, which emphasizes working with communities on safety and service matters. In line with this attitude, the Gardaí's overarching goals include preventing crime and antisocial behavior, decreasing fear of crime, and improving the overall quality of life of citizens. Community policing efforts generally feature several common characteristics: collaboration with the community, proactive problem solving, and a decentralized organizational structure. While the relation to community policing is more straightforward for the other core features, the role of decentralization is worth discussing. The diffusion of decision-making power to the bottom ranks of the hierarchical pyramid allows officers who interact most with citizens to have the discretion necessary to identify creative, customized solutions to a community's problems. The Gardaí count these fundamental characteristics among their ten pillars of community policing, which inform all aspects of their community policing efforts.

The Gardaí engage in a variety of initiatives that reflect this philosophy and facilitate achieving the aforementioned goals of community policing. Values aligned with community policing have influenced Gardaí practices since its creation, and the implementation of formal initiatives specifically modeled after community policing strategies can be traced to the early 1980s. These first steps into community policing were neighborhood watch-style initiatives for urban and rural areas designed to empower citizens as investors in community safety by allowing them to participate directly in crime control activities. As of 2011, there were more than 3,500 such programs implemented across the nation. More recently, Local Policing Fora (LPF) and Joint Policing Committees (JPC) solidify community partnerships by giving members of the public informal and formal channels through which to consult on crime-related problems and solutions. JPCs are now established in all local authority areas under the jurisdiction of the Gardaí, while the more informal LPF are active at the neighborhood level in six such areas. In an effort to realize organizational transformation, the Gardaí was restructured, creating community policing-specific offices and assigning over 1,000 officers to community policing duties. Community policing teams are currently assigned to every district in Ireland, increasing the likelihood that each member of the public may recognize and form relationships with their own Gardaí officers.

Police–Citizen Interactions

Police–citizen interactions in Ireland are shaped by the organization's fundamental principle of policing by consent, rather than by force, as well as community policing practices. In this tradition, uniformed patrol officers typically do not carry firearms. They are armed with a collapsible baton and pepper spray. Specialized units that respond to high-risk emergency situations are also trained and carry heavy arms, for example, the emergency response unit (ERU) and Regional Support Units (RSU). In 2016, the Gardaí formed an Armed Support Unit (ASU) that specializes in high visibility patrolling. In this unit, the officers' firearms are kept in the locked trunk of their vehicle, meaning they are not armed during their foot patrols. The general public appears to be evenly split in their beliefs about arming patrol-level officers. A news poll indicated that 44 percent were in favor arming the entire police force, whereas 43 percent were against such action (*The Journal* 2017). Despite this, the Garda Commissioner declared that the Gardaí will remain a primarily unarmed force.

Police–citizen interactions involve a relatively low amount of violence. For example, in 2014 and 2015, there were slightly fewer than 300 nonfatal assaults on Garda officers each year, that is, about 23 assaults per 1,000 officers (An Garda Síochána 2015). Further, there are relatively few citizen homicides of police officers. Only two Garda officers have been killed in the line of duty since 2013. Additionally, there are very few killings of citizens by police, as only one person died in police custody in 2015.

Another way to understand the nature of police–citizen interactions in Ireland is to examine community attitudes toward law enforcement. The Garda Research Unit conducts an annual survey of a nationally representative sample of 6,000 Irish citizens (An Garda Síochána 2016). In 2016, trust and confidence in the Garda as an institution was positive with 88 percent of respondents reporting mid-to-high levels. Additionally, 79 percent of victims reported crime to the police, indicating that the community is participating in community safety. However, public perceptions of police effectiveness fell between 2015 and 2016. Approximately 50 percent of respondents considered the police to be effective in combating crime. On the other hand, 51 percent considered the Garda to be a world-class force. Further, in reference to community policing efforts, only 35 percent of respondents believed the police patrolled their area regularly.

Notable Scandals

Since the early 2000s, there have been several official inquiries into police misbehavior, however, the most substantial of these has been the Morris Tribunal led by Justice Frederick Morris. This tribunal investigated a slew of allegations levied against Gardaí personnel for actions taken during the 1990s. Outlined in the Tribunal's eight reports, these allegations include Gardaí officers directly engaging in the planting of homemade explosives and firearms to facilitate multiple false arrests and to further occupational advancement, in-custody mistreatment of several unlawfully arrested people, extortion and hoax bomb phone calls to effect entrapment, initiation of a lengthy campaign of harassment against a family, mishandling of confidential informants, and misidentification of a homicide investigation. In addition to finding evidence of this alleged misbehavior, the Tribunal also found evidence of generally improper investigation practices, attempts to retroactively conceal wrongdoing, and the failure of police managers to properly address such behavior once brought to light. The Tribunal concluded that while some Gardaí officers engaged in outright criminal behavior, its senior management was also profoundly negligent in their duty to appropriately investigate the behavior of their officers. Further, the Tribunal found that in some instances, senior police management possessed full knowledge of wrongdoing and either failed to take appropriate remedial action or actively aided in covering up the behavior. The Tribunal found that police accountability within the Garda Síochána was seriously deficient.

The significance of the Morris Tribunal is reflected in the repercussions it brought for policing in Ireland. Most notably, the Garda Act of 2005 was passed in response to the findings of the Morris Tribunal and other publicized controversies. Principal changes included the establishment of two independent oversight mechanisms: the Garda Síochána Ombudsman Commission, which investigates public complaints levied against police, and the Garda Síochána Inspectorate, which addresses issues of operational and administrative efficiency and effectiveness. The Act also requires the Garda Commissioner to send the minister a policing plan every year and a strategy statement every three years. Finally, the Act established the JPCs, which allow citizens to consult with police on issues related to crime and disorder.

After the passage of the Garda Act, a number of policing scandals arose in Ireland. These ranged from negligent management, policy breaches, mistreatment of whistleblowers, and mishandling of evidence. In 2016, the Gardaí enacted a

---

Notable Police Errors

On the same day in 2017, the Gardaí publicly admitted two law enforcement gaffes. They first revealed that 14,600 citizens were wrongfully convicted of failing to pay a traffic citation despite having never received notice of one. They have since worked to set aside those convictions and provide compensation for the costs associated with these cases. The Gardaí then admitted that their computer system inflated the number of roadside breath tests conducted between 2007 and 2012. Of the recorded 1,995,000 breath tests, nearly half (937,000) never occurred, which affects police estimates of drunk-driving prevalence.

Modernization and Renewal Program that should take full effect by 2021. The Garda Commissioner has stated that the chief priority of this program is to effect cultural transformation within the Gardaí. The plan involves civilianization, the hiring of 500 additional civilian employees, a 200 million euro update to their technology systems, decentralization of authority, enhancing community partnerships, a victim-centered approach, and a focus on community policing.

Further Reading

An Garda Síochána. 2015. *Annual Report of An Garda Síochána 2015*. Dublin, Ireland: An Garda Síochána. https://www.garda.ie/en/about-us/publications/annual%20reports/an-garda-siochana-annual-reports/2015-annual-report-revised.pdf.

An Garda Síochána. 2016. "An Garda Síochána Public Attitudes Survey 2016." https://www.garda.ie/en/Information-Centre/Quarterly-Public-Attitudes-Surveys/An-Garda-Siochana-Public-Attitudes-Survey-2016.pdf.

An Garda Síochána. 2018. http://www.garda.ie.

Central Intelligence Agency. 2018. "The World Factbook." https://www.cia.gov/library/publications/resources/the-world-factbook/.

Conway, Vicky. 2014. *Policing Twentieth Century Ireland: A History of An Garda Síochána*. New York: Routledge.

The Journal. 2017. "Should All Gardaí Be Armed? The Nation's Split on the Question." April 26, 2017. http://www.thejournal.ie/article.php?id=2734928.

JAPAN

Japan comprises a group of islands between the North Pacific Ocean and the Sea of Japan to the east of North and South Korea and China. It consists of four main islands and thousands of islets. The country has over 126 million people, 98 percent of whom are ethnic Japanese. It is an economically advanced country with a gross domestic product of USD 42,000, which is slightly higher than its neighbor South Korea (USD 39,500) (Central Intelligence Agency 2018). In the nineteenth century, Japan was a military and economic power in Asia, but its dominance ended with defeat in World War II (1939–1945). Since then, Japan has built a strong democracy and capitalist economy. It has low crime rates and has developed a democratic model of policing through positive community interactions.

Structure and Practices

As the United States occupied Japan following World War II, American officials introduced Western policing practices to the country. A new constitution was formed that emphasized citizens' rights and a nonauthoritarian, decentralized view of law enforcement. Every town with 5,000 residents or more was required to develop its own autonomous police department. This resulted in the creation of 1,600 separate forces (Dammer and Albanese 2014). Each force answered to a public safety commission, ensuring that the people, not the government, controlled the police. In 1954, the Police Law was ratified, establishing the current system and changing the face of policing in Japan. Contemporary policing in Japan is both centralized and localized. The National Police Agency (NPA) operates at the national level and prefectural police departments work at the local level. These agencies are responsible for general policing duties, which include crime investigation and prevention, maintenance of public order and safety, and traffic enforcement. Other specialized law enforcement agencies that have limited jurisdictional police powers, such as the Maritime Safety Agency, the Japan Coast Guard, and the Narcotics Control Department, are also part of Japanese law enforcement.

The police organizations operating at the national level in Japan are the National Public Safety Commission (NPSC) and the NPA. The NPSC is a six-person independent body that acts as a check against excessive police power over citizens in Japan. A commissioner general, who is appointed by the NPSC and the prime minister, leads the NPA. NPA specializes in police training and education, communications, research, and the coordination of prefectural policing efforts. In terms of law enforcement activities, the NPA generally deals with national security and protection. For instance, the Imperial Guard provides protection services for the royal family and security at imperial facilities. There are seven Regional Police Bureaus located in major cities that help the NPA supervise and support police activities in the prefectures, including training and communications facilities. The NPA employs approximately 7,700 personnel, of whom 2,100 are police officers, 900 are members of the Imperial Guard, and 4,800 are civilians (National Police Agency of Japan 2016).

The bulk of policing in Japan occurs at the local level and is performed by prefectural police. A prefecture is a smaller, local district similar to a county. Each of the forty-seven prefectures in Japan has its own autonomous police force. There are approximately 287,000 employees in the forty-seven prefectural police forces, of which 258,600 are police officers and 28,300 are civilians (National Police Agency of Japan 2016). There are approximately 21,000 female police officers and 12,500 female civilian staff (Dammer and Albanese 2014). Prefectural police officers operate from local police stations and substations throughout their jurisdiction. In addition to performing general policing duties, prefectural police departments have militarized units. A notable example is the riot police, or *kidotai*, composed of 10,000 officers who specialize in crowd control, counter-terrorism, and emergency rescue (Dammer and Albanese 2014).

Japanese police have embraced community policing, with a strong emphasis on service to local communities. Their aim is to enmesh officers in the daily lives of the community, increase community awareness of police officers, and provide quick response during emergencies. A notable, unique practice that illustrates this point is the implementation of the police box system, which dates back to 1881. Police boxes are small police substations, often comprising a single room, deployed along police beats across the nation. Those in urban areas are called *koban* and their rural counterparts are *chuzaisho*. There are 6,200 koban and 6,400 chuzaisho (National Police Agency of Japan 2016). These highly visible stations are designed to integrate the officer into the community and give citizens maximal access to police services. These officers either stand guard in front of their box or patrol their beat, visiting homes and businesses. In addition to emergency response and crime prevention, they provide various community-focused services, including counseling, conflict mediation, youth mentorship, and the handling of lost or found items.

To supplement these efforts, the police have created an assortment of groups in which citizens can actively engage in crime prevention efforts with police. There are currently 48,000 such groups in Japan (National Police Agency of Japan 2016). Police also provides guidance for youth both in and out of school. Such guidance involves dispensing advice about various topics, such as general safety lessons, crime prevention, and sexual education. In-school efforts focus strongly on crime prevention and drug awareness education. Outside school, the police are heavily involved in counseling, education, arts, sports, self-defense, and other pro-social activities with youth. Police officers also attend local community events.

Treatment of Suspects

Japan boasts a relatively low overall crime rate and an exceptionally high conviction rate. In 2014, 99.8 percent of all prosecutions resulted in a conviction. Some argue that this may be a product of the relatively broad procedural powers granted to police investigators and a strong focus on obtaining confessions (Terrill 2016). These factors may together create an atmosphere in which suspects are at a risk of having their civil liberties violated. For instance, Japanese police officers may stop and question citizens if they look suspicious or are believed to have witnessed a crime. In 2017, Japan passed a controversial bill that expanded police power by criminalizing the planning of serious crimes. While presumably intended to combat terrorism as they prepared to host the Olympics, critics argued that this law infringed upon civil liberties, such as privacy rights and free speech. Additionally, police investigators may detain and interrogate a suspect for up to twenty-three days without formally charging them with a crime. Further, these suspects do not enjoy the right to have legal representation during questioning, and the procedures for securing court-appointed legal representation come into effect only after one has been formally indicted.

In addition to these broad procedural powers, investigators and prosecutors tend to focus on obtaining confessions rather than exploring other evidence. In fact, nearly 90 percent of all criminal prosecutions in Japan are founded upon a confession from the suspect (*The Economist* 2015). As further evidence of this pressure for confessions, in a 2010 survey of prosecutors, 30 percent reported that a not-guilty verdict would hurt their career and 25 percent admitted that a superior had ordered them to draft a confession statement that differed from the facts reported to them by the defendant. As a result, some investigators have engaged in ethically questionable, if not illegal, methods to secure confessions. While physical abuse is rarely reported, more commonly reported tactics include yelling, intimidating gestures, sleep deprivation, shaming, drafting false confessions, and other

Police and Organized Crime

Boryokudan is the term used to denote any criminal organization in Japan, although they are commonly referred to as *yakuza*. Though the number of people involved has fallen, *boryokudan* still poses a significant problem for police. In 2015, there were 46,900 members distributed across twenty-one distinct organized crime groups. However, 70 percent of all organized crime members belong to one of the four most powerful groups in the country. They engage in common organized crime activities, including drug, firearms, and human trafficking, gambling, extortion, and fraud. Turf wars and other violent conflicts between *boryokudan* groups are especially problematic. In 2015, police arrested 21,643 organized crime members in 38,482 criminal cases.

forms of coercion. Besides infringing upon a suspect's civil liberties, critics argue that these tactics also result in false confessions and wrongful convictions.

Police–Citizen Interactions

In the years following World War II the Japanese police enjoyed high levels of public confidence. However, this changed by the 1990s when the police were embroiled in a wave of highly publicized scandals. Many of these scandals share the common theme of senior management attempting to cover up serious wrongdoing by police officers. In Kanagawa, senior officers attempted to cover up acts of sexual harassment, extortion, hazing, drug use, and prostitution engaged by prefectural police officers. Five officers, including the prefectural chief, were indicted but received lenient sentences. Further, the NPA chief resigned. In Chiba, a woman was raped by police officers on multiple occasions and pressured to receive hush money in exchange for her silence. Senior NPA officers, including the chief, agreed to cover up the incidents. Finally, the Niigata police mishandled a kidnapping case and attempted to falsely take credit for finding the victim. The NPA and Niigata police chiefs resigned amid negative public backlash.

As a result of these controversies, public confidence was shaken and attitudes toward police fell precipitously. According to one poll at the time, 60 percent of adults stated their trust in police had declined in recent years, and 45 percent said they did not trust the police at all. Police officers also noted that citizens were less cooperative with investigations than in the past. The police responded by actively trying to restore public satisfaction to formerly high levels. After the cases of misconduct came to light, the NPA instituted a series of reforms, which included measures to bolster numbers of police box officers and counselors, enhance inspections of prefectural police forces, increase transparency, and improve handling citizen complaints against police officers. As a result, some contend that the police have restored their positive reputation. A recent survey revealed that public confidence in the police as an institution has risen consistently from 2000 to 2009.

Restricted firearms usage also shapes the nature of police–citizen interactions. Though authorized to carry a firearm while on patrol, and in other strictly defined scenarios, Japanese police officers very rarely use these weapons. As a result, very few citizens are injured or killed by police gunfire. Lethal violence against police officers is also relatively low. Only six Japanese police officers were feloniously killed in line of duty between 2004 and 2010. Additionally, only seventeen were killed in on-the-job accidents. Japan has very strict gun control laws. Shotguns and air rifles are the only weapons that citizens may legally own; handguns are banned outright. As a result, gun ownership is far lower than in comparable countries. In 2007, there were 0.6 guns per 100 people in Japan compared to 88.8 guns in the United States. Therefore, there are relatively few armed citizens threatening violence against police.

Japanese police organizational characteristics also impede firearm usage. Departments impose strict regulations regarding the use of firearms by their employees. In fact, police in Japan did not even arm themselves with guns until their occupation by the United States following World War II. Officers are not permitted to carry their guns off-duty; instead they must be stored at the police station. Though they undergo more extensive firearms training than their U.S. counterparts, Japanese police officers emphasize other means of self-defense, such as martial arts over the use of guns. Officers fear stigmatization stemming from inappropriate firearm usage.

Further Reading

Central Intelligence Agency. 2018. "The World Factbook." https://www.cia.gov/library/publications/resources/the-world-factbook/.

Dammer, Harry R., and Jay S. Albanese. 2014. *Comparative Criminal Justice Systems.* 5th ed. Belmont, CA: Wadsworth.

The Economist. 2015. "Extractor, Few Fans: An Overreliance on Confessions Is Undermining Faith in the Courts." December 3, 2015. https://www.economist.com/news/asia/21679489-overreliance-confessions-undermining-faith-courts-extractor-few-fans.

Johnson, David T. 2014. "Policing in Japan." In *SAGE Handbook of Modern Japanese Studies,* edited by James D. Babb. Thousand Oaks, CA: Sage Publications, Inc.

National Police Agency of Japan. 2016. *Police of Japan.* Tokyo, Japan: National Police Agency of Japan. http://www.npa.go.jp/english/index.html.

Terrill, Richard J. 2016. *World Criminal Justice Systems: A Comparative Survey.* 9th ed. New York: Routledge.

JORDAN

The Hashemite Kingdom of Jordan is a constitutional monarchy situated in the Middle East, sharing borders with Syria, Iraq, Saudi Arabia, Israel, and the West Bank. The population of 10.5 million people is 69.3 percent Jordanian, 13.3 percent Syrian, 6.7 percent Palestinian, 6.7 percent Egyptian, and 1.4 percent Iraqi. Arabic is the official language, and 97.2 percent of the population is Muslim. Jordan's economy is much weaker than its neighbors because of a lack of oil and natural resources. The country relies heavily on foreign aid. Its gross domestic product per capita is USD 9,200 compared to USD 16,700 in Iraq and USD 36,400 in Israel (Central Intelligence Agency 2018). Its government is stable, especially compared to other countries in the region. As a monarchy, the king is bestowed with both executive and legislative powers. Jordan's geographic location surrounded by less stable governments has created a refugee crisis for the country and heightened concerns about terrorism, both of which challenge policing operations.

Policing Structure

In the Kingdom of Jordan, policing is centralized at the national level, and the Public Security Force (PSF) performs general police duties. This organization operates under the purview of the Ministry of Interior via the Public Security Directorate. Notably, control of the PSF transfers from the Ministry of Interior to the Ministry of Defense during times of war and to the military governor general during times of martial law. The PSF is divided geographically into three primary divisions: metropolitan (Amman), rural (small towns and villages), and desert units. The hierarchically structured, paramilitary organization is headquartered in the nation's capital city of Amman, where the government maintains administrative control and fulfills technical functions. At the top of the command chain is the director general of Public Security. The king typically appoints someone to this position on the basis of military experience and loyalty to the crown. There are ten regional security directorates, which are further subdivided into fifty-nine smaller security centers. While the PSF is considered a technologically modernized force, rural areas tend to be less modernized than urban ones. This is illustrated by the PSF's utilization of camel-mounted patrol in desert areas.

The King Abdullah II of Jordan has been in power since 1999. During his reign, he has introduced some democratizing elements into the government and legal system, including community policing initiatives. (Department of Defense)

The Law for Public Security was passed in 1965 and identifies police duties with which the PSF is charged. These include preserving public order and protecting lives, honor, and property; preventing, investigating, and arresting perpetrators of criminal offenses; administrating prisons and guarding prisoners; implementing laws and regulations; receiving and handling lost property; supervising and controlling traffic; maintaining order and peace in public places; and fulfilling other duties defined by laws. Police personnel also perform various special tasks, such as guarding shrines, locating missing persons, and assisting immigrations and customs officials.

The operations of the PSF are divided broadly into administrative, judicial, and support functions. Administrative functions include tasks related to general law enforcement, order maintenance, and crime prevention. Judicial police officers conduct criminal investigations, apprehend suspects, and assist the prosecutor's office. Support police fulfill duties related to supporting police operations, including communications and logistics, as well as training and public affairs.

The Special Police Force (SPF) is an elite unit within the PSF that focuses on the prevention of, and response to, terrorism. Additionally, the General Intelligence Department (GID), the gendarmerie, the Civil Defense Directorate, and the military share responsibility for preserving national security. The GID is a civilian agency that reports directly to the king. It has been granted broad powers in collecting intelligence in the name of combating terrorism. In addition to its security function, the gendarmerie is also responsible for maintaining public order and riot control.

With approximately 8,180 police officers in Jordan, there is a ratio of 142 police officers for every 100,000 citizens in the kingdom (Kurian 2006). It is primarily a male-dominated profession. However, it is notable that Jordan is the first country in the region to allow women to join the police. It opened its female police academy in Amman, welcoming its first female cadet in 1972. By 2015, the training institute had graduated fifty-four cohorts of female police cadets from its six-month program. The PSD is increasing its numbers of female police officers, stating that evaluations have shown that such officers are equally capable of carrying out police duties and outperform their peers in various respects. These officers come from varying backgrounds and are distributed to a variety of PSD units accordingly. Female officers in the PSF tend to work primarily in the police laboratory, prisons, public relations, and accounting units. Relatively few fulfill patrol, traffic, or border security functions, although this number seems to be increasing gradually over time.

Refugee Crisis

Various refugee crises have impacted Jordanian security in recent decades. These pose a problem for the police as significant increases in the population and cramped living conditions in refugee camps set the stage for crime and violence and stretch the resources of the PSF. Notable examples of such crises include the Palestinian, Iraq, and Syrian crises. Between 1948 and 1967, Jordan received large numbers of Palestinian refugees. Jordan also received more than 500,000 refugees in the twelve years following the United States-led invasion of Iraq. Then, four years into the Syrian refugee crisis, Jordan hosted 1.4 million refugees. This growth in population strains police resources and can lead to conflict between Jordanians and refugees. For instance, some locals blame refugees for a variety of social ailments, such as a rising cost of living, rent inflation, and diminishing job opportunities.

In response to the Syrian crisis, the PSF has launched community patrol initiatives in Jordan's two primary refugee camps, Za'atari and Azraq. The Za'atari camp alone hosts 80,000 people. Police efforts include establishing an onsite Community Police Station that is open twenty-four hours per day, seven days per week. Officers also perform foot patrols and wear yellow vests to increase visibility during patrols. This practice is designed to promote face-to-face interactions between the police and refugees, as well as solicit community input regarding crime and safety problems. The PSF hopes that these proactive patrols will identify problems and help intervention before they escalate.

Terrorism

Terrorism is another significant problem facing police in Jordan. While past decades witnessed terrorism at the hands of nationalist Palestinian guerrilla movements, the current threat largely comes from radical Islamist terror organizations. Since 2015, Jordan has witnessed several terror attacks that tend to target police and security personnel. For instance, in 2015, a former police officer shot and killed five people, among them were two Americans, at a police training facility in Amman. In another incident, approximately twenty people were killed in an explosion near the northeastern border. A few months later a gunman fired shots at personnel in a GID office. Several terrorists fired upon police in Karak, resulting in at least ten deaths and twenty-nine injuries. Jordan has also experienced a growth in homegrown terrorism. For example, it is estimated that between 2,000 and 4,000 Jordanians have fled the nation to join the Islamic State of Iraq and the Levant (ISIL, also known as ISIS) since 2013 (Yom and Sammour 2017). As of 2013, police have arrested sixty-eight Jordanians with ties to the Syrian conflict. Consequently, Jordan is among the nations that contribute the most recruits to foreign terrorism.

As mentioned above, the primary agencies responsible for policing terrorism are the SPF and GID. In response to the threat of terrorism, Jordan has increased border patrols, focused on hotspots near refugee camps and urban areas, and introduced legislation that expands governmental power to combat terrorism. Jordanian police have also reacted to terror attacks by performing crackdowns and mass arrests of suspected terrorists. For example, the police arrested more than 700 people under suspicion of terrorism following the attack in Karak. Jordanian police have been successful in many of their terrorism prevention efforts, having foiled several planned attacks.

Police–Citizen Relations

The PSF is viewed favorably and respected by the general public in Jordan. A contributing factor to positive police–citizen relations is the use of public relations campaigns by the PSF. Another factor is the implementation of community policing efforts, especially in refugee camps. Evaluations of policing initiatives are encouraging. Of the refugees surveyed who were aware of community policing, 74 percent agreed that it made the camp safer and 59 percent reported absolute or moderate trust in the police (British Embassy Amman 2015). This represents an improvement over baseline perceptions of safety in these camps.

Jordan has made strides toward the protection of human rights via changes to both its constitution and criminal procedure law. One example is a ban on the practice of torture and the use of any confession resulting from it. An additional example is the recent legislative change that guarantees the right to appeal for anyone who experiences pretrial detention. Despite this, human rights abuses at the hands of police agents continue to plague Jordanian police, posing a threat to positive police–citizen relations. In 2014, there were seventy-five citizen complaints regarding the use of torture in police stations (Syria Needs Analysis Project 2014). Further, five police officers were arrested for their alleged involvement in the torture and death of a man in custody in 2015. In 2017, other police officers were arrested for their involvement in the in-custody death of an eighteen-year-old detainee. Reports have also surfaced alleging the abuse and mistreatment of youth housed in juvenile detention centers. Other violations include the use of arbitrary arrests and prolonged detentions.

The investigation and sentencing of officers for human rights violations or corruption tend to be opaque and rarely result in convictions. The Special Branch Unit (SBU) within the PSD investigates allegations of abuse by police personnel. Citizens may also file complaints against the police with PSD's Ombudsman Bureau or a police prosecutor. In a move toward democratic policing, the PSD also established a Transparency and Human Rights Bureau to receive, review, and investigate citizen complaints about misconduct exhibited by PSD personnel. This initiative aims to provide greater public information regarding investigations of such allegations and the sentencing of perpetrators. Similarly, in 2009, the government bestowed civilian prosecutors with the ability to assist in the investigation of human rights abuses.

Police officers in Jordan are armed with a variety of weapons, including tactical batons, handguns, rifles, and other automatic firearms. In more populated areas, specialized police officers are equipped with heavier weaponry and riot gear. Security personnel in Jordan, particularly the gendarmerie, have been criticized for heavy-handed measures taken to disperse nonviolent protests and public demonstrations. In 2011, at a pro-democracy rally, violence between demonstrators and counter-protestors erupted and the riot police were called in to disperse the crowd. The riot police used water cannons and other weapons in an attempt to break up the protestors. In the end, at least one hundred demonstrators were hospitalized and one was killed (Kadri and Bronner 2011). In 2012, police officers allegedly beat and injured thirty protestors. Finally, in 2014, gendarmerie officers allegedly used excessive force to disperse a crowd of eighty to one hundred protestors, injuring eleven severely enough to require medical attention.

Further Reading

British Embassy Amman. 2015. "UK-Supported Community Police Project Making Jordan's Za'atari Camp Safer for Syrian Refugees." *Government of the United Kingdom*, August 2, 2015. https://www.gov.uk/government/news/jordanian-police-making-the-camp-a-safer-place-say-zaatari-residents.

Central Intelligence Agency. 2018. "The World Factbook." https://www.cia.gov/library/publications/resources/the-world-factbook/.

Kadri, Ranya and Ethan Bronner. 2011. "Riot Police in Jordan Clear Camp of Protestors." *New York Times*, March 25, 2011. http://www.nytimes.com/2011/03/26/world/middleeast/26jordan.html.

Kurian, George Thomas. 2006. "Jordan." In *World Encyclopedia of Police Forces and Correctional Systems*. 2nd ed. Vol. 1, edited by George Thomas Kurian, 536–39. Farmington Hills, MI: Thompson Gale.

Syria Needs Analysis Project. 2014. "Jordan: Baseline Information." Assessment Capacities Project. https://www.acaps.org/sites/acaps/files/products/files/16_jordan_baseline_information.pdf.

Yom, Sean and Katrina Sammour. 2017. "Counterterrorism and Youth Radicalization in Jordan: Social and Political Dimensions." *Combating Terrorism Center Sentinel* 10 (4): 25–30. https://ctc.usma.edu/counterterrorism-and-youth-radicalization-in-jordan-social-and-political-dimensions/.

SLOVENIA

The Republic of Slovenia is a parliamentary democracy and representative republic located in Central Europe, east of Italy, south of Austria, and north of Croatia. The population of just over two million people comprises mostly Slovenes (83.1 percent) with minorities from Serbia, Croatia, and Bosnia-Herzegovina. It has a strong economy with a gross domestic product per capita of USD 34,500, comparable to its neighbor Italy (USD 38,200) (Central Intelligence Agency 2018). Slovenia is a relatively young democracy, having achieved independence from the Socialist Federal Republic of Yugoslavia in 1991. It is now a member of the North Atlantic Treaty Organization (NATO), European Union, and Eurozone. As part of its transition from a communist government to a democracy, Slovenia significantly reorganized its police to reflect democratic policing principles.

Structure and Practices

Policing in Slovenia is highly centralized, with the hierarchically structured Slovenian National Police (SNP) responsible for fulfilling the bulk of police tasks. The Police Act of 1998 granted the SNP autonomy and outlined its police powers. The SNP is a national agency that operates under the Ministry of the Interior, which is responsible for all national security and public safety issues. As such, the SNP performs police duties at the national, regional, and local levels. The General Police Directorate trains, coordinates, and supervises the entire police force. It is headed by the Director General of Police. Next, there are eight police directorates across eleven regions who oversee and coordinate policing activities at the local level. These local tasks are carried out by police stations that are headed by commanders. The SNP is headquartered in Ljubljana, the nation's capital and the largest city, and utilizes ninety-eight police stations across eleven police directorates. There are also a few other public police agencies in Slovenia, such as municipal warden services, the judicial police, and the financial administration. However, these agencies have limited jurisdictions and the SNP is the primary general policing force in the country.

According to the Police Act of 1998, the police in Slovenia perform the following tasks: protecting the life and property of citizens; investigating violations of the law and arresting perpetrators of criminal offenses and other wanted persons; maintaining public order, controlling and regulating traffic; protecting national borders, fulfilling tasks defined by regulations on foreigners; protecting specified persons and buildings; and carrying out other tasks defined by laws or secondary acts. The investigation of serious offenses is carried out at the national and regional levels, while less serious crimes and issues related to order maintenance and community security are addressed by local level police officers. More than 90 percent of all police tasks are carried out locally (Kolenc 2003).

The SNP employed 8,054 personnel members in 2015 (Slovenian National Police 2015). Of these, 65.8 percent were uniformed officers, and 37.7 percent had more than a high school education. This is equivalent to approximately 338.9 police officers per 100,000 citizens in Slovenia. Illustrating the major role played by the SNP in Slovenia's security sector, it is a larger organization than the Slovenian Armed Forces, which employed 7,074 personnel members in 2011 (Meško et al. 2013).

In line with the principles of democratic policing, the SNP is highly concerned with transparency, professionalism, and community policing. One effort to increase professionalism was creating the post of the Director General of Police. Prior to this, the Minister of the Interior was the top position within the police force, which politicized the entire policing institution. Now, the position is a professional one carrying a five-year term, and the entire force is perceived as an autonomous professional organization isolated from political influence.

Community Policing

Despite embracing community policing principles, there are some challenges with its implementation. These mainly involve the inflexible, legalistic mentality assumed by most police officers that clashes with community policing's call for flexibility in finding tailor-made solutions to community problems. The bulk of SNP officers seem resistant to the role of social service provider. For instance, the SNP appoints specific officers to perform preventive community policing tasks rather than diffusing the principles of community policing throughout the entire organization. As noted above, police stations are responsible for policing at the local level. These units are further divided into police districts, which aim to carry out community policing activities focused on crime prevention and the provision of social services. Additionally, community policing officers are increasingly required to perform other tasks that hinder their ability to create lasting community relations or fulfill community policing duties. Finally, though community policing efforts resulted in the creation of local safety councils, the community rarely provides input regarding suggesting and implementing solutions to community problems of safety and disorder.

The degree of centralization that characterizes policing in Slovenia is also a hindrance to community policing. It impedes local municipal governments from meaningfully influencing community safety, crime prevention, and law enforcement. While the SNP saw such centralization and hierarchical structuring as a means to effect police reform in the new republic, such characteristics of a police agency oppose the principles of community policing.

One method by which local governments can influence policing in Slovenia is through the creation of municipal warden services. The Local Self-Government Act allows municipal mayors to create formal autonomous security organizations within their local jurisdiction. Municipal wardens typically engage in tasks related to traffic control and safety, order maintenance, protection of property, and peace-keeping. They also meet with community members, institutional leaders, and the SNP in local safety councils. In 2011, there were seven city warden services, fourteen municipal warden services, and 148 municipal wardens (Meško et al. 2013). Additionally, 169 municipalities engaged in intermunicipal warden services. Though this legislation is intended to involve the local community in police issues, as noted above, the community and municipal wardens tend to defer to the SNP for safety and crime-related matters.

Another issue facing the SNP is the dramatic rise of private policing in Slovenia. This includes the entire industry of licensed personnel who perform private security services, such as in-house security, protection, transportation, and alarm monitoring. The Private Security Act grants these officers powers exceeding those granted to ordinary citizens. For example, they are permitted to use physical force and other coercive measures to detain persons found to have violated the law. Not only are there nearly as many private police personnel in Slovenia as there are public police, the number of private police is also increasing quickly. In 2010, there were approximately 0.84 private security officers for every one police officer (Meško et al. 2013). In 2011 6,500 private security officers operated out of 117 private security agencies in Slovenia. Additionally, there were eighty-four private detectives operating out of five registered firms. Overall, because private security is a rapidly growing sector in Slovenia, cooperation and coordination between public police and private security is an issue that challenges the operation of the SNP.

Police–Citizen Relations

Public opinion toward the police has varied significantly since the republic gained independence. Between 1991 and 2000, public trust spiked and declined several times. In 1993, only 20 percent of the public indicated trust in the police (Meško et al. 2013). This increased threefold to nearly 60 percent in 1994, but then fell for several years to about 33 percent. Since 2000, public trust in the police has remained relatively stable, hovering above 50 percent. The police are viewed more favorably than other social institutions, such as the media and the government. During similar time periods, public trust in either of these institutions was below 10 percent.

The Police Act authorizes SNP officers to use firearms under certain circumstances, but such use is extraordinarily low in Slovenia. For example, in 2000, police officers only used firearms in nine instances, with only one fatality (Pagon 2006). This number is similar to the average number of occasions in the past decade. There are a couple of possible reasons for this relatively low number. First, Slovenia boasts strict gun control laws, which result in relatively few citizens owning firearms. Another reason is that crimes involving firearms are relatively low in Slovenia. For instance, firearms were used in less than 14 percent of all robbery cases in 2000 (Pagon 2006). Thus, police have fewer opportunities to engage in violent, gun-related incidents with the public. This results in a relatively low number of civilian and police deaths due to gun violence.

Instances of violations of human rights at the hands of the SNP have declined significantly in the past several decades. For instance, on average, greater than 80 percent of police searches of premises were conducted without a warrant in the 1980s under the "exigent circumstances" rule (Meško et al. 2013). By 2001, the number of warrantless searches dropped to 1 percent. Supporting this trend is the finding that there were no arbitrary or extrajudicial killings of citizens committed by police or other governmental agents in 2015. The primary reason is Slovenia's new constitution written after its independence in 1991, which emphasized protecting human rights. It created the Constitutional Court and the Ombudsman to provide oversight of police practices and shifted police away from practices that violated civil liberties. Later legislation further influenced criminal investigations by excluding illegally obtained evidence from trial and limiting police powers to perform identity checks or stops and frisks. Finally, civilian oversight was introduced in 1998 to provide the community with a voice in resolving complaints against inappropriate conduct.

Further Reading

Central Intelligence Agency. 2018. "The World Factbook." https://www.cia.gov/library /publications/resources/the-world-factbook/.

Kolenc, Tadeja. 2003. *The Slovene Police*. Translated by Miha Granda. Ljubljana, Slovenia: Ministry of the Interior of the Republic of Slovenia, Police, General Police Directorate. https://www.policija.si/images/stories/Publications/book_slovene-police.pdf.

Meško, Gorazd, Branko Lobnikar, Maja Jere, and Andrej Sotlar. 2013. "Recent Developments of Policing in Slovenia." In *Handbook on Policing in Central and Eastern Europe*, edited by Gorazd Meško, Charles B. Fields, Branko Lobnikar, and Andrej Sotlar, 263–86. New York: Springer-Verlag.

Pagon, Milan. 2006. "Slovenia." In *World Police Encyclopedia*. Vol. 2, edited by Dilip K Das, 751–55. New York: Routledge.

Slovenian National Police. 2010. *Annual Report on the Work of the Police (2009)*. Ljubljana, Slovenia: Ministry of the Interior of the Republic of Slovenia, Police, General Police Directorate. https://www.policija.si/eng/about-the-police/tasks-and-goals/758 -statistics/95678-statistics.

Slovenian National Police. 2015. "About the Police." *Ministry of the Interior*. https://www .policija.si/eng/about-the-police.

TURKEY

Turkey is a country of eighty-one million people that straddles the European and Asian continents, with southern Europe to its north, Middle East to its south, and Central Asia to its East. Approximately 70 percent of the population is Turkish and 19 percent is Kurdish. Almost the entire population is Muslim (Central Intelligence Agency 2018). The Republic of Turkey became a sovereign nation in 1923 and is a presidential republic. There have been many periods of military rule and autocratic tendencies, which is reflected in the country's policing structure and practices. Its interesting geographic location also makes it susceptible to terrorism and organized crime, which are persistent policing challenges.

Structure and Practices

Policing is highly centralized in Turkey. Standard policing duties, such as crime prevention, investigation, patrol, and order maintenance, are fulfilled by the central government primarily through two police forces: the Turkish National Police (TNP) in urban areas and the Gendarmerie in rural villages. The TNP is the nation's civilian police force and is answerable to the Ministry of Interior and the General Directorate of Security. The Gendarmerie is a military force that primarily polices rural villages and areas, falling under the purview of the Turkish Armed Forces (TAF). This force is subordinate to the Ministry of Interior for policing functions and the Ministry of Defense for military functions. Both forces operate under the same organizational structure that is divided into principal, support, and advisory units. In this hierarchical structure, power resides at the top with the General Director of Police and uniformed line officers occupying the bottom tier. In 2009, the TNP consisted of nearly 193,000 employees. Of these, 175,000 were sworn police officers and 18,000 were civilians. At the same time, the Gendarmerie employed approximately 300,000 personnel. This equates to a total law enforcement ratio of one police officer per 146 citizens (Goldsmith 2009).

Despite being so centralized, Turkey lacks a national public order or public order training policies. Instead, these are established at the local level. Turkey is divided into eighty-one provinces, which are further divided into districts. The police in each province answer to the governor, who is appointed by the central government. Provincial police forces each have their own headquarters, training programs, and communications systems. It should be noted that Gendarmerie police are trained through the TAF, not provincial training academies. The head officer of each provincial force is the Director of Security or Police Chief, who is an employee of the central government. All police personnel in these forces are appointed by the central government.

Though the country is formally a democracy, the policing style of Turkey is more reflective of an authoritarian regime. Rather than policing by consent, which is indicative of democratic policing, the police exercise coercive control. Turkish police engage primarily in a traditional, reactive style of policing, prioritizing armed law enforcement and order maintenance over service provision. Police officers are not involved in the daily lives of their community as they spend their time responding to emergency calls and effecting arrests. This model leaves no room for community input or participation in crime prevention or community safety activities.

One problem facing the police in Turkey is the unclear relationship between the military and police institutions. Though the Gendarmerie was designed to police only rural areas, they can now be found operating and performing armed patrols in more urban towns. They technically do not possess the legal authority to do so. This occurred, in part, because of urbanization, which has transformed many rural villages, formerly under the jurisdiction of the Gendarmerie, into urban areas. It may also be due to the growing threat of terrorism and extremist violence. The specter of terrorism has permitted the Gendarmerie to operate with broader powers in the name of national security. This jurisdictional confusion may waste resources, as both forces respond to the same incident or it may produce a situation in which neither force responds to an emergency because each assumes the other should have jurisdiction. There is generally a lack of cooperation between the two forces. The Gendarmerie often engages in police action without the consent of the TNP or other civilian oversight mechanisms.

Threat of Terrorism

Terrorism has historically been a major concern for the Turkish police as a threat to national security. Bordering countries including Syria, Iraq, and Pakistan exacerbate the problem as they support both foreign and domestic terrorism organizations. Turkish police fight left-wing, right-wing, and separatist terror groups whose motivations are ideologically, politically, religiously, and ethnically motivated. This threat is especially problematic in the southeastern region of the nation. With approximately 5,000 to 10,000 members, the largest ethnically motivated terror organization within Turkey is the Kurdish nationalist organization Partiya Karkaren Kurdistan (PKK). Violence perpetrated by the PKK has resulted in the deaths of over 40,000 people since 1984 (Gumrukcu 2016). The Gendarmerie reports that forty-six security personnel were killed in clashes with the PKK and another 209 were injured.

The government has responded to this threat, particularly that of Kurdish insurgency, with legislation that gives police expanded powers to combat terrorism. For example, in 2015, Parliament passed security laws that allow police to use firearms when confronting public demonstrations, criminalize covering one's face during protests, and prohibit the carrying of dangerous items such as fireworks, marbles, or slingshots. The laws also provide the police with enhanced wiretap abilities, increased search and seizure powers, and the authority to detain suspects for twenty-four-to-forty-eight hours without prosecutorial or judicial approval. Critics argue that these controversial laws sacrifice civil rights, for example, the freedom of speech, and may be used to marginalize certain ethnic and religious groups. Another response to terrorism was the creation of the Special Operations Department, or *Polis Özel Harekât Dairesi*, and other similar police units. With the principal mission of fighting terrorism, this branch receives specialized training and utilizes advanced, military weaponry.

The summer of 2016 saw a violent attempted military coup that resulted in more than 250 fatalities (Bendix 2017). The central government blamed the Gulen movement as the responsible party. Named after a U.S.-based Islamic cleric, the Gulen movement was officially labeled a terrorist organization. Immediately after the failed coup, the prime minister fired more than 100,000 government employees, including military and law enforcement officers, for allegedly having ties to Gulen and the coup attempt (Nordland and Timur 2016). By November 2016, an additional 15,000 employees were dismissed, including 404 Gendarmerie and 7,500 TNP police officers. These dismissals continued into 2017 with 2,303 more police officers. By July 2017, one year after the attempted coup, approximately 150,000 government employees had been fired for their alleged ties to Gulen and terrorism (Bendix 2017).

Police–Citizen Relations

Due to the style of policing in Turkey, the police and public do not interact much except during emergency or crowd control situations, which are typically adversarial in nature. Despite the coercive nature of policing in Turkey and its history of military coups, the public has historically exhibited supportive attitudes toward the police and the central government in general. In fact, the military and the police are consistently the two most highly respected institutions in the country. In 2010, 68 percent of the country viewed police favorably (Terrill 2016). Though this number fell to 55 percent in 2014, the police and military remain the two most favorably viewed institutions. Additionally, citizens tend to be supportive of Turkey's militaristic efforts to combat terrorist activities, particularly those of Kurdish separatists.

Turkey has a history of public demonstrations resulting in clashes between citizens and police. In addition to regular political protests, the increasing migration of poor, rural citizens to secular, urban cities presents frequent opportunities for violent encounters. All Turkish police are issued a firearm, a practice that began in the 1980s. They are also granted collective discretion in maintaining order during public events. This means that the team policing an event has the power to decide what level of force should be employed. In circumstances where the law is unclear about how to respond to a situation, the lead officer makes the decision. Critics are quick to point out that this often results in extensive level of force being used during the course of normal policing duties and while controlling crowds (Goldsmith 2009). They also argue that excessive force is disproportionately used against minority groups, such as Kurdish immigrants, whose population is estimated to be between ten and twenty million (Terrill 2016). A recent example of such force occurred in 2013 in Istanbul when police used tear gas and water cannons to disperse a peaceful protest in Gezi Park. Police were criticized for stifling the right to peaceful protest and for using excessive force. This event sparked a wave of protests, with hundreds of thousands of people in several major cities opposing such force by what is perceived as an increasingly authoritarian government.

Scholars point out that Turkey's security forces have a history of other human rights violations, with some referring to it as the worst record of any free nation (Terrill 2016). This is largely due to the authoritarian style of policing, the wide powers granted to police, institutional corruption, and the lack of accountability and transparency. Police have been accused of unlawful arrests, torture, prolonged detentions, and extrajudicial killings. Critics argue that police rely too heavily on "third-degree" tactics, such as torture, and fail to properly analyze and follow the evidence. The installation of CCTV cameras in police stations in 2012 has decreased the frequency of such tactics, though instances allegedly still occur offsite. Between 2001 and 2003, 40,000 police officers were disciplined for corruption-related actions and 1,000 were dismissed from service (Terrill 2016).

Further Reading

Bendix, Aria. 2017. "Turkey Dismisses Thousands of Police, Civil Servants, and Academics." *The Atlantic*, July 14, 2017. https://www.theatlantic.com/news/archive/2017/07/turkey-dismisses-thousands-of-police-civil-servants-and-academics/533754.

Central Intelligence Agency. 2018. "The World Factbook." https://www.cia.gov/library/publications/resources/the-world-factbook/.

Goldsmith, Andrew. 2009. "Turkey: Progress towards Democratic Policing?" In *Policing Developing Democracies*, edited by Mercedes S. Hinton and Tim Newburn, 31–49. New York: Routledge.

Gumrukcu, Tuvan. 2016. "Turkey Village Guard Killed in Militant Clash, Aerial Operation Underway." *Reuters*, September 21, 2016. https://uk.reuters.com/article/uk-turkey-security-kurds-idUKKCN11R20K.

Nordland, Rod, and Safak Timur. 2016. "15,000 More Public Workers Are Fired in Turkey Crackdown." *New York Times*, November 22, 2016. https://www.nytimes.com/2016/11/22/world/europe/turkey-erdogan-coup-fired.html?mcubz=1.

Terrill, Richard J. 2016. "Islamic Law." In *World Criminal Justice Systems: A Comparative Study*. 9th ed., 568–690. New York: Routledge.

Chapter 9: Gun Control

Janet P. Stamatel

OVERVIEW

According to the United Nations Office on Drugs and Crime (UNODC), firearms were used in 54 percent of all known homicides around the world in 2017. In 2016, the global firearm homicide rate was 2.54 per 100,000 people, but it ranged from 66.6 per 100,000 in El Salvador to 0.02 in Romania. The highest proportions of homicides committed with guns are concentrated in Latin America, with Puerto Rico at 92 percent, El Salvador at 83 percent, and Jamaica at 81 percent; whereas the lowest proportions are found in Europe, Asia, and Africa, with Romania and Tanzania at 1 percent, the Czech Republic and Mongolia at 2 percent, and Morocco at 3 percent (UNODC 2019). Guns are often used in homicides involving gangs or robberies, although they are also fairly common in intimate partner homicides and family violence.

It is very difficult to track the number of firearms globally because many are obtained and transferred illegally and because many countries do not keep detailed records of registered firearms. In 1999, the Small Arms Survey research center was established in Geneva, Switzerland to systematically collect and analyze information about small arms and light weapons around the world and remains the primary source of information on this subject internationally. The term small arms and light weapons (SALW) is used to cover both military-grade and commercial firearms. Small arms typically refer to weapons used by individuals, such as revolvers, self-loading pistols, rifles, assault rifles, sub-machine guns, and light machine guns. Small arms and firearms are often used interchangeably, although some experts use small arms to distinguish military weapons from domestic firearms. Light weapons usually refer to larger, military-type weapons often used by a small crew of people, such as heavy machine guns, grenade launchers, and antitank and antiaircraft guns and missile systems.

In 2017, the Small Arms Survey estimated that there were approximately 1 billion firearms across 230 countries and territories around the world, 84.6 percent of which were in civilian possession. The United States is estimated to have the highest number of civilian guns at 393,300,000 with India in second place with an estimated 71,100,000 civilian guns. There are also approximately 22.7 million firearms owned by police around the world, with Russia having the largest police holdings at 2,430,000 guns, followed by China with 1,970,000 guns. Finally, there are about 133 million weapons owned by militaries around the world, with Russia possessing about 30,300,000, followed by China with 27,500,000 (Karp 2018).

Although Americans tend to frame gun control as a domestic problem, there are international laws regulating SALW. In 2000, the United Nations (UN) passed the Convention against Transnational Organized Crime that was accompanied by three protocols dealing with trafficking in persons (see chapter 5), the smuggling of migrants, and the illicit manufacturing and trafficking of firearms. The last protocol is referred to as the Firearms Protocol that was ratified in 2001 and went into effect in 2005. The Protocol has several provisions regarding the criminalization of arms offenses, the confiscation and disposal of illegal weapons, the establishment of marks and standardized tracing systems, and the export, import and transportation of arms across countries. It is a legally binding agreement for all parties that have ratified it. Additionally, the UN adopted the Programme of Action (PoA) to Prevent, Combat, and Eradicate the Illicit Trade in Small Arms and Light Weapons in All Its Aspects in 2001. This is a document that establishes normative standards for controlling SALW, with a particular emphasis on the human and socioeconomic consequences of unregulated weapons.

The countries included in this chapter illustrate a variety of challenges both with implementing international protocols and with national gun control and violence reduction strategies. The three developed countries (Australia, Canada, and Sweden) have very different discourses about gun control than the developing countries (Albania, Honduras, Pakistan, Papua New Guinea, and Somalia). Australia and Canada introduced major firearms control reforms in the aftermath of mass shootings, which is similar to how the problem is framed in the United States. Sweden has a unique approach to firearm ownership because of how they organize national security, and firearm violence in Sweden is more strongly related to suicide and domestic violence than mass shootings. In the developing countries, weak states mean that governments are either unable to pass strong firearms controls or unable to enforce them. These countries also have significant problems with organized crime (Albania and Somalia), youth gangs (Honduras and Papua New Guinea), terrorism (Pakistan), and ethnic violence (Papua New Guinea), which fuel illegal arms trafficking and the use of firearms in the commission of violence.

Further Reading

Karp, Aaron. 2018. *Estimating Global Civilian-Held Firearms Numbers*. Briefing Paper. Geneva, Switzerland: Small Arms Survey.

Parker, Sarah, and Marcus Wilson. 2016. *A Guide to the UN Small Arms Process: 2016 Update*. Handbook. Geneva, Switzerland: Small Arms Survey.

UNODC (United Nations Office on Drugs and Crime). 2019. "Global Study on Homicide." https://www.unodc.org/unodc/en/data-and-analysis/global-study-on-homicide.html.

ALBANIA

Albania is a small country of three million people located in Southeast Europe, northwest of Greece and south of Montenegro and Kosovo, and across the Adriatic

Sea from Italy. About 83 percent of the population is ethnic Albanian and 57 percent are Muslim. Albania became a communist country after World War II (1939–1945). It had limited political and economic ties to other communist countries and adopted an isolationist stance to international relations until the 1990s when it began transitioning to a democratic, capitalist country with the collapse of the communist system in Eastern Europe. Contemporary Albania is a parliamentary republic, but its stability is challenged by rampant corruption.

Decades of isolation from the global community hindered the country's ability to modernize and build a robust economy, so Albania is still one of the poorest countries in Europe. Its GDP per capita is USD 12,500, which is comparable to Venezuela and Cuba, but less than half of neighboring Greece (USD 27,800) (Central Intelligence Agency 2018). A weak government, struggling economy, and geographic proximity to military conflicts have created conditions ripe for illegal weapons possession and trafficking.

Economic Collapse and Weapons Theft

As of 2017, Albania had an estimated 350,000 privately owned firearms, which means that 12 percent of the population was armed compared to 21,750 firearms among the military and 19,000 with the police. Only 2.17 percent of private guns in Albania were registered (Alpers and Picard 2019). The proliferation of illegal guns in Albania became a widespread problem in the late 1990s when the economy crumbled.

Between 1989 and 1991, the communist political and economic system collapsed in Eastern Europe due to economic stagnation and popular protests against government oppression. The countries of Central Europe (Czechoslovakia, Poland, and Hungary) were the first to shed communism, but other countries in the region soon followed, including the Soviet Union in 1991. The political tide also caught up with Albania in 1991 when student and labor protests resulted in the first multiparty elections in the country. Unlike other Central Eastern European countries that had political ties with Western nations and strong informal economies supported by emigrant remittances, decades of isolation did not prepare Albanians for a transition to democracy or to free markets. Rebranded communists initially remained in power and subsequent democratic elections were marred by election fraud. Moreover, corruption was widespread.

At the same time, Albania lacked resources, infrastructure, energy supplies, and a skilled labor force to rebuild the economy. Between 1992 and 1997, the country was supported by foreign aid from the United States and Western Europe, remittances from thousands of Albanians who left the country after 1991 in search of better economic opportunities, and illegal trade in oil, arms, and drugs. There was no foreign investment, very little production, high unemployment, and a weak banking system.

As cash started to flow into the country from family members living abroad or illegal sources, Albanians did not trust banks to deposit their money and looked for investment opportunities to grow their savings. Savvy entrepreneurs convinced average citizens, who had no experience with capitalism, to invest their money with promises of 4–6 percent interest rates. As early investors started to see their accounts grow, word spread quickly about this easy way to make money. More and more people gave their life savings to these investment firms, even selling their homes and land to generate more cash to invest.

Unfortunately, the investment firms were pyramid schemes. Interest was paid from deposits from new investors and money from illegal smuggling. As long as new money continued to flow from these sources, investors would get the interest that they were promised. By 1997, there were seventeen known pyramid schemes operating in the country. One of the largest was VEFA Holding, which had 6,500 employees across seventeen foreign branches and USD 6 billion in assets, with much of the wealth suspected to have come from illegal arms sales (Abrahams 2015). It was estimated that one-third of the Albanian population invested USD 1.2 billion into these schemes by 1997 (Abrahams 2015).

Income from illegal activities slowed with the end of the Bosnian War in 1995, so the schemes needed to keep attracting new investors to stay afloat. They were unable to do so and they collapsed by 1997, which meant that the investors lost all of their money. Citizens were outraged not only about the loss of their life savings but also at the government for colluding with these investment companies and the media for not warning the public about the potential risks of such investments.

Protests sprouted around the country and quickly turned violent. Citizens over-ran military depots and looted weapons and ammunition. The depots were typically guarded by young, poor, underpaid soldiers who provided little resistance against the angry mobs. It was estimated that 549,775 weapons, 160,000,000 explosives, and more than one billion rounds of ammunition were stolen from approximately 1,300 military stockpiles (Grillot 2010; Ruvina 2019). Additionally, 1,542 people were killed because of the violence, which was greater than the number of homicide victims between 1991 and 1996 combined (Ruvina 2019).

To make matters worse, the Kosovo War from 1998 to 1999 became another source of weapons for Albania. Kosovo was a part of Yugoslavia until the end of communism that divided the country into six independent nations. The region of Kosovo also sought independence, but Serbia objected. Kosovo is located on the northwest border of Albania, and the population of nearly two million people is 93 percent ethnic Albanian and 95 percent Muslim (Central Intelligence Agency 2018). The conflict between Serbia and Kosovo escalated to a war, which brought more weapons to the region. Intervention by the North Atlantic Treaty Organization (NATO) brought an end to the war. Kosovo is now a partially recognized state with the UN supporting its independence, but Serbia still objects to this move. This ambiguous status means that Kosovo cannot join international arms treaties and the country has no weapons control laws. In 2006, it was estimated that there were 400,000 small arms in Kosovo and only 34,000 were legally owned (Grillot 2010). Weak border controls and law enforcement in both Kosovo and Albania make weapons transfers between the two countries relatively easy.

Gun Control

Gun violence remained high for several years after 1997, but has since declined. In 1998, the gun homicide rate in Albania was 17.62 per 100,000 people, which declined to 3.56 by 2000 and 1.70 by 2013; however, the percentage of homicides committed with a gun did not decrease dramatically. In 2001, about 79 percent of all homicides were committed with a firearm, which decreased to 61 percent by 2011 (Alpers and Picard 2019).

The 1997 pyramid scheme led to the resignation of President Sali Berisha (1944–). The new government under President Rexhep Meidani (1944–) sought to quickly regain control of the country and reduce the level of violence. The government worked to reclaim the stolen weapons through amnesty programs. In 1998, the first gun amnesty law was passed to encourage voluntary surrender and registration of guns, and police were tasked with going door-to-door asking civilians to turn over their weapons. A second amnesty was passed in 2003. Between 1997 and 2005, the government successfully collected 222,918 weapons, about 41 percent of what had been looted in 1997, along with 1,539,828 explosives (Ruvina 2019).

Subsequent governments have passed tighter gun control laws to reduce the numbers of illegal weapons. In 2007, Albania passed a new Law on Weapons that specified rules for importing, exporting, licensing, and brokering weapons. In 2009, the State Export Control Authority was given oversight over licensing companies exporting military equipment and the power to monitor arms trades. In 2016, the Illicit Weapons Possession Act strengthened penalties for illegal gun ownership. Illicit possession of a weapon in motor vehicles and public spaces was punishable by three-to-seven years in prison. Outlawed possession of a gun at home was punishable by one-to-three years in prison. Unauthorized gun production, purchases, sales, or trades were punishable with five-to-ten years in prison. Altering or removing identifiers on weapons was punishable by one-to-five years in prison. The 2016 law was also accompanied by an amnesty period and public relations and education campaigns, such as #AlbaniaWithoutWeapons and "Don't Shoot but Love."

Further Reading

Abrahams, Fred. 2015. *Modern Albania: From Dictatorship to Democracy in Europe*. New York: New York University Press.

Alpers, Philip, and Mike Picard. 2019. "Albania—Gun Facts, Figures and the Law." Sydney School of Public Health, The University of Sydney. GunPolicy.org, 2 October. https://www.gunpolicy.org/firearms/region/albania.

Arsovska, Jana. 2015. *Decoding Albanian Organized Crime: Culture, Politics, and Globalization*. Berkeley, CA: University of California Press.

Central Intelligence Agency. 2018. "The World Factbook." https://www.cia.gov/library/publications/resources/the-world-factbook/.

Grillot, Suzette R. 2010. "Guns in the Balkans: Controlling Small Arms and Light Weapons in Seven Western Balkan Countries." *Southeast European and Black Sea Studies* 10 (2): 147–71. https://doi.org/10.1080/14683857.2010.486945.

Ruvina, Leida. 2019. "Arms up, Guns Down. Analyzing the Clash between the Narratives of State and Media Actors on Light Weapons Control in Albania (2017)." *European Journal of Interdisciplinary Studies* 5 (2): 74–91.

AUSTRALIA

Australia is an island country in Oceania, south of Indonesia and Papua New Guinea and northwest of New Zealand. The population of 23.5 million is ethnically diverse, with English (25.9 percent) and Australian (25.4 percent) being the largest ethnic groups. Australia was colonized by the British in the early 1800s and became a Commonwealth in 1901. It is currently an independent, parliamentary democracy that recognizes the Queen of England as the head of state. Australia has an advanced market economy that benefits from the country's natural resources. Its GDP per capita is USD 50,400, which is comparable to Taiwan and Germany (Central Intelligence Agency 2018). Australia's political history as a former British colony, along with its present status as a highly developed democratic, capitalist country, makes it a nice comparison for the United States. This is especially true because of gun control differences between the two countries. Australia's swift, decisive response to mass shootings is often contrasted with American indecision and political disputes.

Port Arthur Turning Point

Australia has historically had lower homicide rates than the United States. In 1990, the homicide rate in Australia was 2.2 per 100,000 compared to 9.3 in the United States. This pattern has persisted even with declining homicide rates in the United States since the 1990s. The low point for homicide in the United States was 4.5 per 100,000 in 2014, which was still four times higher than Australia (1.0 per 100,000) (UNODC 2018). In 1995, the proportion of homicides committed with a gun was 25 percent compared to 6 percent in the United States (Alpers, Rossetti, and Picard 2019).

On April 28, 1996, Martin Bryant, a twenty-eight-year-old from Hobart, Tasmania drove sixty miles to Port Arthur to commit mass murder. Port Arthur was a penal colony in the 1830s. It is now a World Heritage site and a popular tourist destination. Bryant was armed with two semiautomatic rifles when he entered the Port Arthur Historic Site. He began shooting people in a café, then continued his shooting spree in the gift shop and parking lot. As he drove away, Bryant continued to shoot people on the roadways and at tollbooths. By the time he was arrested, he had killed thirty-five people and wounded eighteen others. The number of deaths was roughly half of the homicides across the country in a year (Chapman 2013).

Prior to this incident, there had been ten other fatal shootings with five or more fatalities between 1987 and 1996. The incident with the largest number of fatalities in 1987 occurred when eight people were killed and five were injured in Melbourne during a shooting at a post office. In the same year, another shooting spree in a suburb of Melbourne killed seven and wounded nineteen (McPhedran and Baker 2011). As horrible as these events were, they did not match the scale of the atrocity at Port Arthur. The number of victims and the sheer cruelty of Bryant became a tipping point for Australian tolerance for gun violence.

The day after this tragedy, the Australian Prime Minister John Howard (1939–) announced that he would introduce comprehensive gun control legislation. Twelve days later, the federal government, six state governments, and two territorial governments came to an agreement about reforming firearm laws. The National Firearms Agreement addressed gun sales, licensing, registration, and storage.

The federal government had already banned semiautomatic weapons in 1991, and states and territories administer most other gun laws. The 1996 law banned additional weapons that were originally designed for military combat and not necessary for sport shooting or hunting. In particular, the law banned self-loading, center-fire rifles, self-loading pump-action shotguns, and self-loading rim-fire rifles. Some exceptions to the ban were allowed for sports and farming. To remove these banned weapons and other illegal firearms, the government offered a twelve-month buyback amnesty program. They paid market prices for guns voluntarily surrendered by citizens during the amnesty period. The program was funded by a one-time income tax levy. Additionally, there were no penalties for illegal weapons that were turned in during the buyback program, but stiff penalties applied after the amnesty ended. In 1997, Australians surrendered 640,401 guns and the average payout was USD 475 (Chapman 2013).

Additionally, the law required the registration of all firearms and owners had to be licensed. Licenses are divided into six categories depending on the types of guns and their uses. The easiest license to obtain is the Category A for .22s, shotguns, and air rifles, none of which can be semiautomatic. Category B is for center-fire rifles, excluding semiautomatics, and require a valid reason for needing one, such as certain kinds of hunting. Category C licenses are restricted to farmers who can own a semiautomatic shotgun limited to five shots or a .22 limited to ten shots. Category D licenses are for semiautomatic guns and rifles and can only be obtained by professional shooters with a registered business. Category H handgun licenses are only available to members of target pistol clubs who compete at least eight times a year. Finally, Category G licenses are for gun collectors who attend at least one professional meeting a year.

The minimum age to obtain a firearm license is eighteen years, and new applicants are required to take a gun safety course. Applicants have to provide a reason for owning a gun, and personal protection is not considered a valid reason. People who have been convicted of a violent crime or have been subjected to a domestic violence restraining order in the last five years are not eligible to obtain a license. Licensed gun owners are also required to obtain a separate permit for each new gun purchase, which is subject to a twenty-eight-day waiting period. Firearm sales are only allowed by licensed dealers who are required to keep sales records. Mail and Internet gun sales are prohibited.

The goal of the National Firearms Agreement was not eliminating guns, but reducing the volume and restricting types of weapons in civilian hands. The public support for sweeping reforms was directly shaped by the appalling Port Arthur massacre and a desire to ensure that the victims "did not die in vain." Politicians also made direct comparisons between Australia and the United States and urged citizens not to let their country "go down the American path" (Chapman 2013). Between 1988 and 2005, the proportion of households in Australia with at least one gun decreased from 25 percent to 6.2 percent (Alpers, Rossetti, and Picard 2019).

Between 1997 and 2001, over 6.5 million weapons were surrendered. Evaluations of the effectiveness of the law on gun violence have produced mixed findings, depending on the period included in the study and how gun violence is defined. The evidence regarding mass shootings, however, is compelling. There were thirteen fatal shootings with five or more victims in Australia between 1979 and 1996 and none between 1997 and 2016. The average rate of firearm deaths between 1979 and 1996 was 3.6 per 100,000, which declined to 1.2 per 100,000 on average between 1997 and 2013 (Chapman, Alpers, and Jones 2016). The average firearm suicide rate for 1979 to 1996 was 3.0 per 100,000 compared to 0.99 on average from 1997 to 2013. However, a study comparing mass shootings, defined as four or more victims, from 1980 to 2009 between Australia and New Zealand did not find a difference between the two countries, despite different firearms laws (McPhedran and Baker 2011).

Handgun Legislation

Another shooting tragedy spurred the next major gun control law in Australia. In 2002, an international student from Hong Kong went on a shooting spree at Monash University in a suburb of Melbourne, where he killed two students and injured five others. The offender, Huan Yun Xiang, was armed with six loaded handguns. This incident prompted the passage of two new gun control laws. The National Handgun Control Agreement of 2002 aimed to reduce the availability and use of high-powered handguns that were easy to conceal, as well as to increase the penalties for the illegal possession of handguns. The same year the National Firearms Trafficking Policy Agreement was also passed, which standardized the regulation of firearms manufacturing across the country and increased penalties for illegal possession of all firearms. A national handgun buyback program was administered in 2003, which resulted in the surrender of 68,727 guns (Chapman, Alpers, and Jones 2016).

In 2018, Australia experienced another mass shooting with a murder-suicide in a small tourist town where a man shot and killed six family members, including four children, before killing himself. Two other shooting incidents in 2019 have renewed debates about gun control in Australia.

Further Reading

Alpers, Philip, Amélie Rossetti, and Mike Picard. 2019. "Australia—Gun Facts, Figures and the Law." Sydney School of Public Health, The University of Sydney. GunPolicy .org, 1 July. https://www.gunpolicy.org/firearms/region/australia.

Central Intelligence Agency. 2018. "The World Factbook." https://www.cia.gov/library/publications/resources/the-world-factbook/.

Chapman, Simon. 2013. *Over Our Dead Bodies: Port Arthur and Australia's Fight for Gun Control.* Sydney, Australia: Sydney University Press.

Chapman, Simon, Philip Alpers, and Michael Jones. 2016. "Association between Gun Law Reforms and Intentional Firearm Deaths in Australia, 1979–2013." *JAMA* 316 (3): 291–99. https://doi.org/10.1001/jama.2016.8752.

McPhedran, Samara, and Jeanine Baker. 2011. *Mass Shootings in Australia and New Zealand: A Descriptive Study of Incidence.* SSRN Scholarly Paper ID 2122854. Rochester, NY: Social Science Research Network. https://papers.ssrn.com/abstract=2122854.

UNODC (United Nations Office on Drugs and Crime). 2018 "Crime Data." https://dataunodc.un.org/crime.

CANADA

Canada is the third largest country in the world in terms of landmass, but shares a border with only one country, the United States. It has a population of nearly thirty-six million people that is ethnically and religiously diverse. Eighty-one percent of the population lives in urban areas, and much of the northern and western parts of the country are sparsely populated. The Canadian government is a federal parliamentary system with ten provinces and three territories. It is part of the Commonwealth of Nations with fifty-three other former British colonies and recognizes Queen Elizabeth II (1926–) as the Canadian monarch. Because of the geographic dispersion of the population across such a large landmass, the role of firearms in Canadian society is controversial and shaped by the physical environment of its residents. This means that it can be challenging to get all of the provinces and territories to agree on gun control policies at the federal level.

Number and Types of Guns

In 2017, there were an estimated 12,708,000 legal and illegal guns in Canada, which corresponds to 34.7 out of 100 people owning a private firearm. In contrast, the Canadian military has approximately 234,000 guns and the police have 103,000. The rate of civilian gun ownership in Canada is much lower than the United States (120.5 per 100 people), but higher than Mexico (12.9 per 100 people) (Alpers and Rossetti 2019). The most common firearm in Canada is a rifle, followed by shotguns and handguns. In 2016, just over two million Canadians had a gun license, or 5.9 for every 100 people.

Canada has a low homicide rate compared to the United States and Mexico. In 2017, the total homicide rate was 1.85 per 100,000 people, and the rate of gun homicides was 0.75 per 100,000 people. The rate of all gun deaths, which includes homicide, suicide, and accidents, was 2 per 100,000 in 2013. Of the 266 gun homicides in Canada in 2017, 54.5 percent were committed with a handgun and 32 percent with a long gun (Alpers and Rossetti 2019).

Gun Legislation

Gun control policies in Canada have a long history. Even during the colonial period, there were restrictions on gun possession, mainly to prevent access to Aboriginal Peoples. During the early years of modern Canada's history, gun laws were usually aimed at preventing certain ethnic, racial, or political groups from obtaining arms.

In the 1970s, as violent crime was increasing sharply in the United States, Canadians engaged in debates about how to avoid a similar situation, which led to discussions about gun control. In 1977, Bill C-51 was passed, which established mandatory background checks for anyone wanting to purchase a gun and required new buyers to obtain a Firearms Acquisition Certificate. The law also increased penalties for crimes committed with firearms and granted police extended search and seizure powers regarding firearm cases. Generally speaking, farmers, hunters, and target shooters opposed gun control legislation, whereas people living in the large, urban areas of the country were more likely to support it. The debates in the 1970s and 1980s were very polarizing, and none of the major political parties wanted to pursue the issue any further.

The gun control debate was renewed in the wake of a mass shooting in 1989. Marc Lépine, a twenty-five-year-old who had been denied admission to the École Polytechnique, blamed women for taking engineering education and employment opportunities from men like himself. On December 6, 1989, Lépine entered a classroom at the college with a rifle and ordered all the men out of the room. He then shot the remaining women in that class and in other locations at the school before committing suicide. Lépine killed fourteen women that day and injured ten others. During his rampage, he blamed feminists for ruining his life (Bindel 2012).

As a result of this incident, women's groups became outspoken advocates for gun control, bringing attention to the numerous female victims of gun violence beyond the Montreal massacre. An École Polytechnique student named Heidi Rathgen and a Ryerson business professor named Wendy Cukier joined forces to create the Coalition for Gun Control to unite various proponents of stricter gun control legislation. Though there was still a considerable amount of resistance to more gun control, the tide turned in 1990 when a police officer was shot and killed over a land dispute between a developer and Aboriginal Peoples.

By 1991, politicians had enough momentum to pass Bill C-17, which added several public safety measures. This law enhanced screening procedures for Firearm Acquisition Certificates by requiring professional references, spousal approval, photo identification, and mandatory safety training. The law also introduced a compulsory twenty-eight-day waiting period for a firearm certificate, prohibited fully automatic weapons, and added restrictions to magazine capacity.

A third gun control law was passed in 1995 that politicians claimed would prevent Canada from adopting the violent gun culture of the United States. Bill C-68 required all gun owners to obtain a license, and not just new purchasers. Two types of licenses replaced the Firearms Acquisition Certificate: one for possession only (POL) and the other for possession and acquisition (PAL). Additionally, a license was required for purchasing ammunition. The new law also strengthened the license screening process, including notification of spouses and common law partners, and required the completion of a Canadian Safety Firearms Test. Once again, penalties were increased for crimes involving firearms.

The most controversial part of Bill C-68 was the required registration of all rifles and shotguns by 2003. Registration of handguns had been regulated since 1934, but long guns had not been subject to such a process. The legislation created the Canadian Firearms Center that would maintain this registry. Gun owners, particularly farmers and hunters in the western provinces, raised concerns that the government might eventually use the registry to take weapons away from citizens. As Aboriginal People also objected to the new law because it violated their treaty rights, a separate set of regulations was implemented for them. Finally, provincial governments objected to the cost of maintaining a registry. Attempts to repeal the registry in the early 2000s failed, but in 2012, the Canadian government passed Bill C-19 that eliminated the long gun registry and only required registration for restricted firearms.

In 2015, Canada passed a Common Sense Firearms Licensing Act (Bill C-42) to loosen some of the licensing provisions and eliminate the possession-only license. However, a shooting in 2018 turned the tide again toward more gun restrictions. A man opened fire in a residential neighborhood in Toronto, killing two people and wounding thirteen others. This incident ignited a debate about gun control, this time focusing specifically on handguns. The majority of Canadians supported a total ban on handguns in urban areas to reduce this kind of violence. Opponents of this idea argued that more legislation would not stop the flow of illegal guns into the country, especially from the United States. In contrast, proponents of a handgun ban showed that half of all crimes using a handgun that could be traced were legally obtained guns that owners sold to others illegally (Samuel 2018). A handgun ban has not been passed yet in Canada. In 2019, legislators passed Bill C-71, which required background checks of an applicant's life history, not just the most recent five years, and requiring businesses to keep sales records of guns for twenty years.

Effectiveness of Gun Control

The research to date evaluating the effectiveness of Canada's various gun control efforts has produced mixed results depending on the periods and outcomes included in the studies. One study measuring the effectiveness of Bill C-17 passed in 1991 showed that the percentage of suicides committed with a firearm between 1984 and 1990 was 31.2 percent, and the percentage between 1991 and 1998, after the law was passed, was 24.5 percent. Additionally, suicide by other means only increased slightly between the two periods. In contrast, the same study only found a slight difference in the percentage of homicides committed with a firearm seven years before (33.7 percent) and seven years after (32.9 percent) the passage of the law (Bridges 2004). Another study examined the long-term trends of firearm homicides between 1974 and 2008 and did not find any effects of gun control Bills

C-51, C-17, or C-68 on the frequency of gun homicides, which could be related to the fact that these laws probably did not affect the availability of illegally owned guns (Langmann 2011).

Further Reading

Alpers, Philip, and Amélie Rossetti. 2019. "Canada—Gun Facts, Figures and the Law." Sydney School of Public Health, The University of Sydney. GunPolicy.org, 2 October. https://www.gunpolicy.org/firearms/region/canada.

Bindel, Julie. 2012. "The Montreal Massacre: Canada's Feminists Remember." *The Guardian*, December 3, 2012, sec. World News. https://www.theguardian.com/world/2012/dec/03/montreal-massacre-canadas-feminists-remember.

Bridges, F. Stephen. 2004. "Gun Control Law (BILL C-17), Suicide, and Homicide in Canada." *Psychological Reports* 94 (3): 819–26. https://doi.org/10.2466/pr0.94.3.819-826.

Central Intelligence Agency. 2018. "The World Factbook." https://www.cia.gov/library/publications/resources/the-world-factbook/.

Langmann, Caillin. 2012. "Canadian Firearms Legislation and Effects on Homicide 1974 to 2008." *Journal of Interpersonal Violence* 27 (12): 2303–21. https://doi.org/10.1177/0886260511433515.

McPhedran, Samara, Jeanine Baker, and Pooja Singh. 2011. "Firearm Homicide in Australia, Canada, and New Zealand: What Can We Learn From Long-Term International Comparisons?" *Journal of Interpersonal Violence* 26 (2): 348–59. https://doi.org/10.1177/0886260510362893.

Samuel, Sigal. 2018. "Canada Is Raging against Gun Violence—But Not Like America." *The Atlantic*, July 28, 2018. https://www.theatlantic.com/international/archive/2018/07/canada-gun-control-debate/566102/.

HONDURAS

Honduras is a part of the Northern Triangle in Central America, east of Guatemala and north of El Salvador. The population of just over nine million people consists of 90 percent mestizo and 7 percent Amerindian, and the official language is Spanish. Honduras was home to the Mayans until the Spanish conquered them in the sixteenth century. It remained a Spanish colony until gaining independence in 1821. The nineteenth and twentieth centuries were characterized by political instability and economic struggles. However, Honduras was able to avoid the violent political conflicts that erupted in El Salvador, Guatemala, and Nicaragua in the 1970s and 1980s. Today Honduras is a presidential republic that has been relatively stable since the last coup in 2009. The Honduran economy relies heavily on agricultural and clothing exports, primarily to the United States, and remittances from emigrants living abroad. Its GDP per capita is USD 5,600, which is comparable to Nicaragua, but lower than El Salvador and Guatemala (USD 8,000) (Central Intelligence Agency 2018). The country suffers from high unemployment and income inequality. Firearm violence is very common due to the availability of weapons from decades of conflicts in surrounding areas, its geographic location as a transshipment point for drug trafficking between South and North America, and a large, poor, young population.

Weapons and Sources

In 2017, it was estimated that there were 1,171,000 privately owned firearms in Honduras, corresponding to a rate of 14.10 guns for every hundred people. This number is about ten times the number of firearms in the Honduran military (107,720) and about forty times those owned by the police (29,000). About 41 percent of these guns (475,000) were registered (Alpers, Rossetti, and Salinas 2019).

Illegal weapons in Honduras come from both domestic and international sources. Within Honduras, illegal guns are lost or stolen from citizens or national stockpiles. The State Armory under the direction of the Defense Ministry is responsible for regulating weapons imports and selling domestic firearms, but it has been criticized for poor record keeping and a lack of transparency (Nowak 2016). Additionally, guns are smuggled into Honduras from a number of countries, including Brazil, Guatemala, Russia, and the United States. Porous borders with Guatemala and El Salvador facilitate arms trafficking and those countries also have large numbers of illegal weapons.

Smuggling across borders tends to take place in small quantities where they are often disassembled and the parts are hidden among traffickers' personal belongings to avoid detection. In 2012, the majority of firearms seized by the Honduran National Police were pistols and revolvers, with a much smaller number of rifles. Illegal firearms in Honduras are relatively cheap. In 2013, 9 mm pistols sold for USD 45 to 350 on the black market compared to USD 900 to 2,000 through legal channels. AK-47s could be purchased illegally for as little as USD 200 (Nowak 2016).

Gun Violence

The countries in the Northern Triangle have some of the highest homicide rates in the world due to long histories of political conflict, persistent poverty, weak governments, drug trafficking, and a large supply of illegal weapons. Homicide rates in Honduras are often the highest of the three countries, although this varies somewhat by year. According to the UNODC, the homicide rate in Honduras in 1990 was ten deaths per 100,000 people, which was comparable to the United States at that time. After than year, homicide rates began to decline steadily in the United States, but rose sharply in Honduras. By 2000, the homicide rate in Honduras was 48.7 per 100,000. It peaked at 85 per 100,000 in 2011 and then began to decline to 41.7 by 2017. The overwhelming majority of homicide victims are young males. At the peak of the violence in 2011, the homicide rate for fifteen- to nineteen-year-old males was 246.6 per 100,000, which declined to 167.4 by 2016. In 2011, the homicide rate for males aged thirty to forty-four was 301.8, which decreased to 173.4 by 2016 (UNODC 2018).

Firearms account for much of the violence in Honduras. In 2006, the firearm homicide rate was 32.3 per 10,000, which rose to 72 by 2011 and then declined to 43.5 by 2016 (UNODC 2018). Between 2005 and 2015, the proportion of all homicides committed with a firearm ranged between 74 and 85 percent (Alpers, Rossetti, and Salinas 2019). One study conducted in 2001 found that of the 1,609 youths and young adults killed by violence in Honduras that year, 82 percent involved a firearm. Of those deaths, 36 percent were committed with AK-47s, 27 percent with homemade weapons, and 25 percent with 9 mm pistols (Yacoub, Arellano, and Padgett-Moncada 2006).

There are many social factors that cause high rates of violence, such as rapid urbanization, enduring poverty and inequality, and political instability. These factors have all been present in Honduras. In the 1980s and 1990s, the government created Export Processing Zones where international corporations were incentivized to manufacture goods for export. Many American companies, especially clothing firms like Maidenform and Oshkosh B'Gosh, built assembly plants and shipping facilities in these areas, which were typically located near large cities or ports. As a result, urban migration increased rapidly in Honduras as poor, rural residents moved to the cities for work.

These Export Processing Zones created new jobs for Hondurans but did not alleviate the persistent poverty in the country. Additionally, export-based economies like that of Honduras are sensitive to global market fluctuations. The global recession in the late 2000s hurt the Honduran economy. Between 2007 and 2016, the percentage of people living in poverty increased from 58.3 percent to 66.2 percent and the percentage of unemployed youth increased from 4.9 percent to 8.2 percent (Berg and Carranza 2015).

Violence in Honduras and the rest of the Northern Triangle is also related to the international drug trade. When the United States increased antinarcotics law enforcement efforts in Mexico and the Caribbean, drug trafficking cartels rerouted shipments through Central America. Honduras has become a key transshipment point for cocaine trafficking and a major produce of amphetamine-type substances (ATS), such as methamphetamine, amphetamine, and ecstasy. As a result of the drug business, higher homicide rates are concentrated along drug transit routes along the Honduran coast to Guatemala.

Gangs and Guns

Urbanization, poverty, and drug trafficking are causes of violence in many countries, yet violence is still more frequent in Honduras than most other countries. The extreme rates of homicide and other forms of violence in Honduras can be attributed largely to gangs and firearms. Youth gangs first developed in Honduras in the 1980s when rapid urbanization brought large numbers of poor young people to urban areas, weakening their social ties to families and communities. These loosely formed groups were typically involved in minor crimes, such as vandalism and assault. During the 1990s, several factors changed the nature of gangs and the level of violence. First, the United States began mass deportations of convicted offenders who were not citizens, particularly to Central American countries. The Northern Triangle received more than 90 percent of gang deportations (Rodgers,

Muggah, and Stevenson 2009). In 1993, the United States deported 1,676 Hondurans with a criminal history, which rose to 3,820 in 1997 (Rivera 2013). Deportees were often gang members from Los Angeles, who did not necessarily speak Spanish fluently, had few social connections in Honduras, and had limited economic opportunities. Not surprisingly, they formed gangs, had extensive knowledge of drugs and firearms from their experiences in the United States, and had social connections to American gangs.

Second, there is a large, poor, uneducated youth population in Honduras, which gangs have used to recruit new members. These youths seek out gangs for protection and group belonging. The larger gangs often have violent initiation rituals for new members, socializing the youth toward violence.

The two largest gangs, or *maras*, in Honduras are the 18th Street Gang (M-18) and Mara Salvatrucha (MS-13). Territory disputes between them are often violent. Most members of these two groups are armed, in part because they often provide security for drug traffickers in the country. The gangs are also known to participate in *sicariato* or contract killings. Gangs own AK-47s and are armed with explosives, such as fragmentation grenades.

Firearms are pervasive and visible in Honduran society. They cause widespread fear among the public and reduce the willingness of communities to engage with gangs or with youth more broadly. Citizens feel powerless against gangs and have little faith in the government's ability to protect them. Private security guards have become popular, especially in cities.

When Ricardo Maduro (1946–) took over the presidency from 2002 to 2006, he introduced several security policies to lower the levels of violence in the country. In 2003, the government passed a zero-tolerance law that raised the maximum prison sentence for gang membership to twelve years. It was later raised again to thirty years. The government also launched Operation Thunder to better control firearms and to reform the justice system. The government mandated a buyback program for high-caliber firearms, paying USD 52 for each weapon (Berg and Carranza 2015). Many citizens did not participate in the buyback because they were not convinced that the government could ensure their safety. In 2004, El Salvador, Guatemala, and Honduras entered into a cooperative agreement to prosecute gang members residing in neighboring countries.

These policies put a lot of gang members in prison, but they did not reduce violence. Instead, gangs became better organized and more violent. Between 2003 and 2004, gangs killed over eleven people, decapitated the victims, and left notes to President Madura demanding that he ease the law enforcement efforts against them. In 2003, gang members also attacked a bus, killing fourteen people and wounding eighteen others, again leaving a threatening note to Maduro.

After 2006, another round of violence prevention strategies was implemented. This time they focused on compliance rather than punishment and aimed to incentivize young people to avoid or leave gangs. For example, the government received a violence prevention grant from the World Bank to decrease the number of firearms in civilian hands and to try to change attitudes toward violence and weapons among young people. Another program called "A Smile without Violence" aimed to support businesses run by former gang members. Although homicide rates decreased between 2011 and 2017, they are still very high and most are still unsolved.

Further Reading

Alpers, Philip, Amélie Rossetti, and Daniel Salinas. 2019. "Honduras—Gun Facts, Figures and the Law." Sydney School of Public Health, The University of Sydney. GunPolicy .org, 17 July. https://www.gunpolicy.org/firearms/region/honduras.

Berg, Louis-Alexandre, and Marlon Carranza. 2015. *Crime, Violence, and Community-Based Prevention in Honduras*. Research Report 97642. The Justice, Security, and Development Series. Washington, DC: International Bank for Reconstruction and Development/The World Bank.

Central Intelligence Agency. 2018. "The World Factbook." https://www.cia.gov/library /publications/resources/the-world-factbook/.

Nowak, Matthias. 2016. *Measuring Illicit Arms Flows: Honduras*. Research Note. Geneva, Switzerland: Small Arms Survey.

Rivera, Lirio Gutiérrez. 2013. *Territories of Violence: State, Marginal Youth, and Public Security in Honduras*. New York: Palgrave Macmillan.

Rodgers, Dennis, Robert Muggah, and Chris Stevenson. 2009. *Gangs of Central America: Causes, Costs, and Interventions*. Occasional Paper 23. Geneva, Switzerland: Small Arms Survey.

UNODC (United Nations Office on Drugs and Crime). 2018. "Crime Data." https:// dataunodc.un.org/crime.

Yacoub, Sophie, Sergio Arellano, and Dennis Padgett-Moncada. 2006. "Violence Related Injuries, Deaths and Disabilities in the Capital of Honduras." *Injury* 37 (5): 428–34. https://doi.org/10.1016/j.injury.2005.12.001.

PAKISTAN

Pakistan is a country of nearly 208 million people in South Asia. It borders the Arabian Sea to the south, China to the north, India to the east, and Iran and Afghanistan to the west. The two largest ethnic groups are Punjabi (44.7 percent) and Pashtun (15.4 percent), and 96.4 percent of the population is Muslim. Pakistan was part of colonial British India in the eighteenth and nineteenth centuries and became a separate state when Britain withdrew from the area in 1947. British India was initially partitioned into two states, Pakistan and India, with Pakistan having an eastern and western region. In 1971, eastern Pakistan became the independent nation of Bangladesh. The Partition of India led to a dispute over the region of Kashmir to the northwest of Pakistan that resulted in four military conflicts between Pakistan and India, and it remains a persistent source of tension between the two countries. Pakistan is also an economically underdeveloped country. It has a GDP per capita of USD 5,400, lower than the neighboring India (USD 7,200), and 30 percent of the population in Pakistan lives below the poverty line (Central Intelligence Agency 2018). Pakistan's conflicts with India, its geographic proximity to two countries with strong legacies of violence and drug trafficking (Afghanistan and Iran), and entrenched poverty have created conditions ripe for arms production and trafficking.

Weapons and Sources

According to the UN Small Arms Survey, the estimated number of civilian firearms in Pakistan was almost forty-four million in 2017, which is more than double the number in 2007 of eighteen million. This means that the number of guns per hundred people rose from 11.6 in 2007 to 22.3 in 2017. Pakistan has the fourth largest civilian firearm holdings, behind the United States, India, and China. Only six million of the nearly forty-four million firearms in Pakistan are registered (Karp 2018).

These weapons come from both international and domestic sources. The influx of SALW into Pakistan became a problem during the Soviet-Afghan War (1979–1989) when the Soviet Union sent troops to support the ruling communist party in Afghanistan and instead installed a puppet government. Islamist Afghan guerrilla groups, known as *mujahedeen*, fought the Soviet invasion in a brutal, decade-long war. Fighters from other Muslim countries, including Pakistan, assisted the *mujahedeen* militarily and the governments of Pakistan, Saudi Arabia, and the United States provided financial support against the communist invasion. Stockpiles of Soviet weapons were captured by the *mujahedeen* during the war. Not only did the war filter weapons into Pakistan, but it created a "Kalashnikov culture." The Russian automatic rifle used during the war was called an *Avtomat Kalashnikova*, automatic Kalashnikov, named after inventor Mikhail Kalashnikov (1919–2013) and popularly known as AK-47s. Possessing a Kalashnikov became a symbol of power and status in the tribal areas of Pakistan, increasing the demand for firearms.

After the U.S. invasion of Afghanistan in 2001, weapons from the United States and NATO forces were stolen or redirected to black markets in Pakistan. The Khyber Pass in northwest Pakistan is a mountainous road linking Afghanistan and Pakistan that has been central for trade since the Silk Road connected the East and the West in the second century BCE. It is also a key passage for the transnational movement of illicit goods, which include drugs and weapons. Illegal arms trafficked from other parts of the world, notably Vietnam and the Middle East, are frequently found in black markets in the Khyber Pakhtunkhwa province.

There are also domestic producers of firearms in Pakistan. Some of them are state-owned enterprises, while others are private manufacturers licensed and regulated by the government.

Illegal guns in Pakistan are trafficked illegally from other countries and are produced domestically. Illegal gun ownership surged during the Afghan War, which contributed to a growing gun culture that equated weapons with power and status. (Corel)

However, the most famous gun producers are located in the town of Darra Adam Khel in northern Pakistan. This cottage industry of hand-produced weapons has been operating since the nineteenth century. The local people claim that a gunsmith from the British Army deserted during the Murree Rebellion of 1857 and taught the local tribesmen how to make firearms.

Although local weapon production was originally intended to provide arms for community defense, it soon grew into a profitable trade business, especially given Darra's access to major roadways to Peshawar, Islamabad, and Kabul. There are an estimated 2,500 gunsmiths in the area who make hundreds of weapons a day (Ahmad 2012). Most craftsmen today come from other parts of the country, but the arms dealers and shopkeepers are locals from Darra who have been in the arms business for generations.

Gunsmiths make counterfeit weapons and ammunition to match any commercially available weapon, including self-loading service rifles. Although domestic weapons have been sold to Taliban insurgents and private militia, locals claim that such organized groups prefer commercial weapons because Darra steel is not weapon grade, so the combat weapons are of substandard quality. Nonetheless, business is still strong because the cost of Darra weapons is significantly lower than foreign originals. For example, an M16 rifle costs about USD 214, or one-fourth of the commercial price. An AK-47 costs about USD 72 and a pistol is only USD 21 (Hashim 2019).

Until recently, Darra's gun industry was not regulated by the state. Darra was located in a Federally Administered Tribal Area that was not subject to Pakistani criminal and constitutional laws. In May 2018, the tribal area was merged with the Khyber Pakhtunkhwa province, which now brings it under federal control. It is not clear yet how this change will affect Darra Adam Khel's arms production.

Gun-Related Violence

The easy access to firearms in Pakistan is related to levels of both interpersonal and political violence. Pakistan does not provide official statistics on the percentage of homicides due to firearms, but a local study of gun violence sheds some light on the problem. In a study of gun deaths in Peshawar, just north of Darra Adam Khel, forensic specialists noted that 91 percent of the cases involved high-velocity weapons. Men were six times more likely than women to be a victim of gun violence, and one-third of the victims were young men between the ages of twenty and twenty-nine years (Marri and Bashir 2010).

The widespread availability of weapons also makes it more challenging for governments to resolve conflicts, such as in Kashmir. The area of Kashmir borders northeastern Pakistan, northern India, and western China and has been disputed territory since the Partition of India in 1947. India gained control over most of the region, despite the fact that the majority of the population is Muslim. India and Pakistan fought two wars over the territory in 1947 and 1965, and nearly 50,000 people have died in related violence since 1989 (Guy et al. 2019).

Malala Yousafzai

Malala Yousafzai was the daughter of a school administrator who grew up in the Swat Valley of Pakistan at a time when the Pakistani Taliban was fighting for control over the area and aimed to eliminate education for girls. At age eleven Malala began blogging about her experiences as a female student. She wrote under a pseudonym but was eventually identified. As a result, when she was fifteen years old, a Taliban gunman shot her in the head while riding a bus home from school. She survived the shooting and became an international spokesperson for girls' education. She was awarded the Nobel Peace Prize in 2014 along with Kailash Satyarthi for advocating for children's rights.

Pakistan also has a large amount of terrorist activity. Its proximity to Afghanistan has allowed the Taliban to take refuge in northern Pakistan, especially in tribal areas that were not under government control until very recently. Al-Qaeda also has a strong presence in Pakistan, as well as a number of other known terrorist groups. In 2018, there were 691 deaths due to terrorism in Pakistan, which was a significant decrease from 5,496 in 2014. About half of the fatalities in 2018 were civilians (SATP 2019).

Gun Control

The 1965 Pakistan Arms Ordinance requires gun owners to be licensed by the state. However, in 2017, only six million of Pakistan's estimated forty-four million civilian guns were registered (Karp 2018). One study reported that 80 percent of the firearm licenses issued in Punjab between 1988 and 1995 were done so without proper verification of the person applying for the license (Munir 2011). When Pervez Musharraf (1943–) became president in 2001, he implemented a plan to deweaponize the country. He stopped the issuance of new arms licenses and banned the public display of firearms. The government also tried to employ gunsmiths in Darra Adam Khel in state-owned arms facilities to reduce the availability of illegal weapons. Finally, the government created a new computerized weapons registry. Many of the provinces objected to this plan because they thought it would reduce security in their regions.

In 2012, the Pakistani government passed an updated Arms Policy specifying the criteria for obtaining a gun license. The law categorized weapons as Prohibited Bore (revolver or pistol over 0.46 inches bore, rifle 303, all automatic and semiautomatic rifles, rifle G-111, Stengun, and Carbine) and Non-prohibited Bore (shotgun, other revolvers and pistols, other rifles, sword). Only the prime minister of the country can issue licenses for Prohibited Bore weapons, whereas the minister for interior or other authorized government officials can issue Non-prohibited Bore licenses. All licenses require criminal history background checks. Licenses are valid for five years. Minors, people with documented serious mental health problems, and convicted criminal offenders are not allowed firearm licenses.

Further Reading

Ahmad, Riaz. 2012. "The Way of the Gun: The Legendary Gunsmiths of Darra Adam Khel." *The Express Tribune*, November 4, 2012. https://tribune.com.pk/story/458310 /the-legendary-gunsmiths-of-darra-adam-khel/.

Central Intelligence Agency. 2018. "The World Factbook." https://www.cia.gov/library /publications/resources/the-world-factbook/.

Guy, Jack, Katie Hunt, Nikhil Kumar, and Helen Regan. 2019. "Why Kashmir Means So Much to Both India and Pakistan." *CNN*, February 28, 2019. https://www.cnn.com /2016/09/30/asia/kashmir-explainer/index.html.

Hashim, Asad. 2019. "Darra Adam Khel: Pakistan's Dying Gun Bazaar." *Al Jazeera*, February 4, 2019. https://www.aljazeera.com/indepth/features/darra-adam-khel-pakistan -dying-gun-bazaar-190204090518478.html.

Karp, Aaron. 2018. "Estimating Global Civilian-Held Firearms Numbers." Briefing Paper. http://www.smallarmssurvey.org/fileadmin/docs/T-Briefing-Papers/SAS-BP-Civilian -Firearms-Numbers.pdf.

Marri, Murad Zafar, and Muhammad Zahid Bashir. 2010. "An Epidemiology of Homicidal Deaths Due to Rifled Firearms in Peshawar Pakistan." *Journal of the College of Physicians and Surgeons—Pakistan* 20 (2): 87–89.

Munir, Muhammad. 2011. "The Role of Light Weapons in Creating Internal Instability: Case Study of Pakistan." *Journal of Political Studies* 18 (2): 243–60.

SATP (South Asia Terrorism Portal). 2019. "Pakistan: Assessment-2019." https://www.satp .org/terrorism-assessment/pakistan.

PAPUA NEW GUINEA

Papua New Guinea is a country in Oceania, north of Australia and west of the Solomon Islands. It occupies the eastern half of the island of New Guinea, as well as smaller populated islands to the east. The western half of New Guinea, called West Papua, belongs to Indonesia. About 85 percent of the population lives on the mainland and 40 percent of those people live in the Highlands, which is a mountainous region that spans the width of the country and is covered in tropical rainforests. Only one-fifth of the population of seven million people lives in urban areas (Alpers 2005).

The population of Papua New Guinea is ethnically, religiously, and linguistically diverse. There are hundreds of ethnic groups speaking 839 languages. The largest ethnic groups are Melanesian, Papuan, Nerito, Micronesian, and Polynesian. English is one of the three official languages, although it is only spoken by about 2 percent of the population (Central Intelligence Agency 2018).

Papua New Guinea was colonized by Germany and the United Kingdom in the 1800s and was transferred to Australia in 1902. The country gained independence in 1975, although it is still part of the Commonwealth of Nations. It is formally a parliamentary democracy, but the national government has struggled to centralize authority over the entire country. The unstable government and difficult terrain have hampered economic development. The country is rich in natural resources, but the lack of infrastructure and challenging physical environment have limited the government's ability to build a strong economy around mineral or gas exports. The GDP per capita is USD 3,700, which is much less than neighboring Indonesia (USD 12,400). The majority of the population lives on subsistence farming (Central Intelligence Agency 2018).

Although Papua New Guinea is not heavily involved in the illicit arms trade, the country has experienced significant gun violence. The root causes of firearm violence are weak government, clan fighting, political violence, and gangs. The poor functioning central government means that obtaining accurate data on gun availability and firearm violence is difficult, although experts agree that violence in Papua New Guinea has been on the rise and that firearms are a major contributor to the problem.

Firearms Availability

Firearms slowly became available in Papua New Guinea in the 1980s as the police and military began importing weapons from the United States, South Korea, Singapore, and Great Britain. During the same period, homemade firearms were used in tribal conflicts in the Highlands. The situation changed in the 1990s as politicians became a source of manufactured firearms. Politicians supplied military-style rifles to constituents in exchange for votes and to provide security during and after elections when violence was common.

As of 2017, 79,000 estimated firearms were owned by civilians compared to 7,200 military firearms and 4,800 police guns. This means that 1 percent of the population owned a gun. This number is low compared to other countries. For example, the rate of civilian gun ownership in Australia was 13.7 percent in 2016. However, the government in Papua New Guinea has been criticized for poor record-keeping and the large number of known incidents of gun violence reported through the media and informally suggests that the numbers of guns are underestimated. Only 34 percent of known civilian firearms are registered (Alpers and Wilson 2019).

A 2004 study of guns in the Southern Highlands of Papua New Guinea provides important insights about the types, sources, and uses of illegal firearms in a part of the country that has experienced considerable violence. The most coveted commercial weapon in the region is the military-issue M16 assault rifle, followed by the AR15 assault rifle. The Australian-made self-loading rifle (SLR) is the most expensive high-powered rifle on the black market. The most commonly owned weapon in the Southern Highlands is the 12-gauge shotgun. Handguns are relatively rare and are perceived as "toys of the elite" (Alpers 2005). There has been evidence of hand grenades and grenade launchers used in tribal conflicts. Homemade versions of single-shot shotguns, smoothbore pistols, and long guns also exist, but their quality does not compare to commercially manufactured guns.

Unlike many other countries that obtain weapons through international arms trafficking networks, this is not the primary source of illicit firearms in Papua New Guinea. There is some international arms trafficking from Australia and the Solomon Islands, as well as the international sea lanes passing the country. However, most illegal civilian firearms are stolen from within the country. Guns acquired for the military and police are either redirected into civilian hands or they are stolen from raids on armories or thefts from prisons. It was estimated that only 43–45 percent of M16s obtained by the military in the 1980s and 1990s remained in government armories. Additionally, between 20 and 50 percent of AR15s cannot be accounted for in police stocks across the provinces (Alpers 2005).

The average cost of a handmade gun in Papua New Guinea is USD 60, which is significantly cheaper than commercial weapons on the black market. M16s and AR15s average USD 3,000 each and pump-action shotguns cost about USD 2,700 on the black market. The Australian SLR sells for about USD 4,050. The most expensive weapon is the MAG machine gun, which ranges from USD 6,600 to 15,000 on the black market. The less popular handgun costs only USD 950 (Alpers 2005).

Firearm Violence

The most recent public data on homicides in Papua New Guinea shows a rate of 10.42 per 100,000 people in 2010, and the number of firearm-related deaths nationally has not been reported to the UN (Alpers and Wilson 2019). Experts agree that homicides are severely underreported in Papua New Guinea, in part, because citizens have to pay to register deaths with government authorities. Additionally, ethnic fighting is usually not included in official homicide statistics.

Violence is concentrated in the two largest cities in the lowlands and in the Southern Highlands. The two largest urban areas in the lowlands are the National Capital District and Lae. In 2010, the known homicide rates in these areas were thirty-three and sixty-six per 100,000, respectively (Lakhani and Willman 2014). In the National Capital District, about 65 percent of violence occurs in areas known as "settlements," which are low-income neighborhoods on the outskirts of major urban areas that developed to accommodate periods of rapid urbanization in the 1970s.

A victimization survey conducted in the National Capital District and the Southern Highlands in 2004 and 2005 found that domestic violence was the most frequent offense, followed by intergroup fighting and armed assault. In the National Capital District, 18 percent of people reported experiencing domestic violence and 12 percent noted armed assault. Attempted murder and murder were more common in the Southern Highlands, with 9 percent and 5 percent of people reporting these crimes, respectively, compared to 1 percent and 3 percent in the National Capital District. Additionally 23 percent of respondents in the Southern Highlands and 19 percent in the National Capital District reported that their victimization experiences involved firearms (Haley and Muggah 2006).

Survey respondents were also asked if they had ever seen different kinds of weapons. In the National Capital District, 66 percent of households had seen a homemade shotgun and 28 percent had seen a factory shotgun or a handgun. Additionally, 16 percent reported seeing an M16 or AR15. Finally, 8 percent had seen an SLR, .22, or a hand grenade. The percentages were similar for the Southern Highlands, with the exception of fewer people (only 3 percent) having seen a hand grenade (Haley and Muggah 2006).

Causes of Firearm Violence

Given the highly diverse nature of the population of Papua New Guinea, people are organized along clan or tribal lines. The country's independence in 1975 was driven mostly by Australia's withdrawal from the island, as opposed to a united, nationalist sentiment for independent governance. As a result, national leaders never really succeeded at centralizing power, and they are often ignored or challenged by local power structures and tribal leaders. As crime began to increase in the 1960s and 1970s as a result of some urbanization and modernization efforts and then again in the 1990s with the large-scale introduction of firearms, the government responded with reactive policing methods, including mandatory curfews and use of force. These policies were interpreted as remnants of colonial control and caused resentment among citizens.

When the country experienced a period of rapid urbanization between 1966 and 1977, young men left rural areas in search of better economic opportunities in large cities. They often resided in low-income settlements and had few social ties in the cities. This situation gave rise to youth gangs, known as *raskols*. At that time, these gangs were mostly involved in petty crime and served as support groups for marginalized young men. However, by the late 1970s, *raskolism* became more violent due to the growing marijuana trade and the government's inability to control crime and social disorder. As firearms started to infiltrate the country in the 1980s, violence continued to grow. Corrupt politicians became involved in the gun trade, offering weapons for votes or for protection against rivals. Guns are also used to resolve tribal conflicts in the Highlands and disputes regarding mining operations.

From a legal perspective, Papua New Guinea has quite restrictive gun laws. The Firearms Act of 1978 was passed shortly after independence, and the Firearms Amendment Act was passed in 1996 in response to increasing illicit gun supplies. Automatic weapons are fully prohibited and semiautomatic firearms and handguns are prohibited unless they were licensed prior to 1999. Rifles and shotguns are permitted to licensed owners who must establish a genuine reason for gun ownership, which includes self-defense, and who must pass background checks. Licensed owners are also only allowed one firearm. However, in practice, these laws are ignored, mainly because they are seen as being imposed upon the clans by "outsiders," which includes the national government.

Further Reading

Alpers, Philip. 2005. *Gun-Running in Papua New Guinea: From Arrows to Assault Weapons in the Southern Highlands*. Special Report. Geneva, Switzerland: Small Arms Survey.

Alpers, Philip, and Marcus Wilson. 2019. "Papua New Guinea—Gun Facts, Figures and the Law." Sydney School of Public Health, The University of Sydney. GunPolicy.org, June. https://www.gunpolicy.org/firearms/region/papua-new-guinea.

Central Intelligence Agency. 2018. "The World Factbook." https://www.cia.gov/library/publications/resources/the-world-factbook/.

Dinnen, Sinclair. 2001. *Law and Order in a Weak State: Crime and Politics in Papua New Guinea*. Honolulu: University of Hawaii Press.

Haley, Nicole, and Robert Muggah. 2006. *The Scourge of the Gun: Armed Violence in Papua New Guinea*. Geneva, Switzerland: Small Arms Survey.

Lakhani, Sadaf, and Alys M. Willman. 2014. *Trends in Crime and Violence in Papua New Guinea*. 75057. Research and Dialogue Series. Washington, DC: The World Bank.

SOMALIA

Somalia lies on the eastern coast of Africa bordering the Gulf of Aden to the north, the Indian Ocean to the east and south, and Djibouti, Ethiopia, and Kenya to the west. The majority of the 11.3 million people is Somali and Sunni Muslim. A twenty-year civil war destroyed the formal government and economy of the country, and for decades Somalia was known as a "failed state" or a "lawless state." In 2012, a federal government regained control over the country, although it is still considered a "fragile state." Somalia is economically underdeveloped with no steady government revenue, large foreign debt, and no formal banking system. The economy runs informally with livestock as the most valuable commodity. The capital of Mogadishu has shown promising signs of investment and development, which has not yet spread to the rest of the country (Central Intelligence Agency 2018). The devastating civil war and political crisis brought thousands of SALW into the country, most of which are in civilian hands. The proliferation of weapons has allowed organized crime groups to flourish and threatens to undermine the fragile stability in the country.

War and Weapons

Somalia's history of violence precedes the civil war to the colonial period. In the nineteenth century, the lands of Somalia were divided among European colonizers: British Somaliland, Italian Somalia, French Somaliland, Ogaden controlled by Ethiopia, and part of northern Kenya. Many Somalis did not welcome foreign influences and united under Sufi leader Mohammed Abdullah Hassan (1868–1920), known as Sayyid Mohamed. Hassan organized the Dervish movement that fought against foreign powers and Ethiopian sympathizers from 1892 to 1920. Hassan's goal was to unite all Somalis under a single Muslim state. The Dervish movement acquired weapons from Sudan and the Ottoman Empire to continue the resistance over twenty years, but they were defeated once the British military began using air forces.

Following World War II (1939–1945), Somalia lost the Ogaden territory to Ethiopia, as well as the land in northern Kenya, and French Somaliland became the independent country of Djibouti. In 1960, the remaining partitions of British Somaliland in the north and Italian Somaliland in the south united to form the independent Somali Republic. Democracy lasted less than a decade, and by 1969 a military coup installed an authoritarian socialist government. The United States provided military assistance to Somalia in the 1960s, but less than what they gave neighboring Ethiopia and Kenya, so Somalia turned to the Soviet Union instead to build its military.

The Soviet Union increased Somali troops from 4,000 in 1960 to 12,000 in 1970 and 37,000 by 1977. The Soviet military also provided training and weapons, including tanks and fighter aircraft (Mohamoud 2006). Despite this rapid military expansion, Ethiopia's army was still six times larger than Somalia's. In 1977, the two countries fought a war over Ogaden. Realizing how outnumbered they were, Somalia quickly recruited 200,000 young, untrained men to fight in the war. Most soldiers deserted and took their military weapons home. When Somalia lost the war, the Soviet Union abandoned them.

In 1978, the Somali government spent 13.8 percent of its GDP on the military compared to 5.7 percent on education and 2 percent on health (Mohamoud 2006). Large-scale corruption and embezzlement bankrupted the country, leaving the majority of the population impoverished. By 1983, the military received 20 percent of the national budget. The extreme poverty and military defeat meant that the government lost a lot of legitimacy. The Somali government returned to the United States for financial support, but it was much less than what the Soviet Union had provided. In the 1980s, armed insurgent groups organized along clan lines challenged the authority of the central government.

By 1991, resistance groups succeeded in overthrowing the military regime of Siad Barre (1919–1995), but then the various rebel groups turned on one another, leading to a brutal civil war in which approximately 30,000 people died from violence and another 300,000 people died from subsequent starvation and disease (Mohamoud 2006). Military arsenals were looted by rebel groups, and lack of a central government allowed for a free trade of weapons and ammunition.

Lack of Weapons Control

By 1992, the UN launched a military intervention in Somalia, sending 37,000 troops, of which 26,000 were Americans (Mohamoud 2006). The UN operation did not disarm gangs, militias, or warlords, leaving a large quantity of available weapons among the population. The UN mission was unsuccessful and when warlords turned against peacekeepers, the UN withdrew its forces by 1995.

In 1992, the UN Security Council imposed an arms embargo on Somalia to curb the influx of new weapons into the country. Member nations of the UN were expected to adhere to the embargo, but in reality it was frequently violated and not enforced by the UN. Countries including Egypt, Eritrea, Ethiopia, Iran, Libya,

Saudi Arabia, Syria, Uganda, and Yemen had violated the embargo, as well as Hezbollah from Lebanon. The United States was also accused of supplying money and weapons to groups helping their war against terrorism.

Weapons within Somalia were frequently redirected to militant groups. Members of the Somali National Army or Somali Police Force often also belonged to clan-based militia, so they could divert government supplies to rebel groups. Desertion rates for both the army and the police were very high due to lack of pay and deserters often took weapons home with them. The majority of weapons were Kalashnikov-type rifles, other kinds of automatic rifles, pistols, light and heavy machine guns, and other weapons, such as rocket-propelled grenades. Between 2004 and 2011, the UN Somalia and Eritrea Monitoring Group documented 455 cases of arms transfers or seizures resulting in 50,000 weapons (Carlson 2016).

Fighting among warlords continued through 2011, although the level of violence ebbed and flowed with different peace initiatives. By 2012, a new federal government took control over the country, although there are still some violent conflicts with remaining insurgent groups. The hope of stable governance is threatened by the large number of SALW still in the country. The estimated number of civilian firearms in 2017 was 1,145,000 or 12.4 guns per hundred people, which was a significant increase from the estimated 750,000 guns in 2007. Only 14,000 of the civilian firearms are registered. The number of firearms in the hands of the Somali army (37,620) and the police (8,000) pales in comparison (Alpers, Wilson, and Rossetti 2019).

Guns and Piracy

The widespread availability of firearms in Somalia means that criminal organizations also have easy access to weapons. Gangs have used armed violence and the threat of violence to run protection rackets for illegal economic opportunities, such as illegal fishing or burning of trees for charcoal. They also extort bribes from motorists on roadways. Most notoriously, armed organized crime groups engage in the very profitable crime of piracy.

The geographic location of Somalia makes piracy a very attractive activity. Cargo ships in the Indian Ocean are routed through the relatively narrow passage of the Gulf of Aden to the Red Sea through the Suez Canal in Egypt to reach the Mediterranean Sea and European markets. Piracy increased after the collapse of the government in 1991, and even more so in the early twenty-first century as poverty worsened and weapons were easily available.

Typically small boats approach cargo ships, and if the pirates are able to board successfully, they hold the crew for ransom. It is difficult to capture a ship, but the monetary rewards can be very large. Between 2008 and 2012, Somali pirates captured about 3,000 hostages. The estimated ransom in 2011 was five million dollars per vessel (Petrig 2013). Some reports have claimed that young men who board the ships can earn USD 10,000 to 15,000 each for a successful ransom. Local communities participate in and profit from these crimes. Warlords supply arms and

Criminal gangs have acquired illegal weapons to facilitate piracy off of the coast of Somalia. It is a high-risk criminal activity that can bring large monetary rewards. However, recent military interventions by other nations have decreased the success of such attacks. (U.S. Navy photo by Mass Communication Specialist 2nd Class Jason R. Zalasky/Released)

Captain Phillips

In 2009, four Somali pirates hijacked the American-flagged cargo ship *Maersk Alabama* in the Indian Ocean. The pirates were armed with AK-47s while the ship's crew was not armed. The pirates were able to board the ship and take the captain, American Richard Phillips, hostage. The pirates had Captain Phillips in a lifeboat for several days before U.S. Navy Seals were able to rescue him. Three of the pirates were shot and killed and one surrendered, who was eventually sentenced to thirty-three years in prison for his role in the hijacking. The dramatic event was captured in the 2013 movie *Captain Phillips* starring Tom Hanks as the captain.

---

equipment to pirates in exchange for a percentage of the ransom. Communities also guard and feed hostages for a fee. Most hostages are treated reasonably well because the large ransom payments are dependent upon crews being kept alive.

After numerous high-profile hijackings, the international community developed a fairly effective antipiracy strategy in 2009. They identified a transit corridor that would be protected by various navies. Although they could not escort ships through the corridor, there was a sufficient naval presence to offer assistance to ships in distress. The strategy did not affect the number of attempted piracy attacks, but it did reduce their success rate by 50 percent (Petrig 2013).

Another antipiracy strategy is to have armed security on the cargo ships. Some countries such as France, Spain, Italy, and Russia assign law enforcement officials to protect the crew against piracy. Other countries and corporations rely on private maritime security companies. Arming private citizens to protect ships raises numerous legal complications. There are no international standards regarding the transfer of weapons on and off ships or their onboard carriage and storage, which means that domestic laws apply and may not be approved in areas through which ships transit. For example, the Suez Canal Authority requires guards to hand over their weapons as ships pass through the canal before they returned.

Further Reading

Alpers, Philip, Marcus Wilson, and Amélie Rossetti. 2019. "Somalia—Gun Facts, Figures and the Law." Sydney School of Public Health, The University of Sydney. GunPolicy .org, 12 September. https://www.gunpolicy.org/firearms/region/somalia.

Carlson, Khristopher. 2016. *Measuring Illicit Arms Flows: Somalia*. Research Note. Geneva, Switzerland: Small Arms Survey. http://www.smallarmssurvey.org/fileadmin/docs/H -Research_Notes/SAS-Research-Note-61.pdf.

Central Intelligence Agency. 2018. "The World Factbook." https://www.cia.gov/library /publications/resources/the-world-factbook/.

Mohamoud, Abdullah A., and Abdullah M. Mohamoud. 2006. *State Collapse and Post-Conflict Development in Africa: The Case of Somalia (1960–2001)*. West Lafayette, IN: Purdue University Press.

Mwanika, Philip Arthur Njuguna, and Lyn Snodgrass. 2013. "Dynamics and Politics of Small Arms and Light Weapons in Violent Conflicts: Arms Control and Its Challenges in Somalia." *Africa Insight* 43 (1): 61–76.

Petrig, Anna. 2013. "The Use of Force and Firearms by Private Maritime Security Companies against Suspected Pirates." *International & Comparative Law Quarterly* 62 (3): 667–701. https://doi.org/10.1017/S002058931300016X.

SWITZERLAND

Switzerland is a relatively small, land-locked country in Western Europe surrounded by France Germany, Austria, and Italy. The population of 8.3 million people is predominantly Swiss and Christian, although there are four language areas in the country: German, French, Italian, and Romansh. Switzerland is the sixteenth wealthiest country in the world with an economy supported largely by financial services and high-tech manufacturing. Its GDP per capita is USD 62,100, which is higher than all its neighbors (Central Intelligence Agency 2018).

The Swiss government has been remarkably stable. The Swiss Federation was founded with three cantons in 1291 and slowly expanded until the 1700s. It was briefly occupied by France under Napoleon Bonaparte (1769–1821), but it became fully independent in 1815. Switzerland became a federal republic in 1848, with the central government sharing power with twenty-six cantons. The Swiss government has maintained a policy of armed neutrality that has directly and indirectly affected the country's stance toward gun ownership and gun control.

Gun Ownership

Switzerland is often used as an example to support gun ownership in the United States because it is a country with a high rate of gun ownership but a low homicide rate, so gun supporters make the simple inference that guns are not the cause of violent crime. However, gun ownership is both highly regulated in Switzerland and is strongly related to violence. These facts are well established in the criminological literature, but are often left out of gun control debates.

The International Crime Victims Survey conducted in four waves between 1989 and 2005 asked respondents whether anyone in the household owned a handgun, shotgun, rifle, or air rifle. In 1989, Switzerland had the highest prevalence of gun ownership among the twelve countries that participated in the survey that year, with 32.8 percent of respondents claiming to have a gun in the household. That percentage increased to 35.7 percent between 1999 and 2003, but declined by 28.6 percent by 2005. In that last wave of the survey, Switzerland dropped to second place in gun ownership among twenty-five European countries, with Finland at the top with 37.9 percent of the population owning a gun (Duquet and Val Alstein 2015).

The UN Small Arms Survey uses expert assessments of firearm availability to estimate the rate of gun ownership around the world. In 2007, Switzerland had the highest civilian rate in Europe with 45.7 percent, whereas Romania had the lowest with 0.7 percent. The European average was 15.7 percent (Duquet and Van Alstein 2015). By 2017, the gun ownership rate in Switzerland dropped to 27.6 percent, and it was ranked eleventh among European countries. It is important to note that gun ownership in Europe is much lower than in the United States. In 2018, the civilian gun ownership percentage in the United States was 120.5 percent, meaning that there were more guns than people. The United States had the highest civilian gun ownership rate, with war-torn Yemen in second place with 52.8 percent of the population armed (Karp 2018).

Gun Usage and Gun Control

Switzerland does not have a standing army. Instead it relies on a civilian militia that can mobilize quickly and efficiently when necessary. Military service is mandatory for men aged eighteen to thirty-four years and is voluntary for women or older men. All members of the armed forces receive eighteen weeks of basic training and are recalled six times over ten years for nineteen days of training. Many people in the armed services keep their military issued weapons at home during their service, although more recently some cantons have allowed reservists to keep guns and ammunition in local gun depots instead of private homes. Of the 36 percent of

Swiss respondents in the 2005 International Crime Victims Survey who reported having a gun in the household, 63 percent had a gun for military purposes only, 13 percent for sports, 4 percent for self-protection, and 3 percent for hunting (Killias and Markwalder 2012).

Before 2007, members of the armed services were given a sealed box of ammunition to keep at home along with their service weapon. They were subjected to annual inspections to ensure that the seal remained intact. However, in 2007, the government passed a law that reservists could no longer keep ammunition at home. Additionally, ammunition for army guns is not available for sale in stores. The standard automatic army rifle is also long and heavy, so it is not easy to conceal or carry without notice. Only army officers and select specialists are issued handguns.

Reservists who are in good standing at the end of their military service are allowed to purchase their service weapons. However, a 2003 law made this practice more restrictive by increasing the fee for the weapon and requiring the person to obtain a gun permit. In the 1990s, approximately 90 percent of reservists kept their weapons after their service, which dropped to 43 percent in 2004 and 23 percent by 2007 (Killias and Markwalder 2012).

The changes in gun and ammunition laws in 2003 and 2007 assisted the decline in gun ownership in Switzerland in the twenty-first century. Additionally, changes in the structure of the army and domestic defense also contributed to this decrease. In the 1990s, the Swiss army had 625,000 soldiers, but after the end of the Cold War, the country downsized its militia to 220,000 by 2004 and 140,000 by 2016 (Killias and Markwalder 2012). It did this by lowering the upper age limit for mandatory service from fifty in the 1990s to thirty years old. The military also decreased the number of mandatory training days for army members. The government passed a law in 2016 to further reduce the military to 100,000 soldiers, but it also has increased the military budget to improve training and efficiency (Brueck 2019). The country relies on other methods of national defense including the ability to quickly demolish all roads, roadways, bridges, and tunnels in the country.

Aside from military weapons, the Swiss are allowed to own private weapons. Gun control measures are regulated by the cantons, but all require a permit to purchase a gun. Background checks are also extensive and include criminal history, mental health, and substance abuse checks. Another permit is required to carry a weapon outside the home and is typically reserved for people who work in security. Permits for handguns are initially valid for six months, which must be renewed every three months. Permit holders must also pass firearm safety and usage tests. Additionally, ammunition can only be purchased by the permit holder.

Firearm Violence

Homicides in Switzerland are quite rare. In 2017, the homicide rate was 0.5 per 100,000 people compared to 5.4 per 100,000 in the United States (UNODC 2018). The relatively high gun ownership rate and very low homicide rate have led some to argue that guns do not contribute to interpersonal violence. However, this argument ignores two important points. First, homicide rates are low across Western European countries for numerous reasons unrelated to weapons, including strong economies, low economic strain, stable and inclusive governments, and high levels of social support. Second, analyses of homicide and suicide cases in Switzerland demonstrate that firearms contribute significantly to violence.

One study of all homicide cases in Switzerland between 1980 and 2004 showed that 46 percent of all homicide victims had been shot. Of homicides involving a firearm, 38 percent of the weapons were illegal, 33 percent were privately owned, 22 percent were military issue, and 7 percent were handguns. Additionally, 46 percent of all homicides in Switzerland had intimate partners, children, or other family members as victims, which was higher than the Netherlands (29 percent) and Finland (35 percent) (Killias and Markwalder 2012).

Another analysis of homicide and suicide cases showed that 69 percent involved a firearm. Of the firearm cases, 66 percent had female homicide victims. Of those cases, 48 percent had victims who were wives or girlfriends of the offender, and 32 percent had victims who were children of the offender. Family violence is more likely to occur in homes where Swiss firearms are typically located. In contrast, male homicides are more likely to occur in public places where firearms are not readily available (Grabherr et al. 2010).

Violent acts involving firearms are also more likely to be fatal than those involving other weapons. Guns make it easy for offenders to overcome resistance from victims and allow swift actions that reduce opportunities for victims to talk with offenders or to otherwise seek assistance. They also make it easier to harm multiple people at the same time and to kill without much forethought or planning. Hospital data from Switzerland showed that only 16 percent of gunshot victims survived their wounds compared to 51 percent of serious violence cases that did not involve a firearm (Killias and Markwalder 2012).

Finally, Switzerland has a high rate of suicides by firearm compared to other European nations. Between 1998 and 2007, 23.6 percent of suicides in Switzerland were committed with a gun. More specifically, 32.6 percent of male suicides and 3.4 percent of female suicides were due to gunshots (Ajdacic-Gross et al. 2010). The percentage of suicides among men aged twenty to forty-nine years has declined over time, likely in response to the declining availability of guns due to changes in the military. In 1995, 38 percent of men in this age group committed suicide with a gun, which declined to 33 percent in 2004 and 24 percent in 2008. Additionally, suicides by other methods did not increase during this period to compensate for the reduction in firearm availability (Killias and Markwalder 2012).

Further Reading

Ajdacic-Gross, V., M. Killias, U. Hepp, S. Haymoz, M. Bopp, F. Gutzwiller, and W. Rössler. 2010. "Firearm Suicides and Availability of Firearms: The Swiss Experience." *European Psychiatry* 25 (7): 432–34. https://doi.org/10.1016/j.eurpsy.2010.04.006.

Brueck, Hilary. 2019. "Switzerland Has a Stunningly High Rate of Gun Ownership—Here's Why It Doesn't Have Mass Shootings." *Yahoo News*, August 5, 2019. https://news.yahoo.com/switzerland-stunningly-high-rate-gun-142300639.html.

Central Intelligence Agency. 2018. "The World Factbook." https://www.cia.gov/library/publications/resources/the-world-factbook/.

Duquet, Nils, and Maarten Van Alstein. 2015. *Firearms and Violent Deaths in Europe*. Brussels, Belgium: Flemish Peace Institute.

Grabherr, Silke, Stephan Johner, Carine Dilitz, Ursula Buck, Martin Killias, Patrice Mangin, and Thomas Plattner. 2010. "Homicide-Suicide Cases in Switzerland and Their Impact on the Swiss Weapon Law." *The American Journal of Forensic Medicine and Pathology* 31 (4): 335–49. https://doi.org/10.1097/PAF.0b013e3181ce9f3e.

Karp, Aaron. 2018. *Estimating Global Civilian-Held Firearms Numbers*. Briefing Paper. Geneva, Switzerland: Small Arms Survey.

Killias, Martin, and Nora Markwalder. 2012. "Firearms and Homicide in Europe." In *Handbook of European Homicide Research: Patterns, Explanations, and Country Studies*, edited by Marieke C. A. Liem and William Alex Pridemore, 261–72. New York: Springer. https://doi.org/10.1007/978-1-4614-0466-8_16.

UNODC (United Nations Office on Drugs and Crime). 2018. "Crime Data." https://dataunodc.un.org/crime.

Chapter 10: Punishment

Janet P. Stamatel

OVERVIEW

How societies elect to punish people who break the most serious rules of behavior has varied greatly over time and across countries. Historically, criminal punishments tended to be more physical in nature than they are today (e.g., hanging, crucifixion, drawing and quartering, whippings), although many countries still use corporal punishment regularly, and some would argue that punishments have become more humane as societies have become more civilized. There is a wide variety of punishments employed in criminal justice systems around the world today, but some countries tend to emphasize certain forms over others. Punishment practices are shaped by two overarching factors: the type of legal system and the dominant philosophy of punishment.

There are three main forms of legal systems in the world. The civil law system, also known as the Romano-Germanic system, dates back to the Roman Empire. It emphasizes the written laws (codes) that clearly specify crimes and associated punishments and supports an inquisitorial process for determining innocence or guilt, where a judge leads the fact-finding investigation in search of the truth. This system can be found in many Western European and Latin American countries. In contrast, common law relies more on customs rather than codes. These customs are still written as laws, but there is more room for interpretation, and the use of the law in previous cases is important for current interpretation of the law, which is called precedent. The common law family is also typically associated with an adversarial legal process where lawyers compete to advocate for their interpretation of the facts of the case. This legal system can be found in the United Kingdom, the United States, and many of the former British colonies. The third type of system is sacred law, which derives all laws directly from religious teachings. The most common example of the sacred system today is Islamic law, in which citizens see laws and punishments as directives from God with little room for interpretation. In practice, many countries have mixed legal traditions that borrow from these three families of law, particularly in places with a colonial history. These legal systems influence how criminal punishments are administered because they outline the scope of available punishments and the amount of discretion that criminal justice actors, such as judges, have in meting out punishments. This chapter provides examples of all three legal families: the civil law system is used in Hungary,

Rwanda, and Sweden; the common law system dominates Malaysia, Singapore, the United States, and Trinidad and Tobago; and the Islamic legal system can be found in Saudi Arabia and to a lesser extent in Malaysia.

Another important factor influencing the types of criminal punishments administered in a country is the perceived goal of punishment. There are five primary philosophies regarding the aims of punishment. First, punishment can be seen to *deter* future crimes either by the offender who is being punished (specific deterrence) or by demonstrating to the general public the consequences of breaking laws (general deterrence). Second, punishment can be used to *incapacitate* people who are harmful to society, particularly through imprisonment. Third, punishment serves as *retribution*, or a way for an offender to pay back a particular victim or society for the harm caused in breaking the law. Fourth, punishment can be used to *rehabilitate* offenders to correct their behavior and make them more productive members of society. Finally, punishment can be used to *restore* the social bonds that were broken through the criminal act; it can be a process of healing for offenders, victims, and society. These goals are not mutually exclusive and most countries embrace all these aims, although to varying degrees and for different types of crimes. Countries also change their primary goals of punishment over time in response to changing political priorities and social conditions.

The countries included in this chapter were selected to highlight differences in both legal systems and punishment philosophies. Hungary illuminates the complexities of reforming legal philosophies and systems in the midst of radical political changes. Malaysia is an example of a country that espouses strict punishments, including corporal punishment, and that struggles to balance a secular legal system rooted in British law with Islamic legal code. Rwanda illustrates how countries use punishment to achieve justice after mass atrocities, such as genocide, and how punishment can restore damaged social bonds. Saudi Arabia is a classic example of a country that subscribes fully to Islamic law, which is often perceived as very punitive. Sweden is known for having a rather humane and lenient punishment system, although there have been pressures to change to a stricter system. Singapore and Trinidad and Tobago are both former British colonies known for their punitiveness. Finally, the United States is unusual in its excessive use of incarceration to punish criminal offenders.

HUNGARY

Hungary is a landlocked country in Central Europe, bordering seven countries, with Slovakia to the north, Austria to the east, and Romania to the west. The majority of the nearly ten million people are of Hungarian ethnicity and identify with Christianity, primarily Catholicism. Hungary was a part of the Soviet communist political bloc from 1945 to 1989, until the communist system in Eastern Europe collapsed (Central Intelligence Agency 2018). Since then, Hungary has transitioned to a democratic country with a free market and has experienced a growing economy. This major social transformation has reshaped the criminal justice system to be more consistent with democratic principles and to conform to European Union standards. However, political parties have disagreed as to the proper balance between law and order, on the one hand, and human rights, on the other hand, and this tension is reflected in penal policy changes since 1989.

Socialist Legal System

From medieval times until the nineteenth century, Hungary was ruled by a monarchy and followed customary law, where cultural traditions guided judicial practices. In 1868, the Kingdom of Hungary joined the Habsburgs of Austria to form the Austro-Hungarian Empire. This union brought the civil law system (also known as Romano-Germanic) to Hungary, which still shapes the current legal system. A key feature of civil law is the codification of laws, leaving little room for interpretation or discretion. The first criminal code of Hungary was formally introduced in 1878. The civil law system also follows an inquisitorial process, where the investigative stage is quite lengthy and controlled by judges pursuing the truth. This is quite different from the adversarial model in the United States, where lawyers compete over the interpretation of the facts of a case.

The end of World War I in 1918 also brought an end to the Austro-Hungarian Empire. As a result of the Treaty of Trianon (1920) that laid out the formal terms of surrender of Hungary, the victorious Allied Powers redefined Hungary's borders, and over 70 percent of its land was redistributed to surrounding countries. Hungary was politically and militarily weak and aligned itself with Italy and Germany. When World War II broke out in 1939, Hungary joined the Axis Powers two years later. Once again Hungary was defeated in 1945, leaving the country under the control of the Soviet military.

Hungary remained an independent country, but its political and economic systems and military were heavily controlled by the Soviet Union, which forced Hungary to adopt communism. The constitution of 1949 had no protections for citizens' rights including the right to a fair trial. In 1950, the communist government of Hungary adopted a new act to the criminal code that introduced elements of the socialist legal system. Although this revised arrangement retained the key features of the civil legal system, it treated the law as a tool to achieve communist political, economic, and ideological goals. For example, the impact of criminal offenses on the rest of the society and on public order became very important because it reinforced the communist value of communitarianism. Additionally, offenses against communal (state) property and the common good, such as stealing from the workplace, were treated very seriously because they undermined the goal of common ownership and equality.

The first full Criminal Code of the communist period was passed in 1961, a Criminal Procedure Code was introduced in 1973, and a Penal Code in 1978. These new laws reinforced the communist influence on the criminal justice system. Economic offenses were prioritized and new laws were introduced to restrict personal freedoms, such as speech and travel. Imprisonment also became an important tool to protect society against criminal offenders. In the 1980s, half of the adult offenders were sentenced to prison and 25 percent to unconditional imprisonment, although prison sentences were usually short. Only 1 percent of sentences during that time exceeded five years (Lévay 2012).

Democratization and Human Rights

Decades of poor economic performance and political unrest brought an end to communism in Hungary and other Central and Eastern European communist countries in 1989, which eventually led to the collapse of the Soviet Union in 1991. Hungary's political revolution was peaceful, and the new leaders quickly expressed the desire to make Hungary a democratic, capitalist country and to eventually join the Western European countries in the European Union. A constitutional government that prioritized the rule of law replaced the socialist legal practices. Changes to the Hungarian constitution in 1989 explicitly protected civil and human rights, and laws were enacted to limit government abuse of power, especially with respect to punishment.

One of the first legal changes made by the new government was the creation of a Constitutional Court, which ruled in 1990 that the death penalty was unconstitutional because it violated the constitution's provision of "the right to life" (Toth 2013). During communism, the death penalty could be applied for intentional homicide, as well as for eight types of political crimes, two offenses of public order, and eleven military crimes (Lévay 2012).

The Hungarian Criminal Code was significantly revised in 1993 to decriminalize many acts (e.g., prostitution), reduce mandatory punishments, and give judges more discretion in sentencing. For example, the minimum prison stay was reduced from three months to one day. Additionally, the revised code introduced alternative sanctions to incarceration, including treatment for drug offenders. Legal changes also provided more rights for the accused, such as the right to a fair trial, as well as humane prison conditions. These provisions brought Hungary in compliance with the European Convention for the Protection of Human Rights and Fundamental Freedoms.

During the early 1990s crime rates were increasing in Hungary as they were in most post-communist countries in Central and Eastern Europe as a result of the social upheaval caused by major political and economic changes. When a center-right political party gained power in 1998, it introduced criminal justice reforms that embraced a "get tough" approach toward criminals, which emphasized punishment over treatment and minimized the sentencing power of judges. In 1999, a law was passed allowing for life imprisonment without parole and the statutory minimum prison sentence was increased from one day to two months. As a result, the prison rate rose from 140 per 100,000 people in 1998 to 178 per 100,000 by 2002 (Lévay 2012).

The 2002 and 2006 elections brought the Socialist Liberal Party into power that annulled many of the 1998 criminal justice reforms, opting instead for more inclusionary practices. In particular, the 2003 changes to the Penal Code reduced custodial sentences, encouraged the use of alternative sanctions, and gave more discretionary power to the judiciary. As a result, the prison rate decreased to 147 per 100,000 by 2006. The Penal Code was amended again in 2006 to introduce social justice policies, such as mediation and restorative justice, and to add explicit victim protections to the law. These reforms were passed, in part, to conform to the practices of the European Union.

The subsequent elections in 2010, 2014, and 2018 saw the victory of a Center Right Party again, led by Prime Minister Viktor Orbán (1963–). Orbán has increasingly amassed control over the country by limiting the powers of the Constitutional Court and eliminating several government regulatory bodies. His political rhetoric emphasizes Christian nationalism, legality, and security. He has spread fear about the "Islamization of Europe," taking an exclusionary stance toward refugees. Under his leadership, the Hungarian Criminal Code was revised in 2012 to impose stricter laws on illegal immigration, emphasize social order over personal rights, and increase protections for children (Fekete 2016).

Contemporary Penal System

The Hungarian Penal Code has provisions for the following sanctions: imprisonment, confinement, community service, fines, disqualification from a profession, revocation of driving privileges, bans from certain places, and expulsion for noncitizens. There are twenty-nine prisons, two educational facilities, and one hospital in the country for custodial sentences. As of 2017, there were 16,947 people imprisoned at a rate of 173 per 100,000 people. About 18 percent of the incarcerated population was awaiting trial. Only about 7 percent of detainees are women, and less than 0.5 percent are juveniles (Institute for Criminal Policy Research 2017). In 2011, only 2 percent of the prisoners were serving a life sentence, and 17 percent were serving sentences longer than five years (Karsai and Szomora 2015). The law allows for life sentences for thirty criminal offenses, but in practice it is only applied in intentional homicide cases. Life imprisonment can only be applied to offenders who are at least twenty years old and is mandatory for violent recidivists. Parole is an option for some incarcerated offenders.

In addition to these punitive sanctions, the Hungarian Penal Code also provides for preventative measures, such as admonition, probation, fines, forfeiture of assets, and compulsory psychiatric treatment. For felony offenses, probation is only an option if the offense would have resulted in a prison sentence of less than three years. Probation generally lasts from one to three years.

Further Reading

Central Intelligence Agency. 2018. "The World Factbook." https://www.cia.gov/library/publications/resources/the-world-factbook/.

Fekete, Liz. 2016. "Hungary: Power, Punishment and the 'Christian-National Idea.'" *Race & Class* 57 (4): 39–53. https://doi.org/10.1177/0306396815624607.

Institute for Criminal Policy Research. 2017. "World Prison Brief." http://www.prisonstudies
   .org/world-prison-brief-data.
Karsai, Krisztina, and Zsolt Szomora. 2015. *Criminal Law in Hungary*. Austin, TX: Kluwer.
Lévay, Miklós. 2012. "Human Rights and Penalization in Central and Eastern Europe: The
   Case of Hungary." In *Resisting Punitiveness in Europe? Welfare, Human Rights and Democ-
   racy*, edited by Sonja Snacken and Els Dumortier. London, UK: Routledge.
Toth, Zoltan J. 2013. "The Capital Punishment Controversy in Hungary: Fragments on
   the Issues of Deterrent Effect and Wrongful Convictions." *European Journal of Crime,
   Criminal Law and Criminal Justice* 21: 37–58.

MALAYSIA

Malaysia is a country in Southeast Asia with over thirty-one million people. It borders Thailand and Indonesia in the South China Sea. Malaysia was a British colony
until it gained independence in 1957. It is a federal constitutional monarchy, consisting of thirteen states and three federal territories. Malays and indigenous peoples are the largest ethnic group, followed by Chinese, Indian, and others. About
60 percent of the population is Muslim, almost 20 percent Buddhist, and about
10 percent Christian. It is a secular state, although Islam is the official religion
(Central Intelligence Agency 2018). Civil law and Islamic law coexist in a complicated relationship. Tensions between secular and religious views toward punishment are a defining feature of Malaysian criminal law. Human rights activists often
criticize Malaysia for using both corporal punishment and the death penalty.

Legal System

Islam spread into the Malay region in the early fifteenth century and melded with
ancient customary laws to form the legal system of Malaysia prior to British occupation. In the nineteenth century, this system was replaced with a British penal
code. The current legal system is still modeled after English common law. The
federal constitution outlines penalties for federal offenses, although states can also
enact criminal laws, as long as they do not contradict the constitution. Sharia law,
based on Islamic religious principles, also applies to Muslims in Malaysia, primarily with respect to family and religious matters, although the boundaries between
government and Sharia law have been frequently contested. Sharia stems from
the writings of the Qur'an and Sunnah, as well as other religious doctrines, and
can be applied to all areas of life, which include public safety, marriage and family, property arrangements, and religious practices. Sharia law is believed to come
from God, not government rulers, and it supersedes other laws in its strictest interpretation. In contrast to Saudi Arabia, Malaysia is not a theocracy and does not
have a legal system based fully on Sharia law. Instead, Malaysia is a secular state,
and government laws passed at the federal level are given primacy. Additionally,
Islam is the official religion of Malaysia, but people are allowed to practice other
religions. About 60 percent of Malaysians are Muslims and Sharia laws and courts

only apply to them, whereas government law applies to all Malaysians regardless of their religious preferences.

Types of Punishments

Under the federal penal code, punishments for crimes include fines, probation, restitution, corporal punishment, imprisonment, and the death penalty. Fines are applied for minor offenses, such as low-level corruption or public disorder, and are also levied along with prison sentences. Community service is not directly specified as a punishment for certain crimes, but it can be applied at the discretion of judges. This is not a common practice in Malaysia, although the Criminal Procedure Code allows for a maximum of 240 hours of community service to be applied to young offenders aged eighteen to twenty-one years.

The incarceration rate in Malaysia is 167 prisoners per 100,000 population. Of the 50,000 prisoners, less than 7 percent are women and about 2 percent are juveniles. There are thirty-five prisons in the country and three juvenile detention centers (Institute for Criminal Policy Research 2017).

Whipping, or caning, was introduced under British colonial rule and is still part of the federal constitution. It is typically administered in addition to a prison sentence. For example, aggravated assault carries a maximum penalty of three years in prison, a fine, whipping, or any combination of two of these three punishments. Whipping is a possible punishment for theft, extortion, robbery, and sexual assault, among other offenses.

The execution of a whipping penalty is very specific to not cause unnecessary injury to the offender. The cane is made of rattan and cannot be more than a half-inch thick. The maximum number of strokes is twenty-four for an adult and ten for a juvenile. Offenders must be certified as being able to withstand the punishment by a medical examiner. Historically, whipping was only applied to male offenders under fifty years old. However, in 2010, Malaysia carried out this punishment on women for the first time. In three separate cases, women convicted for extramarital sex received four-to-six strokes each.

Corporal punishment, like whipping, is controversial both within Malaysia and the international community. A 2012 survey of Malaysians reported that 53 percent thought whipping was "barbaric," 67 percent said it was "ineffective," and 77 percent thought it was "impractical." The human rights group Amnesty International classifies whipping as torture and claimed that it had reached "epidemic proportions" in Malaysia in 2010, with an estimated 1,200 canings per month (McCurry 2010). Some legal scholars, however, have argued that the strict rules regarding the application of whipping ensure that it is just and humane and that the punishment is consistent with Sharia principles regarding punishment, reformation, and deterrence (Shariff et al. 2012).

Recent whipping examples include a 2018 case of a twenty-five-year-old man who argued with his mother over money and then hit her on the head, causing an injury requiring three stitches. The man was convicted of assault and sentenced to seven years in prison and three strokes with a cane. In the same year, two police-men were convicted of armed robbery. One received a sentence of eleven years in prison and four lashes, whereas the other was sentenced to thirteen years in prison and six lashes.

The death penalty is also administered in Malaysia. It is one of twelve countries that have mandatory death sentences for certain crimes, including murder, attacks against the monarch, and discharging a firearm in the commission of another crime. The death penalty was also mandatory for drug trafficking until November 2017 when the Parliament passed a law allowing other punishments to be applied for those crimes. The death penalty can be issued at judges' discretion for cases of abduction, arms possession or trafficking, and treason.

Almost half of the countries in Asia still administer the death penalty. Malaysia had the third highest number of people with a death sentence (1,042) in 2016, behind Bangladesh (1,645) and Pakistan (6,000). In 2016 alone, Malaysia had issued thirty-six new death penalties and executed nine people. The Malaysian government has been criticized by human rights groups for what has been called "secretive" executions, as offenders and their families are given very little notice when the executions are going to be administered (Amnesty International 2017). For example, a water seller was convicted of discharging a firearm during the course of a robbery in 2009, which is subjected to a mandatory death penalty. On May 22, 2017, the offender's family was given a letter by the prison informing them that they should visit him the following day because they were going to administer the execution in 24 hours.

In 2018, a new political party called Pakatan Harapan (Alliance of Hope) won control of the government, and Prime Minister Mahathir Mohamad (1925–) prom-ised to introduce criminal justice reforms to improve human rights in Malaysia. He placed a moratorium on the death penalty with the intention to introduce a law to abolish it. It is not clear yet whether he will have the political backing to succeed.

Religious Tensions

In 1993, the legislature of the Malaysian state of Kelantan passed the Hudud Bill, which is still causing controversy in the country. Under Islamic law, *hudud* offenses are "crimes against God" that have fixed punishments derived from religious texts. The seven *hudud* offenses include theft, robbery, unlawful sexual intercourse, slan-derous accusation of unlawful sexual intercourse, drinking liquor, rebellion and apostasy. Punishments for these crimes are severe, with very little room for judicial discretion. For example, the punishment for a first theft offense is amputation of the right hand at the wrist; the punishment for unlawful sexual intercourse for a married person is stoning to death; and the punishment for apostasy for someone unwilling to repent is death.

The bill caused considerable controversy not only because of its severe nature but because it pitted the secular state against Islamic law. Malaysian states are not allowed to issue punishments that exceed federal guidelines. As Sharia law also only applies to Muslims, the Hudud Bill would result in unequal treatment of offenders committing the same crime based on their religious affiliations. Additionally, legal scholars disagree as to the offenses that are considered *hudud* (Haneef 2010). In 2016, the Pan-Malaysian Islamic Party introduced a Hudud Bill in Parliament for approval at the federal level, but a vote on the bill was tabled.

Further Reading

Amnesty International. 2017. *Death Sentences and Executions 2016*. London: Amnesty International. https://www.amnestyusa.org/reports/death-sentences-executions-2016/.

Central Intelligence Agency. 2018. "The World Factbook." https://www.cia.gov/library/publications/resources/the-world-factbook/.

Haneef, Sayed Sikandar Shah. 2010. "Discourse on Hudud in Malaysia: Addressing the Missing Dimension." *Journal of Islamic Law and Culture* 12 (2):131–44. https://doi.org/10.1080/1528817X.2010.574393.

Institute for Criminal Policy Research. 2017. "World Prison Brief." http://www.prisonstudies.org/world-prison-brief-data.

McCurry, Justin. 2010. "Malaysia Criticised over Canings." *The Guardian*, December 6, 2010. http://www.theguardian.com/world/2010/dec/06/caning-malaysian-prisons-amnesty-international.

Shariff, Ahmad Azam bin Mohd, Mazupi bin Abdul Rahman, Hayatullah Laluddin, Tengku Noor Azira bt Tengku Zainudin, Anita binti Abdul Rahim, and Nazurabinti Abdul Manap. 2012. "Whipping Punishment under Islamic Criminal Law: Perception and Misconception in Malaysia." *Advances in Natural and Applied Sciences* 6 (8): 1263–67.

RWANDA

Rwanda is a relatively small country in east-central Africa, bordering the Democratic Republic of the Congo, Uganda, Tanzania, and Burundi. Its population of almost twelve million people comprises three main ethnic groups: Hutu, Tutsi, and Twa. The majority of people are Christians. It has a mixed legal system, with strong influences of civil law from the colonial period mixed with customary law. It is a relatively poor country, with a GDP per capita of USD 2,100, comparable to Afghanistan and Mali. The economy was ruined because of the 1994 genocide, but it has been steadily rebounding in the twenty-first century (Central Intelligence Agency 2018).

Rwanda was a Belgian colony that gained independence in 1962. In the twentieth century, there were a series of violent conflicts between the Hutu and Tutsi groups that culminated in the genocide of 1994. The numerically dominant Hutu and Tutsi groups became increasingly segregated under the colonial rule of Germany followed by Belgium. The colonizers created artificial divisions between the two groups and favored the Tutsi. A dispute over independence from Belgium culminated in the Rwandan War (1959–1962) between the two ethnic groups, with the victorious Hutus taking control of the independent country in 1962. Hundreds of thousands of Tutsis fled the country, some of whom formed rebel groups that returned in the 1990s. This backdrop of ethnic violence set the stage for the

Rwandan Civil War in 1990 that ended in genocide. This mass atrocity created a criminal justice system crisis in a country with limited financial resources, which led to some innovative approaches to punishing offenders and administering justice after enormous tragedy.

Genocide

Between 1990 and 1993, the Rwandan Civil War pitted the Hutu-led government against a rebel group of Tutsi refugees living in Uganda. The cease-fire was short-lived as fighting renewed after April 6, 1994 when President Juvénal Habyarimana's (1937–1994) plane was shot down and he was killed. Habyarimana was a Hutu, and the Tutsis were initially blamed for his death. This led to one hundred days of intense violence targeting Tutsis, politically moderate Hutus, and the smallest ethnic group of Rwanda called the Twa. Approximately 800,000 to one million people were brutally murdered, and the international community eventually recognized the mass atrocity as genocide.

In July 1994, the main rebel group, called the Rwandan Patriotic Front, led by Paul Kagame (1957–) defeated the Hutu government forces. Peace was restored with some assistance from the United Nations. The country was faced with the unprecedented challenge of how to bring justice to the victims of genocide, punish the offenders, and maintain a tenuous peace while trying to rebuild the country, both politically and economically. In 1994, just before the conflict, there were 10,000 people in prison in Rwanda, but this number jumped to 125,000 by 1999 as the country adjudicated those accused of participating in the genocide. This was about 10 percent of the male Hutu population (Drumbl 2000). To deal with both the severity of the crimes and the excessive number of offenders, Rwanda adopted three mechanisms of justice.

International Criminal Tribunal for Rwanda

Mass atrocities, such as genocide, are violations of international law, so the United Nations Security Council established the International Criminal Tribunal for Rwanda (ICTR) on November 8, 1994 to prosecute crimes of genocide, crimes against humanity, and war crimes. These acts were codified as international crimes through the Geneva Conventions of 1949 following the mass atrocities of World War II. According to these laws, genocide is defined as acts intended "to destroy, in whole or in part, a national, ethnical, racial, or religious group" (Article II).

The ICTR focused on prosecuting senior military and government officials, as well as religious and media leaders who were responsible for organizing, funding, and inciting the mass violence that occurred in Rwanda. Between 1995 and 2012, the ICTR issued ninety-three indictments, of which sixty-two cases resulted in convictions and fourteen in acquittals. The ICTR had limited options for sentencing for the guilty, including life in prison, a fixed prison term, fines, and/or forfeiture of proceeds or property. Rwandan prisoners were sent to countries that complied with international standards regarding the treatment of prisoners, often Mali or Benin. They would be eligible for parole after serving twenty-five years of life sentences or two-thirds of a finite sentence.

International Criminal Tribunals, such as the ICTR, are controversial because national and international ideas of justice are not always aligned. The international tribunals seek retribution from offenders, document a historical record of the mass atrocities, express collective horror and disapproval of such acts, and aim to prevent future atrocities. However, the structure and nature of international tribunals may conflict with the country's goals and values with respect to administering justice and building peace. In this case, the Rwandan government did not agree with the ICTR's prohibition against the death penalty, as well as the fact that sentences could be served in other countries. The ICTR also faced administrative challenges and charges of corruption; nevertheless, it was the first international court to convict offenders of genocide and the first to recognize rape as a means of committing genocide.

Rwandan Criminal Courts

As a developing country experiencing significant political turmoil since independence, Rwanda did not have a particularly well-developed criminal justice system prior to the genocide. In 1994, there were 700 judges and magistrates, of which only fifty had any formal legal training. Many of these professionals were Tutsis who either died in the genocide or fled the country. This left about twenty lawyers with a formal legal training to deal with a massive number of cases against people who had participated in the genocide (Drumbl 2000).

The government passed the Organic Law of 1996 to administer justice in the aftermath of the genocide and restore peace. The law divided offenders into four categories: organizers and people in authority who planned and/or committed systematic murders and who were not prosecuted by the ICTR; people aside from the first category who committed murder or other serious crimes leading to death; those committing other serious personal crimes; and those committing property crimes.

The law encouraged confessions for offenders in all categories, except the first, through reduced sentences to expedite the processing of a large number of offenders. However, most prisoners awaiting trial did not believe they had committed a crime and instead thought they were prisoners of war. By 1999, 125,000 people were accused of crimes related to the genocide, and only 1,274 were adjudicated (Drumble 2000). The prison capacity for Rwanda prior to 1994 had only been 45,000. This meant that many of the accused could spend a significant portion of their lives in overcrowded prisons simply *awaiting trial*. Additional resources were invested in the criminal justice system to improve the speed and efficiency of case processing. In 2000, the Rwandan courts tried 2,406 people, resulting in 34 percent sentenced to prison for one-to-twenty years, 30.3 percent sentenced to life in prison, 14.4 percent sentenced to death, and 19 percent acquitted. Despite the additional resources, in 2005, it was estimated that 60,000 suspects were still in prison awaiting trial, and that it could take eighty years to prosecute all of them. Suspects convicted of the most serious crimes (category 1) could receive the death penalty through the Rwandan court system until 2007 when it was abolished.

Gacaca

In 2001, the Organic Law was amended to recognize *gacaca* courts to prosecute cases that occurred between 1990 and 1994 related to ethnic conflicts. *Gacaca* means "lawn" or "grass" and refers to a traditional means of resolving disputes outdoors in the community so that local leaders presided and the public could witness the proceedings. Under the Organic Law, *gacaca* courts could try offenders accused of offenses in all categories of offenses, except the most serious ones.

Local governments in Rwanda comprise cells up to 500 people, which are grouped into larger units called sectors, which are subsequently grouped into communes or small towns. Each cell elected twenty people to serve *gacaca* courts, and those people then elected judges for the sector, and, in turn, sector judges elected judges for the communes. Political and religious elites, as well as lawyers, could not be selected for *gacaca* courts. Cells were allowed to try cases of theft and vandalism; sectors could try assault cases; and only communes tried murder

This billboard advertises the *gacaca* courts used in Rwanda to assist with the administration of justice in the wake of the Rwandan genocide. These grassroots courts employed a community justice model to process over a million cases. (Robin Kirk)

cases. Once again, offenders were encouraged to confess before the trial to receive a reduced sentence. Offenders convicted in a *gacaca* court could appeal their sentence to a traditional Rwandan court.

Gacaca courts were seen not only as a way to expedite court processing but also as a means to expose the truth of what transpired during the genocide and to promote peace and reconciliation. Critics of the process warned of bias and unfair trials. One of the unexpected results of the *gacaca* courts was the number of additional offenders who came to light during proceedings. Between 2005 and 2012, the *gacaca* courts tried approximately 1.2 million cases (Human Rights Watch 2011).

Further Reading

Central Intelligence Agency. 2018. "The World Factbook." https://www.cia.gov/library /publications/resources/the-world-factbook/.

Drumbl, Mark A. 2000. "Sclerosis: Retributive Justice and the Rwandan Genocide." *Punishment & Society* 2 (3): 287–307.

Human Rights Watch. 2011. *Justice Compromised: The Legacy of Rwanda's Community-Based Gacaca Courts.* New York: Human Rights Watch. https://www.hrw.org/report/2011/05 /31/justice-compromised/legacy-rwandas-community-based-gacaca-courts.

Pruitt, William R. 2017. "Crime and Punishment in Rwanda." *Contemporary Justice Review* 20 (2): 193–210.

Schabas, William A. 2009. "Post-Genocide Justice in Rwanda: A Spectrum of Options." In *After Genocide*, edited by Phil Clark and Zachary D. Kaufman, 207–28. New York: Columbia University Press.

United Nations. n.d. "United Nations International Criminal Tribunal for Rwanda." http:// unictr.unmict.org/.

SAUDI ARABIA

Saudi Arabia is a country in the Middle East situated between the Red Sea and the Persian Gulf. An absolute monarchy rules over twenty-eight million people, the vast majority of whom are Muslims. It is the birthplace of Islam, as the Prophet Mohammed was born in Mecca in 570. In 622 he moved to Medina, where he unified the tribes of Arabia under Islam. Saudi Arabia has a significant amount of influence in the Muslim world because of this history and internationally because of its oil-rich economy. It has a GDP per capita of USD 54,500, similar to the United States (USD 59,800) (Central Intelligence Agency 2018).

The modern Kingdom of Saudi Arabia was created in 1932. It is a theocracy in which government and religion are inseparable. Instead of a constitution, religious texts serve as the rules for governing. In 1992, Saudi Arabia passed the Basic Law of Governance in an effort to codify fundamental tenets of the state as is typical of modern governments. Article 1 of the Basic Law states that "The Kingdom of Saudi Arabia is a sovereign Islamic State. Its religion is Islam. Its constitution is Almighty God's Book, the Holy Qur'an, and the Sunnah (Traditions) of the Prophet (PBUH)." Additionally, Article 8 proclaims "Governance in the Kingdom of Saudi Arabia is based on justice, *shura* (consultation) and equality according to Islamic

Sharia" (Royal Embassy of Saudi Arabia, n.d.). Religion and law are fundamentally intertwined in Saudi Arabia.

Sacred Legal System

Unlike the common law system practiced in the United States and the United Kingdom, which emphasizes legal precedent, or the civil law system used in much of Europe, which relies on codified laws, Saudi Arabia is a prime example of a sacred legal system, whereby laws are derived directly from legal sources and believed to be decreed by God. Sharia, or Islamic law, literally means "the way" or "the straight path" (Moore 1987, 62). It consists of rules for behavior that have been revealed by God, primarily through religious texts of the Qur'an and the Sunnah. Countries that employ Islamic law vary in the degree to which other religious sources and interpretations can influence the legal system. Saudi Arabia practices Wahhabism, which does not recognize nontextual sources of law and adopts a strict application of those texts.

These religious texts serve as a moral code for Muslims, as well as the basis for some penal codes. Serving God and submitting to his will in all aspects of life are governing ethical principles that put the individuals' needs and wants behind those of the religious community. Crimes, a subcategory of sins, are violations of this edict to serve God and should be punished. Because crimes are seen as offenses against God, public opinion is not tolerant of criminal behavior and generally supports harsh punishments.

Crime and Punishment

Islamic law identifies three types of crimes, which then determine the types of punishments that are allowed. The most serious crimes are *hudud*, which are crimes against Islam. Their punishments are prescribed in religious texts and cannot be subject to discretion. The punishments are harsh to reflect the seriousness of the offenses with respect to religious doctrine. The seven *hudud* offenses include theft, armed robbery, unlawful sexual intercourse, slanderous accusation of unlawful sexual intercourse (defamation), drinking liquor, rebellion, and apostasy. Four of those crimes (armed robbery, unlawful sexual relations, rebellion, and apostasy) are punishable by death. The punishment for theft is amputation of the right hand for a first offense and amputation of the left foot for a second offense. Falsely accusing someone of improper sexual intercourse results in a whipping of eighty lashes, and drinking liquor carries a penalty of forty-to-eighty lashes.

The second type of crime are *qisas*, which can be serious crimes like murder, but their punishments are considered the right of the people rather than the right of God, like the *hudud*. The emphasis of these crimes in on retribution for the injured party, and the Qur'an emphasizes forgiveness and financial compensation for these offenses. All other crimes fall into the third category of *ta'zir*. These offenses are not directly specified in religious texts and judges determine their penalties.

In Saudi Arabia, the balance of judicial power between religion and state depends to a large extent on the type of legal matter. Islamic law clearly dominates in matters of personal law, such as marriage, divorce, and inheritance. Islamic law and the government share responsibility over criminal matters, as determined by the types of offenses involved. The government is largely responsible for all other types of legal issues, such as taxation, immigration, and traffic laws.

Saudi Arabia does not publish detailed statistics about sentencing decisions, although there is some public information for the most serious punishments. In 2016, Saudi Arabia was ranked third highest in death penalty executions with 154, behind Pakistan (567) and China (thousands). Of those executed in 2016, three were women and 76 percent were Saudi Arabian nationals. The death penalty was administered for the offenses of murder (eighty-one), terrorism (forty-seven), drug-related crimes (twenty-four), kidnapping and torture (one), and rape (one). In that same year, more than forty people were issued a death sentence and about forty-four were awaiting execution. Saudi Arabia, Iran, and Iraq were responsible for 95 percent of all executions in the Middle East and North Africa (Amnesty International 2017).

As of 2013, the prison population rate was 161 prisoners per 100,000 people, which ranks the country ninety-fifth in the world. About 6 percent of prisoners were female, less than 1 percent were juveniles, and about 72 percent were foreigners. More than half of prisoners were awaiting trial (Institute for Criminal Policy Research 2017).

Human Rights Issues

Human rights activists heavily criticize punishments for *hudud* crimes in most countries that practice Islamic law. In 2016, Saudi Arabia carried out a mass execution of forty-seven persons convicted of terrorism, most of whom were beheaded. The United Nations Committee on the Rights of the Child criticized this decision for four of the offenders who were under eighteen years old. Human rights activists argue that imprisonment without trial and the application of the death penalty

---

Lifting the Ban on Women Drivers

In 2017, women in Saudi Arabia were finally granted the right to drive. For decades women activists had been advocating for a change in the law. The latest social media campaign about the issue started during the Arab Spring in 2011 and led to Crown Prince Mohammed bin Salman announcing an end to the ban against female drivers. However, before the law went into effect in the summer of 2018, several prominent women activists involved in this movement were arrested for "suspicious contacts with foreign entities" and "working to destabilize the kingdom." The suspects have been held in jail without formal charges against them.

are weapons of the Saudi government to quell political dissent. Reporters have documented dozens of political dissidents who have been arrested within the last year, many of whom were women's rights activists. An American, Walid Fitaihi, who has dual American-Saudi citizenship was arrested in 2017 and released after twenty-one months in prison without ever knowing why he had been arrested. Upon his release, he told reporters that he had been tortured in prison. In another case, a Saudi cleric, Salman Al-Awdah, was arrested in 2017 for tweeting that he hoped political tensions between Saudi Arabia and Qatar would end peacefully. He was charged with thirty-seven crimes including mocking the government. He was scheduled to appear in court in 2019 without legal representation to hear if he would be sentenced to death for his crimes, but his hearing was postponed.

Saudi Arabia has also been criticized for its use of corporal punishment, which can be administered to children as well as adults. In 2009, a Sri Lankan man and woman were found guilty of adultery in Saudi Arabia and initially sentenced to death by stoning. The Sri Lankan Ministry of Foreign Affairs filed an appeal, and the sentence was reduced to a whipping of 700 lashes and six years in prison. In 2016, the United Nations Convention against Torture criticized the use of corporal punishment in Saudi Arabia, particularly with respect to whipping and amputation. That report specifically cited the case of Ra'if Badawi, a blogger who was arrested in 2012 for "insulting Islam" in his writings. He was sentenced to ten years in prison, 1,000 lashings over the course of twenty weeks, and a fine. He was whipped fifty times in a public square in 2015, but subsequent whippings were postponed due to health concerns.

Defenders of Saudi Arabia's punishment practices note that *hudud* punishments are rarely carried out in practice because the severity of the punishments serves as a deterrent against committing crimes. For example, in 2014, a Yemeni man who had been convicted of multiple robberies had his right hand cut off as punishment. This was the only documented case of amputation for theft in Saudi Arabia in that year. Additionally, evidentiary standards for *hudud* crimes are so high that they are often not met. For example, many *hudud* crimes require four eyewitnesses. *Qisa* crimes also allow room for mercy. For example, a man was convicted of murder in 2015 and sentenced to death. However, he spent a year in prison demonstrating that he had reformed, so sheikhs and royals appealed his sentence and the daughter of the victim asked that his life be spared.

Further Reading

al-Rasheed, Madawi. 2010. *A History of Saudi Arabia.* Cambridge, UK: Cambridge University Press.

Amnesty International. 2017. *Death Sentences and Executions 2016.* London: Amnesty International. https://www.amnestyusa.org/reports/death-sentences-executions-2016/.

Central Intelligence Agency. 2018. "The World Factbook." https://www.cia.gov/library/publications/resources/the-world-factbook/.

Institute for Criminal Policy Research. 2017. "World Prison Brief." http://www.prisonstudies.org/world-prison-brief-data.

Moore, Richter H., Jr. 1987. "Courts, Law, Justice, and Criminal Trials in Saudi Arabia." *International Journal of Comparative and Applied Criminal Justice* 11 (1–2):61–67.

Royal Embassy of Saudi Arabia. n.d. "Basic Law of Governance (1992)." https://www .saudiembassy.net/basic-law-governance.

SINGAPORE

Singapore is a geographically small island nation situated between Malaysia and Indonesia. It consists of nearly six million people, most of whom are ethnic Chinese. It is a parliamentary republic run by a single political party, the People's Action Party, since its independence from Britain in 1965. It is one of four Asian Tiger economies, in addition to Hong Kong, South Korea, and Taiwan, that quickly developed into high-income economies after independence from colonizers. It has a GDP per capita of USD 94,100, the seventh highest in the world (Central Intelligence Agency 2018). Singapore officials attribute much of this economic success to a strict law and order society. As such, Singapore is known for its tough criminal justice system and harsh criminal punishments.

Law and Order Society

Singapore has a global reputation of being an exceptionally clean, safe, and orderly country. This is attributed, in part, to what are referred to as "Asian values," a culture that emphasizes hard-work, frugality, discipline, and sobriety. These values are seen as key to both individual success and, more importantly, to the economic development of the nation. Additionally, Singapore is a collectivist society that places the needs of the community above those of the individual. These values are central to the philosophy of justice shaping the criminal justice system in Singapore. Crime and justice are seen as relational concepts rather than individualistic, which means that crime is seen as a violation of the victim and societal relations and punishment is designed to protect the community. This system stands in sharp contrast to the Western model of justice that emphasizes due process and the protection of individual rights.

The importance of the rule of law in Singapore also creates a predictable and orderly society that is amenable to economic growth, which is how the ruling political party justifies its strict criminal justice practices. Even seemingly small infractions can incur tough penalties to reinforce society's disapproval of law-breaking activities. Fines are commonly used to send a message to less serious offenders that their actions are not socially acceptable. For example, a charge of jaywalking can result in a fine of SGD 500 (approximately USD 380), as can eating or drinking on public transportation, or feeding animals in a national park. Chewing gum and smoking on public transportation can be punished by a fine of SGD 1,000 and stealing wi-fi is a SGD 5,000 fine (Radics 2014). This practice has resulted in Singapore's nickname as "a fine city."

Singapore is a clean, orderly city-state known for its wealth and high standard of living. As a strict law-and-order society, police issues heavy fines for small infractions that disrupt this order, giving it the nickname of "a fine city." (Tananuphong Kummaru/Dreamstime.com)

Harsh Punishments

Singapore has an incarceration rate of 213 per 100,000 people, which ranks it 63 out of 222 countries. This rate has been fairly steady since 2006. Of the 12,219 people incarcerated in fourteen institutions in the country in 2016, 10.5 percent were female, 3.2 percent were minors, and 9.9 percent were foreigners (Institute for Criminal Policy Research 2017). About two-thirds of those incarcerated were convicted of drug offenses, and about four-fifths of them have had prior drug charges.

Singapore also practices corporal and capital punishment, which are legacies of British colonialism. Caning is a possible punishment for over thirty-five criminal offenses and is a mandatory punishment for rape, drug trafficking, illegal money lending, and overstaying visas by foreigners. Caning can be only applied to males between eighteen and fifty years old. In 2013, there were 2,300 caning sentences, which was significantly lower than the peak of 6,400 in 2007 (Radics 2014). Caning is a familiar part of the culture and used in other social institutions, such as families and schools, so most citizens are not opposed to the practice. However, caning violates international law through Article 5 of the Universal Declaration of Human Rights, Article 7 of the International Covenant on Civil and Political Rights, and the Convention against Torture. Because Singapore views international law and domestic law as separate legal systems, the country does not adhere to international law unless it is explicitly incorporated into domestic law.

Caning an American Student

In 1993, American Michael P. Fay was a teenager living in Singapore with his parents. He and some fellow high school students were arrested for stealing road signs and spray-painting cars. Fay was charged with vandalism, mischief, and possessing stolen goods. He confessed to the crimes and was sentenced to four months in jail, six strokes with a cane, and a fine of USD 2,555. Americans were outraged by the caning sentence, and President Bill Clinton asked the Singapore government for clemency on Fay's behalf. The government responded by reducing the caning sentence to four strokes and releasing him from jail after eighty-three days, after which Fay returned to the United States.

Singapore is one of three nations in Southeast Asia that administers the death penalty, along with Malaysia and Vietnam. In 2017, eight people who had received death penalty sentences in Singapore were executed by hanging, all of whom had been convicted of drug crimes. In the same year, there were fifteen new death penalty sentences, 80 percent of which were for drug crimes, and over forty people had been sentenced to the death penalty in previous years but had not yet been executed. The 2017 numbers of executions and new death penalty sentences were double those of 2017. However, these figures are much lower than previous years. For example, between 1993 and 2003 Singapore executed 174 people. It is not clear if the country is now administering this punishment less or if it is not reporting all of its executions to avoid scrutiny by the international community (Amnesty International 2017).

Singapore is one of eleven countries that has a mandatory death penalty sentence for the most serious criminal offenses, including terrorism-related offenses that result in death, drug trafficking, the manufacture of illegal drugs, and mutiny. Certain categories of offenders convicted of these crimes are exempt from the death penalty, including minors under eighteen years old, pregnant women, and the mentally ill. In the last few years, some high-profile death penalty cases involving foreigners generated considerable negative attention, encouraging criminal justice officials to review the mandatory death penalty policy for drug offenses, but the Singaporean courts upheld the law permitting its use. In 2012, the country amended the use of the mandatory death penalty for some offenses to give judges more discretion to opt for life imprisonment with caning instead of the death penalty. The vast majority of citizens support the death penalty, especially for murder and drug trafficking.

Drug Laws

Singapore has a global reputation for its "zero-tolerance" policy toward drugs that includes strict law enforcement and severe penalties. The country first passed the Drugs (Prevention and Misuse) Act of 1969 soon after gaining independence from

Britain. In the 1970s, heroin became a problem in the country affecting approximately 20,000 users (Lindsey and Nicholson 2016). This led to a sharp law enforcement response and the passage of the Misuse of Drugs Act of 1973 that allowed death penalty for certain drug offenses. As a result, drug use fell sharply in the country. For example, in 1994, police arrested 208 people per 100,000 for heroin-related offenses, which declined to 86 per 100,000 in 2011 (Lindsey and Nicholson 2016).

Currently, Singapore does not produce narcotics, and drug use among residents is fairly low, which makes drug trafficking the country's primary concern. Drugs are seen as a threat to economic success, national security, and the overall welfare of the population. Harsh penalties are designed to deter drug offenses, For example, illegal trafficking of more than 15 grams of diamorphine, 30 grams of cocaine, 250 grams of methamphetamine, or 500 grams of cannabis could result in the death penalty. Trafficking of between 330 and 500 grams of cannabis is punishable by a minimum sentence of twenty years imprisonment and fifteen stokes with a cane, and a maximum sentence of thirty years to life and fifteen strokes. Trafficking of other serious (Class A) drugs not listed above carry a minimum sentence of five years and five strokes and a maximum sentence of twenty years and fifteen strokes. Producing diamorphine, cocaine, or methamphetamine could also result in the death penalty. Convicted offenders can be rewarded for good behavior in prison with a one-third reduction of their prison sentences or after serving twenty years of a life sentence.

Drug possession carries a minimum sentence of two years in prison beyond the first offense and a maximum penalty of ten years in prison, SGD 20,000 fine, or both. Suspected or known drug users are arrested and subjected to mandatory drug detention centers run by the Singapore prison system. According to the Misuse of Drugs Act, a person can be remanded to such a center if they are "reasonably suspected to be a drug addict" (Ann et al. 2017). In 2014, there were 6, 527 people incarcerated for drug-related offenses, 707 were held in remand for drug-related offenses, and 1,400 were detained in drug rehabilitation centers (Lindsey and Nicholson 2016). Drug users are typically detained for a minimum of six months, with a maximum of two years. Treatment is compulsory and entails detoxification, behavioral change programs, and relapse prevention plans. Once addicts are released from mandatory rehabilitation, they are monitored extensively for up to two years to try to prevent relapse. First-time arrests for drug use do not always result in a criminal record, but multiple arrests often warrant lengthy prison sentences.

Further Reading

Amnesty International. 2017. *Death Sentences and Executions 2016*. London: Amnesty International. https://www.amnestyusa.org/reports/death-sentences-executions-2016/.

Ann, Lim Li, Connie Ong, Mohd Salihin Subhan, Benjamin Choy, and Tan Tee Seng. 2017. "Activism on Arbitrary Detention, the Suspension of Law." In *A History of Human Rights Society in Singapore 1965–2015*, edited by Jiyoung Song, 70–95. London, UK: Routledge.

Central Intelligence Agency. 2018. "The World Factbook." https://www.cia.gov/library /publications/resources/the-world-factbook/.

Institute for Criminal Policy Research. 2017. "World Prison Brief." http://www.prisonstudies .org/world-prison-brief-data.

Lindsey, Tim, and Pip Nicholson. 2016. *Drugs Law and Legal Practice in Southeast Asia: Indonesia, Singapore and Vietnam*. Oxford: Hart Publishing.

Radics, George Baylon. 2014. *Singapore: A 'Fine' City: British Colonial Criminal Sentencing Policies and Its Lasting Effects on the Singaporean Corporal State*. SSRN Scholarly Paper ID 2484259. Rochester, NY: Social Science Research Network. https://papers.ssrn.com /abstract=2484259.

SWEDEN

Sweden is a country of approximately ten million people located in Northern Europe between Norway and Finland. It is a part of Scandinavia, along with Denmark and Norway, which is a group of Northern European countries sharing a North Germanic heritage. Sweden is run by a parliamentary constitutional monarchy and is part of the European Union. It is a relatively wealthy country with a strong welfare state. It has a GDP per capita of USD 51,200, comparable to Germany (USD 50,800) and the United States (USD 59,800) (Central Intelligence Agency 2018). These characteristics of Sweden's geographic location, cultural heritage, and current political and economic systems have contributed to the country's attitudes toward criminal punishment, particularly its rather unique approach to incarceration. Experts often use the term "Scandinavian exceptionalism" when referring to the criminal justice systems in Sweden, Denmark, and Norway, as these countries are characterized by low rates of imprisonment, humane prison conditions, and low levels of political involvement in criminal justice policies.

Sentencing Practices

The most common criminal punishment is a fine, which is given in about half of all criminal convictions. Other punishments include a suspended sentence, probation, or community service, all of which can be given along with a fine. Prison is the final alternative, which is only used for the most serious offenses. Similar to other European Union countries, Sweden has abolished the death penalty. According to the Swedish National Council for Crime Prevention, in 2016, the proportion of convicted offenders fined was 58 percent, whereas 11 percent were waived prosecutions, 11 percent were prison sentences, 9 percent were suspended sentences, and 10 percent other types of sanctions (brå 2017).

In 2017, the World Prison Population List ranked Seychelles as the country with the highest rate of incarceration, with 738 people imprisoned for every 100,000 people in the population and the United States was the second highest with 666 per 100,000. Sweden is ranked 191 out of 222 countries on the list with an imprisonment rate of fifty-seven per 100,000. It is at the low end of incarceration rates for Northern European countries. Lithuania (235 per 100,000), Latvia (218), and

Estonia (205) are at the high end; Ireland (78) and Norway (74) are in the middle of this group; and Sweden has the second lowest incarceration rate just above Iceland (38). About 6 percent of Swedish prisoners are women, less than 1 percent are juveniles, and about 31 percent are foreigners (Institute for Criminal Policy Research 2017).

In 2016, 22 percent of those given prison offenses were convicted of theft crimes, 13 percent for serious violent crimes, 25 percent for drug offenses, and 12 percent for road traffic offenses, primarily driving under the influence of drugs or alcohol (brå 2017). The most frequent sentence duration in 2016 was two months maximum and the second most common was six months maximum. Only 9 percent of sentences were longer than two years, and only eleven people total were sentenced to life in prison (brå 2017). Prisoners are eligible for parole after serving two-thirds of their prison sentence. Parolees are often required to participate in some kind of prisoner reentry program, such as a substance treatment facility, halfway house, work release program, or electronic monitoring.

Prison Conditions

Most prisons in Sweden are small, with less than a hundred inmates, which means that most prisoners are assigned to prisons that are fairly close to their homes. Family visits and conjugal visits are strongly encouraged to maintain strong family bonds during incarceration. About 20 to 30 percent of prisoners are assigned to open prisons, with minimal security. Many prisoners in these facilities are allowed to leave during the day, typically to work. They are often allowed to wear their own clothes rather than prison uniforms, and they interact with custodial staff regularly. The remaining prisoners are sent to closed prisons with controlled entrances and exits and overall higher levels of security.

The guiding philosophy of punishment in Sweden is to maintain as normal a life as possible. Swedes believe that the punishment of incarceration is the loss of *liberty only*, not the loss of a normal life with family, education, work, and society. As a result, prison conditions are very humane and prisoners have a good quality of life. There is no overcrowding nor are there major health problems. There is a large staff for a small number of prisoners, and regular interactions between staff and prisoners are encouraged. Prisoners are typically active in education, work, and treatment programs. Prisoners even give input on how the prison is run. Swedish prisons emphasize security much less than Anglo-American prison systems. They also consider how the physical design of facilities can affect prisoners' psychosocial development, encouraging reflection and remorse rather than punishment.

Criminal Justice Decision-Making

Unlike the United States, where public opinion has a strong influence on criminal justice policies, populism in Sweden has been less important than expert input and evidence-based policies. Legislative decisions include long periods of deliberation by experts on the topic under consideration. Criminal justice policies are designed to be humanitarian and practical, rather than aimed at gathering political support. In 1974, the Swedish National Council for Crime Prevention was established to provide knowledge and expertise to inform crime policies.

Public opinion data show that Swedes tend to be less punitive than other Europeans. For example, among people from fifteen European countries who were asked about their attitudes toward crime and punishment, Swedes were most likely to approve of crime prevention programs and were less supportive of longer prison sentences (Demker et al. 2008). A study conducted by the International Crime Victims Survey asked people in a number of countries what type of punishment they would support for a two-time burglary offender: fine, prison, community service, suspended sentence, or other punishment. Thirty-one percent of respondents supported prison and 47 percent chose community service. Their support for prison was higher than some countries such as Portugal (9 percent) and Austria (10 percent), but lower than others such as England and Wales (51 percent) and Malta (52 percent) (Mayhew and Van Kesteren 2002). Swedes generally agree that incarceration is harmful and should be reserved for the most serious criminal offenders. However, there does seem to be a shift in popular attitudes with Swedes now more likely to be dissatisfied with the criminal justice system than in the past.

Recent Trends

Experts have noted some evidence that Sweden is moving toward a more punitive model of punishment. While crime control had historically been an apolitical issue, a new political party that emerged in 1991 called New Democracy challenged that pattern with an anti-immigration and anticrime platform. In 2010, another party called Sweden Democrats also made crime, punishment, and immigration central to their platform. This pattern raises concerns that expert knowledge on criminal justice matters may become devalued in favor of a more populist approach.

Additionally, starting around 1989, the courts shifted from a more rehabilitative approach toward punishment to one of "just deserts" (von Hofer and Tham 2013). This led to an increase in punishments administered and an emphasis on proportionate punishments. The goal was to make penal decision-making more uniform. In 1999, parole conditions were also tightened so that offenders had to serve two-thirds of their sentences prior to parole, whereas in the past it had been only half.

Around the same time, the media in Sweden became privatized and an independent voice weighing in on criminal justice issues. The victims' rights movement also took hold in Sweden, which emphasized offender accountability and victim redress. Sweden's low-tolerance drug policy fueled discussions about traditional moral values and encouraged a repressive attitude toward crime control. Finally, in 2004, there were three highly publicized prison escapes that resulted in tighter security measures, particularly at maximum-security prisons. In one case, an offender who had been convicted of killing two police officers walked out of the prison carrying a gun and a mobile phone that had been smuggled in by a guard.

He left the prison with three other inmates, but all were recaptured within a few days. Thus, though there is some evidence of a more punitive turn in Sweden's penal policies since before the 1980s, they have not fundamentally changed the overall nature of "Scandinavian exceptionalism" in Sweden, especially compared to other countries.

Further Reading

brå. 2017. "Swedish National Council for Crime Prevention." https://www.bra.se/bra-in -english/home/about-bra.html.

Central Intelligence Agency. 2018. "The World Factbook." https://www.cia.gov/library /publications/resources/the-world-factbook/.

Demker, Marie, Ann Towns, Göran Duus-Otterström, and Joakim Sebring. 2008. "Fear and Punishment in Sweden: Exploring Penal Attitudes." *Punishment & Society* 10 (3): 319–32.

Institute for Criminal Policy Research. 2017. "World Prison Brief." http://www.prisonstudies .org/world-prison-brief-data.

Mayhew, Pat, and John Van Kesteren. 2002. "Cross-National Attitudes to Punishment." In *Changing Attitudes to Punishment*, edited by Julian V. Roberts and Mike Hough, 63–92. Devon, UK: Willan Publishing.

von Hofer, Hanns, and Henrik Tham. 2013. "Punishment in Sweden: A Changing Penal Landscape." In *Punishment in Europe*. Palgrave Studies in Prisons and Penology, edited by Vincenzo Ruggiero and Mick Ryan, 33–57. London: Palgrave Macmillan. https:// doi.org/10.1057/9781137028211_3.

TRINIDAD AND TOBAGO

The Republic of Trinidad and Tobago consists of two islands in the Caribbean to the northeast of Venezuela. The islands are home to 1.2 million people, primarily of East Indian and African descent due to its complex colonial history. Trinidad and Tobago were first colonized by the Spanish in the early sixteenth century, then by the French in the late eighteenth century, before being conquered by Britain in 1908. The Spanish and French brought African slaves to the islands. The British ended slavery, but instead contracted East Indians, Chinese, and Portuguese laborers to work on the islands under an exploitative system of indentured servitude.

The English-speaking country gained independence from the United Kingdom in 1962 and is part of the Commonwealth Caribbean. It is one of the wealthiest islands in the Caribbean due to petroleum and natural gas production, as well as tourism. The GDP per capita is USD 31,300, roughly double that of neighboring islands Granada (USD 15,100) and Barbados (USD 18,600) (Central Intelligence Agency 2018). Trinidad and Tobago is a parliamentary republic with a common law legal system. Although it is a fully independent nation that maintains its own criminal justice system, the island-nation shares a legal history with the United Kingdom, as well as some limited judicial roles. Similar to many countries in the Caribbean, Trinidad and Tobago has been experiencing relatively high crime rates in the twenty-first century and has traditionally responded with harsh punishments.

Crime and Punitiveness

Though crime in many Caribbean nations has been historically high due to gang activity, drug trafficking, and a lack of criminal justice resources, the twenty-first century brought an upswing in violent crime in Trinidad and Tobago that became a matter of grave concern among policymakers and the public. Official crime data recorded 30.4 murders per 100,000 people in 2013, which was about six times higher than the United States. That same year, the robbery rate was 221, burglary was 222, serious assaults and shootings were 40.5, and rape was sixteen per 100,000 people. The number of murders peaked at 547 in 2008, then dropped slightly to 407 in 2013. Between 2000 and 2010, the average murder rate in Trinidad and Tobago was 25.1 per 100,000 people, which was second among Caribbean countries after Jamaica (50.3), but double that of Barbados (9.5), Grenada (10.2), Dominica (10.3), and Antigua and Barbuda (11.9). The main contributors of the high homicide rate in Trinidad and Tobago are gang activity and domestic violence. The number of known gangs in the country increased from 60 in 2009 to 102 in 2012 (Seepersad 2016). In 2018, the police commissioner cited excessive illegal weapons in the country as a contributing factor to the high violent crime rate.

The fear of crime, particularly violent crime, and a growing sense of insecurity have prompted the public to push policymakers to take a tougher stand on crime. Several opinion pieces in the country's newspapers have called for public floggings and hangings of criminals to deter crime. Citizens of Trinidad and Tobago generally hold more punitive attitudes toward criminals than residents of other Caribbean countries. For example, a survey of residents of seven Caribbean countries conducted between 2010 and 2011 found that respondents in Trinidad and Tobago more strongly supported harsher punishments for criminals, including the death penalty, than those in other surveyed countries. Respondents in Trinidad and Tobago also supported progressive criminal justice responses to crime, such as job creation and poverty reduction, but not necessarily more so than residents of other Caribbean countries in the survey (Maguire and Johnson 2015).

Punishment Philosophy and Practices

In 1967, the courts of Trinidad and Tobago acknowledged five aims of punishment: retribution, general deterrence, specific deterrence, prevention, and rehabilitation. In determining which goals should guide a sentencing decision, judges are encouraged to consider numerous factors, including how frequently the crime occurs in the country, the circumstances of the particular criminal act, the criminal record of the offender, and whether the offender pled guilty. Judges have a wide range of punishments that can be administered. On the more lenient end of the spectrum, judges can discharge the conviction without punishment, suspend the sentence, or require probation, fines, and/or community service. On the harsher end of the punishment options, judges can sentence offenders to corporal punishment, imprisonment, or death. In 2014, the government passed the Administration of Justice Bill to allow offenders who were serving a sentence of more than six years in prison the possibility of parole.

Corporal punishment is typically reserved for violent crimes, such as sex offenses, serious assault, and robbery. It is administered in addition to other punishments, such as imprisonment. The aim of corporal punishment is to illustrate society's moral outrage for the crime. It is only administered to males over eighteen years old, typically consisting of a whipping with a tamarind or birch rod, usually less than twenty-four strokes. Offenders must clear a medical exam before the punishment is administered. The United Nations Human Rights Committee prohibits corporal punishment.

According to the World Prison Brief (2017), the incarceration rate in Trinidad and Tobago in 2015 was 270 per 100,000 people, which ranked the country 42 out of 222. There were 3,667 people in prison, of which 61 percent were awaiting trial. Only 2.6 percent of inmates were female, 4.8 percent were juveniles, and 3.1 percent were foreigners. There are four standard prisons in Trinidad and one in Tobago. Additionally, Trinidad has a remand prison for those awaiting trial, a women's prison, a youth training center, and a correctional rehabilitation center. In 2014, the government invested TTD 727.8 million (approximately USD 107.8 million) to upgrade Prison Service facilities (Seepersad 2016).

Until 2011, the death penalty was a mandatory sentence for murder and treason convictions in Trinidad and Tobago, as was the case for all Commonwealth Caribbean countries. However, a series of legal challenges regarding the constitutionality of the death penalty led to a change to make it an optional sentence. Historically, the country had a globally high rate of death sentences and executions, although since the 1990s, relatively few executions have been carried out, with the last execution in 1999. The method of execution used in Trinidad and Tobago is hanging. According to Amnesty International, in 2016, there were no executions in Trinidad and Tobago, two people were given a death sentence, and thirty-three people were already under a death sentence.

Given the high violent crime rate in the country, the public has been calling for more executions. In 2008, Trinidad and Tobago voted against a United Nations resolution calling for a global moratorium on the death penalty. The people currently serving a death sentence are in various stages of the appeals process. As an independent nation, Trinidad and Tobago has a Court of Appeal that is part of its Supreme Court. However, some cases can be appealed to the Judicial Committee of the Privy Council in London, which is a holdover from colonial times. For example, in January 2018, the Privy Council heard a death penalty case from Trinidad in which a mentally ill man was convicted of killing another inmate. This means that while the United Kingdom does not allow death penalty, the Privy Council still rules on death penalty cases from the British Overseas Territories and the Commonwealth Caribbean nations.

In 2001, several Caribbean countries formed the Caribbean Court of Justice, which is located in Port of Spain, Trinidad. This court has two functions. First, it is an international court with exclusive jurisdiction over matters related to the

Caribbean Community (CARICOM) and its related economic and trade agreements. Second, it is a municipal court of last resort for civil and criminal matters designed to replace the Privy Council to provide justice that is more representative of the culture of the people in the region. As of 2015, Barbados, Belize, Dominica, and Guyana have replaced the Privy Council in London with the Caribbean Court of Justice, whereas other countries still use both courts.

Although punitive policies have been the hallmark of criminal justice in Trinidad and Tobago for decades, experts have questioned the effectiveness of this approach. The government is planning more preventative approaches to address the crime problem. It is also in the process of developing a restorative justice policy to better facilitate offenders' reintegration into communities. Incarcerated offenders also noted the need to improve educational and vocational programs in prisons to better prepare them for reentry upon release.

Further Reading

Central Intelligence Agency. 2018. "The World Factbook." https://www.cia.gov/library/publications/resources/the-world-factbook/.

Institute for Criminal Policy Research. 2017. "World Prison Brief." http://www.prisonstudies.org/world-prison-brief-data.

Maguire, Edward, and Devon Johnson. 2015. "The Structure of Public Opinion on Crime Policy: Evidence from Seven Caribbean Nations." *Punishment & Society* 17 (4): 502–30.

Seepersad, Randy. 2016. "Crime and Violence in Trinidad and Tobago: IDB Series on Crime and Violence in the Caribbean." Technical Notes. Inter-American Development Bank. http://publications.iadb.org/handle/11319/7772.

Seetahal, Dana S. 2014. *Commonwealth Caribbean Criminal Practice and Procedure*. Abingdon, UK: Routledge.

Sumter, Melvina, Elizabeth Monk-Turner, and John Rougier. 2012. "Offenders' Perceptions of Reentry Needs in Trinidad and Tobago: An Exploratory Study." *International Criminal Justice Review* 22 (3): 297–308. https://doi.org/10.1177/1057567712454881.

UNITED STATES

The United States is a country of over 325 million people located in North America. It is a diverse society in terms of race, ethnicity, and religion. It is the nineteenth wealthiest country in the world with a GDP per capita of USD 59,800 (Central Intelligence Agency 2018). Despite being a global promoter of democracy, the United States has been heavily criticized for some of its punishment practices, particularly mass incarceration, which many perceive as violating human rights and undermining democratic principles. The United States is also one of two highly developed nations that still applies the death penalty, with Japan being the other one.

Punitiveness and Populism

The U.S. criminal justice system is different from other highly developed democracies in two important respects. First, criminal punishments tend to be highly punitive, which is consistent with popular beliefs about social responses to crime.

Second, public opinion plays a significant role in shaping criminal justice policies. Since the 1970s, the criminal justice system has moved away from attempts to rehabilitate offenders toward practices that emphasize retribution and incapacitation. Additionally, criminal justice policies have taken a very emotional tone that tends to emphasize the pain and suffering of victims and evokes a tough response to crime. These policies have been shaped less by criminal justice experts and more by political action committees aiming to appease voters.

An example of these trends can be found in a wave of legislation in the 1990s to punish sex offenders, including requiring them to register with law enforcement after release from prison, notifying communities of the location of registered sex offenders, and restricting where ex-offenders could live after their release. These laws added postrelease punishments for this particular group of offenders. They were strongly shaped by public opinion regarding sex offenders rather than by expert knowledge on this type of crime. Most of these laws were named after victims of heinous, highly publicized crimes, and many of the victims' families were actively involved in getting the legislation passed (e.g., the 1994 Jacob Wetterling Crimes against Children and Sexually Violent Registration Act and the 2006 Adam Walsh Child Protection and Safety Act of 2006).

Americans are generally known for having punitive attitudes toward criminal offenders and for supporting long prison sentences. The International Crime Victims Survey asked people in a number of countries what type of punishment they would support for a two-time burglary offender: fine, prison, community service, suspended sentence, or other punishment. Fifty-six percent of American chose imprisonment, compared to 37 percent of Australians, 22 percent of Italians, and 12 percent of French, although Americans favored this option less than people in most of the African and Asian countries surveyed (Mayhew and Van Kesteren 2002). Most Americans still believe that rehabilitation should be a goal of incarceration and that prisoners should receive treatment to help them rehabilitate.

Death Penalty

The use of the death penalty in the United States has varied considerably over time and across states. Since the death penalty was reinstated in 1976 after a brief hiatus, the United States has executed 1,466 people. The most executions (ninety-eight) took place in 1999, and the number of people executed has been steadily declining since 2009. In 2017, twenty-three people were executed and almost 3,000 others were on death row. Thirty-one states allow a death penalty sentence, and most executions take place in southern states (Death Penalty Information Center 2018).

The use of the death penalty in the United States has been controversial for numerous reasons. Some have argued that it violates the eighth amendment of the Constitution that bans cruel and unusual punishment. While the Supreme Court has upheld its use in general, in 2005, it ruled that it could not be used for offenders who were less than eighteen years old when they committed their offense. A second controversy concerns whether the death penalty is administered fairly. Research has shown that African Americans are disproportionately sentenced to the death penalty, especially when their victims were white (Death Penalty Information Center 2018). Finally, human rights activists have been concerned about cases where the defendants were wrongfully convicted. For example, the Innocence Project works to exonerate innocent people on death row through DNA testing.

Mass Incarceration

The United States implements a wide range of criminal penalties including fines, probation, parole, community service, electronic monitoring, substance abuse treatment, incarceration, and the death penalty; although it is best known internationally for its excessive use of incarceration. In 2015, over 6.5 million American adults were under correctional supervision. This rate of 2,710 per 100,000 people in the population was the lowest since 1994. Just over half of these offenders (56.2 percent) were on probation, 22.6 percent were in prison, 12.9 percent were on parole, and 10.8 percent were in a local jail (Kaeble and Glaze 2016).

Of the over two million people incarcerated in the United States in 2015, 9 percent were in federal prisons, 59 percent in state prisons, and 32 percent in local jails. In 2015, the United States had the largest number of people incarcerated (2,145,100) in the world and the second highest incarceration rate of 666 per

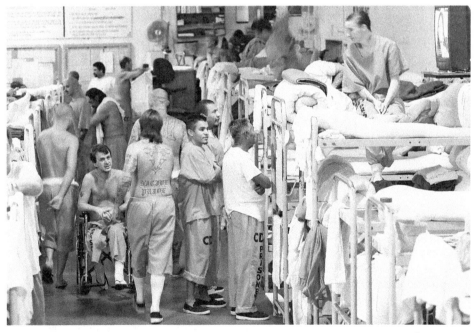

One consequence of mass incarceration in the United States is the overcrowding of prisons, as shown in this example from California. (California Department of Corrections and Rehabilitation)

100,000 people, only trailing Seychelles, a country of small islands off of the east coast of Africa. Almost 10 percent of prisoners in the United States are women, less than 1 percent are juveniles, and about 5 percent are foreigners (Institute for Criminal Policy Research 2017).

Between the early 1900s and 1980, the number of incarcerated people in the United States was slowly rising to about a half a million people. From 1980 to 2010, however, the number increased quickly and sharply to reach about two million people. This growth was historically unprecedented and catapulted the United States to the top of the world prison list, above nondemocratic countries with notoriously high incarceration rates, such as China and Russia. Experts began referring to this huge increase as "mass" incarceration and labeled it an "epidemic." After rising steadily since the 1970s, the incarceration rate in the United States began to decline in 2010.

In response to a rising violent crime rate after World War II, the United States implemented a number of "get tough" policies that contributed to this trend. Famously, President Nixon's War on Drugs, which began in 1971 and was continued by subsequent presidents, significantly increased the number of nonviolent drug offenders in both state and federal prisons. In the 1980s, truth-in-sentencing laws were passed to ensure that prisoners spent their full sentences in prison rather than being released early on parole. In the 1990s, three-strikes laws were passed to punish repeat offenders with longer sentences. Mandatory minimum sentences, especially for drug crimes, also prevented judges from being too lenient in sentencing. As a result of these criminal justice reforms since the 1970s, more people were receiving prison sentences for longer periods of time.

As a result of the War on Drugs, almost half of all offenders in federal prison were convicted of a drug charge. In contrast, just over half of those in state prisons committed a violent crime (52.9 percent), 19 percent committed a property

---

Minority Overrepresentation in Prison

Given that 13 percent of Americans are black and 17 percent are Hispanic, the fact that 38 percent of state prisoners are black and 21 percent are Hispanic has generated a debate about whether incarceration is applied fairly. In 2016, African Americans were incarcerated in state prisons more than five times the rate of whites, and in twelve states more than half of the prison population was African American. Popular opinion assumes that minorities commit more crimes and therefore are incarcerated more than whites. However, research has shown that implicit bias in decision-making by criminal justice practitioners, unequal application of criminal justice policies, and structural disadvantage in non-white communities are largely responsible for this pattern.

The Sentencing Project. 2016. "The Color of Justice: Racial and Ethnic Disparity in State Prisons." http://www.sentencingproject.org/publications/color-of-justice-racial-and-ethnic -disparity-in-state-prisons/.

crime, and almost 16 percent were incarcerated for a drug offense (Wagner and Rabuy 2017). Seventy percent of people in local jails were awaiting trial and not yet convicted.

Mass incarceration has drawn criticism both domestically and internationally on a number of points. Most notably, it has resulted in disproportionate imprisonment of African Americans and Hispanics. It has also led to overcrowding and poor living conditions in many prisons. The privatization of the prison industry raises concerns about putting profits over civil rights. Additionally, states are becoming more aware of the financial burden of mass incarceration. It is estimated that the United States spends about eighty billion per year on correctional populations. In 2010, states spent an average of USD 31,000 per inmate (Henrichson and Delaney 2012). Coupled with the social costs of mass incarceration, particularly on children of the incarcerated and on urban communities, several states are shifting away from relying so heavily on this form of punishment, which has contributed to the declining rates of incarceration in the United States since 2010.

Further Reading

Central Intelligence Agency. 2018. "The World Factbook." https://www.cia.gov/library /publications/resources/the-world-factbook/.

Death Penalty Information Center. 2018. "Facts about the Death Penalty." https://files .deathpenaltyinfo.org/documents/pdf/FactSheet.f1581367854.pdf.

Henrichson, Christian, and Ruth Delaney. 2012. *The Price of Prisons: What Incarceration Costs Taxpayers*. New York: Vera Institute of Justice.

Institute for Criminal Policy Research. 2017. "World Prison Brief." http://www.prisonstudies .org/world-prison-brief-data.

Kaeble, Danielle, and Lauren Glaze. 2016. *Correctional Populations in the United States, 2015*. NCJ 250374. Washington, DC: U.S. Department of Justice, Bureau of Justice Statistics.

Mayhew, Pat, and John Van Kesteren. 2002. "Cross-National Attitudes to Punishment." In *Changing Attitudes to Punishment*, edited by Julian V. Roberts and Mike Hough, 63–92. Devon, UK: Willan Publishing.

Wagner, Peter, and Bernadette Rabuy. 2017. *Mass Incarceration: The Whole Pie 2017*. North Hampton, MA: Prison Policy Initiative. https://www.prisonpolicy.org/reports/pie2017 .html.

Selected Bibliography

Arjomand, Said Amir, and Nathan J. Brown. 2013. *The Rule of Law, Islam, and Constitutional Politics in Egypt and Iran*. New York: SUNY Press.

Brown, R. Blake, and The Osgoode Society. 2012. *Arming and Disarming: A History of Gun Control in Canada*. Toronto, ON: University of Toronto Press.

Central Intelligence Agency. 2018. "The World Factbook." https://www.cia.gov/library/publications/resources/the-world-factbook/.

Chakraborti, Neil, and Jon Garland. 2009. *Hate Crime: Impact, Causes and Responses*. Thousand Oaks, CA: SAGE.

Dammer, Harry R., and Jay S. Albanese. 2013. *Comparative Criminal Justice Systems*. Belmont, CA: Cengage Learning.

Das, Dilip K., and Michael Palmiotto. 2006. *World Police Encyclopedia*. New York: Routledge.

Deer, Sarah. 2015. *The Beginning and End of Rape*. Minneapolis, MN: University of Minnesota Press.

Garland, David. 2001a. *The Culture of Control: Crime and Social Order in Contemporary Society*. Chicago, IL: University of Chicago Press.

Garland, David, ed. 2001b. *Mass Imprisonment: Social Causes and Consequences*. Thousand Oaks, CA: SAGE.

Haberfeld, M. R., and Ibrahim Cerrah, eds. 2007. *Comparative Policing: The Struggle for Democratization*. Thousand Oaks, CA: SAGE.

Huhn, Sebastian, and Hannes Warnecke-Berger, eds. 2017. *Politics and History of Violence and Crime in Central America*. New York: Palgrave Macmillan.

Ingelaere, Bert. 2016. *Inside Rwanda's Gacaca Courts: Seeking Justice after Genocide*. Madison, WI: The University of Wisconsin Press.

James, Erica Caple. 2010. *Democratic Insecurities*. Berkeley: University of California Press.

Kelly, J. T., T. S. Betancourt, D. Mukwege, R. Lipton, and M. J. VanRooyen. 2011. "Experiences of Female Survivors of Sexual Violence in Eastern Democratic Republic of the Congo: A Mixed-Methods Study." *Conflict and Health* 5 (1): 25. https://doi.org/10.1186/1752-1505-5-25.

Kethineni, Sesha, ed. 2014. *Comparative and International Policing, Justice, and Transnational Crime*. 2nd ed. Durham, NC: Carolina Academic Press.

Mecka, Gledina. 2017. "European Union Criminal Law—Towards a European Criminal Code." *Academic Journal of Business, Administration, Law and Social Sciences* 3 (1): 79–85.

Mitchell, Margaret, and John Peter Casey, eds. 2007. *Police Leadership and Management*. Sydney, Australia: Federation Press.

OHCHR (Office of the High Commissioner United Nations Human Rights). 2019. https://www.ohchr.org/EN/pages/home.aspx.

Payan, Tony. 2016. *The Three U.S.-Mexico Border Wars: Drugs, Immigration, and Homeland Security*. 2nd ed. Santa Barbara, CA: ABC-CLIO.

Perry, Barbara. 2001. *In the Name of Hate: Understanding Hate Crimes*. New York: Routledge.

Rafter, Nicole. 2016. *The Crime of All Crimes: Toward a Criminology of Genocide*. New York: New York University Press.

Roulstone, Alan, and Hannah Mason-Bish, eds. 2012. *Disability, Hate Crime and Violence*. New York: Routledge.

Schabas, William A. 2011. *An Introduction to the International Criminal Court*. Cambridge, UK: Cambridge University Press.

Sloth-Nielsen, Julia, ed. 2013. *Children's Rights in Africa: A Legal Perspective*. New York: Routledge.

"Small Arms Survey." n.d. http://www.smallarmssurvey.org/.

Totten, Samuel, and Eric Markusen. 2013. *Genocide in Darfur: Investigating the Atrocities in the Sudan*. New York: Routledge.

UNODC (United Nations Office on Drugs and Crime). 2019a. "Global Study on Homicide." https://www.unodc.org/unodc/en/data-and-analysis/global-study-on-homicide.html.

UNODC (United Nations Office on Drugs and Crime). 2019b. https://www.unodc.org/.

Weitzer, Ronald. 2014. "New Directions in Research on Human Trafficking." *The ANNALS of the American Academy of Political and Social Science* 653 (1): 6–24. https://doi.org/10.1177/0002716214521562.

Zimring, Franklin E., Maximo Langer, and David S. Tanenhaus. 2017. *Juvenile Justice in Global Perspective*. New York: New York University Press.

About the Author and Contributors

Author

Janet P. Stamatel, PhD, is an associate professor of sociology and an affiliate of the Center for Equality and Social Justice at the University of Kentucky. Her research combines political sociology with global criminology to examine how macro-level factors, such as political regime changes, affect crime rates across different countries. She has written many articles explaining the differences in criminal behavior, particularly violence, across countries. She is also the co-editor of *Crime and Punishment around the World*, Vol. 2. The Americas, with Hung-En Sung.

Contributors

Joseph M. Calvert, PhD, earned his doctorate in sociology from the University of Kentucky and works at the Center for Health and Human Services Research in Cincinnati, Ohio.

Kathleen Ratajczak is a PhD candidate in sociology at the University of Kentucky.

Chenghui Zhang is a PhD candidate in sociology at the University of Kentucky.

Index